Poetry and Music in Medieval France

In *Poetry and Music in Medieval France* Ardis Butterfield examines vernacular song in medieval France. She begins with the moment when French song first survives in writing in the early thirteenth century, and considers a large corpus of works which combine elements of narrative and song, as well as a range of genres which cross between different musical and literary categories. Emphasising the cosmopolitan artistic milieu of Arras, Butterfield describes the wide range of contexts in which secular songs were quoted and copied, including narrative romances, satires and love poems. She uses manuscript evidence to shed light on medieval perceptions of how music and poetry were composed and interpreted. The volume is copiously illustrated to demonstrate the rich visual culture of medieval French writing and music. This interdisciplinary study will be of interest to both literary and musical scholars of late medieval culture.

CAMBRIDGE STUDIES IN MEDIEVAL LITERATURE

General editor
Alastair Minnis, *University of York*

Editorial board
Patrick Boyde, *University of Cambridge*
John Burrow, *University of Bristol*
Rita Copeland, *University of Pennsylvania*
Alan Deyermond, *University of London*
Peter Dronke, *University of Cambridge*
Simon Gaunt, *King's College, London*
Nigel Palmer, *University of Oxford*
Winthrop Wetherbee, *Cornell University*

This series of critical books seeks to cover the whole area of literature written in the major medieval languages – the main European vernaculars, and medieval Latin and Greek – during the period c. 1100–1500. Its chief aim is to publish and stimulate fresh scholarship and criticism on medieval literature, special emphasis being placed on understanding major works of poetry, prose, and drama in relation to the contemporary culture and learning which fostered them.

Recent titles in the series
Margaret Clunies Ross *Old Icelandic Literature and Society*
Donald Maddox *Fictions of Identity in Medieval France*
Rita Copeland *Pedagogy, Intellectuals and Dissent in the Later Middle Ages:*
Lollardy and Ideas of Learning
Kantik Ghosh *The Wycliffite Heresy: Authority and the Interpretation of Texts*
Mary C. Erler *Women, Reading, and Piety in Late Medieval England*
D. H. Green *The Beginnings of Medieval Romance: Fact and Fiction, 1150–1220*
J. A. Burrow *Gestures and Looks in Medieval Narrative*

A complete list of titles in the series can be found at the end of the volume.

Poetry and Music in Medieval France

From Jean Renart to Guillaume de Machaut

ARDIS BUTTERFIELD

CAMBRIDGE
UNIVERSITY PRESS

CAMBRIDGE UNIVERSITY PRESS
Cambridge, New York, Melbourne, Madrid, Cape Town, Singapore, São Paulo, Delhi

Cambridge University Press
The Edinburgh Building, Cambridge CB2 8RU, UK

Published in the United States of America by Cambridge University Press, New York

www.cambridge.org
Information on this title: www.cambridge.org/9780521622196

First published 2002
This digitally printed version 2008

A catalogue record for this publication is available from the British Library

ISBN 978-0-521-62219-6 hardback
ISBN 978-0-521-10092-2 paperback

To my mother, and the memory of my father

Contents

List of illustrations   *page* ix
List of musical examples   xii
Acknowledgements   xv
Bibliographical note   xviii
List of abbreviations   xix

Prologue   1

I   Text and performance

1 Song and written record in the early thirteenth century   13

2 The sources of song: chansonniers, narratives, dance-song   25

3 The performance of song in Jean Renart's *Rose*   64

II   The boundaries of genre

4 The refrain   75

5 Refrains in context: a case study   87

6 *Contrafacta*: from secular to sacred in Gautier de Coinci
   and later thirteenth-century writing   103

III   The location of culture

7 'Courtly' and 'popular' in the thirteenth century   125

8 Urban culture: Arras and the *puys*   133

vii

Contents

9 The cultural contexts of Adam de la Halle: *Le Jeu de Robin et de Marion*   151

IV Modes of inscription

10 Songs in writing: the evidence of the manuscripts   171

11 *Chant/fable: Aucassin et Nicolette*   191

12 Writing music, writing poetry: *Le Roman de Fauvel* in Paris BN fr. 146   200

V Lyric and narrative

13 The two *Roses*: Machaut and the thirteenth century   217

14 Rewriting song: chanson, motet, *salut* and *dit*   224

15 Citation and authorship from the thirteenth to the fourteenth century   243

VI Envoy: The new art

16 The *formes fixes*: from Adam de la Halle to Guillaume de Machaut   273

Epilogue   291

Glossary   296

Appendix   303

Notes   314

Bibliography   339

Index of manuscripts   361

General index   366

List of illustrations

1 (a) The layout of a trouvère song in a romance: Gace Brulé,
'Ne sont pas achoison de chanter' in Gerbert de Montreuil,
Le Roman de la violette, BN fr. 1374, fol. 168r. The stanza
is written in red.

(b) The layout of a trouvère song in a chansonnier: Gace
Brulé, 'Ne sont pas achoison de chanter' in BN n. a. fr.
1050, 'Clairambault', fol. 51r.   *page* 32

2 'Le Jeu du Chapelet' [The Game of the Circlet of Flow-
ers] in Jacques Bretel, *Le Tournoi de Chauvency*, Oxford,
Bodleian Library, MS Douce 308, fol. 113r.   44

3 A sequence of six dance-songs (each marked out by an
enlarged initial) beginning with the refrain *'En non Deu'*,
in Jean Renart, *Le Roman de la rose*, Rome, Biblioteca
Apostolica Vaticana Reg. 1725, fol. 70r.   52

4 (a) 'La danse robardoise', showing a lady holding up a
mirror, in Jacques Bretel, *Le Tournoi de Chauvency*, Oxford,
Bodleian Library, MS Douce 308, fol. 123r.

(b) Ivory mirror back, showing courtly scene with dancing and a circlet of flowers, French, fourteenth century,
Victoria and Albert Museum.   60

5 *'J'ai joie ramenee chi'*, a refrain in Jacquemart Giélée, *Renart
le Nouvel*, as presented in the four manuscripts of the *roman*:

(a) BN fr. 25566, fol. 127v
(b) BN fr. 372, fol. 17v
(c) BN fr. 1593, fol. 18r (with added discantus)
(d) BN fr. 1581, fol. 18r (blank staves)   84

6 (a) *Kurzmotetten* (Motet 435), showing two refrains and a tenor: '*Renvoisiement / Ensi doit on aler / Hodie*', BN fr. 12615, fol. 191 v (top initial).

(b) The same two refrains, '*Renvoisiement*' and '*Ensi doit dame aler*' (separated by a third refrain, '*Se j'ai amé*', not shown) in *La Court de paradis*, BN fr. 25532, fol. 333v.   98

7 (a) Initial N of a refrain, showing a figure dancing (a 'performative marker'), with blank staves to the right, in Tibaut, *Le Roman de la poire*, BN fr. 2186, fol. 29r.

(b) Ballade, with spaces left for staves in the first stanza, and refrain picked out with a paraph in the final stanza, in Jehan Acart de Hesdin, *La Prise amoreuse*, BN fr. 24391, fol. 138r.   182

8 Text and gloss from the *Traduction et commentaire de l'Ars amatoria d'Ovide*, Paris, Bibliothèque de l'Arsenal 2741, fol. 11r, showing different sizes of script (larger for the text, and smaller for the gloss). A refrain is cited in the far-right column, picked out by a paraph and signalled by the label *chancon* written in the margin.   185

9 Refrain in Girart d'Amiens, *Escanor*, BN fr. 24374, fol. 68r, marked out by an enlarged initial, spaces left for staves, and an 'end of section' design filling in the last line of song in the left-hand column.   188

10 A page from *Aucassin et Nicolette*, BN fr. 2168, fol. 75r, showing a *laisse* flanked by two prose sections. Three sections of music are provided, two at the start, and the third at the end of the *laisse*, together with the rubrics 'Or se cante' for the *laisse* and 'Or dient & content & fabloient' for the prose.   194

11 (a) The first semi-lyric piece, 'Amour dont tele est la puissance', in *Le Roman de Fauvel*, BN fr. 146, fol. 24r, showing two notated refrains. It begins at the top of the middle column, with a picture and enlarged initial.

(b) The second, strophic semi-lyric piece, 'Han Diex ou pourrai je trouver', *Le Roman de Fauvel*, BN fr. 146, fol. 26v, with notated refrains, flanked by two converse pictures of Fauvel first with a horse's head and human body, and second, kneeling before Fortune, with human head and horse's hindquarters. 210

12 *Lay*, with notation, in Guillaume de Machaut, *Remede de Fortune*, BN fr. 1586, fol. 26r, with picture showing the Lover writing on a scroll. 218

13 A page from the *chanson avec des refrains* 'Bele Aelis' by Baude de la Kakerie, BN fr. 12615, fol. 50v, showing a mixture of notated and unnotated lines, with refrains (and first lines of strophes) marked out by enlarged initials, including '*Ne vos repentez mie de loiaument amer*'. 234

14 (a) Carole in Guillaume de Machaut, *Remede de Fortune*, BN fr. 1586, fol. 51r, with notated virelai below.
(b) 'La karole d'amours', *Le Roman de la Rose*, BL Royal MS 20. A. XVII, fol. 9r. 264

15 Adam de la Halle, polyphonic rondeaux, BN fr. 25566, fol. 34r. 274

List of musical examples

Ex. 1 *Cui lairai ge* (vdB, refr. 387): a comparison of its musical sources, ed. M. V. Fowler, 'Musical Interpolations in Thirteenth- and Fourteenth-Century French Narratives', 2 vols. (Ph.D diss., Yale University, 1979), II, 344. *page* 80

Ex. 2 *Ne vos repentez mie* (vdB, refr. 1375): a comparison of its musical sources, ed. M. V. Fowler, 'Musical Interpolations in Thirteenth- and Fourteenth-Century French Narratives', 2 vols. (Ph.D diss., Yale University, 1979), II, 359. 81

Ex. 3 *Bon jor ait* (vdB, refr. 285): a comparison of its musical sources, ed. M. V. Fowler, 'Musical Interpolations in Thirteenth- and Fourteenth-Century French Narratives', 2 vols. (Ph.D diss., Yale University, 1979), II, 354. 83

Ex. 4 *Nus n'a joie s'il n'aime par Amours* (vdB, refr. 1391): a comparison of its musical sources in *Renart le Nouvel* (line 2346), ed. M. V. Fowler, 'Musical Interpolations in Thirteenth- and Fourteenth-Century French Narratives', 2 vols. (Ph.D diss., Yale University, 1979), II, 465. 84

Ex. 5 *Ainssi doit on aler* in Motet 435 (ed. Tischler, *Earliest Motets*, II, 1506): a comparison of its musical sources. 90

Ex. 6 'D'une amour quoie et serie': comparison of the first line and refrain of a *contrafactum* by Gautier de Coinci with the first two lines of the model by Gilles de

[Viès] Maisons, ed. J. Chailley, *Les Chansons à la Vierge de Gautier de Coinci (1177/78(-1236)* (Paris, 1959), No. 11.   107

Ex. 7   'Hui matin a l'ajournee': comparison of opening of Gautier's song with the *clausula* model ((Wolfenbüttel, Herzog August Bibliothek 677) W_1), and motet version ((Wolfenbüttel, Herzog August Bibliothek 1099) W_2), including the *hoquet* passage, ed. J. Chailley, *Les Chansons à la Vierge de Gautier de Coinci (1177/78(-1236)* (Paris, 1959), No. 12.   110

Ex. 8   'Ja pour yver': comparison of opening, and first refrain, of Gautier's song with the model by Blondel de Nesle, ed. J. Chailley, *Les Chansons à la Vierge de Gautier de Coinci (1177/78(-1236)* (Paris, 1959), No. 13.   111

Ex. 9   *'Par chi va la mignotise'*: refrain from *Le Jeu de la Feuillée*.   148

Ex. 10   *Le Jeu de Robin et Marion*: comparison of two melodies *'Je me repairoie du tournoiement'* and *'Vous perdés vo paine, sire Aubert'*, Adam de la Halle *Le Jeu de Robin et Marion*, trans. and ed. Shira I. Schwam-Baird; music ed. Milton G. Scheuermann, Jr, GLML 94A (New York, 1994), Nos. 2 and 4.   157

Ex. 11   *Aucassin et Nicolette, laisse* 9: a possible reconstruction, from J. Stevens, *Words and Music in the Middle Ages* (Cambridge, 1986), p. 226.   193

Ex. 12   Bamberg MS, Motet No. 43, ed. Gordon A. Anderson, *Compositions of the Bamberg Manuscript: Bamberg, Staatsbibliothek, Lit.115 (olim Ed.IV.6)*, CMM 75 (American Institute of Musicology, 1977).   230

Ex. 13   Richard de Fournival, 'Onques n'amai', lines 1–2, 8–9, ed. F. Gennrich, *Altfranzösische Lieder*, 2 vols. (Tübingen, 1955–56), II, 40–41.   251

Ex. 14   Comparison of Adam de la Halle, rondeau *'Diex, comment porroie'* (refrain), ed. N. Wilkins, *The Lyric Works of Adam de la Hale: Chansons, Jeux Partis, Rondeaux, Motets*, CMM 44 (Rome, 1967) and Guillaume de Machaut, rondeau *'Quant je ne voy'* (refrain), ed.

Leo Schrade, *Oeuvres complètes*, PMFC 2–3, repr. in
5 vols. (Monaco, 1977).   275

Ex. 15 Adam de la Halle, Motet No. 6 (opening) and rondeau
No. 6, ed. N. Wilkins, *The Lyric Works of Adam de la
Hale: Chansons, Jeux Partis, Rondeaux, Motets*, CMM
44 (Rome, 1967).   281

Ex. 16 Adam de la Halle, Motet No. 10 (ending) and rondeau
No. 11, ed. N. Wilkins, *The Lyric Works of Adam de la
Hale: Chansons, Jeux Partis, Rondeaux, Motets*, CMM
44 (Rome, 1967).   282

Ex. 17 Adam de la Halle, Motet No. 1 (opening) and rondeau
No. 5, ed. N. Wilkins, *The Lyric Works of Adam de la
Hale: Chansons, Jeux Partis, Rondeaux, Motets*, CMM
44 (Rome, 1967).   282

Ex. 18 Jehan de Lescurel, 'A vous, douce debonnaire' (polyphonic version), ed. N. Wilkins, *The Works of Jehan
de Lescurel*, CMM 30 (Rome, 1966).   285

Acknowledgements

Many friends and colleagues have sustained and encouraged me through the long drawn-out pleasures and pains of producing this book. John Stevens, through a carefully placed chance remark, first engaged my interest and curiosity in French refrains: his subtle, exacting standards of scholarship across the disciplines of English, French and musicology have been a constant inspiration ever since. I particularly regret that having discussed so much of it with me he did not live to see the book in print. I have been fortunate in the generosity, both personal and intellectual, of colleagues in French and musicology. I owe thanks to Jane Gilbert, and Nancy Freeman Regalado, and especially to Simon Gaunt and Sarah Kay, for their supportive reading of my work in various drafts, their conversation, intellectual energy, and friendship. Among friends in musicology, three in particular, Margaret Bent, Daniel Leech-Wilkinson and Suzannah Clark, have shown me intellectual support on a truly grand scale. I have also learnt much from many stimulating conversations over the years with Christopher Page and Mark Everist. My heartfelt thanks for the opportunities all these scholars, and many others, have provided of lively dialogue in and across their various specialisms. Many colleagues and friends in English have given me the benefit of their learning, wide reading and intellectual agility. I owe a particular debt to Tony Spearing, David Wallace and Alistair Minnis for their unflagging encouragement of this book from its earliest stages. Alistair, as editor, has shown great patience and loyalty towards the project. More recently, I have benefited from Henry Woudhuysen's usual (that is, rare) meticulousness in his reading of a medievalist's efforts. Thanks, too, to Daniel Karlin, Philip Horne and other colleagues in English at UCL. John Sutherland and David Trotter have been not only tolerant but warmly encouraging of my research in discipline(s) remote from theirs. Felicitas Köhnen has kindly taken time out of her own research to help me in the last stages of preparing the book for press.

I acknowledge with gratitude the three institutions to which I have belonged, Trinity College, Cambridge, Downing College, Cambridge, and University College, London. Each has provided a very distinctive academic environment in which to carry out research: I could not have wished for better. Thanks are due to the British Academy and the British Academy Neil Ker Fund for two separate grants towards manuscript research; and the Chambers Fund of University College, London for assistance with publishing costs. Research for the book has been carried out principally in Cambridge, Paris and London, as well as various European libraries. It has been a privilege and delight to spend so many hours in the Salle des manuscrits at the Bibliothèque Nationale, and to make use of the extraordinary facilities of the Cambridge University Library and the British Library. My thanks also to John Allen at University College London Library. Several friends have been generous with hospitality in Paris: I would particularly like to acknowledge Monique Bergeret, Cathérine Axelrad and Gérard Bricogne.

The following libraries have kindly granted permission to reproduce material from their collections: in Paris, the Bibliothèque Nationale and Bibliothèque de l'Arsenal; Vatican Library; Bodleian Library, British Library and the Victoria and Albert Museum. Small amounts of material scattered through the book have previously appeared in essay form: I am grateful to Edinburgh University Press, and the publishers named below for reprinting permissions. Respectively, a couple of paragraphs in Chapters 1 and 7 appeared in 'Medieval Genres and Modern Genre-Theory', *Paragraph*, 13 (1990), 184–201; part of Chapter 11 in '*Aucassin et Nicolette* and Mixed Forms in Medieval French', *Prosimetrum: Crosscultural Perspectives on Narrative in Prose and Verse*, ed. Joseph Harris and Karl Reichl (Cambridge: D. S. Brewer, 1997), 67–98; part of Chapter 9 in 'Pastoral and the Politics of Plague in Machaut and Chaucer', *Studies in the Age of Chaucer*, 16 (1994), 3–27; part of Chapter 10 in '*Mise en page* in the *Troilus* Manuscripts: Chaucer and French Manuscript Culture', in *Reading from the Margins: Textual Studies, Chaucer, and Medieval Literature*, ed. Seth Lerer (Huntington: Huntington Library Press, 1996),

49–80; published simultaneously as *Huntington Library Quarterly*, 58 (1995), 49–80. Parts of Chapters 10, 12 and 14 contain material that appeared in 'The Refrain and the Transformation of Genre in the *Roman de Fauvel*', *Fauvel Studies: Allegory, Chronicle, Music and Image in Paris, Bibliothèque Nationale MS français 146*, ed. Margaret Bent and Andrew Wathey (Oxford: Clarendon Press, 1998), 105–31. I thank Oxford University Press for permission to reprint material in this revised form.

I owe most of all to the many friends and family who have helped in countless ways, often without realising it, with their good humour, faith, musical gifts, distance from academic life, and many small and larger acts of kindness. For creating particular moments of blissful relaxation away from the book, thanks to Dana and Tom and their unquenchable love of Italian art and wine. Help with child care deserves special mention, especially from Doreen Clark, Claire Heard, Elizabeth Illsley, Emma Stone, successive Roehampton students and valiant, and long-suffering Putney and Cambridge friends. It is hard to thank my parents adequately for their constant encouragement, practical wisdom and unfailing generosity; my parents-in-law have also been heroic, my brother sympathetic. Finally, my very very special thanks to Thomas and Daniel for their wonderful vitality, intellectual companionship, comedy, philosophy, and everything else they have given to me (including the ability to stay awake at all hours); and to Brian, graceful to the end.

Bibliographical note

Refrain texts are italicised throughout, partly to reflect the various means by which scribes highlight refrains in manuscripts.

Wherever possible, for ease of reference, music examples are taken from published editions. No attempt has been made, therefore, to co-ordinate different editorial policies.

Unless otherwise indicated, translations are mine, and manuscripts are located in Paris, Bibliothèque Nationale de France, Richelieu-Louvois, and referred to with the following abbreviations: fr. (fonds français), lat. (fonds latins) and n. a. fr. (nouvelles acquisitions françaises).

List of abbreviations

BBSIA	*Bulletin bibliographique de la société internationale arthurienne*
BECh	*Bibliothèque de l'école des chartes*
CCM	*Cahiers de civilisation médiévale*
CFMA	Classiques français du moyen âge
CMM	Corpus mensurabilis musicae
CSM	Corpus scriptorum de musica
EMH	*Early Music History*
FMLS	*Forum for Modern Language Studies*
Gennrich	Friedrich Gennrich, ed., *Rondeaux, Virelais und Balladen aus dem Ende des XII., dem XIII. und dem ersten Drittel des XIV. Jahrhunderts, mit den überlieferten Melodien*, 3 vols.: vols. I and II, GRL 43 and 47 (Dresden, 1921, and Göttingen, 1927); vol. III, SMMA 10 (Langen bei Frankfurt, 1963)
GLML	Garland Library of Medieval Literature
GRL	Gesellschaft für romanische Literatur
HLF	*Histoire littéraire de la France*
JAMS	*Journal of the American Musicological Society*
JEGP	*Journal of English and Germanic Philology*
JRMA	*Journal of the Royal Musical Association*
M	Friedrich Gennrich, *Bibliographie der ältesten französischen und lateinischen Motetten*, SMMA 2 (Darmstadt, 1957)
MD	*Musica Disciplina*
MHRA	*Modern Humanities Research Association*

MLQ	*Modern Language Quarterly*
MLR	*Modern Language Review*
MMMA	Monumenta monodica medii aevi
MQ	*The Musical Quarterly*
New Grove	*The New Grove Dictionary of Music and Musicians*, gen. ed. Stanley Sadie, 29 vols. 2nd edn (London, 2001)
NM	*Neuphilologische Mitteilungen*
PL	*Patrologia Latina*
PMFC	Polyphonic Music of the Fourteenth Century
PMM	*Plainsong and Medieval Music*
PMLA	*Publications of the Modern Language Association of America*
PRMA	*Proceedings of the Royal Musical Association*
R	*G. Raynauds Bibliographie des altfranzösischen Liedes, neu bearbeitet und ergänzt von Hans Spanke*, I, ed. Hans Spanke (Leiden, 1955; reprinted with index, 1980)
RILM	Répertoire international de littérature musicale
RISM	Répertoire international des sources musicales
SATF	Société des anciens textes français
SMMA	Summa musicae medii aevi
SP	*Studies in Philology*
TLF	Textes littéraires français
Tobler-Lommatzsch	*Altfranzösisches Wörterbuch*, ed. Adolf Tobler and Erhard Lommatzsch, 10 vols. (Berlin, 1925–76)
vdB	Boogaard, Nico H. J. van den, ed., *Rondeaux et refrains du XIIe siècle au début du XIVe* (Paris, 1969)
ZFSL	*Zeitschrift für französische Sprache und Literatur*
ZRP	*Zeitschrift für romanische Philologie*

Prologue

Vernacular song in medieval France was one of the greatest cultural achievements of the Middle Ages. The art of the troubadours in the early twelfth century created a movement that spread into all the major European languages and has absorbed readers and singers in every subsequent period of history, including our own. Not only the art of medieval song but all kinds of literary and musical production throughout the European medieval period found focus in France.

This book starts with the story of how French vernacular song was first recorded in writing. The surviving evidence points to a romance author, Jean Renart, who, in the early decades of the thirteenth century, seems to have given crucial impetus to a process of gathering together and writing down secular French and Occitan songs that continued throughout that century and into the next. Renart gains the credit partly because he claimed it at the start of his romance: in fact, several figures, including Gautier de Coinci, were working in the early part of the thirteenth century towards similar aims. The consequences of this activity were enormous. From this point on, song became an increasingly literate art. This is not to say that the words necessarily gained a more privileged position than the music, for music itself became an increasingly literate art. Changes in music arose directly out of the way it was written down. What may seem to have been a simple process of copying down the words and music of a song, worked subtly to change the nature of song.

Song survives in Renart as a written object, not on its own terms, but in the context of a romance narrative. Songs were collected together, as a separate genre, or set of genres, only later in the thirteenth century. The status of these early song transcriptions thus prompts various questions. Understanding song requires understanding song in romance: we are forced to put together two genres we normally keep separate. The context of narrative also provides special circumstances for interpreting the form in which the songs have been transcribed: poetry and music, words and notes, song and narrative are presented together, each influencing and shaping the other. Such considerations set up the parameters of this study. How do we understand the written character of secular song in this century? How does it relate to the changing character of narrative? What broader connections can we perceive between the different types of written context for song?

Material for this book has been selected rather differently from previous studies. My aim is to include the kinds of genre where poetry and music meet most creatively: these often include works, especially from the thirteenth century, which are little discussed, such as *Le Tournoi de Chauvency* and *L'Estoire de Joseph*. Others, though well known to modern scholars, including the trouvère chanson and motet, Jean Renart's *Roman de la rose*, *Aucassin et Nicolette*, Adam de la Halle's *Le Jeu de Robin et de Marion*, and Guillaume de Machaut's *Remede de Fortune*, have hardly been discussed in relation to one another. The reason for this variety and novelty of juxtaposition is partly a deliberate attempt to raise questions about how such works are most illuminatingly viewed. The argument of the early chapters of this book is that the generic contexts for song in the thirteenth and early fourteenth centuries are much more varied, heterogeneous and hybrid than we have come to expect. The modern history of song forms has largely been made possible by taking the songs out of the contexts in which they were produced and received. In parallel with more recent work which has sought to deepen our understanding of the social, intellectual and spiritual attitudes towards secular song in this period, the aim of my study is to put the songs back into their formal and generic contexts.[1] The results often disturb the categories we have subsequently assigned to them.

Song emerges not as a single, hermetically sealed genre, but as one that is infiltrated and extended by all sorts of other elements, or else itself abbreviated and inserted into seemingly extraneous settings. I am interested in the way in which poetry and music do not turn out to exist in separate worlds, but constantly intermingle in surprising juxtapositions. The same is true of song and narrative. Our modern determination to see the poetic as somehow divorced from the musical is constantly confounded in this period. Finding the terms to describe the fluctuations and subtleties of their relationship is not easy. A common language often divides musicologists and literary scholars. The term 'source', for example, means 'manuscript' to the former, and 'textual origin'[2] to the latter. I use it largely to mean 'manuscript', but with the added implication (conflated with the literary usage) that a manuscript is an important primary representation of the material it contains. I have tried to create fresh juxtapositions of material – and terminology – in order to suggest new ways of writing musical and literary history. This partly arises because some of the most famous works, such as *Aucassin et Nicolette*, *Robin et Marion* and *Le Roman de Fauvel* each seem *sui generis*: they make us rethink history because they do not seem to fit in to received notions of either musical or literary tradition.

No history of medieval French vernacular song has yet been written. In the current state of research, this is unsurprising: vernacular song intersects with so many other areas of writing and composition that the topic becomes very hard to delimit and to master from the necessary range of perspectives. Some issues remain unresolved, such as the complex interrelations between Latin and vernacular writing, or the interpretation of rhythm in musical notation. Perhaps most challenging of all is the way that song form changes between 1100 and 1350. In a radical shift, the formerly dominant monophonic (single-voiced) trouvère chanson gives ground to the polyphonic (multi-voiced) rondeau and ballade: simultaneously (is it a cause or a symptom?) musical notation becomes far more visually detailed and rhythmically communicative, and narrative takes on a new flexibility and authorial confidence in its use of the first person. The change in song is so radical that it is hard to characterise without taking into account a vast range of factors involving music and words, several of which have yet to be properly isolated. Research on individual genres is still in its early stages: it is only very recently, for example, that the repertory of motets has started to receive general discussion. Assessments are still needed of how different groups of motets relate to one another and to other instances of early polyphony, such as the polyphonic *formes fixes* (rondeau, ballade and virelai), as well as to monophonic song. The evidence for the earliest stages of polyphony in the important collection of songs in Oxford, Bodleian Library, MS Douce 308 and *Le Roman de Fauvel* needs reviewing. Work on the large body of refrain material is recent and growing.

This book focuses selectively within two broad areas: the written contexts for secular song in the thirteenth century, and the nature of change in song and narrative between the thirteenth and fourteenth centuries. The (manuscript) sources for vernacular song in medieval France are numerous. The most familiar (at least to music scholars) are the great song books (chansonniers) of the thirteenth and fourteenth centuries. The less familiar (at least to music scholars) include a wide range of writings that might loosely be called 'narrative', such as romances, sermons, *jeux*, *dits*, treatises and translations. In some compilations, one repertory of song will be cited within another: this is true, for example, of *motets*, *pastourelles* and *saluts d'amour* in which occur refrains and rondeaux. Some songs are included in proverb collections. Of all these contexts, romances and first-person narratives on love are the most substantial in length and number, and comprise upwards of seventy works between the thirteenth and early fifteenth century. Several previous studies, in recent years, have concentrated on narratives containing songs.[3] They have largely been written from a literary perspective, and have tended to take narrative as their reference point. Song in narrative thus looks like an oddity, or at any rate something which needs explanation. I have increasingly come to think that this view should be reversed. Narrative is only one of the many contexts for song in the medieval period, and it makes better sense of both narrative and song to broaden the terms of comparison.

For example, Jean Renart, as the author of the first French narrative to cite songs, needs to be compared not only with other romance authors, but also to be viewed as a song compiler and editor in his own right. Until his role in the transmission of song is put in a wider perspective, the significance of his work is hard to assess. Literary scholars are unanimous in acclaiming *Le Roman de la rose* of Guillaume de Lorris and Jean de Meun as the most seminal vernacular narrative of the thirteenth century. Yet, notwithstanding Zink's brilliant (but localised) study of the two *Roses*, we need a more inclusive sense of how Renart's influence on the form of later love narratives compares with that of Guillaume de Lorris and Jean de Meun.[4]

'Form' is perhaps a key word. The 'formalism' of the 1950s and 1960s has had a well-documented (and, in part, well-justified) period of decline in favour of new research into social history, the composition of audiences, manuscripts as evidence of contemporary reading practices, feminism and psychoanalysis. It may be appropriate now to reassess its importance. Considerations of form have been so successfully superseded that we have few means left of distinguishing different types of 'lyric' writing from 'narrative' writing, or from writing that combines the two. This book tries to put form back on the agenda, not least because it is a main distinguishing characteristic of the two *Roses*, and uses it as a starting point for thinking about all the different ways we might try to approach thirteenth-century writing.

Yet this is not a formalist study. If a single word could sum it up it would be 'contextual'. What I have tried to do is develop, cumulatively, ways of understanding song by showing how far its different contexts shape and transform it. I include in 'context' recognising where song is part of some larger whole, of a 'source' in all senses of the word: another song, a sermon, a narrative or a compilation, a manuscript page, a performance, an intellectual tradition, a social environment, a set of generic assumptions. It has not, of course, been possible to look at every kind of context with every example. Beginning with the context of narrative, I try to gain a sense of how novel Renart really is, how novel his methods are for transmitting song, and how far the newly transcribed song genres in his *Roman de la rose* have been subjected to change within their romance setting.

Having taken account of the large differences of style between the various song genres cited by Renart, I turn to the most commonly cited genre of song: the refrain. In the usual dictionary definition a refrain is 'a phrase or verse occurring at intervals, especially at the end of each stanza of a poem or song'.[5] Yet in thirteenth-century and much fourteenth-century composition, refrains – short phrases of text or melody or both – have a far more flexible formal role. Most distinctively, they are cited not just within works, but across them, the same refrain appearing in as many as six or seven contexts from a variety of genres. Some two thousand refrain texts and around five hundred melodies have been collected from the thirteenth to the early fourteenth century, from widely diverse genres and contexts. Refrains are constantly fascinating. They throw up fundamental questions about French vernacular production, and in the process question our ways of categorising what we read from this period. For example, the division of works as either 'musical' or 'literary' looks particularly uneasy with respect to refrains: they infiltrate both descriptions equally, but inhabit neither exclusively. They raise questions about genre – how they function generically, and how they affect other kinds of writing and our classifications of them. They are so pervasive a feature of vernacular writing that they prompt us to ask why they are there, what medieval authors found interesting about them, and what they tell us about patterns of creativity more generally. More than this, they are the fundamental building block of medieval song forms: the use of the refrain is largely what distinguishes one kind of song from another. It has been said that when the history of vernacular song comes to be written it will have to take due account of the refrain.[6] This book is not claiming to be that history but it does try to show how central refrains are to the writing of that history. To trace the branching pathways of refrain-citation is to discover a new perspective on genre. One particular aim is to use this perspective to open our eyes to parallel compositional activities in both musical and poetic contexts.

The structure of the book is broadly chronological, but not rigidly so. It is also designed to allow certain issues to develop from more than one perspective. For instance, much recent work on medieval French song has circled around the opposing terms 'courtly' and 'popular'. Included in these terms is both a sense of the specific social circumstances of an author and his audience, and a reference to style and register. The *grant chant courtois*, as troubadour and trouvère song is often called, encapsulates both meanings of courtly, in that it is produced for and within an aristocratic society, and is also a complex, highly wrought musical and poetic construct. Dance-song, on the other hand, has a more nebulous definition, since it survives largely in aristocratic productions, yet in forms which are simple, brief and minimally structured. If we are to learn anything of genuinely popular poetic or musical culture in the Middle Ages, then dance-song would seem to gesture towards it in its simplicity, lack of innate rhetorical pretension, and public function. Yet the transmission of dance-song in genres and settings that allude to sophisticated and wealthy social practices heavily qualifies any description of it as 'popular', and has given rise to John Stevens's usefully compromising term 'courtly-popular'.[7] Several chapters, notably from Sections I–III, explore the limits of these terms in an attempt to trace as closely as possible the cultural associations that govern song citation and shape its form and meaning.

Such an enquiry is pursued in Section III in an attempt to consider the 'culture' of song in more specifically social terms. The pun in the title of the section ('The Location of Culture'), borrowed from Homi Bhabha, draws attention to the way that culture is ambiguously, yet powerfully related to place.[8] Arras, through its *confrérie* and *puy*, stands out as an area of exceptional importance in the production of later thirteenth-century writing, and the invaluable work of Ungureanu and Berger lays the groundwork for realising how Arras functioned as a literary and musical centre. Much work remains to be done, especially on manuscript provenance, but I hope, nevertheless, that my selection of Arras as a type or model of the importance and interest of social context to these hybrid works will serve to indicate ways in which further research on this and other geographical centres might develop. For the first time, to my knowledge, an attempt is made to link a group of hybrid works geographically, and think through the aesthetic consequences of this association.

The second half of the book turns to the question of how to characterise the change between late thirteenth-century and mid-fourteenth-century writing. I have concentrated on three areas: the manuscript presentation of a wide range of works that transmit song, the changing formal distinctions between song and narrative, and the curious way a developing polemic about authorship arises out of material that is powerful through being both anonymous and public. The argument in each of these sections goes back to the early thirteenth century in order to locate the connections between thirteenth- and fourteenth-century writing as firmly as possible. A key motif of these chapters is the idea of a boundary: I explore the ways in which the differences between genres are articulated through *mise-en-page*, through form, register, social and sexual difference, words and music, the private and the public, the authored and the anonymous. The section finishes with some reflections on the practice of citation. Song very often has the function of a citation. Yet this can cause confusion. How do we know – amidst a patchy manuscript record – whether a chanson or a refrain is newly composed for its context, or already well known? I look at the ways refrain-citations border on cliché, on common, proverbial forms of speech and contrast this with various seemingly contradictory strategies in thirteenth- and fourteenth-century writing for using refrains and other song genres to bolster a notion of *auctoritas*.

The greatest poet-composer of either century, Guillaume de Machaut, provides a final point of reference for the book. All three topics in the second half – manuscript layout, the relations between song and narrative, and the nature of authorship – are crucially developed by Machaut to an outstanding extent. Machaut currently enjoys a renaissance of interest amongst literary scholars (his importance having been long recognised by musicologists): yet apart from some major fourteenth-century studies he still tends to be approached through an interest in narrative stimulated by the *Roman de la rose* of Lorris and Jean de Meun, or else through Chaucer. The aim here, by contrast, has been to situate him from both a literary and musical perspective within the context of such gifted practitioners in the art of writing music and poetry as Gautier de Coinci and the author(s) of *Le Roman de Fauvel*.

The book begins and ends with discussion of texts and performance. In common with many other scholars from the past two decades, my work has sought to reconstitute the page of the scribal manuscript as an authentic object in its own right.[9] There has been and continues to be much to learn from the manuscript page about the cultural perceptions of those who produced it. My particular effort here is to try to connect this approach to textual history with material that involves music as well as words. Thinking about song stimulates us to think about the way in which medieval writing relates to an event, and not merely to an original form of writing. What we are trying to deduce from the physical marks on the page is not only what someone, perhaps the author or a scribe under his supervision, originally wrote, but also what a work was like in performance. This question is familiar to those who try to decipher musical notation, it is less frequently asked of words. Literary scholars tend to think of transmission as a matter of relaying, more or less accurately, a form of words; in the case of song it is more a matter of relaying a living context.

A manuscript's written transmission of a work is a highly elusive form of evidence. We need to be aware of its partiality. As *written* evidence, it presents to us only one version of the complex negotiations in these works between their production and reception. For instance, songs are often copied in ways that obscure our sense of how they might have been received by a medieval audience. Jean Renart's *Le Roman de la rose* contains the claim that it can be both read and sung, yet the single surviving manuscript makes no provision for music. By its nature, any manuscript is (in some form) a rewriting of its own 'evidence', and we need to be sensitive to the shifting relations between the 'oral' and the 'literal' that each one presents.[10] It seems likely that medieval manuscripts present something more intangible than an 'ur-text', that is, a range of kinds of writing that at one extreme may represent literate communication at its furthest from an oral event, and at the other may approximate to an oral event with uncanny closeness.

Works that mix song and narrative are of peculiar interest because of the way in which they internalise the conditions of performance. By enclosing performances of songs within the performing context of the *roman* as a whole, they could be said to inscribe oral events, not just forms of language. In this way they illustrate in microcosm some of the complexities of the process by which live performances of medieval works were transliterated, and transformed. The mixed nature of the media – song and text – provides a constant juxtaposition, if we could only learn to observe it, between different forms of orality, or (equally) of literacy. When we have words and music together as in song per se, and as in song cut into narrative, writing functions as more than one medium, representing more than one kind of sound. The author who explores this rich potential of writing more sophisticatedly than any other in either century is Guillaume de Machaut, whose works provide a glittering display of literary and musical collaboration. His *Remede de Fortune* and *Le Voir Dit* are examples of writing where poetry and music forge together the sound of the page and the silence of the imagination. This partnership, as I shall argue in the first chapter, is already presaged in the early decades of the thirteenth century with some of the first surviving records of vernacular song.

PART I

Text and performance

I

Song and written record in the early thirteenth century

Medieval works present acute problems of interpretation by their intimate associations with the circumstances of public performance. These circumstances, full of the contingency, risk and social tension of human exchange, and brought about by the physical presence of the people engaged in the act of communication, seem to be inherently irreproducible. Yet our knowledge of the predominantly oral culture of the medieval period derives largely from literate sources, that is, from sources that are all forms of reproduction of works experienced in irreproducible conditions. We are faced, then, with the difficulty – even the impossibility – of trying to bring to life the social and material context of a work from the resistant medium of a manuscript copy.

Manuscripts bear a relation to the works they reproduce that is different from the modern book. Whereas the modern novel, for example, *is* to a major extent the book itself, in that the conditions of its writing and of its reception share the same medium, the medieval work is represented by the medieval manuscript only in a distorted and incomplete form. There is a lack of consistent relation between the scribes and the works they are reproducing: each manuscript has its own contingency of production that adds to that of the conditions of performance of the work. This situation is complicated by the absence of any hard distinction between the oral and the written. In theory, the scribe may be transcribing an oral event directly 'from life', but in practice, most kinds of composition in the Middle Ages are produced, performed, received and reproduced in conditions which pass through various intermediary stages not just between the oral and the written, but between public and private, individual and communal, and active and passive involvement on the part of authors, performers, audiences and scribes.

Disentangling these stages proves to be a familiar crux in the interpretation of musical manuscripts: few types of source show more clearly the problems of interpreting a newly formulated means of representing in writing an essentially oral event. If we consider the nature of this oral event more closely, we could say that song occupies a place between the temporal or ephemeral, and the iterable. Every song is a unique, singular performance, and an inherently repeatable event. A stanzaic song combines both elements by being constructed from a repeated form that produces a temporal but also recurrent pattern of sound. At an early stage in the thirteenth century, vernacular song is, for the first time, consistently committed to writing. This introduces a new kind of tension between the temporal event and the text. It would be more accurate to say that not one kind but many kinds of tension are produced. For instance, there is the question of how closely, or rather, how loosely, the written notation corresponds to the various characteristics of musical sound. Modern scholars have still found no means of determining the rhythm of medieval song from pre-mensural notation: there is little consensus over whether this indicates that rhythm (in our sense) is lacking in medieval song, or whether it is an element that existed but that scribes did not think it necessary to record in writing, or again, whether our uncertainty is merely a result of our failure to understand the precise parameters of flexibility in the notational symbols. Such features as duration and tempo are notoriously difficult to render in written form, and indeed remain so in modern notational practice in the gap between performance and modern performing editions (of all periods of music).[1]

A further question concerns the discrepancies between the date of composition of a piece and the date of its surviving transcription. Troubadour song was first written down often at least a century after it was composed, and we have little way of knowing whether the surviving pieces of writing represent an attempt to preserve a historically 'authentic' image of troubadour song or a free thirteenth-century reinterpretation, even re-creation of that repertory. In addition, the surviving forms of transcription may be relying at least as much on written as on oral traditions. The difficulty of connecting the written form to the oral event in medieval music is exacerbated again by the complexities of relation between the writing down of the words and the writing down

14

of the melodies. Often these two types of writing (as now) were carried out by different scribes who did not always coordinate their work, so we may have one view of a song from the words, and another from the music, yet both occurring on the same manuscript page.[2] The tensions between text and event in medieval song are not those of a straightforward dichotomy: as soon as a song becomes a text, its nature as an oral event is altered.

Many complex and fluctuating forms of reaction to developing literacy existed in the medieval period, and as M. T. Clanchy, for example, has emphasised, sharply differing perceptions existed of the relative trustworthiness of oral or written media. Clanchy dwells on the extraordinary co-existence in the twelfth century of new claims for the authenticity of writing with a rise in forgeries. Such a situation bears eloquent witness to the power of written over oral testimony, not in terms of access to truth (for this is granted to orality, especially in legal contexts), but in the potential of writing for exploitation.[3]

For medieval readers, then, as well as for modern, trying to interpret a written text thus involves taking account of the slipperiness and imprecision of the relation of writing to action. But are we to conclude that the conditions of performance are simply irretrievable? Paul Zumthor implies this when he describes a medieval text as 'une forme vide' rather than 'parole pleine'.[4] Since the texts lack all those features of sound, gesture, timing and occasion which constitute 'l'aspect corporel des textes médiévaux', he argues, they are inherently fragmentary (p. 12). This is because the performance context is not a merely contingent adjunct to the text but a complex of circumstances that are directly constitutive of its form. If he is right, however, that performance is an intrinsic aspect of a medieval work, then perhaps we should think again about the nature of the surviving text. Rather than decide too quickly that it is 'fragmentary', we might ask whether the text does not in fact contain some sense of the work's character in performance, whether performance is not in some way inscribed within the text rather than irrecoverably absent from it?

One way of reading the text as a performance is to understand it generically. Such an argument is taken up by Jameson, for instance, for whom genre is an attempt to 'specify the proper use of a particular cultural artifact' by acting as a substitute for the 'indications and signals (intonation, gesturality, contextual deictics and pragmatics)

15

which ensure [the] appropriate reception [of the speech acts of daily life]'.[5] If we learn to interpret the genre of a work we will find ourselves uncovering just those corporeal features that Zumthor describes as inherent but absent. This is part of Jameson's belief that in an oral context recognition of genre is relatively straightforward. For him, 'as texts free themselves more and more from an immediate performance situation' generic rules become correspondingly difficult to enforce.

Jameson's attempt to bring genre and performance together is nonetheless confused. It is strangely simplistic of Jameson to regard the speech acts of everyday life as easy to receive appropriately – an issue to which Bakhtin's work on speech genres gives more full and subtle account.[6] Medieval compositions strongly suggest that the sociolinguistics of the oral are not *ipso facto* transparently open to interpretation, still less opaquely closed to misinterpretation. The physical presence of a poet-performer in the public transmission of a medieval work sets up barriers rather than open routes to interpretation (for instance, by making an audience question the relation between the 'I' of the work, and the 'I' of the performer). Furthermore, the suggestion that genre acts as a *substitute* for performance signals, while evidently partially true, leaves little room for understanding how, in that case, genre operates in an oral context. One reason why speech acts are not always easy to interpret is precisely because of the complicating factors of genre in an oral exchange. Genre is not merely a substitute for performance signals but a kind of performance signal.

Jameson's point is obscured because, like Zumthor, he creates a polarity between the oral and written, by saying that oral contexts simplify problems of interpretation whereas written contexts ambiguate them. Yet as Clanchy and others have made clear, throughout most of the medieval period literate factors are already at work in many oral contexts. While it is right to point out that works were orally performed, this does not mean that they were orally composed, but that oral performance is in some way itself shaped by texts. Although Zumthor is at pains elsewhere to distinguish between different degrees of orality, his description of a medieval text as 'une forme vide' as opposed to 'parole pleine' appears to forget this. Rather than appeal, however implicitly, to a notion of the Middle Ages as an Edenic pre-literate world of pure speech acts we need to take more direct cognizance of the intricate interrelations in the period between oral and literate processes of composition. Here I will be rejecting the polarity which results from seeing performance as a 'real presence' in a lifeless text, in favour of understanding medieval culture as already and (certainly by the early thirteenth century) as always functioning in a borderline area in which constant negotiations take place between public and private, vocal and aural, physical and abstract concepts of communication. This, rather than Jameson's, is the context in which I see genre operating, as a means whereby such distinctions are examined, articulated and represented.

Nowhere are the negotiations between genre, performance and writing more delicate than in the *romans* which contain songs, to which I propose to give the French term *romans à chansons*. As works of mixed genre, they keep passing across the boundaries of the oral and the literate. By setting songs into a narrative they enclose already existent social forms within a fictional narrative frame and in so doing treat these oral forms in a literate way, that is, as texts. This leads them in a variety of novel and far-reaching directions. In this opening section, I explore two broad areas. The first is the difficulty of interpreting questions of performance through the actual manuscripts that have survived. I take account not only of the fact that the manuscripts of the *romans à chansons* (like all manuscripts) are textual not oral witnesses, but also of their particular character as mixed forms of transmission, since they incorporate the medium of song as well as of speech. I argue that the problems of transmission in these works turn out to involve a particularly intriguing version of the balance between the oral and the literate in the period, and not just to be arcana of literality.

Examples are drawn from works throughout the thirteenth century, with special reference to the earlier *romans*. I consider them within two fundamental, and widely used categories: the 'courtly' (or 'aristocratisant', in Bec's terms) and the 'popular' (or 'popularisant').[7] These are useful, if imprecise terms, and indicate, albeit crudely, a central social division in the perception of song production evident from Renart on. During the course of the next chapters, both terms will come under increasing scrutiny. This social dimension is my second main area of discussion. Here I begin by comparing the ways in which 'courtly' and 'popular' song come to be transmitted in writing. I consider how the writing down of 'courtly' song in the *romans* compares with other thirteenth-century song anthologies, taking into account that writing may include the copying of music as well as of words. The writing down of 'popular' song raises further issues. By containing many unique examples of 'popular' song in the form of refrains and *rondets de carole*, the *romans* act as a primary source. The demands of interpreting this source have not always been acknowledged. I reopen questions surrounding the nature of dance-song, the formation and articulation of refrains, and the relation between refrains and *rondets*; all the while with an eye to the determining importance of the romance context as a perspective for understanding the written form of these songs.

The final chapter in this section continues this second main area of discussion. Here I consider more directly how performance is a social action, with its own set of social constraints derived from the relation between performer and audience. Concentrating on Renart's *Le Roman de la rose ou de Guillaume de Dole*, I show how his work, by enclosing a wide range of lyric genres, internalises a correspondingly diverse set of social practices, and that this provides him in turn with a subtle means of commentary upon competing forms of communication in the period.

First of all, as a necessary introduction to these issues of performance, transmission and audience, I begin with the Prologues to the earliest *romans à chansons*. Conceived precisely as an introduction to this new genre by their medieval authors, they illuminate for us in terms that are worth careful re-examination the assumptions and expectations that these poets both held and sought to cultivate.

PROLOGUES

Jean Renart's Prologue to his *Le Roman de la rose ou de Guillaume de Dole* (composed probably *c.* 1210) has received much critical attention.[8] Here I want to stress that the establishment of this new kind of work – the combining of songs and romance – goes hand in hand with a new self-consciousness about the significance of writing songs. His first words explain that his new work not only mixes two genres (*conte* and *chans*) but that the function of mixing them is to preserve the songs as *written* forms:

> Cil qui mist cest conte en romans,
> ou il a fet noter biaus chans
> por ramenbrance des chançons...
> (1–3)

> He who has turned this story into a romance, and who has caused fine
> songs to be notated in it for the sake of recording songs in memory... [9]

Some uncertainty exists over the meaning of 'il a fet noter biaus chans'. Against the received opinion of most of the work's editors,[10] that it means 'where he had fine melodies copied', Michel Zink has argued that Renart is referring to singing rather than copying, and hence translates the line as 'where he had beautiful melodies sung by the characters'.[11] But he does not take this to mean that the romance was performed with music. Zink believes that the key word in these opening lines is 'ramenbrance'. Renart's interest in music is literate rather than oral: 'These are melodies that reverberate only within the fiction of the romance but that call to mind the memory of actual songs' (p. 109).

Zink's argument is subtle, yet one might have several reasons for demurring from his reasoning. He questions the meaning of 'copied' by saying that 'for an author of a romance to allude to a copyist working on his directions would be unique, in this context' (p. 107). But, as everyone who has written on Renart in recent years has agreed, including Zink himself, this romance is indeed a unique work, with unique aims. Uniqueness is precisely what Renart claims, and indeed his Prologue is a highly idiosyncratic piece of writing compared to the usual introductory remarks to a *roman d'aventure*. Some kind of flattering reference towards a patron is common, as in Chrétien de Troyes' *Li Contes del Graal* or *Chevalier de la charrette*.[12] Renart sets his work apart from the rest by insisting on the crucial transforming effect of the songs upon the work's style and performance. He promotes his poetic method and medium rather than the story to follow.[13] It would not be surprising if this novel decision involved him in some novel attempts to enable the form of the work to exist.

Zink goes on to say that Renart cannot be 'thinking of a copyist who specialises in musical scores' because 'the unique manuscript of the romance has no scores' (p. 107), an argument that is reiterated by Regina Psaki.[14] This is specious reasoning. Renart's *Rose* survives in a late thirteenth-century manuscript, in which it is copied alongside two romances by Chrétien and another by the mid-thirteenth-century author, Raoul de Houdenc. We have no way of knowing what stage in the transmission of Renart's work this manuscript represents; when we also recognise the patchy nature of music copying it is impossible to rely on its absence here as evidence that music was not transmitted in writing in an earlier version, or, even more speculatively, that music was never intended to be part of the performance experience of the romance.

Zink's evidence that 'noter' means 'perform' is obscure.[15] He rather admits, with disarming candour, that it is the meaning that he prefers to find: 'one could prefer to see in the "noter" of v. 2 not the verb derived from *notare* but the one derived from the noun *nota* – that is, *noter*, meaning "to sing, to interpret musically"' (p. 108). But perhaps the problem here is the implicit need to find a preference. It is more significant that *noter* has a double reference. In a pun that survives in modern French and English, a 'note' is both a sound and a sign. To notate is at once to add music to a text and to set music into writing. In a period in which vernacular song is only just beginning to be more widely copied, the shifting reference of 'noter' between 'to interpret musically' and 'to record in writing' indicates the wider truth that the distinction between these two activities is not yet clear cut. 'To record in writing' *is* 'to interpret musically'. The writing down of song involves turning something oral into something written, but also something written (the romance) into something that encounters the oral (the songs). It weakens the radical nature of Renart's work to see it as a purely literary game. It is a much more difficult balancing act between the oral and the performed, and the written and the read, in all their different permutations.

We can see this from the complex prevarications of Renart's rhetoric in his prologue. Zink talks of the impression we gain 'of vague stammerings with awkward repetitions'. I see it rather as a delight in apposition and paradox, as a careful and brilliantly incremental series of contrasting pairings, 'conte et chans', 'los et pris', 'chans et sons', 'chante et lit', 'chanter et lire', 'conte et chante', 'd'armes et d'amors', designed to intensify the work's main claim to novelty, that it can be both sung *and* read:

> Ja nuls n'iert de l'oïr lassez,
> car, s'en vieult, l'en i chante et lit,
> et s'est fez par si grant delit
> que tuit cil s'en esjoïront
> qui chanter et lire l'orront,
> qu'il lor sera nouviaus toz jors.
> Il conte d'armes et d'amors
> et chante d'ambedeus ensamble. . .
> (18–25)

> No one will ever leave off from hearing it, because if one wishes to, one can both sing and read it, and it is composed so delightfully, that all those who hear the work being sung and read will have pleasure in it; it will always be novel to them. It tells of arms and of love and sings of both at the same time. . .

The division between 'conte et chans' is neither simple nor single: Renart's headlong couplings join together as much as they distinguish the activities of hearing, singing, reading, narrating and composing. Zink makes the same hard-line distinction between the oral and the written as Zumthor and Jameson, but written music is no more or less evanescent than written words. The word 'nota', for a musical note, already testifies to its literateness: conversely, a written romance, like music, vanishes in performance. The earliest versions of Renart's *Rose* have already vanished, and the single surviving script only approximates to them. The musical note is a sign, a *signifié* contradictorily denoting a *signifiant*. For musical notation to be present in the manuscript would, in that sense, be a literate event, not an oral one.

Renart's finely calibrated movements between making appeals to the songs as forms of oral musical performance and as a written verbal record illustrate the complex position held by the *roman à chansons* amongst the competing claims of orality and literacy. These earliest *romans à chansons* give us a glimpse of genre in the making, that is, genre in the process of being composed, constructed and given a physical shape. Renart defines the terms of this process with care and ingenuity: his *Roman de la rose*, as a work which newly combines *chans* and *conte*, creates new parameters for its reception, since it gives the genre of chanson a new mode of musical transmission, at once oral and written. But this mediating role of the work between oral and literate modes is further complicated by the influence of the two genres upon each other: the romance acts as a kind of stage for the production of the songs, but a stage which subtly alters and contains the songs, just as the songs, in turn, modify the nature of their narrative frame. Urged by Renart to notice how well the words of the songs fit those of the narrative ('toz les moz des chans, / si afierent a ceuls del conte' [all the words of the songs belong so well to those of the story] (28–29)), we are being asked to observe how far (and how successfully) he has bent the two genres towards each other. The modes of transmission of each genre are each altered by their juxtaposition: by re-producing the genre of the chanson, the romance enables the songs to gain a literate context and itself a new means of oral performance.

Nancy Durling writes of the paucity of surviving thirteenth-century reaction to Renart's *Rose* (p. 3). Apart from the frustratingly uncommunicative manuscript copy, only one work, *Le Roman de la violette* (*c.* 1228–30) by Gerbert de Montreuil, seems to imitate Renart's directly. It contains a comparable number and range of pieces (Renart's *Rose* has forty-eight, the *Violette* has forty), and some of the lyrics are identical. Both romances also have a similar plot (the flower in the title of each work plays the same role in each story). Moreover, Gerbert models his Prologue on Renart's: he puts forward the same reasons for the novelty and value of his *roman*, using similar rhetoric:

> Et s'est li contes biaus et gens,
> Que je vous voel dire et conter,
> Car on i puet lire et chanter
> (36–38)[16]

> And this story which I want to recite and tell to you, is fine and noble because it can be both sung and read.

I want to bring two further works into the discussion. Gautier de Coinci's *Les Miracles de Nostre Dame* (*c.* 1218–36), at first sight, is a work which belongs in a quite different context from the *Rose* and the *Violette*.[17] It is a vast collection of Marian legends in which, in the second and third redactions of the work (composed from *c.* 1219), groups of songs are set between the two books. Yet though the songs' texts are religious, musically they are *contrafacta*, modelled structurally upon and set to the melodies of a large range of trouvère chansons, *pastourelles* and refrains.[18] In generic range then, the songs are closely analogous to those in Renart's *Rose* and *Le Roman de la violette*.

This provides some evidence to suggest (as Chailley argues) that Gautier (like Gerbert de Montreuil) is also directly imitating Renart, and although the dates of both works are insufficiently established to make this certain, much in Gautier's manner in his Prologues (which introduce each book) suggests that he has a work such as Renart's *Rose* in his sights. In common with Renart and Gerbert, Gautier gives considerable emphasis to the performance of the songs, particularly as he claims he is performing them himself to the accompaniment of a 'vïele' (I, Pr 2, p. 22, lines 56–58).[19] His words match theirs in his reference to the contrast the songs will provide to the reading out of the legends: 'Un petitet, s'il ne vos grieve, / Ainz que plus lise, veil chanter' [For a little, if it does not trouble you, before I read more, I wish to sing] (I, Pr 2, p. 20, lines 16–17). Moreover, a substantial proportion of the numerous manuscript copies of the *Miracles* does contain musical notation.[20] This shows that music for vernacular song was transmitted around the date of Renart's *Rose*; it also raises the possibility that Gautier himself may have used a (now-lost) copy of Renart's work which had music written into it, as Renart asserts.[21] (The situation is less clear for the *Roman de la violette*, as I will go on to discuss.)

The third thirteenth-century work that recalls Renart's Prologue is *Aucassin et Nicolette*. The (anonymous) singer begins by announcing the names of his two main characters, but then immediately turns to the sung/spoken feature of the narrative:

> dox est li cans, biax li dis
> et cortois et bien asis.
> (8–9)[22]

Sweet is the melody, fine the words, courtly and well arranged.

Again, he draws the audience's attention to the work's impending generic contrasts ('dox est li cans, biax li dis'). *Aucassin* also survives in a single copy, but this time with music for each *laisse*. Although there is no consensus over its date, this use of a shared rhetorical trope suggests that the author is writing within the same generic horizon as Jean Renart, Gerbert de Montreuil and Gautier de Coinci.[23] It shows that Renart's work fits into a tradition in which music was more than a merely metaphorical presence in a text.

Renart's *Rose* is unique, but not isolated. It belongs with a larger thirteenth-century ambition to incorporate song within the medium of writing. The history of this ambition shows it to have been full of fits and starts, shaped partly by practical exigencies, and by the specialist nature of music copying. In the next two chapters, the precise nature of this fluctuating semi-oral, semi-literate relation between songs and narrative will be examined more closely by means of our only surviving evidence: the writings themselves.

2

The sources of song: chansonniers, narratives, dance-song

The writing down of song shapes the history of song. This is true in certain obvious ways: without writing, musical history would be invisible as well as inaudible. Many would argue that even with the aid of writing, the music of the past is strictly inaudible, as music of the *past*. Nonetheless, the desire to retrieve an aural image of the sound of early music powerfully motivates us to decipher medieval notation, even if we recognise that our resulting image is inescapably modern.[1] For while writing is the vital link between present and past, it is also the primary impediment. The differences between the ways in which music was written in the thirteenth century and modern notation are not merely cosmetic.[2] When we translate old writing we lose the representational relation between old writing and sound, yet if we do not translate it we run the risk of never grasping that relation in our own terms (the only terms, some would argue, that we can ever claim to understand). Writing presents to us the challenge of understanding as clearly as we can the relation between song as an event, and song as a set of written marks. It would be a mistake to think that one has automatic precedence over the other. Literacy affects the nature of music as much as it does of speech and poetry.

The early thirteenth century marks the moment when medieval vernacular song first came to be written down with any degree of consistency. The chansonniers began to be compiled around the middle of the century: some twenty major collections survive that continued to be copied until well into the fourteenth century, and in the case of troubadour manuscripts, as far as the sixteenth. Chansonniers do not represent the earliest surviving context for vernacular song, however. Written copies of songs first survive in any number in less expected places such as romances or sermons. In describing the history of these contexts, as I remarked earlier it is important to distinguish between the dates at which songs were composed, the dates of composition or compilation of the works into which they were copied, and the dates of the surviving manuscripts. Differences between any or all of these dates create anomalies that are often complicated to unravel. Apart from a single early twelfth-century witness from St Martial de Limoges,[3] one of the first written records of a troubadour song is Jaufre Rudel's 'Lanquan li jorn son lonc en may' [In May when the days are long] in Renart's *Rose*. Since the unique copy of the *Rose*, however, is late thirteenth century, priority in surviving manuscript terms comes with the version of 'Lanquan li jorn' in fr. 1374, a copy of the *Roman de la violette* that dates from before 1250.[4]

The early thirteenth-century date of composition of Renart's *Roman de la rose* (even allowing for the latest possible estimate of *c*. 1228) gives it singular, primary significance in the history of medieval song genres. The *chanson de toile*, the *rondet de carole*, and the independent refrain are all genres which survive in written form for the first time in this romance.[5] Many individual examples of these genres are unique to the narrative; others belong to genres not known from any other context, such as the *chanson d'éloge* and *tornoi de dames* (so named by Félix Lecoy). I commented earlier on the new mode of transmission for secular song provided by narrative in the early thirteenth century: this gains further significance when we realise that narrative contexts represent some of the earliest stages by which lyric genres were recorded in writing.

Before claiming too much for Renart, it should be remembered that another narrative source of songs is provided by the Arthurian prose romances, for which the earliest surviving manuscripts predate even the *Violette*. These contain a unique song genre, the Arthurian *lai*. They are also a repository for many other kinds of experimental speech genres. The earliest, the prose *Tristan* (the oldest manuscript is dated *c*. 1230), is a vast compilation, still only partially edited, within which are interleaved nearly ninety verse set-pieces.[6] Seventeen of these are *lais*, written out with music: as well as 'lai' they are given other titles in the manuscripts such as 'lettre en semblance de lai de Morgain à Artus' [a letter in the form of a lay from Morgain to Artu]. The Arthurian *lais* constitute a genre peculiar to the prose romance; they do not occur independently in other sources, and their form, usually an extended series of monorhyming quatrains, is not paralleled outside Arthurian romance.[7] They may well predate Renart's *Rose* in composition, forming a distinct branch in the process of copying song, and one that again included the copying of music, though confined to a single genre.[8]

How do narratives such as Renart's *Roman de la rose* and Gerbert's *Roman de la violette* compare with the chansonniers as sources of medieval secular song? In what sense could these *romans à chansons* be regarded as early forms of chansonniers? These questions have hardly been asked from a musicological point of view.[9] Conversely, until recently, literary historians have been able to find little more to say about the presence of the songs in these narratives than that they have a decorative, entertaining function.[10] It is time to reconsider the narratives from both perspectives. What can we learn about attitudes towards secular song in the early thirteenth century from the fact that the desire to anthologise and record song is first shown among romance authors? In what way do the later compilers of chansonniers share in such attitudes? Is there any evidence of mutual influence between compilers and romance authors?

For the purposes of direct comparison with the chansonniers it may be helpful to summarise the range and extent of song types found in narratives throughout the thirteenth and early fourteenth century. Here I consider both their literary and their musical transmission. In many respects, the pattern is far from consistent. The two earliest *romans à chansons*, *Le Roman de la rose* and *Le Roman de la violette*, contain the widest spectrum of genres, and in that sense approximate most closely to the chansonnier anthology model. The forty-eight songs (of which one is repeated) in the *Rose* include citations from trouvère chansons, troubadour *cansos*, dance-songs, including some independent refrains, *chansons de toile*, *pastourelles*, 'chansons dramatiques', a 'chanson d'éloge', a 'tornoi de dames' and an otherwise unidentifiable extract of narrative song. The *Violette* follows closely behind with forty citations – with an extra four in the variants – of which twenty-five are refrains, and the rest from trouvère chansons, occitan *cansos*, a *chanson de toile* and an epic fragment.[11]

Gautier de Coinci's *Miracles*, as we have already noted, make up another early thirteenth-century anthology, the sacred song texts being attached to secular melodies from chansons, *pastourelles* and refrains.[12] However, after this group, most of the inset lyrics to be found in secular (and some sacred) narratives throughout the thirteenth century are independent refrains, together with a smaller proportion of *rondets*. After Renart the quotation of *grands chants* becomes more rare. The most important exceptions in the thirteenth century are Jakemés' *Roman du castelain de Couci* and the anonymous *Chastelaine de Vergi*, both of which cite songs by the twelfth-century trouvère, the Châtelain de Couci. Late thirteenth- or early fourteenth-century narratives which cite chansons, or other longer lyric genres include *Meliacin*, a revised version of Adenet le Roi's *Cleomadés* by Girart d'Amiens, which has twenty-four songs (including several chansons), *Le Romans de la dame a la lycorne et du biau chevalier au lyon* and Nicole de Margival's *Le Dit de la panthère d'amours*. Some twenty narratives cite refrains exclusively, sometimes in very large numbers (there are around sixty-five in *Renart le Nouvel* and forty-nine in Baudouin de Condé's *Prison d'amours*), or only one or two (as in *Galeran de Bretagne* or Baudouin's *Li Contes de la rose*).[13] An important group, dating from the 1280s and 1290s, was produced in or near Arras, or has connections with works produced in Arras and nearby *puy* towns.[14]

Thus although credit is usually given (at his own request) to Jean Renart for instigating the whole French vernacular tradition of setting songs into narrative, his influence (on the authors of *romans à chansons*) was not straightforward: one might note the disparity of survival between the single manuscript of the *Rose*, the four copies of the *Violette* and nearly thirty of Gautier's *Miracles* with songs, of which thirteen have music. Gautier de Coinci's importance, especially in the history of *musical* transcription of vernacular song, deserves reassessing given the far wider dissemination of his work. Renart's narrative stands out, nonetheless, for its pioneering collection of diverse sung material, one that no other thirteenth-century work subsequently equals. This position is emphatically challenged in the fourteenth century by Chaillou de Pesstain's extraordinary feat of hybridisation in his version of the *Roman de Fauvel* (169 musical pieces are set into the narrative). In a further change of direction, poets such as Nicole de Margival, Guillaume de

Machaut and Jean Froissart set large numbers of the new *formes fixes* into their *dits*.

Broadly, the thirteenth century begins with the creation of anthology narratives, containing a mixture of higher and lower style songs. This is followed by a shift in practice towards the large-scale citation of refrains, interspersed with a few works citing *grands chants* (usually single stanzas), and then a radical generic change from the turn of the century in which narrative authors start to include the new *formes fixes* with a renewed emphasis on diversity.

The musical transmission for these inset songs is equally various. No music exists in the romances for *grands chants*. (They are given musical notation only in the *contrafacta* sources, that is, in Gautier de Coinci's *Miracles* and in a late thirteenth-century Latin work by Adam de la Bassée, the *Ludus super Anticlaudianum*.)[15] The two genres that are copied with music in thirteenth-century narratives – outside the unique *laisses* in *Aucassin et Nicolette* – are the Arthurian *lai*, and, far more ubiquitously, the refrain.[16] With the exception again of Adam's *Ludus*, and just two songs in the *Miracles*, all this music is monophonic: polyphony does not occur substantially in narrative before the *Roman de Fauvel* manuscript Paris BN fr. 146 (*c*. 1316–18).[17] Altogether, music is recorded for just under a quarter of the song citations, a proportion that compares well with the general patterns of survival of music in the troubadour and trouvère chansonniers.[18]

There are many, perhaps conflicting, inferences to be drawn from such observations: it is always difficult to generalise convincingly on the basis of scanty and partial evidence such as the presence or absence of musical notation, or the surviving copies of any one work or type of work. One place to begin might be by comparing directly, and in more detail, the nature of chansonniers and of romance as types of context for song. I propose first to consider how *grands chants* are presented in chansonniers and in romance.

WRITING 'COURTLY' SONG

My first example is a widely circulated song by Gace Brulé, 'Ne sont pas achoison de chanter' (R787).[19] First quoted in *Le Roman de la violette*, it is subsequently copied in twelve chansonniers. Gerbert de Montreuil gives the first stanza:

> Ne mi sont pas ochoison de canter
> Pres ne vergiés, plaseïs ne buisson;
> Quant ma dame mi plaist a commander,
> N'i puis trouver plus loial ochoison,
> Et molt m'est bon que sa valour retraie,
> Sa grant biauté et sa coulour veraie,
> Dont Dex li volt si grant plenté donner
> Que les autres m'en couvient oublïer.
> (5790–97)

> Neither fields nor orchards, gardens or woods give me an occasion to sing; but if it pleases my lady to command me, I cannot find a more loyal occasion, and it is all the more fitting that I rehearse her worth, her great beauty and her pure colour which God desired to give her in such abundance that others are driven from my mind.

Comparing the *mise-en-page* in general terms, first of all, we find that the two earliest copies of the *Violette* (fr. 1374 (*c.* 1240) and fr. 1553 (1284)) present the stanza rather differently. In fr. 1374, where it appears on fol. 168r in the upper half of the first column, the song text (in common with all the other songs in the romance) is written in red (see Fig. 1(a)). Space is left for an enlarged (and presumably illuminated) initial at the start of the song, and for another at the first line of narrative immediately following. There is no preparation for music. The stanza is written in prose, with punctuation separating each verse line. In fr. 1553 (fol. 320v) there is neither distinction in ink colour, nor any preparation for music, but again enlarged initials are used to mark the beginning of the stanza and the resumption of the narrative: here the initials alternate in red and blue and have filigree decoration that extends the length of the columns. The stanza is lineated as verse.

When we look now at the layout of this song in chansonniers we find variety rather than a uniformly distinct approach. The song is not generally copied with music, for instance.[20] The following three chansonniers (fr. 24406, *Trouvère* MS *V* (end thirteenth / beginning fourteenth century); n. a. fr. 1050, 'Clairambault', *Trouvère* MS *X* (late thirteenth century); and fr. 20050, the 'Chansonnier St Germain', *Trouvère* MS *U* (from *c.* 1250)) are representative in their range. Only one,

'Clairambault,' has musical notation for the song. This, in common chansonnier format, is written on four-line staves above the first stanza, with subsequent stanzas written as prose, as in *Violette*, fr. 1374, with punctuation separating each verse line (see Fig. 1 (b)). Fr. 24406 has empty five-line staves for the first stanza; the 'Chansonnier St Germain', however, has not been prepared for music at all; instead the whole song is written out as continuously lineated prose in a single column, the verse lines marked out by minor initials. There is not only variation from chansonnier to chansonnier, but also considerable discontinuity within individual collections. This is particularly marked in the 'Chansonnier St Germain' in which, out of 306 songs, ninety-three are notated, many others have blank staves, others again have spaces for staves, and a whole quire of song texts has no space for music at all.[21]

It is tempting to take a collection such as 'Clairambault' as representative of a notionally standard chansonnier layout: it is beautifully clear and well organised, every song has music and is not only grouped according to author, but individually labelled with the author's name.[22] Yet it is probably more accurate to see it as an articulate version of a genre of layout that ranged between extremes. The now heavily mutilated 'Chansonnier du Roi' (fr. 844, *Trouvère* MS *M*, thirteenth century) is even more rich and elaborate, with fine, enlarged author portraits introducing each group of songs. The Vatican chansonnier (Rome, Biblioteca Apostolica Vaticana, MS Lat. 5232, *Troubadour* MS *A*), also thirteenth century, has author portraits as well as rubrics, and begins on fol. 9 not with a *canso* but a *vida*, written in red. In this manuscript the *vidas*, or miniature poetic biographies take the place of music: a highly literary, even fictional image of the songs is thus created that is in fact typical of southern French and Italian troubadour manuscripts where music usually plays no part in song layout.

This general fluctuation in the presence or absence of music in the chansonniers indicates how little they can be said to present an equally balanced relationship between text and music. Visually, the presence of musical notation, even in those manuscripts where it is consistently given for each song, is far outweighed by the textual presence of the song's subsequent stanzas. Similarly, as I have already commented, it would be naive to assume that songs with music constitute a straightforwardly performative version of those songs.

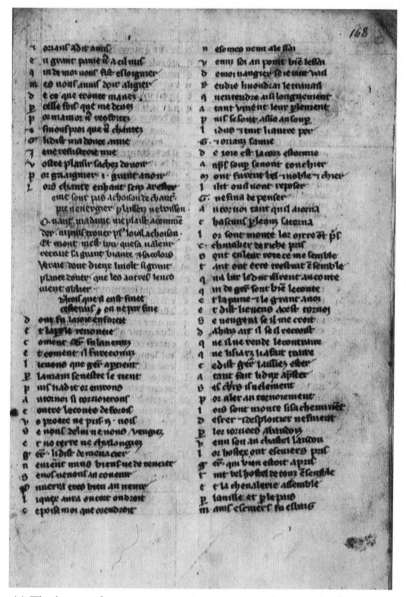

1 (a) The layout of a trouvère song in a romance: Gace Brulé, 'Ne sont pas achoison de chanter' in Gerbert de Montreuil, *Le Roman de la violette*, BN fr. 1374, fol. 168r. The stanza is written in red.

(b) The layout of a trouvère song in a chansonnier: Gace Brulé, 'Ne sont pas achoison de chanter' in BN n. a. fr. 1050, 'Clairambault', fol. 51r.

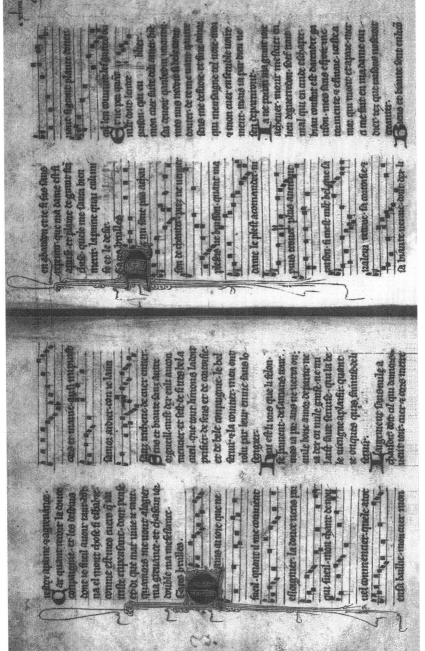

I (cont.)

These points would not need labouring were it not that the *romans à chansons* are so readily taken to contrast sharply with the chansonniers as contexts for song. The contrasts undoubtedly exist, but they should not be overdrawn. This can be seen both by observing the similarities between the layout of the notated songs in Gautier de Coinci's *Miracles* and several chansonnier layouts, and conversely, between the features of *mise-en-page* in the romances without music and the non-musical sections of chansonniers. Several of the *Miracles* manuscripts, notably the wealthy 'Soissons' manuscript (n. a. fr. 24541), fr. 22928, fr. 1536 and fr. 1530 introduce the opening group of songs, in common chansonnier style, with an author portrait of Gautier (sometimes the second group as well at the start of the second book). A particularly interesting mistaken rubric in fr. 2193 even introduces the first song cluster as 'Chans au roy Thiebaut' (fol. 1r) next to a picture of two figures holding a scroll between them. The rubricator appears to have thought he was beginning work on a chansonnier, and has unthinkingly labelled the songs with the name that routinely introduces the bulk of chansonnier compilations.[23] One perhaps telling detail of comparison in the converse case is that red ink is used on the one hand for song texts in one *Violette* manuscript, and on the other for the *vidas* in Vatican Lat. 5232: this gives visual prominence to the way in which the *vidas* in the Vatican chansonnier act as a biographical commentary on the songs, and in the romance, the songs are a commentary on the narrative. In both cases, the overall visual scheme of the manuscript is a careful articulation of textual and intellectual elements, a far cry from any simple sense of a performing script.[24]

The implications of the presence or absence of music in manuscript traditions are indeed difficult to assess. Literary scholars commonly assume that if musical notation is present then a song was sung, and if it is absent that music was not intended. Given the lack of music in romance contexts for *grands chants* compared to the chansonniers, it might seem reasonable to think that the romances imply a more literary, that is, more verbal context and character for song.[25] But these assumptions are misleading. The concentration of musical copying of refrains in romance increases dramatically throughout the thirteenth century. We need to take account of the fact that the gradually changing climate from orality to literacy means that more music was transcribed, an argument that qualifies the belief that connections between lyric and music diminish in the period and that this can be deduced from the surviving books.[26] The absence of musical notation for the *grands chants* should also prompt caution, since it is likely that it was caused at least as much by the relative difficulty of transcribing their melodies (difficulties evident in the chansonniers) as by an increasing disregard for their status as songs rather than texts. The brevity and formal simplicity of refrain melodies made them much easier to copy. On the face of it, then, we may have more grounds, paradoxically, for supposing the absence of music to prove orality and its presence to prove literacy than the reverse.

Simple contrasts are best avoided between the performative and the literary. The beguiling teleology of a large-scale drift towards 'writer-liness' conceals a more fluctuating and self-conscious relationship between text and event, a dynamic dialogue between music and poetry that stimulates creative composition in the thirteenth and fourteenth centuries. Renart's *Rose* is an anthology in which the songs have been chosen with a highly developed sense of their fictive role in a framing narrative: but this approach has much more in common with chanson-nier scribes than is usually assumed. At the same time, too much has been read into the fact that the single surviving copy of the *Rose* lacks music: there is no intrinsic reason for doubting Renart's assertion that he had music copied into his 'novel' work, though he may well have faced greater practical problems than Gautier who had access to a rich and musically literate scriptorium. But more important, perhaps, than any attempt at a simple answer to whether music was originally copied into the *Rose* is to reflect on the way in which the early written history of vernacular song is embedded within narrative. As Renart indicates, this is an immediately complex procedure. Not only does song become text, it does so by being quoted within a larger textual structure. Only after this anchoring in narrative does song come regularly to stand on its own as a written form.

We can trace this process quite directly by considering one of the most quoted of all trouvère songs, 'A vos, amant, plus k'a nule autre gent' [To you, beloved, more than to any other] by the twelfth-century poet, the Châtelain de Couci. He was a particular favourite of romance authors: Renart's *Rose*, the *Roman de la violette*, the *Chastelaine de Vergi*, *Meliacin* and *Le Roman du castelain de Couci* all quote songs attributed to him.[27] Moreover, they tend to quote from the same chansons, and even the same stanzas: thus the *Roman de la violette* and the *Chastelaine de Vergi* both quote Stanza III from 'A vos, amant',[28] a chanson which is also quoted in full in the *Castelain de Couci*; while Renart's *Rose* and the *Castelain de Couci* both quote the first stanza of 'Au nouviel tans que mais et violette' [In the new season of May and the violet].[29] This indicates that the quotation of Gui de Couci's chansons developed into a topos in its own right within the *romans à chansons* composed during the course of the thirteenth century. Whether the *romanciers* created his fame, or whether they merely capitalised on it, is interesting to speculate.

A first point of contrast is between the *Violette* and the *Rose*. Gerbert de Montreuil takes a compiler's approach to song.[30] Gerart, the hero of the *Roman de la violette*, remembers his absent lady Euriaut:

> Et nampourquant, quant l'en souvient,
> De chanter volentés li vient,
> Lors chante halt sans demourer:
>   Par Diu ! amours, grief m'est a consirer...
> (4621–24)

> And nevertheless, when he remembers her, the desire to sing comes upon him, and he then sings loudly without hesitation: 'Oh God, love, it is painful to me to part...'

Since the two lovers in the *Roman de la violette* are indeed far apart at this moment in the plot, the words of this stanza are fitting enough. However, there is little sense that the song has been specially chosen above any other. Similar introductory formulas are used a few lines earlier when Gerart, also thinking of Euriaut, sings a refrain (4473–80). The chanson stanza is no more appropriate to the plot than the refrain, and could equally well be replaced by any other lyric expression of regret or longing.

Renart, by contrast, consistently draws attention to the authorship of the *grands chants* he quotes, though not always with perfect seriousness. A case in point is his use of the first stanza from the Châtelain de Couci's song 'Li noviaus tens et mais et violete' (Lerond, Chansons, No. V). It occurs near the beginning of the romance. The Emperor Conrad has just heard for the first time a report of Lïenor's beauty which has already caused him to fall in love with her. Two stanzas from separate chansons are sung: the first by the Emperor and Jouglet (his minstrel) together, the second by the Emperor alone as he wakes in the morning after a troubled night's sleep and finds the sun streaming down on to his bed.

The pairing of the two stanzas is clearly something of a joke on Renart's part. The first is sung 'en l'onor monsegnor Gasçon':

> Quant flors et glais et verdure s'esloigne,
> que cil oisel n'osent un mot soner,
> por la froidor chascuns crient et resoigne
> tresq'au biau tens qu'il soloient chanter.
> Et por ce chant, que nel puis oublier,
> la bon' amor dont Dex joie me doigne,
> car de li sont et vienent mi penser.
> (846–52)

> When flowers and gladioli and greenery withdraw, and the birds dare not make a sound, each one cries and is fearful because of the cold until the fair weather comes when they are used to singing. Even so I sing – I cannot forget to – of the virtuous love of which God gives me joy, for my thoughts are all of her, and all from her.

The second, sung 'por l'amor bele Lïenor', paints an opposite seasonal picture. Instead of shivering, the nightingales are in full throat, and the flowers are blooming, not retreating from the cold. Naturally the outcome is the same in each case, with the poet inspired to sing of his love. Renart's choice of contrasting stanzas seems designed to show the contrivance of this kind of opening device in a chanson: one moment the birds are singing, the next moment they are not, yet in any case the lover, and especially this lover, is determined to sing. The remark 'en l'onor monsegnor Gasçon' in this light is ambiguous. Even without the second song to qualify it, this stanza by Gace Brulé cannot be felt to fit its narrative circumstances very successfully (except in its last two lines). It is difficult to avoid the conclusion that Renart includes it, with an ironic dig at Conrad's shallow critical opportunism, simply as a foil to the next lyric.

By referring each time by name to the trouvère from whom he is quoting, Renart maintains his distance from them. In the *Roman de la violette* the songs are presented as if they were spontaneous utterances; in the *Rose* they retain their autonomy as expressions of a different experience, uttered by a different person. The character in the *roman* (usually Conrad) does not simply speak through the songs, instead he uses them as an analogy for his own experience, and Renart leaves space in this disjunction between character and poet for his own implied authorial comment. The *grands chants* in the *Rose* are integrated in an experience of reading: Renart writes them into his narrative with an acute sense of their independent social meaning, something which he conveys both through Conrad's choice of each song, and also through his indirect ironic framing of such choices.

The chansonniers follow Renart and Gerbert de Montreuil in varying measure. There are examples, like Gerbert's, of relatively unsophisticated compilation, perhaps most of all in the 'Chansonnier St Germain' which has no apparent order for its songs, but indexes them in that sequence to provide at least a semblance of retrospective organisation. The 'Chansonnier Cangé' (fr. 846), in a more academic, but no less naive a spirit, puts the songs into first-line alphabetical order, an arrangement which obliterates any intellectual association between them. More often, however, the arrangement is by author, a decision which confirms Renart's cultivation of *grands chants* as an authored rather than anonymous genre. Yet it is the hierarchical ranking of authors in several of the chansonniers which most corresponds to Renart's highly developed consciousness of the social location of *grands chants*. In both kinds of context – romance and chansonnier – the songs are not merely gathered together but given precise social calibration. Both Renart as compiler, and certain of the chansonnier compilers are coordinating a carefully cultivated image of the trouvères and troubadours. They appear to be responding to the way in which the *grands chants* have developed as an institution: the songs evidently have a powerful social meaning in thirteenth-century culture which itself becomes an object of cultural scrutiny.

The pattern of influence between the early *romans à chansons* and the chansonniers takes a particularly interesting turn in two further romances, *La Chastelaine de Vergi* (early/late? thirteenth century) and *Le Roman du Castelain de Couci* (*c.* 1300) by Jakemés.[31] They are coupled together as early as the fourteenth century: Froissart, writing in *La Prison Amoureuse*, cites them both as representations of 'des vrais amans', as proverbial in their tragic loyalty as Tristan and Yseult:

> Qu'en avint Tristran et Yseus,
> Qui furent si vrai amoureus ?
> Le castellainne de Vergi ?
> Et le castellain de Couchi,
> Qui oultre mer morut de doel
> Tout pour la dame de Faioel?
> (217–22)[32]

> What happened to Tristan and Yseult, who were such true lovers?
> or the Châtelaine de Vergi? or the Châtelain de Couci who died for
> sorrow in Outremer all for the lady of Fayel?

For the author of the *Livre du Chevalier de La Tour-Landry*, the two
stories were examples of adultery.[33] Deschamps, and later Christine de
Pisan, however, held them in higher esteem. The Chastelaine 'la trés loyal
nommée de Vergy' [the very loyal one called de Vergi] and 'la dame de
Fayel' are listed by Deschamps amongst women of great 'onneur, bonté,
senz, beauté et valour' [honour, goodness, sense, beauty and worth] such
as Hester and Penelope.[34] Christine de Pisan refers to their dignified,
yet extreme response to the misfortunes caused by love.[35]

Each *roman* quotes from chansons attributed to the Châtelain de
Couci. The *Chastelaine de Vergi*, an anonymous work of barely one
thousand lines, quotes just one stanza from 'A vos, amant, plus k'a
nule autre gent'.[36] Jakemés, in the *Castelain de Couci*, makes a more
ambitious tribute to the poet by casting him as the hero of the *roman*, and
allowing him to sing several of his own chansons during the course of the
story.

The *Chastelaine de Vergi* could hardly be described as an anthology;
yet in its approach to song it functions in much the same concentrated
way as the elaborately detailed author portraits in the 'Chansonnier
du Roi'. Our attention is brought to bear on a single poetic statement
that is taken to possess already an intense cultural significance, and yet
which the work as a whole further confirms and enhances. The stanza
acts as a distillation of the emotional dilemma faced by the knight at
the moment when he perceives it most acutely.[37] The knight is caught
between having to confess his secret love, the secrecy of which is the very
condition of its existence, and submitting to a decree which would also

result in permanent separation from his lady. This choice determines the course of subsequent events, for the story remorselessly follows the bleak logic of the knight's situation. As he underlines with a pun on *jeu-parti*, merely by articulating the choice, the knight initiates a tragic end to his love:

> que le geu a parti si fort
> que l'un et l'autre tient a mort;[38]
> (269–70).

> that the game had divided so sharply that both choices led towards death.

It is here that the poet brings in the trouvère's lines:

> Si est en tel point autressi
> com li chastelains de Couci,
> qui au cuer n'avoit s'amor non,
> dist en un vers d'une chançon:
> > Par Dieu, Amors, fort m'est a consirrer
> > du dous solaz et de la compaingnie
> > et des samblanz que m'i soloit moustrer
> > cele qui m'ert et compaingne et amie;
> > et quant regart sa simple cortoisie
> > et les douz mos qu'a moi soloit parler,
> > comment me puet li cuers ou cors durer ?
> > Quant il n'en part, certes trop est mauvés.
> (291–302)

> He is exactly like the Châtelain de Couci, who did not have anything but love in his heart, [and] says in a stanza of a song:
> > Oh God, Love, it is hard for me to part from the sweet solace and company and countenance that the one who was my companion and friend used to show me; and when I consider her simple courtesy and the sweet words that she used to say to me, how can my heart remain in my body? If it doesn't part from it, then truly things are too bad.

The narrative impasse is temporarily filled by the song, yet it is not so much the narrative which is the focus of attention as the song itself, precisely in the way it is assumed to have a meaning which speaks beyond its own horizon.

The work which most implies a counter pattern of influence from the chansonniers back to romance is the *Castelain de Couci*. The formulas which introduce the songs into the narrative are very like those of Renart's *Rose* or the *Roman de la violette* (especially in the dancing scenes where three rondeaux are sung); and yet the overall structure of the work is an entirely new conception in Old French romance. It is clear that this conception in fact derives directly from the very brief Occitan thirteenth-century *vidas* and *razos* of the troubadours written to accompany the songs in a chansonnier such as Vatican Lat. 5232. Jakemés sets the Châtelain de Couci's chansons into a fictional narrative based on the well-known *coeur mangé* legend, where a lover is forced, by a jealous spouse, to eat the heart of his or her beloved.[39] The thirteenth-century biographies of Guilhem de Cabestanh first give this legend a hagiographical twist.[40] Jakemés's innovation is to develop the connection between *vida* and *canso* into a *roman à chanson*. The point of comparison here partly concerns authorship (an issue to which I will return in a later chapter): the trouvère as *auteur* gains more than a separate collection in a songbook, more even than a portrait, he becomes a hero in a romance of his own construction, in the implied narrative of his own corpus of songs. Chansonnier and romance intersect in that whereas the chansonniers have already created the authorial image of the trouvère, and have already given his songs a developed social context, the romance in turn continues the work of anthologising and recording the songs as an identifiable repertory.

The result of setting chansonniers and *romans à chansons* side by side helps us to gain a broader view of the process of putting song into writing in the thirteenth century. The particular importance of the *romans à chansons* in the history of lyric transmission lies in their centrally mediating role between performance and writing. The first part of this book seeks not to contrast song and text, but rather to argue that they cannot be so easily wrenched apart, least of all in this period. The notion of performance, as we perceive it in thirteenth-century writing, is already heavily overwritten with scribal preoccupations; conversely, a text has embedded within it long histories of living social practice. Nowhere is this more subtly and explicitly dwelt on than in works which propel song into an intensely direct dialogue with the complex processes of writing that were already part of the history of narrative. *Romans à chansons* invite us to tease out the double relation in this 'original' narrative context between the text as a representation of song, and the text as a representation of a narrative representation of song.

WRITING 'POPULAR' SONG

Popular song, as it is popularly defined, comes directly from the people: by its nature it is traditional and spontaneous, mobile, dynamic, and oral. In all of these respects it resists writing. Indeed the relation between popular culture and writing is usually claimed to be antipathetic: once it is written down, its essential qualities are lost as directness is replaced by the many-layered intervention of literacy. I have described the *romans à chansons* as passing across the boundaries of the oral and the literate. If it is surprising to find Renart's *Rose* acting as one of the very earliest anthologies of medieval high art song, and hence as a primal location for the turning of *grands chants* into highly literate artefacts, it is even more shocking to discover that it is the first, and often the only surviving site for the written expression of a wide range of lower style, apparently popular songs. The writing down of popular song seems a far more radical shift from the oral to the literate than the passage of high art into literacy. No doubt part of this is a nostalgic myth created by the literate, but there remains a powerful and observable difference between the ways in which high art and low art relate to writing.[41]

When we find, as in the case of the *Rose*, an apparently original source for popular song, the temptation to seek to recover the traces of this elusive culture is irresistible. Renart's *Rose* had immense value for nineteenth- and early twentieth-century scholars who, passionately absorbed by the question of origins, saw the romance as a place to discover *the* origin of popular song. The first and most influential formulation of this enquiry was undertaken by the two great turn-of-the-century French scholars Joseph Bédier and Alfred Jeanroy.[42] Both were intent on recovering a picture of French dance-song in all its primal innocence and unspoilt rural gaiety; the romances were a key resource not only for the songs they contained but also for the way they seemed to gesture with a special directness to a real, social world in which dance-song took place. That the romances were a far from popular (in the sense of lower-class) kind of writing did not, it seems, immediately concern them. The clashes of perspective in these and other sources of song between lower and higher art, the courtly, the popular, and the clerical will be examined more directly in a later chapter.

Here I want to build on the work of Bédier and Jeanroy by focusing on the complexities of interpreting 'popular' song in romance. The major interpretative crux concerns the portrayal of dance-song by means of refrains and *rondets*. So much confusion persists about the nature of refrains that it seems necessary to return (at least briefly) to the questions that taxed Bédier and Jeanroy early last century. They were involved with two separate – though closely connected – issues: one concerning the relation of refrains to dance-song, the other the possibly fragmentary nature of refrains. Although both scholars were perhaps ultimately engaged in a form of social anthropology, they differed in their interpretation of textual evidence, and whether refrains are to be regarded as whole or fragmentary. Jeanroy believed that refrains were fragments of dance-songs now lost, but which would have had a narrative or dramatic character.[43] Bédier saw no reason to believe that refrains were fragmentary. With an ingenious argument based on 'Le Jeu du Chapelet', or the game of the circlet of flowers (see Fig. 2), vividly described in the late thirteenth-century 'courtly' romance, *Le Tournoi de Chauvency*, he demonstrated that refrains could be part of a dance without being part of larger poems, without, in other words, necessarily sacrificing their independence.

This is not the place to rehearse their debate in full; nonetheless certain of the arguments bear re-examination since the issues remain current, and well illustrate the problematic, yet uniquely transitional nature of the narratives as lyric sources.[44] In particular, there has remained a tenacious belief in the fragmentary nature of refrains, and this in spite of the work van den Boogaard and Doss-Quinby have done to correct such a view.[45]

One of the main reasons why it has persisted concerns the connections between refrains and rondeaux. A rondeau's structure is dependent upon a refrain; in addition, we know that the earliest rondeau forms (those found in Renart's *Rose*) were dance-songs, or *rondets de carole*. Since we also have plenty of evidence that refrains accompanied dance-song (at least in some form) it has seemed natural to conclude that an isolated

2 'Le Jeu du Chapelet' [The Game of the Circlet of Flowers] in Jacques Bretel, *Le Tournoi de Chauvency*, Oxford, Bodleian Library, MS Douce 308, fol. 113 r.

refrain implies the existence of a *rondet de carole* based on that refrain.[46] This, in essence, was Jeanroy's view: 'tous nos refrains ne sont que des fragments de rondets' (p. 407). It is still being echoed by Pierre Bec when, discussing the form and origins of the *rondet*, he writes: 'la plupart de nos refrains médiévaux ne sont que des fragments (ou des éléments générateurs?) de rondets'.[47]

Bec's curious mixture of assertiveness and equivocation about whether a refrain is a fragment or whether it is a generating element of a *rondet*, epitomises the uncertainty in modern views of the refrain. Despite the fact that both the refrain and the *rondet de carole* are widely agreed to be constituents of dance-song, the precise relation between the two has hardly been discussed since Jeanroy and Bédier.[48] Moreover, where song forms are discussed, notably by Bec, it is on their own terms. Here, my case is that they need to be considered in the context in which they are transmitted. I will therefore consider the nature and role of refrains both separately in *rondets*, and in romance. This involves trying to discern the nature of both the songs and the *romans* as forms of writing. We need to take account of the way in which the *romans* create their own pressure as a literate, fictional and rhetorical context upon the form of the songs transcribed within them. Renart's *Roman de la rose* is tantalizingly difficult to read in this way, but as I hope to show, the difficulties are indicative of the subtle factors shaping the transformation of lyric genres throughout this period.

Let us begin by examining the presentation of both *rondets* and refrains in Renart's *Rose*. The fact that Renart quotes both independently – for alongside the seventeen *rondets de carole* are three isolated refrains – suggests immediately that he distinguishes between them.[49] In that case, what precisely is a *rondet de carole*, and what is the relation of the refrain to it? The question itself is not as easy as it appears, since it raises the issue of how an oral form is to be understood from its written version. Is it a dance or is it a text, or rather, since it is both, how does its textual form correspond to its social form?

As a dance, the *rondet de carole* (at its simplest) has been described by scholars ever since Gaston Paris and Alfred Jeanroy as a song performed by a group of dancers, linked either in a circle or in a single chain, moving in step to the song.[50] The song itself (according to this description) consisted of refrains sung in alternation with strophic sections, the strophic sections being sung by a soloist or a small group of singers, and the refrains by a chorus comprising the rest of the company of dancers. The soloist or solo group dances alone in the middle of the circle, or leads the dancers in the open chain. This description has been deduced largely in its detail from romances, but also in outline from other sources such as sermons and moralising treatises.[51] Various kinds of textual evidence are used to supply this description. First, it is argued, the variable form of the *rondets* found in Renart's *Rose* (later to develop into the fixed form of the fourteenth-century rondeau) suggests the possibility of an alternating chorus and soloist because it often contains a refrain repeated as a half-line in the middle of the stanza:

> Aaliz main se leva,
> *bon jor ait qui mon cuer a!*
> Biau se vesti et para,
> desoz l'aunoi.
> *Bon jor ait qui mon cuer a*
> *n'est pas o moi.*
> (1579–84; vdB, rond. 9)[52]

Aaliz got up early. *Good day to the one who has my heart!* Beautifully she dressed and prepared herself, under the alder. *Good day to the one who has my heart! He is not with me.*

The repetition of the refrain sets up a principle of alternation all the more marked by the lack of clausal connection between it and the strophic lines, or *additamenta*, as the early fourteenth-century theorist Johannes de Grocheio terms it.[53] The refrain – a brief first-person exclamation of love – interrupts a miniature description in the third person of a pastoral scene. The change in voice between refrain and *additamenta* is characteristic of many *rondets*, including those quoted in other romances. Take for instance:

> C'est la jus, desoz l'olive.
> *La la voi venir, m'amie.*
> La fontaine i sort serie,
> el jaglolai soz l'aunoi.
> *La la voi, la voi, la voi,*
> *la bele la blonde; a li m'otroi.*
> (*Lai d'Aristote*, 303–08; vdB, rond. 17)[54]

It's over there, under the olive tree. *There I see her coming, my beloved.* The fountain springs up clearly and the gladioli under the alder. *There, I see her, I see her, I see her, the beautiful, the blonde one, I give myself to her.*

Again, but even more briefly, there is a sketch of a scene in the *additamenta* – a fountain playing in the alder grove – interrupted by a refrain in the first person, as if by a lover talking of his lady.

But while the typology of *rondets de carole* is usually straightforward – essentially there are two broad strophic types, one describing a pastoral scene 'la gieus' ('over there') in which there is either an olive tree or a fountain (or even both as above), and the other describing Bele Aeliz[55] – the manner of their transcription in the earliest sources is variable. Take the following, quoted by Renart:

> C   est la gieus la gieus qen dit en ces prez.
> vos ne vendrez mie dames caroler. la
> bele aeliz i vet p[or] ioer souz lavert olive
> vos ne vendrez mie caroler es prez q[ue] vos

namez mie. Gi doi bien aler et bien caroler
cariai bele amie
(5427–35;[56] vdB, rond. 15)

It's over there, over there that they are singing in the meadows. *You should never come carolling, ladies.* Beautiful Aeliz goes there to play under the green olive tree. *You should never come carolling in the meadows for you do not love at all. I must indeed go and carol for I have a pretty lover.*

This example appears initially to conform to one of the simpler *rondet* structures in the romance, with an internal, partially repeated refrain in a second voice interrupting the description of a pastoral scene (in which the 'C'est la gieus' and 'Bele Aeliz' types are in fact conflated). However, the last two lines disrupt this scheme. According to Bédier (who follows a reconstruction initially proposed by Jeanroy) they form two extra strophic lines which are to be followed again by the refrain *Vos ne vendrez mie.*[57] But *Gi doi bien aler*, far from belonging to a pastoral landscape, is a phrase which closely resembles other refrains.[58] Other reconstructions are therefore possible, and other hypotheses about how the form came to be transcribed in this way. For example, suppose the manuscript form of this song is indeed fragmentary (in Zumthor's sense); the transcription may represent an abbreviated version of two performances of the song, sung with a second refrain (in the second performance) acting as a reply to the first: '*you* should never come here to carol' but 'I will and must'. Or else, given the disturbance of type in the strophic sections, the manuscript could be attesting, in some confused process of semi-oral, semi-literate transmission, to two distinct *rondets.*[59]

My interest here is less in trying to claim any one reconstruction as superior than in illustrating, through the difficulty of 'reading' these texts, that we need to consider the nature of the romance as 'evidence' afresh. Part of this reconsideration is the question of what exactly the written form of the songs is evidencing. Does the form of the songs reflect the way in which thirteenth-century dance-song was actually performed? Or does it instead reflect the performance practice of the romance, in which such dance-song is represented through the filtering medium of romance? Most likely, perhaps, it constitutes a literate, fictionalised piece of rhetorical description that stands at one remove from the actualities of live performance. One step towards resolving these possibilities would be to clarify the status of the refrain, since the different views about whether it stands alone or whether it implies a *rondet* or larger dance-song interlude in turn implicitly posit different views of the status of the manuscript in relation to what it describes.

Bédier believed that the refrain was the fixed element in the dance-song, and the strophe the part which was renewable ('Les plus anciennes', p. 399). Fixity had two meanings: a repeated and hence constant element within the *rondet*, and second, a traditional tag which the majority of dancers knew, unlike the rest of the song which was known only by the soloist.

The preceding examples of *rondets* in Renart's *Roman de la rose* show that there is a textual basis for a principle of alternation between refrain and *additamenta*. However, it is not the refrain that is the fixed element in the song, but the *additamenta*. As we have seen, in the whole collection of *rondets de carole* in Renart's *Rose*, there are only two types of strophe, one describing Bele Aeliz, and the other a pastoral scene 'la gieus' in which there is either an olive tree or a fountain. Each type is 'fixed' in the sense that it contains its own formula of words, which remains constant from *rondet* to *rondet*. The refrains, on the other hand, while they are repeated within each *rondet*, are not repeated among the group of *rondets* (although they are often used in other contexts).

If the strophic sections remain constant, while the refrains vary from *rondet* to *rondet*, it is inaccurate to describe the strophe as the more complicated, less well-known part of the *rondet*. The strophic sections are commonplace, and highly familiar, the refrains a means of providing individual point to the songs. The refrain acts as the distinguishing semantic feature of each *rondet*, just as it also acts as the *rondet*'s primary structural characteristic. This is presumably why, in the romances, refrains are often assigned to solo singers, rather than a chorus.

Musically, there are further reasons for expecting the refrain to have a key role. Very few examples of rondeau texts survive complete with music from the thirteenth century; for the most part, as I noted earlier, notation survives only for refrains. This indicates that the tune of the refrain is fundamental to the music of the rondeau.[60] The completely notated rondeaux, such as the rondeaux of Guillaume d'Amiens, support this. They have the following schema:

Text	A	B	a	A	a	b	A	B
Music	α	β	α	α	α	β	α	β

Although the words change between soloist and chorus, both the refrain and strophic sections have the same melody. Since the refrain starts the structure, it can thus be said to generate it: it acts as the key to the performance of the whole song.[61]

This discussion of the structural role of the refrain in *rondets* concludes against Jeanroy. Its textual characteristics – clausal interruption, change in voice, change of theme – are precisely of the type that suggests that the refrain, far from being organically integrated into a *rondet*, is a disjunctive element. As the above examples show, not only are the refrains detached semantically from the strophic sections, they form a new sentence structure which is superimposed upon the strophe. There is an accidental relation between a *rondet* and its refrain: across the two strophic types 'C'est la gieus' and 'Bele Aeliz' any refrain could be superimposed. The refrains can hardly, in that case, be thought of as inseparable from the *rondets* in which they occur.

The verbal independence of the refrain within a *rondet*, and musically, its function as the primary generating element of the dance-song, shows that to think of an isolated refrain as a fragment of a *rondet* carries with it misleading assumptions. The form of a *rondet* does appear to encase a refrain in a way which makes the refrain more integral to the song than if the refrain were an independent burden recurring at the end of successive stanzas, as in the later virelai and ballade. Yet we can now see that this is indicative of the dependence of the *rondet* form upon the refrain, rather than, as Bec argues, the other way round.[62]

If we accept that the refrain is indeed autonomous then, in attempting to describe an isolated refrain, there would be little point in general in trying to find a *specific* surviving context from which it could have originated. The pioneering bibliographical work by van den Boogaard has shown that refrains occur in the thirteenth and early fourteenth centuries across a wide range of contexts, including motets and chansons as well as many kinds of narrative genres. For example, the refrain *Ne vos repentez mie / de loiaument amer* [Never repent of loving loyally] appears in seven contexts altogether: as the eleventh rondet in Renart's *Roman de la rose*, in *La Court de Paradis* (an anonymous thirteenth-century sacred narrative), in Gautier de Coinci's *Miracles* (III, 502) and in four *chansons avec des refrains*.[63] None of these could confidently be described as the 'original' source of the refrain, and the textual history of many refrains confirms that the concept of a single original context is in any case inappropriate. This is not to say that there may not be specific instances in which refrains can be identified as 'new', as the invention of a particular poet. On the contrary, the possibility of their existence, together with the difficulty of identifying them, should make us all the more wary of branding refrains in general as shortened forms of *rondets de carole*.

Having concluded that refrains are not simply fragments of *rondets de carole*, it would follow that they cannot, in any simple sense, be fragmentary citations in a romance either. We may test this by considering now their role within romance, especially since the earliest *rondets* first survive in romance. In what way do their characteristics in *rondets* relate to their characteristics in romance?

I want to return to the problems of transcription in the dance-songs of Renart's *Roman de la rose* in order to compare them with a similar description of dance-song in the *Roman de la violette*.[64] The most obvious difference between the two is that whereas Jean Renart quotes *rondets* along with three isolated refrains (a unique combination in thirteenth-century romance), Gerbert de Montreuil quotes only refrains. It has been suggested that here we see the 'birth' of the refrain, since either because of scribal laziness or confidence in readers' memories, refrains represent incipits which readers were expected to fill out for themselves.[65] The true contrast is that Gerbert's work is more unselfconsciously literate than Renart's.

The opening scenes of each romance illustrate this well. The setting in the *Rose* is a *fête champêtre*: the whole court has moved into the forest for a fortnight, and feasts in silken pavilions, hunts, dances and makes love in an extravagant round of sensual pleasure. (Such a court setting – whether indoors or out – commonly signals the citation of dance-song in later *romans à chansons* such as *La Court de Paradis*, *Le Tournoi de Chauvency* and *Renart le Nouvel*.) The first bout of carolling takes place as a group of young courtiers are returning to the pavilions after a leisurely day spent wandering barefoot in the woods, washing in nearby springs and picnicking, the ladies in clothing that gradually becomes ever more dishevelled. On the way, 'li chevalier' begin to sing spontaneously 'ceste chançonete' (see Fig. 3):

> E   non deu sire se nelai,
>   lamor de lui mar lacoi[n]tai
> (291–92)

> *In God's name, sir, if I do not have his love, then cursed be our meeting.*

This refrain prompts a series of songs, a *rondet*, another refrain, and three more *rondets*, some sung by male, some by female soloists. After dinner, later that evening, a more formal sequence begins: the ladies and gentlemen proceed out of the marquees, then position themselves 'main a main... en .i. prevert' (507–08) [hand in hand... in a green meadow] in order to start the *carole*. A lady begins with a *rondet*; her role as soloist is taken by a young squire, who is attached to the 'prevost d'Espire', then by the son of the Count of Aubours and finally, by the Duchess of Austria.

Both passages present a combination of solo and communal performance, though in exactly what manner it is difficult to decide. Dancing is implied, even though the details are cryptic: we are told that the first lady (in the second sequence) steps forward (511) and, after the second rondet, that 'Ceste not pas dure .III. tours' (528) [this did not last more than three turns]. The words 'redit' and 'conmence' and 'reconmence' also allude obscurely to the course of the dancing.[66] Three times, Renart tells us, a new member of the company began to sing before the previous song had finished (293–94). The song citations do not present a clear performance picture either. The two isolated refrains are differentiated formally from the *rondets* – and the refrains within the *rondets* – by being in a rhymed couplet. But there is no consistent division between soloist and chorus, refrain and strophe. The first refrain, *E non Deu*, is sung by the knights as a group, but the second by a single girl, and all the *rondets* by individuals. In one case at least it is the refrain in a *rondet* which appears to have direct relevance to the soloist. In addition, the songs are not attached by rhyme to the narrative octosyllabics, and so could be arranged in any order without causing disruption either to the form of the *roman* or to its plot.

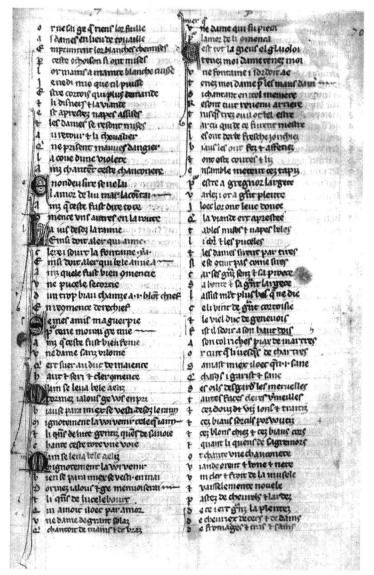

3 A sequence of six dance-songs (each marked out by an enlarged initial) beginning with the refrain '*En non Deu*', in Jean Renart, *Le Roman de la rose*, Rome, Biblioteca Apostolica Vaticana Reg. 1725, fol. 70r.

If we wanted to suppose that a traditional *carole* was being represented here, we would have to assume that the text was indeed fragmentary – even misleading. This is caused partly by the nature of the song forms, and partly by the way in which the mixture of artless informality and orderly sequence, both in the narrative description and in the form of the songs, contributes to a powerful sense of spontaneous, unstructured oral performance. Here, if anywhere, we seem to have an example of a work which gestures in its incompletion towards a more full performance context. But is this a context described by the romance or performed by it? Two of the *rondets* alternate their refrain lines in a chiastic pattern (see Fig. 3):

```
M   ain se leva bele aeliz
    dormez ialous ge vos enpri
b   iause para miex sevesti. desoz le raim
M   ignotement la voi venir cele q[ue] iaim–
et  li gentiz que[n]s de savoie
c   hante ceste tote une voie
M   ain se leva bele aeliz
    mignotement la voi venir
b   ien se para miex se vesti. en mai
D   ormez ialous, et ge menvoiserai—
(310–21)
```

Beautiful Aeliz got up early – *sleep, jealous one, I beg you* – she prepared herself beautifully, dressed even more so, under the branch. *I see her coming gracefully, the one I love!* And the noble Count of Savoy sang this right through: Beautiful Aeliz got up early – *I see her coming gracefully* – she prepared herself beautifully, dressed even more so, in May. *Sleep, jealous one, and I will enjoy myself.*

This is both rhetorically neat (which might imply that the romance is merely describing the scene) and convincingly oral in the ease with which the lines pass from one *rondet* structure into another (which might imply that the romance is revealing performance practice). In this passage (as in oral performance), the two are not mutually exclusive. Ironically, Renart's work gives just enough impression of rhetorical and formal control over its presentation of oral spontaneity to make it hard at times to distinguish its script from one which is testifying, for example, to the reactions of a scribe to an informal oral performance.[67]

The scene in the *Roman de la violette* corresponds precisely (in an indoor setting) to the second sequence of dance-song in Renart's *Rose*: the court has just finished dinner and is in the mood for some carolling. Each lady chooses a knight for the dance. As in Renart's scene, a lady begins:

> Commenche tout premierement
> A chanter ma dame Nicole...
> *Alés bielement que d'amer me duel.*
> (98–99; 104)

Right at the start my lady Nicole begins to sing: *Go beautifully that I may give myself up to love-sorrow.*

Here, however, dance movements are hardly mentioned at all, aside from the odd reference to carolling. Altogether Gerbert chooses to make little concession to spontaneity in his representation of the scene:

> La damoisiele de Couchi,
> Cui Dex fache vraie merchi,
> Qui molt fu avenans et biele,
> A dit ceste canchon nouviele,
> Car ele amoit bien par amor:
> *Seulete vois a mon ami;*
> *S'ai grant paor.*
> Li castelainne de Nïor,
> C'on apieloit Alïenor,
> Molt estoit cointe, un poi brunete,
> Puis a dit ceste cançonnete,
> Qu'ele n'estoit mie esperdue:
> *Aprendés a valoir maris,*
> *Ou vous m'avés perdue.*
> (129–42)

The lady of Couci – to whom God grant true mercy – who was very attractive and pretty, uttered this new song, for she was very much in love: *I go alone to my lover; I am terrified.*

The châtelaine of Nior, who was called Alïenor, was very delicate, and somewhat dark-haired. She then uttered this song, for she was not at all dismayed: *Learn to be worthy, husband, or you have lost me.*

Whereas in the *Roman de la rose*, the songs were linked together to suggest a rudimentary dancing sequence, Gerbert presents each refrain as if it were a distinct, separate performance. The passage is striking not for its impression of spontaneity but its stylisation. Seven singers are described (all female), and each in the same way: the poet informs us first of her identity, then lists her attractive features, and finally (except in two cases) gives a brief emotional reason for her choice of refrain.

The order of singers and refrains is not so much an order of events, as a rhetorical order, and in this case they do seem mutually exclusive. The description is well balanced and has a clear principle of repetition: one singer, one refrain, and three elements of description. Unlike Renart, Gerbert rhymes the refrains with the narrative lines, so that the line immediately preceding a refrain rhymes with the second line of a two-line refrain, or with the last two lines of a three-line refrain.[68] To make the scene even more stylised, the narrative cues between the central three refrains are each of the same length, as if they were five-line strophic sections. For these reasons, it is clear that Gerbert's use of refrains rather than *rondets* is far from haphazard. Instead the refrains fit into a carefully organised rhetorical scheme where, in contrast to the passage in Renart's *Rose*, there is no suggestion of spontaneous whimsicality in the choice of song form. It might be argued that the refrains could still represent abbreviated forms of *rondets*. Yet it would have to be recognised that any sense of abbreviation, if it exists, refers outside the romance. Within the rhetorical terms of the romance, and hence, by implication, within its terms of performance, the refrains are complete.

In trying to understand the negotiations in these romances between what they describe and what they enact, it seems that different modes of performance are actually written into the texts, and 'written' in various senses. Sylvia Huot has discussed how writing acts as a visual representation of speech.[69] There are ways of reading further into the performative character of medieval manuscripts which consider how the manuscripts themselves reflect a complex meeting-ground in the course of the thirteenth century between oral and literate cultures. They raise the acute dilemma of how one is to differentiate in a medieval manuscript between different types of written performance: between writing which is attempting to record a specific oral performance; writing which imitates an oral performance style; and writing which (like the modern novel) is an act of writing rather than performing. The difficulty each time concerns the extent to which the manner of performance is 'visible' from its written version. In the *romans à chansons*, the songs complicate the issue even further, since they raise questions about their own manner of performance, and the extent to which their performance conditions are changed by their context in romance. For the songs are also 'written' in the sense that they are described in the narrative; the performance of each song is circumscribed by the narrative frame of the roman, so that it is always, in some sense, a *mediated* performance, and one which includes the audience's response within the romance.

These *romans* thus internalise the various stages of a song's existence: its production, performance, reception and reproduction. This is a fascinating and difficult process to observe, as the dilemmas it poses turn out to have a much larger resonance than one might expect from problems of transmission. The process is not a naive one. We are witnessing not a direct reflection of the way in which people in the thirteenth century performed trouvère songs, *caroles* and *chansons de toile*, but a view of how a particular poet wished to represent such performances and their cultural signals. At the same time, each *roman* is engaged in the same processes of transmission, a situation which is acutely self-reflexive, since the means by which the *roman* has been transmitted necessarily shapes the view it presents of the transmissive process. Subject to the contingent vagaries of transmission, the *roman* cannot after all be said to exert full control over its self-presentation, and as we shall see, this renders the term 'self-reflexive' inadequate. It is precisely the slippage between these two kinds of semi-orality – the version described by the *roman* and the version which describes it – that I am attempting to examine in this chapter.

The contrast between Renart's *Rose* and the *Violette* is particularly interesting in this respect, since the changes in Gerbert's use of refrains from Renart's seem to indicate a different balance in the two works between the performative and the descriptive. The presence of orality does seem to be stronger in the text of the *Rose*, and even if this is simply caused by poorer transmission there is a sense in which (as I shall argue more fully shortly) the work, by being interested in problems of oral transmission, lends itself to this risk. It would be a mistake, I think, to regard Gerbert's work as a development from Renart's simply because it presents dance-song in a more stylised manner. Renart's understanding of the complexities of the relation between performance, genre and writing has a sardonic subtlety that far outweighs the blandness with which Gerbert rhetoricises song. What we can learn from the *Violette* is the way in which the genre of the refrain lends itself with ease to different kinds of textual presentation.

I have been arguing that one way of resolving the question of whether refrains are complete or fragments of *rondets de carole* in romance versions of dance-song is to examine their rhetorical status, to see whether they form part of the internal or external performance context. Does the generative role that we found refrains to have in *rondets de carole* also apply to their role in romance? I want to approach this question by considering their internal context in romance more closely, and refining the terms 'complete' and 'fragmentary'. As I argued earlier, to say that refrains imply a specific 'original' context is a specious scholarly assumption. But this is not to say that refrains may not imply *some* kind of context. Only a very small proportion of refrains survives outside either a lyric or narrative context in the thirteenth century, for example, in proverb collections or as isolated jottings.[70] In this sense, a refrain's independence is perhaps its most paradoxical characteristic. It is in the curious position of behaving like a genre whose most constant characteristic is its dependence on other genres. When we look at its role in romance in more detail, we find refrains acting with precisely this kind of independence yet dependence in relation to the narrative.

Further examples of refrain-citation in the *Roman de la violette* bear out the fundamental, generating role of refrains. Towards the end of the same opening court scene, Gerart, the hero of the romance, is asked to perform some songs. He obliges with the first strophe of a song attributed to Gace Brulé, and then, as soon as he has finished this, sings a 'cançonnete a karole':

> *J'ai amours fait a mon gré,*
> *Miels en vaurra ma vie.*
> (204–05)

> *I have made love just as I desire, my life is worth more for it.*

Although the refrain is described as a *carole*, Gerart is not dancing to it. Instead he follows it with a speech about his own lady which begins by taking up the words of the refrain:

> Miels en doit valoir sans mentir. . .
> (206)

> It must be worth more because of it, indeed. . .

He concludes his speech with a second refrain:

> Et pour chou qu'il me souvient ore
> De li, chanterai jou encore
> Ceste chançon, pas ne lairai:
> *Dont n'ai jou droit que m'envoise,*
> *Quant la plus biele amie ai?*
> (234–38)

> And because I am reminded of her now, I will sing this song again,
> and not hold back: *Am I not right to enjoy myself, since I have the most*
> *beautiful of lovers?*

The two refrains frame the whole speech, the first prompting it, and the second acting as a rousing rhetorical climax. But the second also has a further, generating function in the plot, since by causing general envy among the rest of the courtiers, Gerart spurs Lisiart, comte de Forez, into the treachery which defines the course of the hero's subsequent adventures. In this example, the refrains thus have a key initiating role, both in the detail of the narrative material and in its larger structure.

In a further example, we find the following refrain syntactically completing an invitation begun in direct speech to dance:

> Apriés cheli une canta,
> Qui clere vois et boin chant a,
> Ele ert ducoise de Bourgoigne;
> Son ami par le main enpoigne,
> Puis li a dit: 'Amis, cantés:
> *Alés cointement et seri,*
>   *Se vous m'amés.*
> (105–11)

> After her another lady, who was the Duchess of Burgundy, sang with
> a clear voice and a fine tune; she grasped her friend by the hand and
> then said to him: 'Friend, sing, *Dance elegantly and smoothly, if you*
> *love me.*

Here the refrain merges so seamlessly into the spoken request that it is difficult to tell whether the Duchess is instructing her lover in song to dance elegantly and gracefully, or whether she is asking him to sing the following song containing that instruction. The delicately implicit mutuality of this performance is suggested by the transitional nature of the refrain between speech and song.

It is in this context (rather than a naïve realist one) that we should situate the character of the refrain-citation in Bédier's model text, Jacques Bretel's *Le Tournoi de Chauvency*. On the face of it, the work is indeed naively realist. Bretel presents his work as an eyewitness account of the tournament. He even tells us the exact date on which he started his book – 8 September – and fills his account with references to the care with which he noted down on the spot the details of what was happening each day (2107–09). All the people present are named with historical accuracy, and the fourteenth-century Oxford manuscript (Bodleian Library, MS Douce 308) provides a visual echo of the text's precision in its numerous heraldic insignia. The tournament is described in meticulous detail, to the extent that historians have frequently used the work to reconstruct actual thirteenth-century practice.[71] Into such an event, songs fit entirely naturally: they are integral to the atmosphere of courtly entertainment to which the whole work is committed, and in which it participates.

However, such a show of verisimilitude has a teasing quality. The spontaneity which Bretel is at pains to present is so highly polished that it is impossible to decide where entertainment is being created by the poet, and where it is being reflected from an actual occasion. This ambiguity about the work is captured by the illustrator in the Oxford manuscript, who shows the lady performing one of the set-piece dances presented in the narrative (fol. 123 r, 2533–602) holding a mirror (see Fig. 4(a)). Unlike Oiseuse in Guillaume de Lorris's section of *Le Roman de la rose*,[72] she is not explicitly described in the dance as holding a mirror, but the object precisely represents the way in which the social and the poetic are mirrored both within and by means of the narrative. Scenes of this kind are represented in mirror cases of the period (see Fig. 4(b)). Take for example the moment just after Bretel's description of a dialogue exchanged on the fourth evening between a knight and a lady. The poet begins by explaining to his audience how he overheard

4 (a) 'La danse robardoise', showing a lady holding up a mirror, in Jacques Bretel, *Le Tournoi de Chauvency*, Oxford, Bodleian Library, MS Douce 308, fol. 123 r.
(b) Ivory mirror back, showing courtly scene with dancing and a circlet of flowers, French, fourteenth century, Victoria and Albert Museum.

the pair talking, and that from admiration, he cannot now forbear from repeating their speeches. Their words follow, given propriety and formality by being presented as two consecutive set pieces. When the 'parlement' is concluded, the lady summons Bretel himself to entertain them with some new compositions. It is a witty moment of double, or even triple reflection, for Bretel shows the pair of courtiers contributing to a piece of entertainment in the same breath as they are asking to be entertained themselves, and contributing not only within the romance to its internal audience but by means of the romance to its external audience of which they may well have been a part.

Bretel's handling of refrains well illustrates such shifts between different modes of performance. On the third evening of the tournament, seven refrains are cited which together depict a series of personal

4 (*cont.*)

encounters within a defined group of courtiers. As in the *Roman de la violette*, where a refrain in turning a spoken request into song unobtrusively moves a private moment into a public register, so here each encounter is private on its own terms, but linked by the refrains into a more stylised, communal activity.

The scene begins with Bretel's isolation of a particular couple, Renaut de Trie and Jehenne d'Auviler, holding each other by the hand as they dance.

Bretel, following every movement and flicker of response, comments with gossipy knowingness:

> En mon cuer pansai: 'Se me samble,
> Dont avenéz vos bien ensamble.'
> (2463–64)

> I thought to myself: 'it seems to me that you go very well together.'

Then follows another couple; the girl makes the advance:

> *Clere blondete sui, a mi –*
> *Lassette, et si n'ai point d'ami!*
> (2478)

> *I am a dazzling blonde, alas, poor little me for I have no lover!*

Bretel calls on someone present to rectify the situation and claim her in song in front of them all. It is Jehans d'Oiseler who obliges, singing 'Si haut que tuit l'ont entendu' [so loudly that all heard him]:

> *Améz moi, blondete, améz –*
> *Et je n'amerai se vos non!*
> (2490)

> *Love me, little blonde, love me: and I will love no one but you!*

The scene continues with an increasing interplay between refrains and speech – the refrains prompting longer spoken replies and these replies in turn being encapsulated in further refrains. The whole occasion thus develops an atmosphere that self-consciously moves between formality and informality, the singing of refrains creating a certain social frisson caused by the playing out of relationships in front of an audience, using words which are at once intimate and impersonal.

This brief examination of refrains in thirteenth-century narrative contexts shows that there existed a considerable continuity between their characteristics in *rondets de carole*, and their characteristics when quoted independently in romance. Just as refrains prove to be a key generating structural element in dance-song, so they often provide textual momentum and pattern in narrative. But more than this, their role in romance suggests new terms for the debate about their complete or fragmentary nature. Their generating potential derives from the way in which they at once imply a context while possessing a certain autonomy. In this sense, they could be thought of, not as fragmentary, but as a kind of shorthand in that they have the rhetorical function of highlighting and epitomising a dramatic or discursive argument, of catching up its different threads into a single, concise moment of expression.

We have also seen in this range of narrative examples different kinds of negotiation between what they describe and what they enact. Different works, it seems, provide a different kind of balance between presenting the oral textually and the textual orally. Refrains once more play a crucial role since they could be said to be inherently transitional forms that move easily between speech and song, formality and informality, individual sentiment and public response. In particular, they act as a pivot between performance and description by liaising between the narrative's internal and external audience. As in *Le Tournoi de Chauvency*, by creating a situation in which the members of the work's likely external audience are able to watch a representation of themselves performing, they enable the poet to show the very process of performance, that is, to show the dynamic of oral relations being constructed through, and by means of its textual representation.

3

The performance of song in Jean Renart's *Rose*

In the final chapter of this section I want to consider performance as a social experience conveyed by genre, and to do so by concentrating on Renart, whose work presents a more intense internalisation of this experience than any other I know from the thirteenth century. This will entail examining the ways in which Jean Renart characterises the social setting of the many lyric genres which he sets into his romance. First, we need to consider the songs' generic range more closely. Renart makes a broad distinction between the *grands chants courtois*, which are performed exclusively by the Emperor Conrad and his personal *jongleur*, Jouglet, and the other, more traditional, anonymous genres which are sung by a large cross-section of the characters in the romance, including courtiers, townspeople, *jongleurs* (male and female) and the principal female characters, Lïenor and her mother. Emmanuèle Baumgartner has argued persuasively that just as Conrad is associated principally with *grands chants*, so Lïenor is associated with the lower register dance-songs.[1] My concern here is to relate that observation to the fact that Renart makes a further distinction between the private circumstances in which *grands chants* are performed, and the public atmosphere which surrounds the dance-songs.

Except towards the very end of the romance, the *grands chants* are sung either by Conrad on his own ('toz seuls'), or in intimate court settings where the audience numbers no more than two or three specially favoured companions. The songs echo his emotional progress throughout the story as he first falls in love with Lïenor, simply from having heard reports of her beauty, then believes he has lost her because of a slur cast on her name by his seneschal, and finally, gains her (and sees her for the first time) once she comes to court and successfully clears her reputation. Many of the occasions are the archetypal lyric settings for thoughts of love: waking up in bed on a brilliant spring morning, listening to birdsong, sitting pensively by a window, or riding on a journey. Of the thirteen trouvère chansons, Conrad personally sings nine (the first with Jouglet). He sings for love of Lïenor, for joy at Guillaume's arrival at his court, to express covertly to Guillaume his love for his sister, and to find comfort from his private anguished reflections ('mout dolenz et mout angoisseus... / Des bons vers mon segnor Gasson / li sovient' [full of pain and anguish... he remembered some fine lines of my lord Gace] (3618, 3620–21)). By contrast, the dance-songs are a public affair, involving not only a large audience, but also an audience which participates in the performance.[2]

We may take as an example the opening scene of Renart's *Roman de la rose* discussed in the last chapter. As I noted then, both sequences of dance-song present a combination of solo and communal performance, and although the exact manner is difficult to deduce, it is clear that each song involves the active participation of the whole group, either by enabling the courtiers to sing or dance communally (like the first refrain sung by all the knights), or by exerting a more subtle communal pressure on each individual to take his or her turn as a soloist. Other quotations of dance-song in the romance confirm this, as for example, the carolling which takes place at Guillaume's lodgings, which created so much noise that the festivities could be heard throughout the town (2360–85).

As Renart presents it, dance-song thus differs radically from the *grand chant courtois* in the relationship it creates between performer and audience. For in dance-song the members of the audience turn out to be the performers, and the performers the audience. Moreover, in this case, a further public dimension is added by the fact that Renart (like Jacques Bretel later in *Le Tournoi de Chauvency*) names members of his contemporary noble audience as the dancers: by this he ensures that the mutuality of the relationship between performer and audience within the romance gains another layer of reciprocity in the relationship between the romance and its external audience. One result is that the external audience can enjoy a simultaneously oral and literate form of participation in the romance. The *grands chants*, by contrast, are sung by fictional characters – Conrad, Guillaume and Jouglet – a situation which conversely redoubles the effect of self-enclosure Renart is at pains to create around them.

But during the course of the romance a change takes place in Renart's presentation of the *grands chants* which disturbs the initially well-defined polarity between them and the dance-songs. Although Conrad begins by performing the chansons himself, he ends by becoming a listener. The turning point appears to be the one song that is not only performed by Conrad but ostensibly also composed by him ('l'emperere en fist lués cez vers' [the emperor immediately composed these stanzas] (3179)). This song 'Quant de la foelle espoissent li vergier' [When the orchards grow thick with leaves] is a turning point in the plot since, as Renart comments portentously, it is the one inauspiciously overheard by Conrad's jealous seneschal and which prompts the latter to try to dishonour Lïenor. It seems of added ironic significance that the only song attributed to Conrad should be the one that brings about the public exposure of his private fantasies. From this moment on, the privacy of Conrad's infatuation with the reported beauty of Lïenor comes under an increasingly public scrutiny, first as Lïenor is wrongfully accused, and then as she vindicates herself through an equally public manoeuvre.

This process of gradual exposure is subtly articulated by Renart through the song citations. After his peak of introspection in 'Quant de la foelle' – as composer as well as performer – Conrad performs three more chansons, two of which are now carefully attributed to well-known trouvères (Gace Brulé and Renaut de Sabloeil), and the third, sung in response to the news of Lïenor's pretended betrayal, an attack on and attempted renunciation of Love. All subsequent *grands chants* are performed *to* Conrad, and the tight circle of known, named performers suddenly widens to include new unnamed characters such as 'un vallet' from the court, and a visiting 'menestrel... de Chaalons'. The circumstances under which Conrad hears the songs also widen: the song sung by the 'menestrel... de Chaalons' is simply one of many sung by a large crowd of minstrels who have congregated at the German court from all regions to earn money ('por aquerre' (4565)). Conrad happens to overhear the song while he is with his barons, and this time Renart comments specifically on the public pressures of the occasion:

> D'une chambre ou li baron sont
> oï l'empereres cest vers.
> Com ses pensers estoit divers
> de ciaus qu'il avoit assamblez!
> (4594–97)

> The emperor heard these lines in a chamber where his barons were
> gathered: how different were his thoughts from those of the people
> he had assembled!

In contrast to the earlier opportunities Conrad has had to express his
reactions in private abandon, he now has to submit to the constraints
of a larger, more formal gathering where the individual response has to
compete with the communal mood.

His penultimate comeback performance, towards the end of the romance, stages the final transition in this public process, since he sings,
not a *grand chant*, but a dance-song:

> De la joie qui l'en rehete
> li est ciz chans dou cuer volez:
>   *Que demandez vos*
>   *quand vos m'avez?*
>   *que demandez vos?*
>   *dont ne m'avez vos?*
>   *—Ge ne demant rien*
>   *se vos m'amez bien.*
> Et li autre en ont tuit chanté:
> *Tendez tuit vos mains a la flor d'esté,*
>   *a la flor de liz,*
>   *por Deu, tendez i!*
> Ce fu *Te Deum laudamus.*
> (5104–16)[3]

> With the joy that was rejuvenating him, this song flew out of his heart:
> *What do you ask for, now that you have me? what do you ask for? do you
> not have me? – I ask for nothing if you love me well.*
>   And the others all sang together: *Stretch out your hands to the flowers
> of summer, to the lily flowers, for God's sake, stretch them out!*
>   This was a *Te Deum laudamus.*

There are significant changes in the whole nature of the performance from his earlier outpourings. Far from being a merely solipsistic exercise, the song expresses a crucial moment of public recognition for Lïenor. The entire scene plays uneasily on the theme of exposure. Lïenor has just proved to the assembled court her innocence and the seneschal's corresponding deceit by the cunning ruse of making a further trumped-up charge against the seneschal. In denying this new charge, he is forced simultaneously to deny the grounds for the charge he has placed against her. Nonetheless the ruse has a price since it also forces her to name herself to the Emperor in front of them all as the girl of the rose: 'Por Deu, sire, oiez la parclose: / je sui la pucele a la rose' [In God's name, sire, listen to this conclusion: I am the girl of the rose] (5039–40). In other words, she has to admit publicly to the one private detail (her rose-shaped birthmark on her thigh) that was formerly her most intimate secret. If the seneschal tries to rape her verbally, Lïenor, it seems, can only redeem herself by verbal prostitution. Somewhat ironically, this act persuades the Emperor of her purity and restores public value to his love. The choice of genre in which he expresses this is crucially apposite since the principle of public response inheres within it in the shape of the refrain. The courtly audience thus performs the song, as well as witnesses it, and this prepares the way (as Renart hints proleptically with the reference to the *Te Deum*) for Conrad to seek its approbation for his marriage.

The new generic alignment now established between Conrad and dance-song is confirmed by the final song citations, which continue to comment ironically on the course of the plot. In the immediate excited aftermath of the 'redemption scene', *grands chants* and the lower register *chanson d'histoire* 'Or vienent Pasques les beles en avril' [Now comes beautiful Easter in April] are sung without the kind of discrimination in performance style shown earlier in the romance. The second of the *grands chants* contains remarks on the importance of maintaining discretion in Love so that no one else, aside from the lover, should suffer (5248–51), a lesson that one would think it is rather too late for Conrad to learn. The last two songs of all clinch the transformation: both are dance-songs, and of the first, sung by 'uns chanterres de vers Touart' [a singer from near Touart] (5422), a count remarks that he knows no one with a better right to sing it than the Emperor (5435–37). 'Voire' [Indeed] agrees Conrad, and promptly sings the second: 'C'est la gieus, en mi les prez' [It's over there, in the meadows], which has the refrain *j'ai amors a ma volenté / teles com ge voel* [*I have love according to my desire, just as I want*] (5444–45). Underlining the point heavily, Renart adds:

> Ceste li rest bone, sanz doute:
> or la puet chanter, qu'il a toute
> honor et joie a cest mengier.
> (5446–48)

> This one suited him well, without doubt: he can now sing it, since he has all honour and joy at this feast.

Renart's choice of dance-song in the climactic scene of the romance marks out the plot's reliance on oral forms of witness. Conrad only falls in love with Lïenor and forms a desire to meet her brother through Jouglet's oral attestation of her beauty and Guillaume's superlative knightly qualities. The songs repeatedly play their part as forms of oral witness in their own right – a role which is often assigned to them in thirteenth-century romance, for instance in *Galeran*, *Sone de Nansai* and the prose *Tristan*. Thus when Conrad seeks further confirmation of Lïenor's desirability from his valet Nicole, who has been sent to invite her brother to the court, Nicole verifies his fulsome praise of her singing by insisting – under cross-questioning from Conrad – that he heard her himself: '– Et que sez tu? – Ge l'ai oïe' [And what do you know of it? – I have heard it [myself]] (1410). Yet, as the verbal combat between Lïenor and the seneschal proves, oral assertions are at once vital and unreliable. Throughout the romance, Conrad only ever has other people's word for his love, and while this eventually seems enough, the previous course of the plot has shown it to be an unsound basis for assessing Lïenor's value as a wife. The shift from *grand chant* to dance-song is not all gain: in passing from a securely closed world of private reaction to the uncertain open arena of public opinion, Conrad learns that if treachery can occur in the former, the latter exacts its own kind of vengeance.

The plot itself hinges on questions of participation, on the precise relation between a physically occurring event and its production, reception and subsequent transmission. The seneschal's scheme tries to separate these stages by creating a story without a basis in fact, yet Lïenor is able to retaliate only by doing the same, which in turn causes an uproar.

The legal process of the case proves complicated: the barons (with justification, as it turns out) support the seneschal against her counter-accusation, yet dare not press their support too far for fear of having their possessions confiscated. Eventually, oral claims and counter-claims are rejected in favour of the ducking-test, which the seneschal passes. Only now, facing the extreme risk of being publicly proved to be false, is Lïenor able to claim her innocence, so that the seneschal, being publicly proved to be innocent, can thereby be shown to be false. The moral contrariness of the situation confounds any easy equation between truth and report; instead, Renart shows the complexity of negotiation between different types of communication and how subject they are to a variety of self-interested social pressures. Conrad's sudden championing of dance-song at the end of this convoluted legal battle only confirms this: after all, he is simply seizing the moment to achieve his own desires, as the refrain which so suits him declares: *j'ai amors a ma volenté / teles com ge voel* [*I have love according to my desire, just as I want*] (5444–45).

Renart's plot is remarkable in the way it scrutinises – through an idealised adventure – the kinds of issue that are at the centre of problems of transmission, and shows them to be of acute social significance. He shows how different modes of performance form part of the means by which the fraught social processes of public life are enacted, and he does this through the inset songs, and in particular through the carefully demarcated generic differences in the songs. Thus where the high register *grands chants* involve one kind of intense, private transmission, the dance-songs require another, far more open and communal. But Renart's real originality is to bring these issues of transmission into the text. He shows that we should not close off the problems they raise as being outside the text, but rather take into account the way in which they are part of the text. The conditions of performance – its whole process of production and reception – not only surround the text, they participate within it, and the interrelations between the oral and the literate, the social and the poetic are in effect negotiated within the plot.

The mixture of genres in the romance articulates these transactions. For by setting the songs within the narrative, Renart not only gives social forms to the genres in performance, he also – in the performance of the whole work – shows the genres to embody (at least fictionally) social forms of performance. The inset genres not only perform, they demonstrate the social context of performance: they have the double function of describing and enacting at one and the same time. The mutuality of this role indicates the way in which genre and performance interact. We are reminded by Renart's *Roman de la rose* that genre need not be thought of as a post-facto 'experimental construct', but that it is a much more dynamic principle that mediates between audience categories of expectation and meaning. Similarly, where we incline analytically to separate out the processes of production and reception, Renart, with far greater social acuity, shows them to be mutual. In his work, reception is written into production.

Yet, as we have seen, this involves a risk. If the work describes the social tensions involved in problems of transmission, it also enacts them, in the sense that it is also vulnerable to being poorly transmitted. Accidents of transmission are of crucial importance in medieval works. The tendency of the modern editorial process, answerable as it is to criteria of reliability and authority, is to see textual difficulties as contingencies which obscure our understanding of the 'real work'. But in some fundamental sense medieval texts *are* accidents, because performances are accidents, that is, single, self-sufficient occasions which can never be repeated. At the same time, as texts they also record and repeat the experience of performance. Throughout the thirteenth century, and particularly in the *romans à chansons*, the way in which performances are being turned into texts is attesting to an attempt to turn the accidental into the controlled, to make the accidental seem reliable, even authoritative.

PART II

The boundaries of genre

4

The refrain

The complexity of generic signification in the thirteenth century is intense. Generic interplay is a dominant characteristic of both verbal and musical composition: new genres are created, and pre-existent genres are set together in a variety of combinations, or else given new boundaries of distinction. Through all this generic mobility, a larger literary change takes place throughout the century. The increasing effort amongst thirteenth-century authors and scribes to produce texts aiming to record and repeat the experience of performance, produces its own textual conditions for new kinds of composition. Any attempt to document this change has to face a bewildering plurality in the surviving mass of compositions: authors create works which allow many different kinds of distinction to be drawn right across such formal and social categories as lyric and narrative, the sung and the non-sung, the courtly, the popular and the clerical.

Issues of generic differentiation will be addressed in this chapter by concentrating further on the tiny detail of the refrain. This small element in thirteenth-century compositional technique has much light to shed on the larger picture of medieval creativity. One reason for this is that refrains bear an intriguingly disruptive relation to the concept of genre. They do not answer easily to any of the criteria that might normally define a poetic form, a song, or even a genre. They have such irregular patterns of metre and rhyme that in many contexts even their overall length remains an open question; they may or may not occur with music or in musical genres; and they are so short, and variable in function that, as we have seen, scholars have been reluctant to accord them more than a fragmentary status, let alone regard them as a genre in their own right. Just as their own characteristics raise questions about genre, they make connections across so many genres in this period, that analysis of even a single refrain allows a glimpse of a much larger creative process.

Many issues concerning refrains bear directly on the ways in which generic differences in the period are articulated. This is in part simply because so large a proportion of works in the thirteenth century contains refrains (van den Boogaard collects nearly 2,000 citations from some 200 rondeaux, 600 chansons, 470 motets and 56 narrative and didactic works). More particularly, by being cited across works as well as within them, refrains possess a seemingly unique ability to speak for a whole range of genres, and to communicate as texts and as melodies.

I discussed in the previous section the way refrains imply a context: they are not merely incomplete scraps of text and music, but elements that are charged in their use. I now want to extend this argument by considering how their passage from work to work and from genre to genre enables them to mix or mediate between genres. This enquiry takes us beyond the citation of refrains in romance. Two kinds of mutually dependent approach are developed in this section and extended throughout the book. First, an effort is made to understand the character of refrains more fully, both on their own terms, and by exploring how they relate to their very varied generic contexts. Second, I argue that the citation of refrains offers us a new means of understanding how genres are perceived in the thirteenth century. Tracing the branching pathways between contexts linked by the same citations proves to be a highly productive way of viewing thirteenth-century writings. Led by the pattern of refrain sources itself, we can make fresh comparisons between genres, works, authors and cultures, and between words and music. We see how dense a supporting network of meaning flows around refrains. Let us begin with the elusive process of defining them.

DEFINITIONS

Perhaps some comment on the functional mobility of refrains is required. In the usual dictionary definition, a refrain is 'a phrase or verse recurring at intervals, especially at the end of each stanza of a poem or song'.[1] Yet in thirteenth-century composition the definition of a refrain widens to a disconcerting degree. It acts formally as a 'refrain' in its most generally used sense only within rondeaux, and in a sub-group of chansons. In rondeaux, the refrain is usually repeated as a half-unit within the stanza (although, as we have seen, this pattern varies considerably in the earliest *rondets* found in Renart's *Roman de la rose*).[2] The chansons which contain refrains are of two types generally designated *chansons à refrains* (or refrain-songs), and *chansons avec des refrains*. In the former, one refrain is repeated at the end of each stanza. This refrain may not be unique to that chanson, but may also occur elsewhere. The *chansons avec des refrains* have a different refrain at the end of each stanza. Each refrain may be quite independent metrically from the other refrains, it may often have a different number of lines, and it may even have a different tune, not only from the other refrains but also from the strophic sections of the song.[3]

The kind of independence possessed by the refrain in a chanson, and especially in a *chanson avec des refrains*, is even more evident in the other two contexts in which refrains appear: motets and long narrative and didactic works. The thirteenth-century motet is a genre of often complex verbal and musical construction, composed of three or even four voices based on a tenor.[4] The tenor is usually a section of liturgical chant, but later in the century, some motet texts are composed entirely in the vernacular, with the tenor taken occasionally from a well-known chanson or refrain. All the voices have separate melodies and texts (a very few specialised examples, the *motets centons*, consisting in a patchwork of refrains joined together).[5] One group of motets, known as *motets entés*, are encased (literally 'grafted') between the two halves of a refrain in such a way that, in many examples, the first line of the refrain forms the first line of any one voice-part, and the last line of the refrain the last line of the part. The thirteenth-century motet composer treats the refrain as a point of departure in a composition intended for a musically educated audience, capable of appreciating the subtlety of his musical and verbal ingenuity.[6]

The use of refrains in motets as independent units of composition acts in some sense as a musical parallel to the use of refrains in romances.

However, it is in the *romans* that the refrain seems most obviously 'out of context' when it is quoted on its own. For here, unlike the other three cases (rondeau, chanson and motet), the refrain is attached not to a song but to a narrative genre, where it is not (usually) repeated at regular intervals.[7] The refrain in a *roman* seems at the furthest remove from a 'refrain' as usually described.[8]

Perhaps the most arresting characteristic of refrains concerns their propensity to be cited *across* all four kinds of context. The same refrain may occur in a motet, a *roman*, a rondeau *and* a chanson. For instance, the following occurs in no fewer than eight different contexts:

> *Cui lairai ge mes amors*
> *amie, s'a vos non?*
> (vdB, refr. 387)

> *To whom shall I give my love, my dear, if not to you?*

Its earliest textual context is one of the *rondets* contained in Renart's *Roman de la rose* (532–37). We also find it in another rondeau (from a Vatican manuscript) which is itself quoted at the end of the first strophe of an anonymous *pastourelle* in another manuscript. The refrain occurs in three further *chansons avec des refrains*: the first quotes it at the end of its third strophe, the second after its seventh strophe, and the third after its fourth strophe. In the second song, one of Gautier de Coinci's pious *contrafacta*, the words 'Mere Dieu' are substituted for 'amie'. In addition to the two rondeaux and the four chansons, the refrain appears in two motets. Finally, it can be found in the commentary to a thirteenth-century French prose translation of Ovid's *Ars amatoria*.[9]

This kind of widespread occurrence is not unusual: thirteen refrains each appear in six or more different contexts (one of which, *Hé, Dieus que ferai*? [*Oh God, what shall I do*?] (vdB, refr. 824), appears in nine separate songs); while many more appear independently at least four times.[10] Such a proliferation of sources is considerable evidence that we are dealing with something other than a subsidiary feature of a stanzaic poem. For a refrain to appear so many times on its own suggests that it was popular and memorable in itself, and not simply by virtue of being part of another work. In this particular refrain (*Cui lairai ge*), one of the eight sources – a *pastourelle* – contains a double incidence of interpolation, in which the rondeau to which the refrain is attached is itself set into a further work. This again is not unusual.[11] The thirteenth century is remarkable for the way in which genres do not exist in isolation but are repeatedly juxtaposed, creating elaborate structures of interpolation and hybridisation.[12]

The cross-contextuality of refrains has various consequences for the ways in which genre operates. The mobility of their citation means that four disparate genres (rondeau, *chanson avec des refrains*, motet and *roman*) are simultaneously brought into relation, enabling comparisons to be drawn between their compositional methods. Refrains form two kinds of connection: one between genres (where two or more works cite the same refrain) and one within a genre, where an inset refrain connects (or distinguishes) different parts of the same work.

MELODIES

So far, we have been considering the variation of a refrain from a largely verbal point of view. But, as we noted earlier, refrains have a musical life as well because they appear in three different song genres (the chanson, motet and rondeau), and also because they are quoted with musical notation in the manuscripts of several romances.[13] How stable, then, is a refrain's musical identity? Do the melodies show a comparable degree and process of variation to the words? Do the melodies and the texts circulate separately or together?

Not as many tunes as verbal texts survive for refrains, which is in keeping with the fact that musical sources are generally rarer than literary ones in the medieval period. Nor have they been collected in a way which compares with van den Boogaard's study of the literary sources. Nonetheless, the refrain tunes which have survived form a substantial repertory.[14] Without a comprehensive bibliographical study of the music we are unable properly to cross-refer the refrain texts with their tunes. But even a cursory comparison of their musical sources shows that the tunes possess considerable variation.

Let us begin by considering two refrains which have a wide range of musical as well as literary sources. The first, *Cui lairai ge* (vdB, refr. 387), as we noted earlier, appears in eight separate contexts. It is found with music in four out of the eight, giving six musical readings (see Ex. 1).[15]

Ex. 1 *Cui lairai ge* (vdB, refr. 387): a comparison of its musical sources

In spite of differences in the opening pitch, all six tunes are recognisably related to each other. Five out of the six begin with a rising seventh (although the *Miracles* (fr. 25532) version does not climb any higher than the first series of thirds) and share the same basic melodic shape in the second half of the melody as well. *Miracles* (Soissons) and Mo are the closest to each other of all the tunes despite being a fourth apart in pitch. They are identical in the second half, and have only slight differences in the first half of the tune. The Munich reading is the next closest: here the peak of the phrase is the octave, rather than the seventh. *Miracles* (Leningrad), *Miracles* (fr. 25532) and Noailles present further variety, *Miracles* (Leningrad), in particular, by being the only version to end one degree above the opening pitch rather than on the opening pitch itself.

Although there is a good deal of variation amongst these musical sources, enough to show that the tune was not rigidly fixed, there are still enough resemblances to show that we are dealing with a single melody, rather than with a set of different melodies. To this extent, then, it seems that *Cui lairai ge* had its own tune; that in popular memory the words and the tune of *Cui lairai ge* formed a single unit.

Let us put alongside *Cui lairai ge* another frequently cited refrain from Renart's *Rose*:

> *Ne vos repentez mie*
> *de loiaument amer.*
> (vdB, refr. 1375)

> *Never repent of loving loyally.*

This appears in seven contexts altogether: as the eleventh *rondet* in Renart's *Rose*, in *La Court de Paradis* (271), *Les Miracles* (III, 502) and four *chansons avec des refrains* (R2041, R839, R1509, R1963). Music survives in various manuscripts for these four songs and is also present in *La Court de Paradis*, a total of seven readings (See Ex. 2).

As with *Cui lairai ge*, three of the melodies immediately stand out as very similar, Roi 20 (fr. 844), Noailles 122 and fr. 12483. There is

Ex. 2 *Ne vos repentez mie* (vdB, refr. 1375): a comparison of its musical sources

little to distinguish them, apart from slight differences in the placing of plicas, and the fact that fr. 12483 is written a fourth lower than the other two. Noailles 50 has some oddities, suggesting an error in transcription, because while its second half is very similar to Roi 127, the first half starts on an E rather than a D, and ends on a B rather than an A. This causes the tune to leap down a sixth in the middle rather than a fifth. Yet despite variation, all the sources described so far present a single tune. The last two sources, Noailles 24 and *Paradis*, however, present further separate tunes, each of which is quite distinct from the other. One rises up from a G to a C; the other descends from a C to a G.

Ne vos repentez mie thus cannot be described in quite the same way as *Cui lairai ge*, as a refrain known by its tune and words together. One pairing of words and melody has some stability among the chansons, but two further tunes also circulated with the same words. It gives some indication of the multiplicity of connections between refrain texts and refrain tunes.

A single set of words may have a different tune in each of the songs in which it occurs. Take as an example the refrain:

> *Bon jor ait qui mon cuer a;*
> *n'est pas o moi.*
> (vdB, refr. 285)

> *Good day to the one who has my heart! He is not with me.*

The earliest textual source for this refrain is the ninth *rondet* contained in Renart's *Rose* (1579–84). We then find it used in the fifth strophe of the 'Bele Aalis' song by Baude de la Kakerie (R1509), and in a motet (M79). Since the manuscript of Renart's *Rose* contains no music, the only musical sources for the refrain are those of the chanson and the motet, the latter supplying two melodies. All three musical citations are different (see Ex. 3).

The last two bear some resemblances in their melodic pitch and shape. Both melodies not only have the same range from C to G, but each half of both melodies is clustered round F–G and D–C respectively. Since the former melody has an 'open' ending on E, while the latter a 'closed' ending on C, they could almost be two melodically balanced halves of a single longer tune. Nonetheless, there would be no possibility of

Ex. 3 *Bon jor ait* (vdB, refr. 285): a comparison of its musical sources

mistaking either of them as a variation of the other, or of mistaking them both as variations of a single 'parent' tune. The tune in the chanson is different again from both. Anyone trying to edit the tunes of this refrain text would be unable to present a single conflated version; they would have either to present all three tunes, or make an arbitrary choice from among them.

This case is not exceptional among refrains (or for that matter among other song genres). There are even examples of refrains in a single work having different tunes attached to them in different manuscripts. *Ne vos repentez mie* has already provided an example of this, since the two manuscripts for one of the chansons (R839) contain different tunes for the same refrain text. The four manuscripts of *Renart le Nouvel* provide a more striking instance. Three of them contain musical notation for the refrains (see Fig. 5). They provide an unusually rich resource of refrain melodies, especially since no two of the manuscripts contain the same number of refrains (fr. 25566 has sixty-five, fr. 1593 has sixty-eight, fr. 1581 has sixty-two and fr. 372 has fifty-nine).[16] In several cases, a refrain text has a different tune in each manuscript. Example 4 contains the three tunes for *Nus n'a joie s'il n'aime par Amours* [*No one has joy if he does not love through Love*] (vdB, refr. 1391).

Renart le Nouvel is an exceptional work. Yet it presents clear evidence that refrains were not exclusively attached to single tunes, evidence which many other works confirm. The existence of several tunes for one verbal text is, in any case, a well-known phenomenon in medieval song.[17] Many complete trouvère songs, such as 'Pour verdure' and 'Li nouviauz tanz et mais et violete' by the Châtelain de Couci, have quite separate melodies in different manuscripts.[18] Whether, conversely, single refrain tunes were

83

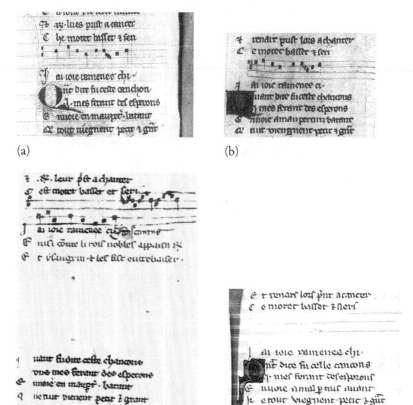

5 *J'ai joie ramenee chi*, a refrain in Jacquemart Giélée, *Renart le Nouvel*, as presented in the four manuscripts of the *roman*:
(a) BN fr. 25566, fol. 127v
(b) BN fr. 372, fol. 17v
(c) BN fr. 1593, fol. 18r (with added discantus and space left below for the illuminator)
(d) BN fr. 1581, fol. 18r (blank staves)

in general attached to a variety of texts cannot yet be ascertained without a full study of the cross-references between them;[19] but we do know of some important sources of *contrafacta* in which French secular refrain tunes are given French religious texts or Latin texts.[20]

To consider the melodies of the refrains as well as their words is to realise that the processes of adaptation were two-fold. Words and

Ex. 4 *Nus n'a joie s'il n'aime par Amours* (vdB, refr. 1391): a comparison of its musical sources in *Renart le Nouvel* (line 2346)

tunes changed, moved, were split and re-formed, not necessarily in synchrony, but undoubtedly with a degree of mutual influence. In the case of refrains we find a different picture emerges from the one that is implicitly drawn by van den Boogaard's bibliography of a set of discrete, neatly categorisable phrases. If a text can be put with several different tunes, and one tune to more than one set of words, then this must affect our attempt to define a refrain. There is no simple way of defining a refrain only by its text or only by its melody, for it may require both text and melody together to define it. The seeming comprehensiveness of van den Boogaard's catalogue has probably distorted our sense of a refrain by making it appear to have clear-cut boundaries. Once we take account of the formulaic nature of the texts and melodies it is possible to see different ways of grouping refrains as large clusters of related formulas where the connections cut across van den Boogaard's categorisation and open it up to new, broader perspectives. The example of *Hareu li maus d'amer m'ochist* [*Alas, the pains of love are killing me*] shows how refrain texts and melodies can have a mobile, fluctuating relationship that creates a large network of interconnecting formulas.[21] The term 'refrain structure' may be a better term for these larger clusters than 'refrain' *tout court*.

But allowing flexibility into our definition of refrains is not to deny that in many contexts, refrains have quite precise parameters. The pattern of refrain-citations shows two contradictory characteristics: a tendency towards instability, since there is a large degree of small-scale variation, yet also towards stability, since these very slightly distinctive features are often themselves repeated exactly. The variation appears to be fluid and seamless, yet refrains are often also insistently discrete.

We do not need, in short, to abandon van den Boogaard, but to realise that the question of how to define refrains has more than one answer. This in turn depends on the approach taken to the question. For instance, to define refrains within chansons is to seek to understand their forms of repetition. Looking at refrains in narratives reveals other means of definition, such as the use of rhyme, the type of speaker, and their proverbial or sententious character; in motets, their relation to clausula and to plainsong. Van den Boogaard's bibliography begins by cataloguing rondeaux, and if a refrain is cited in a rondeau then it is that version of the text which he prints. However, none of these types of context necessarily has an exclusive right of definition.

The next chapter reflects further on these issues by taking a single, widely cited refrain and investigating the full generic variety of its contexts. This is to see how stable the citation remains from context to context, and hence what kind of contextual pressure is exerted by and upon it. Some broader principles of thirteenth-century composition are revealed. The very ubiquity of refrains offers a new means of looking comparatively at a range of genres in a single glance. As short phrases – either textual, melodic or both – that occur in varying patterns of combination and repetition within larger compositional structures, they are a model of the fundamental relationship in medieval creativity between simple, pre-existent compositional units and their complex interlacing in longer constructions. Being able to see authors at work with these units in different genres is a way of gaining a more inclusive and hence more supple sense of how different works are composed ('put together'). We find that boundaries occur in unexpected places and signify in unexpected ways.

5

Refrains in context: a case study

The refrain *Ainssi doit on aler / a son ami* [*This is how you must go towards your lover*] (vdB, refr. 65) occurs in six different works altogether: in a rondeau collected in Paris, BN fr. 12786, at the end of the fifth stanza of a *chanson avec des refrains*, in two motet texts and as one of a large number of inset refrains in two late-thirteenth-century narratives, *La Court de paradis* and *Le Tournoi de Chauvency*. Of the six this refrain appears with music in one of the motets and in *La Court de paradis*. I do not claim any statistical significance for this choice of refrain: it merely serves, as many others would do, to illustrate – with a manageable number of examples – how refrains are cited. I will be trying to establish the degree to which this refrain changes character in the process of re-citation, or conversely changes the character of its various contexts. To what extent is it an agent of change, even disruption, in thirteenth-century genres? What do we learn about generic differences, or similarities, when we follow the traces of refrain-citation?

Ainssi doit on aler undergoes slight verbal and musical variation in its contexts. The degree of verbal change can readily be deduced from van den Boogaard's bibliography, some details of which I reproduce here, supplemented by the melody where the source supplies it.

To begin with the texts (see Table 5.1), three citations are identical (the rondeau and the two motets); of the others, the two *romans* contain simple noun substitutions ('dame' and 'amie' respectively for 'on', with a change in word-order in the latter), while the chanson also includes an adjective ('bele') and has 'va' instead of 'doit on aler'. Even before examining the contexts it is clear that some contextual pressure exists to mould the refrain into slightly different forms. If we compare these

87

Table 5.1 *Ainssi doit on aler* : contextual variations

vdB, refr. 65.	(a) *Ainssi doit on aler*	rondeau (vdB, rond. 168)
	a son ami.	Paris, BN fr. 12786
	(b) *Ainsi va bele dame*	*chanson avec des refrains* (R584.V)
	a son ami.	Paris, BN fr. 22543
		Modena, Bibl.Estense MS R 4.4
		Paris, BN fr. 20050
		Berne, Stadt- und Univ.Bibl.MS 389
	(c) *Ensi doit on aler*	motet (M435)
	a son ami.	Paris, BN fr. 12615 (music)
		Paris, BN fr. 844 (music)
	(d) *Ainsi doit on aler*	motet (M1143a)
	a son ami.	Rome, Biblioteca Apostolica-Vaticana, MS Reg. 1490
	(e) *Ensi doit dame aler*	*La Court de paradis*, line 359
	a son ami.	Paris, BN fr. 25532 (music)
		Paris, BN fr. 837
		Paris, BN fr. 1802
	(f) *Ainsi doit aleir amie*	*Le Tournoi de Chauvency*, line 3186
	a son amin.	Mons, Bibliothèque de la Ville, MS 330-215
		Oxford, Bodleian Library, MS Douce 308

citations with other refrains listed by van den Boogaard (see Table 5.2) we can see that the process of variation extends into many other texts.

All these are listed as separate refrains, yet as a group they contain several interlocking and closely related formulas in various kinds of combination. In the (rearranged) order below, a smooth progression of formulas unfolds from 'Ainsi doit aler' (in refrs. 60, 61 and 62) to 'qui aime' (taken up in refrs. 60, 61 and 74), to 'qui amours maine' (refrs. 73, 72, 70), to 'Ainsi va qui aime/amours' (refrs. 74, 72, 73), and finally, to the new pronoun 'nos' in refr. 70. From this perspective, the variants in the chanson context of refr. 65 ('bele dame' and 'Ainsi va') turn out to exist as separate refrain formulations in their own right (see refrs. 62,

Table 5.2 *Ainssi doit on aler*: comparison with other refrain texts

vdB, refr. 60	*Ainsi doit aler fins cuers qui bien aime.*	*La Chastelaine de Saint Gille*, 22
vdB, refr. 61	*Ainsi doit aler qui aimme par amours joliement.*	*Le Court d'amours*, 31
vdB, refr. 62	*Einsi doit aler qui bele amie a.*	vdB, rond. 1 = Renart's *Rose*, 299, 2518
vdB, refr. 74	*Ensi va qui aime, ensi va.*	(a) M341 (b) *Le Roman de la violette*, 719
vdB, refr. 72	*Ainsi va qui amours demaine a son conmant.*	vdB, rond. 51 = *Le Restor du paon*, 2531
vdB, refr. 73	*Ainsi va qui amors maine et qui bon'amor maintient.*	vdB, rond. 19= *Le Lai d'Aristote*, 464
vdB, refr. 70	*Einsi nos meinne li maus d'amors, einsi nos meinne.*	*Le Roman de la poire*, 1151[1]

and 72–74). Putting a number of citations alongside one another in this way swiftly reveals the indeterminacy of refrain boundaries, the ways in which refrain texts form a kaleidoscope of shifting phrases.

If we look now at the melodies, we find that the three sources (two for one of the motets, and one for *La Court de paradis*) are notably stable. The substitution of 'dame' for 'on' in (e) (*Paradis*) has no melodic counterpart. The only difference among them (apart from the passing note on 'doit' in *Paradis* (fr. 25532)) is that fr. 844 presents the tune a tone lower than the other two manuscripts. I give the music from Tischler's edition of M435, which includes the reading in fr. 25532 (see Ex. 5).

Looking across all these examples raises the question of how best to analyse refrains, since it seems that it would be pertinent to compare not only the contexts of a 'single' refrain-structure, but also those of other semantically related refrains, thereby cutting across van den Boogaard's boundaries of categorisation. Such a comparison would give a wider sense of the processes by which refrains form associative groups, which might in turn indicate some of the principles of choice operating within different generic contexts.[2] Hence in the following discussion, although

Ex. 5 *Ainssi doit on aler* in Motet 435: a comparison of its musical sources

I will concentrate on the six contexts of *Ainssi doit on aler / a son ami*, other refrains – and other contexts – will also be introduced where appropriate.

To what extent, then, does the role and function of *Ainssi doit on aler / a son ami* vary? Where variations exist, can we say that they are generically determined? Glancing at each context in turn, romance, rondeau and *chanson avec des refrains*, the strongly deictic character of the refrain nearly always stimulates some kind of narrative reconstruction of its implied accompanying action. Beginning with romance, perhaps the clearest example of this process occurs in context (f), *Le Tournoi de Chauvency*. The poet-narrator in *Le Tournoi*, reclining in a meadow just outside the castle walls, is watching a great procession of knights issuing out of the castle, headed by Louis de Looz, the host of the whole tournament. He is closely followed by the noble Maucervel; between them rides the Countess of Luxembourg, so excited by the sight of her lover that her sister is prompted to comment in song on the manner in which she is riding:

> Vint la contesce chevauchant
> De Lucembour a grant noblesce;
> Teil joie mainne et tel leesce
> Que nus n'i savroit amender.

Trop la faisoit bon resgarder,
Et la bele Margot, sa suer,
Encommença de jolif cuer
Ceste chançon, cler et seri:
Ainsi doit aleir amie a son ami! [3]
(*Le Tournoi de Chauvency,* 3178–86)

> The Countess of Luxembourg came riding very nobly; she was be-
> having so joyfully and with so much pleasure that no one would have
> known how to increase it. It was so good to look at her, and the beau-
> tiful Margot, her sister, with a joyful heart began this song, in a clear,
> serene voice: *This is how you must go towards your lover*!

The narrative continues with a detailed description of the procession, the
streets filled with people, banners, and shields as the knights ride by to
the accompaniment of singing and great revelry. In such a setting, the
phrase *Ainssi doit on aler* gains a full narrative gloss: 'one goes to one's
lover' riding on a horse, in the rich courtly circumstances of a tournament, acting in public view and hence open to comment. Other
narrative settings reinforce this gloss.

The related refrain *Einsi doit aler qui bele amie a* [*This is how you must
go if you have a beautiful lover*] (vdB, refr. 62) which occurs in a *rondet*
cited twice over in Renart's *Rose* is, in the first passage, part of a dance
sequence and in the second, part of another tournament.[4] This broad
narrative frame is itself open to variation. In *Le Lai d'Aristote*, the *rondet*
containing the refrain *Ainsi va qui amors maine / et qui bon'amor main-
tient* [*This is how it goes with the one whom love leads and who upholds good
love*] (vdB, refr. 73) is sung during a mocking love scene in which the
philosopher Aristotle, having fallen in love with his pupil's lady, is per-
suaded to humiliate himself by carrying her around a garden on his back.
Where in *Le Tournoi* the lady rides towards her lover in a state of joyful
admiration, here in the *Lai d'Aristote*, she rides scornfully *on* her admirer.
The contrast between the scenes illustrates the grammatical fluidity of
the deictic *Ainsi* . . . in that it can be uttered both by the actant (as in the
Lai d'Aristote) and by an observer of the action (as in *Le Tournoi*).

These examples demonstrate some stability in the kinds of contextual referent that authors perceive in this refrain-cluster. Moreover,
the *Lai d'Aristote* citation appears to function precisely by relying on
the audience's prior knowledge of the refrain's conventional narrative

implication: the humour depends on our sense of the inversion – literally and physically – of the refrain's usual meaning.[5]

However, if the narrative meaning ascribed to the refrain remains broadly constant in these *roman* examples, the formal relations between a refrain and its context evidently vary, depending on whether the refrain is set directly into the narrative, or into a rondeau that is set into the narrative. Even within rondeaux, the relation between refrain and strophe varies markedly. Both the *rondets* in Renart's *Rose* and *Le Lai d'Aristote*, for example, fall into the pattern discussed in the last chapter, where the refrain is not integrated into the *rondet*-structure but rather cuts across the strophic sections:

> La jus, desoz la raime
> –*einsi doit aler qui aime*–
> clere i sourt la fontaine,
> y a!
> *Einsi doit aler qui bele amie a.*
> (Renart, *Le Roman de la rose*,
> 295–99 and 2514–18)

> *Ainsi va qui amors*
> Bele Doe i ghee laine.
> Maistre musart me soutient.
> *Ainsi va qui amors maine*
> *et qui bon'amor maintient.*
> (*Le Lai d'Aristote*, 461–65)[6]

> Over there, under the branch – *this is how you must go if you are in love* – the fountain springs up clearly, aiya! *This is how you must go if you have a beautiful lover.*

> *This is how you go if love* – Beautiful Doe washes wool there. Master Fool is carrying me. *This is how it goes with the one whom love leads and who upholds good love.*

In these cases, the meaning of the refrain as a performative gesture is supplied by the narrative that surrounds the rondeau, rather than by the rondeau verses themselves. The rondeau in which vdB, refr. 65 occurs, by contrast, does not occur within a narrative; it forms part of a collection of song texts in the early fourteenth-century fr. 12786.[7] Here refrain and strophe conform, each amplifying the other in a round of semantic affirmation:

> *Ainssi doit on aler*
> *a son ami.*
> Bon fait deporter,
> –*Ainssi [doit on aler].*–
> baisier et acoler;

pour voir le di.
Ainssi [*doit on aler*
a son ami].
(vdB, rond. 168)

This is how you must go towards your lover. It is good to be joyful –
This is [*how you must go*] – and kiss and embrace; I say so truly. *This
is* [*how you must go towards your lover*].

Even within a single genre then, refrains can vary considerably in
function. In the three rondeaux cited above, not only does the relation
between refrain and strophe differ, each refrain has a different form of
repetition: from semi-repetition in the *Rose* example (where the second
part of the refrain alters), to the repetition of one line out of two in the *Lai
d'Aristote*, to the more common rondeau structure (vdB, rond. 168) of a
partial (and exact) recurrence of the refrain in mid-strophe. In the latter,
narrative expansion of the refrain takes place in an embryonic fashion
within the strophe, unlike the former examples where it is provided
wholly by the romance. Such formal variety in the function of the refrain
is characteristic of thirteenth-century rondeaux; only in the fourteenth
century does the form stabilise into the type represented by rond. 168.
In spite of this, it is striking that the impulse to provide a narrative
gloss occurs whatever the form of the rondeau, apparently regardless
of whether the refrain occurs in a romance, in a rondeau, or else in a
rondeau set into a romance.

Ainssi doit on aler / *a son ami* has an openness of reference which
strongly invites narrative reconstruction. As we shall see, this characteristic runs across all the other genres of its surviving contexts. At the
same time, its very openness means that it is capable of receiving quite
varied narrative meanings. Evidence of this is provided by the *chanson
avec des refrains* (context (b)). This type of song differs from the more
common *chanson à refrains* in being characterised by formal disjunction.
There is usually no continuity between the metre and rhyme-scheme
of each stanza and its refrain, and marked formal differences exist between the refrains themselves. The *chanson avec des refrains* is thus a
song type constructed precisely upon the formal disunity among refrains: the play of difference between refrains is no mere by-product of

uncontrolled repetition, but something that is demanded by the form of the song.

This example is a *chanson de mal mariée*, describing from the point of view of an anonymous and hidden observer a conversation between two married sisters. The younger complains to the elder of her double misfortune: her husband blames her for being unfaithful, but she does not even have a lover. Her sister advises her to accept her admirer without delay or scruple; and since just at this point he rides by, young and handsome, the girl immediately stretches out her arms to him, and they begin embracing while the elder discreetly retires. The refrain *Ainssi va bele dame / a son ami* [*This is how a beautiful lady goes towards her lover*] occurs at the end of the fifth stanza:

> Quachiez m'iere soz un ramier
> Pres d'eles por lo meuz oïr.   50
> Atant ez vos un chevalier
> A cheval par lo pré venir
> Qui mout biaus et jones estoit.
> Tant tost com la dame aperçoit
> Del cheval a pié dessendi,   55
> Envers eles lo cors aloit.
> Et quant la tres bele lo voit
> Andeus ses biaus braz li tendi:
>   *Ainsi va bele dame*
>   *A son ami.*
> (R584. V, 49–60; MSS Berne, Stadt- und Univ.Bibl.MS 389 and fr. 20050)[8]

I was hidden in a thicket near to them to hear them better. Suddenly a knight who was very handsome and young came through the meadow on horseback. As soon as he saw the lady he dismounted from his horse, and went towards them. And when the very pretty one saw him, she stretched out both of her beautiful arms to him: *This is how a beautiful lady goes towards her lover.*

Much in this setting recalls the narrative examples: the lovers are courtly, and as in *Le Tournoi*, the lady goes forward in front of watching eyes to meet her knight with an unabashed simplicity of intention. But here the circumstances are more intimate, and the refrain carries a greater weight of erotic reference. Again, as in the *Lai d'Aristote*, the poet plays ironically on the openness of the demonstrative *Ainsi....* '*This*' is how (*thus*) one goes to one's lover ... Hiding behind the lack of specificity in the refrain, the poet leaves the audience to supply the tone of the remark, all the while showing that the openness of meaning in the relation between the refrain and the girl's action makes it vulnerable to innuendo.

To consider how *Ainssi doit* fits in to the larger compositional scheme of the chanson will take us into the workings of *chansons avec des refrains* as a genre. The chanson as a whole, in its different manuscript versions, represents an interesting set of scribal/authorial reactions to the formal instability of refrains. It survives in four manuscripts, including the troubadour chansonnier *R* (fr. 22543), none of which, unfortunately, provides music.[9] The number of stanzas in the sources varies: two manuscripts (Berne and fr. 20050) give seven stanzas, the third (Modena) gives five, while the Occitan source has only the first four. Apart from the seventh stanza in Berne and fr. 20050, the song is tightly organised: the stanzaic lines are all octosyllabic, and in the rhyme-scheme of ababccdccdR, the c and d rhymes are constant throughout. The refrains vary in form, metre and line-length, but even they have been marshalled into a degree of conformity in that they all end with the word 'ami'. The latter introduces a question about the compositional process of the song – were the refrains chosen because they all shared this rhyme feature, or were they specially adapted to conform to it? We can partially answer this by checking their concordances: three are *unica*, but the others survive elsewhere in the same form, implying (though hardly more than that) a principle of choice on the author's part rather than adaptation.

The fifth stanza, nonetheless, illustrates the complexity of the question. For in Modena, it appears under a different guise from Berne and fr. 20050, with the refrain altered and expanded:

> Atant ez vos un chevalier
> Maintenant par les prez venir: 50
> Sor un palefroi chevauchier,
> Et si venoit de grant aïr
> Qui joenes et mout biaus estoit.
> Quant andos les dames connoist,
> A pié de cheval descendi,   55

Et cele qui s'amie estoit,
De tant loing com ele le voit,
Andos ses biaus braz li tendi.
Ensi doit en aler a son ami,
Et plus mignotement que je ne di.
(R584.V, 49–60; Modena, Bibl. Estense MS R. 4.4)

Suddenly a knight comes to the meadows riding on a palfrey, and he was young and very handsome and came at great speed. When he recognised the two ladies he dismounted from his horse, and she who was his lover, from as far away as she could see him stretched out both her beautiful arms towards him. *This is how you must go towards your lover, and more sweetly than I can say.*

The stanza is recognizably drawn from the same material as the one which appears in Berne and fr. 20050: some lines are identical though put in a different order (compare lines 51 and 53 in Berne and fr. 20050 with 49 and 53 in Modena), while others partially overlap. But it is the treatment of the refrain which is particularly intriguing, since not only does the scribe add a unique line (overlooking the formal constraint on the rest of the refrains in the song to end with 'ami'), he also uses a version of the first line which, as we know, was widely used elsewhere. He seems, in short, to be correcting back the refrain to a version that he knew. The differences between these two parallel fifth stanzas are not easy to interpret in terms of the compositional process of the song: clearly no simple copying process is involved, but something more like recomposition, perhaps from memory. The changes in the refrain appear to indicate that the version in Berne and fr. 20050 is an adaptation of a line better known in the form in which the Modena scribe gives it; at the same time, the latter feels free to augment it with a new line, seemingly because he perceives it as incomplete without it.

We can see from this that although the principle of formal disjunction is important to this song, not all the song's 'producers' observed it. Nonetheless similar contingencies of juxtaposition and interconnection are common enough to indicate that associative links between refrains are a crucial feature of thirteenth-century compositional practice.

The last three contexts of vdB, refr. 65 – the two motets and *La Court de paradis* – are a case in point. Each of them elaborates upon *Ainssi doit on aler / a son ami* by means of another refrain. Motet 435 is one of a small number of distinctive pieces usually known as *Kurzmotetten* or refrain motets. These motets consist in one or two refrain texts set over an unpatterned tenor, creating tiny polyphonic pieces of barely more than a few seconds' duration. They are an important attestation to the significance of refrains as independent units of textual and musical material in the thirteenth century. In M435 the following two refrains are put together (see Ex. 5 and Fig. 6(a)):

> *Renvoisiement i voit*
> *a mon ami;*
> (vdB, refr. 1623)
>
> *Ensi doit on aler*
> *a son ami.*
> (vdB, refr. 65)
>
> *Joyfully I go to my lover; this is how you must go towards your lover.*

Compared to other contexts, this example of amplification is minimal, consisting in the abrupt juxtaposition of semantically related texts. The sense of abruptness is caused in part by the overlapping meaning of the texts, and in part by the grammar: the first descriptive statement in the first person not quite connecting with the second, more open-ended third-person observation.

As if in recognition, the author of the second motet (M1143a) puts the same two refrains together, this time with an intervening textual expansion:

> *Renvoisiement i vois a men amie,*
> *Par espaules caviaus blois,*
> Blans plicons, bendes d'orfrois,
> Blance cemise autresi,
> Car c'est li drois;
> Bras sans las,
> Pies sans saulers:
> *Ainsi doit on aler*
> *A son ami.*
>
> *Joyfully I go there to my lover. With fair hair over my shoulders,* white pelisse, bands of gold braid, white chemise as well, for that is right; arms unlaced, feet without shoes; *this is how you must go towards your lover.*

6 (a) *Kurzmotetten* (Motet 435), showing two refrains and a tenor: '*Renvoisiement / Ensi doit on aler / Hodie*', BN fr. 12615, fol. 191 v (top initial).
(b) The same two refrains, '*Renvoisiement*' and '*Ensi doit dame aler*' (separated by a third refrain, '*Se j'ai amé*', not shown) in *La Court de paradis*, BN fr. 25532, fol. 333 v.

As in the other contexts for vdB, refr. 65 there is a strong impulse to provide a narrative motive for the refrain, in this case by particularising the visual and gestural details of the implied erotic movement towards a lover. By this means the author also allows the two refrains properly to connect.

There is no means of knowing whether either of these motets was composed in the knowledge of the other, or even by the same person

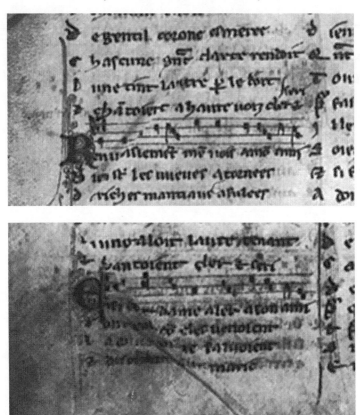

6 (*cont.*)

(they are not copied in the same manuscripts). This makes it all the more tantalising to discover a contiguity between the same two refrains (*Renvoisiement* and *Ensi doit*) in *La Court de paradis*, where they appear on the same folio separated by a third refrain (see Fig. 6(b) and Ex. 5). It is possible that some scheme of influence is at work among the three contexts. My point is more that such details bear witness to the kinds of generative semantic association that take place in thirteenth-century composition, and in particular, to the way in which motet composers sharpen such association into a structural principle.[10]

This examination of the various contexts of *Ainssi doit on aler/a son ami* has uncovered several points of connection, both in the way each supplies a narrative motive for the refrain, and in the details of the way each context is constructed around the refrain. *La Court de paradis* further exemplifies this by providing close points of comparison not only with the motets, but also with the *chanson avec des refrains*.[11] This anonymous thirteenth-century narrative survives in three manuscripts, one of which (fr. 25532) includes musical notation for the nineteen refrains. Like *Le Tournoi de Chauvency* it sets *Ensi doit on aler/a son ami* within a courtly context; however, it translates the secular court into heaven, where the characters are not contemporary members of the nobility but prophets, saints, martyrs and the company of the elect, presided over by the Virgin Mary and Christ. In a bizarrely plotted inversion of the secular court festivities so frequently portrayed in thirteenth-century romance, the author describes Christ as sending out invitations via St Simon and St Jude to a heavenly ball to be held on All Saints Day. As well as the male guests – patriarchs, apostles and martyrs – various groups of women are invited – virgins, widows and faithful married women. Love refrains are sung by the guests as they arrive, and during the dancing, to signify their love of Christ and their joy at the occasion.

The author conducts the religious parody by means of detailed allusions to secular genres. Several of these can be observed by comparing the contexts of this one refrain. For example, the passage containing *Renvoisiement / i vois a mon ami* and *Ensi doit dame aler/a son ami*, with the intervening refrain *Se j'ai amé folement, /sage sui, si m'en repent* [*If I have loved foolishly, I am now wise, and repent of it*] contains a description, framed by the refrains, of the clothing and gestures of the dancing women which recalls both in detail and structure the central section of M1143a, framed as it is by the same two refrains. Even more pointed is the way in which *Ensi doit dame aler/a son ami* in *La Court de paradis* recalls the *chanson avec des refrains*. For in *La Court de paradis* the refrain is given not to a *mal mariée* to sing but to the group of loyal married women. Not surprisingly, both contexts make the same substitution of 'dame' for 'on':

> E vos les dames marïees
> Mout tres richement atornees
> Qui furent avec lor seignors
> En loiauté et par amors...
> Li une aloit l'autre tenant

Et chantoient cler et seri:
> *Ensi doit dame aler*
> *A son ami.*

(*La Court de paradis*, 350–53, 357–60)

> Here were the married women, very richly adorned, who lived with
> their lords in loyalty and love ... Each went along arm in arm and
> singing clearly and serenely: *This is how a lady must go towards her*
> *lover.*

This example shows not a specific allusion but a generic one. Analysis
of the contexts of *Ainssi doit on aler / a son ami* reveals precise manipulations of refrain texts, which seem to rely on well-defined generic expectations about refrain-citation within such settings as a courtly carole,
or a procession by horseback, or the complaints of the *mal mariée*.
In all these cases of irony or parody we appear to find evidence that
authors were well aware of the ability of refrains to mediate between
genres.

To conclude, the pattern of connections among the six contexts of
vdB, refr. 65 indicates some of the complexities of relation that exist
between refrains and other thirteenth-century genres. Clear differences
exist between the formal function of the refrain: the brevity of the
motet treatments[12] contrasts with the full narrative glosses supplied by
the romances and the chanson, and again with the varying forms of
repetition that occur in rondeaux. Some attempt is made in each genre
to connect the refrain by rhyme: this varies, some contexts treating the
refrain as two lines (rond. 168 rhymes with both), others as one line,
and the motets and chanson not just rhyming with 'ami' but repeating
it. To this extent, the genres take a distinctive approach to the refrain.
However, the concept of a single refrain is itself mobile: the formulaic
shifts, substitutions and rearrangements form part of the essential texture
of a refrain, rather than represent deviant versions of a single normative
prototype. In this sense, authors are responding to the character of the
refrain as a semantic and formal structure that is open to all kinds of
creative variation.[13]

Perhaps what is most remarkable is the extent to which compositional principles are shared amongst the genres. In every case, as we have
seen, the surrounding text amplifies the refrain, either by providing a

narrative explanation, by giving details of gesture, movement and dress, or by juxtaposing a semantically parallel text. In three of the contexts the same amplifying text (the additional refrain *Renvoisiement / I vois a mon ami*) is chosen illustrating a principle of generative association amongst refrain texts which we also observed among the producers of the chanson. Wider attention to the pattern of migration of refrains throughout thirteenth-century genres shows this principle to be endemic: the kaleidoscopic character of refrain-citation causes complex associative chains to be formed across works, bringing them into unexpected liaisons.

6

Contrafacta: from secular to sacred in Gautier de Coinci and later thirteenth-century writing

The word *contrafacta* has an unprepossessingly technical sound. It was not used in its modern musical sense in the Middle Ages: the verb *contrafacere* in medieval Latin (*contrefaire* in Old French) means to imitate, counterfeit or forge. The modern usage, apparently first coined in this century by Friedrich Gennrich, has the more neutral meaning of the substitution of a new set of words for an existing tune.[1] Yet it would be misleading to trust this quasi-scientific specificity very far: in practice we are concerned with an area of medieval creativity which is on the edge of a large and shifting cultural process. There are two principal characteristics of this process: one concerns the placing and replacing of words in relation to melodies, the other, since *contrafacta* are often of this kind, the multiple and often fascinatingly contradictory interrelations between sacred and secular.

These aspects of *contrafacta* are difficult to grasp or define in settled ways. The relation between medieval melodies and texts is unstable – at least from a modern perspective – which means that it is often not clear whether the new text is in partnership with a new tune, a free adaptation of an existing tune, or with the existing tune itself. In any case, when we consider how widespread the practice of melodic – and textual – adaptation is in medieval composition, how frequently, for instance, a single text may be copied (though often with significant textual variation) in different manuscripts with several quite distinct melodies, it becomes debatable whether we are viewing one process or several.[2] The relations between sacred and secular provoke further questions. We tend to think now in terms of straightforward opposition, of the sacred, in particular, as a perspective which defines itself against the secular. But examples of *contrafacta* show that to be simplistic. First of all, as Jean Frappier and Pierre Bec have commented, 'chansons pieuses' have no separate generic existence in the twelfth and thirteenth centuries, they come into being 'en marge du lyrisme profane', that is, as parasitic imitations and conversions of already existing secular genres.[3] Rather than two cultures competing on equal terms, vernacular sacred song falls under the shadow of the already powerful tradition of secular song, and hence forms a relationship marked by dependence and intimacy.[4]

Having discussed some of the ways in which refrains form stable, yet also highly flexible, overlapping structures, and then seen how this formal flexibility stimulates various kinds of amplification within different genres, allowing new possibilities of meaning by association and parody, I want to develop this exploration of genre by considering how refrains are used to negotiate the boundaries between the sacred and the secular. *Contrafacta* composition has much in common with refrain-citation: the substitution and juxtaposition of old texts and new tunes, or of new texts and old tunes is endemic to both. By giving access to the minutiae of such procedures, refrain-citation reveals some of the mechanisms by which meaning is made to face both ways along the same cultural axis.

GAUTIER DE COINCI, *LES MIRACLES DE NOSTRE DAME*

The peculiarities of the relationship between sacred and secular song are evident in the earliest *chansons pieuses*, some of the most sophisticated and creative examples of *contrafacta* in the medieval period. These are the songs inserted by Gautier de Coinci between his two books of Marian narratives. Because many copies of the *Miracles* have music (thirteen) the work provides a unique opportunity to observe both aspects of the *contrafacta* process – the placing of text against melody, and the conversion of secular to sacred – at the very moment when the process is being initiated. Its subtlety derives from Gautier's pioneering redefinition of the role of the trouvère and his appropriation of it for a new sacred context. At first sight, he indeed appears to be harshly oppositional. His opening Prologue is careful to define his own songs by negative comparison with secular songs. He refuses to sing 'de risees et de folies' [of farce and folly] (I, Pr 2, p. 22, line 64), of 'Tyebregon et d'Emmelot' (III, 324) or of Marot and Maroye (III, 330), songs which only those bent for hell's torments enjoy. 'Karoles' he describes (in the fiery tones of the preacher Stephen Langton) as 'gabois et legeries' [mockery and trivialities] and 'chans de lecheries' [songs of lechery] (III, 348–50): songs more fit for devils to sing than for clerks.[5] Let us not be like those who cast honey aside for poison and leave Marie for Marot ('Et por Marot Marie laissent', III, 382). The extent to which he draws on secular models can be seen in his delineation of his own role as performer, which is closely analogous to the trouvère's: he composes and sings for the love of his lady ('Et atemprer veil ma viele, / Se chanterai de la pucele' [and I want to tune my viele and sing of the lady] (I, Pr 2, p. 22, lines 57–58)).

However, his work confirms as much as it rejects courtly secular values. His attitude towards the people in his audience has a doubleness which is part of the whole cultural process of *contrafacta*. He wishes to define them in one way (as 'gens letrees' (III, 355), that is, as educated clerics)[6] but can only do so by assuming their secularity: in other words, by desiring them to fulfil the pious character of their clerical calling, he appeals precisely to the courtly tastes he is lambasting, such as a liking for secular song. His tactic is the old ecclesiastical trick of using the very forms of lewd entertainment as the material for his own spiritual performance. The comparison with Renart is irresistible. For instance, Gautier strongly emphasises the novel presence of the songs, choosing a vivid metaphor to describe their relation to his narratives. He will plant them ('En cest livre volrai planter / De lius en lius chançons noveles' [I want to plant in this book, here and there, new songs] (I, Pr 2, p. 20, lines 18–19)), and they will become like sweet-scented flowers scattering fragrance throughout the work (I, Pr 2, p. 21, lines 32–35). While this resembles Renart's rhetoric (compare Renart's 'brodez, par lieus, de biaus vers' with 'volrai planter / De lius en lius chançons noveles'), Gautier supplants the courtly metaphor used by Renart with the ancient sacred symbol of the Virgin: the rose (I, Pr 2, p. 21, line 37).[7]

Without new evidence to confirm the dating of Renart's *Rose* or the *Miracles*, the relationship between the two works can only be conjectured. Similar difficulties attend comparison of Renart's *Rose* and the first part of *Le Roman de la rose* by Guillaume de Lorris.[8] To have two such radical definitions of secular song – one in romance, one in Marian narrative – produced possibly within the same decade, shows the importance of this early part of the thirteenth century for trouvère song. Whether or not Renart's work precedes or follows Gautier's *Miracles* it provides a natural interpretative context for the kind of inversions practised by Gautier on secular song. Both authors are ambivalent towards their implied audiences. We might expect it of Gautier, but Renart is also playing off more than one kind of approach towards courtliness. Keen as he is to promote his romance among courtly listeners, his terms of valuation appeal blatantly to courtly prejudice. In the *Rose*, the 'chans' are 'biaus' (like Renart's ecclesiastical patron 'li biaus Miles . . . de Nantuel') and provide a fitting match for the *roman*, which has the prime courtly subject 'd'armes et d'amors'. The final coup is their exclusivity: they are unintelligible to 'vilains'. However Renart's claims have a certain sharpness. His first metaphor, for example, of the dye adding cost to the cloth has a commercial tang which is faintly disconcerting. With hindsight, we can recognise the latent sarcasm with which Renart later describes the financial excesses of Conrad's court, but even without this, Renart's easy equation of 'renown' and 'expense' produces vague disquiet in an audience not entirely seduced by his exaggerated praise of courtly values. Renart's careful manipulations of prejudice and taste have much in common with Gautier's.

In the only major study to date of Gautier's chansons, Jacques Chailley has concluded that the composition of the songs proceeded in four stages between 1218 and 1236.[9] The first redaction of the *Miracles* contained no songs (they are absent in fifty-three of the surviving seventy-nine manuscripts); in 1219 he began to compose a small group in honour of St Léocade, and by 1223 had completed the second stage of the *Miracles* including nine songs. Eight further songs were finished by 1227; from 1228 to 1236, Chailley argues, there was a final redaction and another cluster of songs. According to the pattern followed in the most carefully executed manuscripts, the *Miracles* take the following form: a general Prologue; a secondary Prologue followed by a cycle of songs; the first book of miracles; a further Prologue followed by a cycle of songs; the second book of miracles. Various manuscripts have further additions: the group of three St Léocade songs, usually added at the end of the first book; a work called 'Les Saluts Notre Dame' which follows the second book; and two versified sermons that are inserted into the second book, 'De la chastée as nonains' [On the chastity of nuns] and 'De la doutance de la mort' [On the fear of death]. Several compilations interpolate a wide range of extra pieces including Latin songs, motets, and French poems on the nativity of the Virgin and Jesus Christ.

Gautier reveals not only a thorough interest in secular song, but also a particular fascination with the dance-song topos of Bele Aelis. As well as several examples of songs modelled on *grands chants* such as Blondel de Nesle's 'L'amours dont sui espris' [The love which has seized me], several others are based on *pastourelles*. In some late songs, including another by Blondel, he even turns a *grand chant* into a *chanson avec des refrains* by adding refrains. The following three songs, all given a relatively late date by Chailley (between 1224 and 1232), and placed in sequence in the Soissons manuscript (n. a. fr. 24541), show Gautier's manner of extending the lower register of his models at its most marked. It is not impossible that these particular songs might be the result of a direct response to Renart's *Rose*.

The first, 'D'une amour quoie et serie' [Of a love elegant and serene] (No. 11 in Chailley) is a *contrafactum* of a melody by Gilles de [Viès] Maisons. I give the first two statements of the melody by Gilles, with the opening of Gautier's song followed by the refrain *Vilainnes genz* (see Ex. 6).

Ex. 6 'D'une amour quoie et serie': comparison of the first line and refrain of a *contrafactum* by Gautier de Coinci with the first two lines of the model by Gilles de [Viès] Maisons

Gilles's melody (for an eight-line strophe rhyming ababbcab) is divided into two sections: an opening ouvert–clos phrase for the first two text lines which is repeated, with slight variation, for the next two, followed by two separate but balanced phrases for the last four lines. The tune begins with a distinctive repeated *d'* that leaps down a fifth and then climbs back to the *d'* before settling at the end of the clos phrase on the *g'*. Gautier models his opening line on the ouvert phrase in the Gilles song, giving a clean, sharp focus to the oscillating fifth. Reinforcing the motif even further, he gives it to the start of a refrain which he adds after each strophe:

> *Vilainnes genz, vous ne les sentez mie*
> *Les douz maus que je sens.*
>
> *Vulgar people, you never know the sweet pains that I feel.*

This refrain is widely cited elsewhere (see vdB, refr. 1840): the text (though not the melody) is also closely related to another refrain (vdB, refr. 1865) which is cited in 'Ja pour hiver, pour noif ne pour gelée' [Never because of winter, snow or frost] and a *rondet de carole* in Renart's *Rose*.

Gautier's use of a refrain has textual as well as musical implications. Picking up the reference to worthiness in the song by Gilles ('Cil n'est pas de chanter dignes / Qui ne chante par deport' [he is not worthy to sing who does not sing for pleasure]), the refrain develops it into a contrast between the worthy and the 'vilaine genz', and is introduced with the same phrasing ('Nest pas dignes'):

> Nus qui aint vilainnement
> Ceste chançon n'encomment:
> Nest pas dignes qu'il en die
> Nes le refrait seulement:
>
> No one who loves vulgarly may begin this song; it is not fitting that he should sing even so much as the refrain.

The witty appropriateness of *this* is that by making the refrain – his major structural change to the song – encapsulate the song's message (and dominate the melody), Gautier makes it unsingable, except, of course, by the worthy. But it is only in the third stanza that he reveals his turn on

'worthiness' – 'N[e] pas Marot mès Marie' [not Marot but Marie . . .] –
so that the unsuspecting singer who might have thought himself worthy
in Gilles's sense is implicitly pulled up short and retrospectively shown to
be singing under false pretences. The structure of the *contrafactum* has a
delayed action in which the process of textual change – the reclamation
of 'digne' from a secular to a sacred sense – is at first teasingly half-
concealed.

'Hui matin a l'ajournee' [This morning at daybreak], a *contrafactum*
of a *pastourelle*, has an interestingly circuitous history. It appears to have
originated as the duplum of a three-voice clausula from the Notre Dame
organum, *Benedicamus domino*. This clausula made its way into at least
two Latin motets, one of which includes a French *contrafactum* in the
form of a *pastourelle*. Thus 'Hui matin' is a kind of double contrafact,
a reversion to piety of a religious text that had been converted into
secularity. The resulting piece, in Gautier's version, has a switchback
quality which is not at all equivalent to what might be construed as an act
of mere cancellation of the song's temporary excursion into frivolity. One
instance is the way that the 'O.o.o.o.o.o' in the refrain, far from being
the spontaneously 'popular' outburst that it seems,[10] has been produced
with academic humour from the *hoquet* passages in the organum, that
is, from the abrupt alternations between voices in the sacred polyphony.
With further subtlety, Gautier plays on the vowel sound 'ot' in his text,
arguing that it is this simple sound that makes all the difference between
virtue and vice: 'tot a un mot' [in a word] one should abandon 'Marot'
for 'Marie' (see Ex. 7).[11]

Such transpositions are even more starkly displayed in 'Ja pour yver,
pour noif ne pour gelee' (see Ex. 8). The melodic model, in this case, is
Blondel de Nesle's 'Li plus se plaint d'Amours mès je n'os dire' [Most
people complain of Love, but I dare not speak].[12] However, again Gautier does more than simply invent a suitably pious text. He creates a
remarkable generic shift from *grand chant* to *chanson avec des refrains*.
The Blondel melody is in characteristic 'higher' style, with elegant,
smoothly flowing stepwise progressions focused initially around the
opening *c'* (which is repeated six times for the first twelve syllables of
text). Gautier's song follows this melody with scarcely any deviation:
to this he puts a text that announces its Marian orientation relatively

Ex. 7 'Hui matin a l'ajournée': comparison of opening of Gautier's song with the *clausula* model (W_1), and motet version (W_2), including the *hoquet* passage

Ex. 8 'Ja pour hiver': comparison of opening, and first refrain, of Gautier's song with the model by Blondel de Nesle

straightforwardly:

> Ja pour yver, pour noif ne pour gelee
> N'iere esbaubiz, periceus, (muz) ne maz
> Que je ne chant de la dame honnouree
> Qui Jhesucrist porta (entre) ses braz.
> Chascun an faiz de la Virge sacree
> Un son nouvel dont tout l'an me soulaz
> Dire puet bien qui a s'amour bien bee:
>> *Vous ne sentez mie*
>> *Les douz maus d'amer*
>> *Ausi com je fais.*

> Never because of winter, snow or ice will I be so dismayed, fearful, mute or defeated that I will not sing of the honoured lady who carried Jesus Christ in her arms. Each year I make a new song to the sacred Virgin from which I draw comfort throughout the year; he who greatly desires her love can well say: *You don't feel at all the sweet pains of love as I feel them.*

The sense of shock or disruption comes with the refrain. In part this is textual: the lines are metrically distinct from the preceding strophe, and the cliché 'Les douz maus d'amer' [the sweet pains of love] is so thoroughly associated with secular love-longing that even the direct references to the Virgin that precede it struggle to purge it of its secularity.

But if this last point remains debatable perhaps, there is no doubt about the stylistic shift that occurs in the music. In common with other *chansons avec des refrains*, the melody changes from its serene, 'higher' style closing phrase to a jaunty, light and self-enclosed tune. When this sense of change is confirmed by the other refrains, each of which is melodically distinct, the result is a song that moves disconcertingly back and forth between two kinds of musical style. In fact, the sequence of refrains detaches itself further and further from the melodic world of the *grand chant*: the pitch range of the third refrain (which comes after the fifth strophe) rises up to a *g'* (the highest pitch in the Blondel melody is *f'*). The register of the final refrain (*Cui donrrai ge mes amours, / Mere Dieu, s'a vous non?* [*To whom will I give my love, mother of God, if not to you?*]), which as we saw in an earlier chapter also occurs in Renart's *Rose* as part of a *rondet de carole*, has the most marked lower style both musically, and from its dance-song romance context (see Ex. 1). As if to counter-balance this stylistic tendency, Gautier converts this last refrain with a deft substitution, so that 'Mere Dieu' is put in for 'amie'.

'Ja pour yver, pour noif ne pour gelee' is framed by two refrains that are cited in Renart's *Rose*: *Cui donrrai ge mes amours* from the seventh *rondet de carole* (532–37), and *Vous ne sentez mie* from the fifth (514–19). Whether or not Gautier was directly influenced by Renart to make these citations, they reveal how far Gautier was interested in overlaying his *grand chant* models with lower style elements. Before creating a religious counterpart to a chanson he gave the original song a much broader and more overt secular base. His creative activity is far from that of a narrow moralist, instead he appeared to wish to make his songs as directly, and 'popularly' appealing as possible, if necessary by scattering them (to use his own metaphor) with well-known refrains. Only after this initial transformation do the songs gain the further benefit of a religious colouring (to use Renart's metaphor). As a consequence, they are richly resourced: able to draw on both kinds of context at once, the religious message is the result of a process of absorption rather than of negation.

This is further evident from perhaps the most curious of all his interpolations to the Marian narratives, the sermon 'De la chastée as nonains' in octosyllabic couplets which finishes with a 62-line piece in heptasyllables beginning 'La fontenele i sort clere' [The spring gushes out clearly].

The latter was described by its earliest editors as a *reverdie pieuse*, but it has been argued by Chailley, and more fully by Koenig, that it cannot really be thought of as a chanson at all.[13] The whole work is addressed to the nuns of Notre-Dame de Soissons ('vos damoyseles, / Vos cloistrieres, vos jovenceles' [you young women, you cloistered women, and young girls] (439–40)), urging them to prize chastity and to welcome the chance to forgo an unhappy earthly marriage in favour of a heavenly marriage with Christ. Towards the end of the address, just before the section beginning 'La fontenele i sort clere', Gautier cites two refrains:

> 'Mal ait cil qui me maria!'
> Ce dïent en lor chançonnetes
> (1096–97)
>
> 'Curses to him who married me!' So they say in their songs

and

> Le commant de la chançonnete
> Face qui est bien vraie amie:
> 'Pour Dieu, ne vos repentez mie,
> Ce dist, de loiaument amer.'
> (1106–09)
>
> Let whoever is a true lover carry out the song's command: *'For God's sake, never repent, so [the song] says, of loving loyally'.*

The first, the traditional cry of the *mal mariée*, is taken with opportune straightforwardness as direct proof of the woes of earthly marriage: the second, however, is punningly reclaimed as a sacred truth about the nature of Christian love. Both set up a framework for the strangely constructed 'pseudo-chanson' that the young nuns are urged to sing (1113–16).

'La fontenele i sort clere' begins as a kind of pious fantasia on the theme of Bele Aelis. It differs from other thirteenth-century sermons on Bele Aelis, which tend to quote a whole *rondet de carole* at the start and then gloss each line systematically.[14] Its idiosyncratic repetitions hint at a regular formal structure but do not fully deliver one. Thus the opening line is repeated with slight variation as 'La fontenele i sourt serie' [The spring gushes out calmly] four times altogether at lines 1117, 1121, 1125 and 1137, while the line 'Dire puet bien tele i a' [A woman who has it can certainly say] is likewise repeated four times at 1120, 1124, 1128 and 1132. The quatrain structure becomes less clearly signalled by formal repetitions after this, although the line 'M'ame ou ciel marïera' [my soul will marry in heaven] at 1160, repeated exactly at 1168 and with variation at 1164, acts as a final refrain. As Koenig points out, however, the poem is not laid out strophically in the manuscripts but as an unbroken verse narrative in common with the preceding sermon and earlier miracles.

The poem thus seems to fall somewhere between a chanson and an elaborate piece of versified narrative, heightened by frequent repetitive patterns (for the most part there are only two rhyme sounds throughout). The repeated lines themselves, especially at the start, are worth further consideration. The line 'La fontenele i sort clere / serie' is a standard element in a *rondet de carole* based on the 'C'est la jus' motif. It occurs, for instance, in the 'strophic' sections of five *rondets de carole* cited in Renart's *Rose*.[15] Phrases common to these *rondets* are repeatedly echoed in Gautier's poem, such as the refrain line *bon jor ait qui mon cuer a!* [*good day to the one who has my heart*] (vdB, rond. 9, *Rose*, 1579) which stands behind 'Bonne aventure ait ma mere' [may my mother have good fortune] (1118, 1123 and 1131). Gautier's use of 'a' as one of his two rhyme sounds recalls and reinforces the verbal structure both of *bon jor ait* and vdB, rond. 1. Moreover, one of the refrains Gautier cites at the end of the sermon is also cited in Renart's *Rose*:

> *Ne vos repentez mie*
> *de loiaument amer*
> (vdB, rond. 11; *Rose*, 2369)
>
> *Never repent of loving loyally.*
> (see Ex. 2)

The emphatic 'ne mie', reinforced by exclamations 'Diex! Diex! Diex! men cuer n'ai mie' [God! God! God! I do not have my heart any longer] (1126) is a frequent motif in Gautier.

That the texture of Gautier's piece is thoroughly interwoven with linguistic features drawn from secular dance-song hardly needs further demonstration. The numerous parallels and citations in common with Renart's *Rose* may well indicate that Gautier saw himself as a direct rival to Renart, intent on replacing romance with a sacred context in which well-known songs could be an equally vital and pleasurable element.[16] But even if he was working quite independently of Renart, it seems clear that he was just as influenced by the powerful current of secular song, and just as intrigued by the possible rapprochements between different registers in that tradition. Perhaps surprisingly, he turns out to be highly innovative in his exploration of those relations: his continual effort to redirect the current of secularity back into religion takes him deep into the linguistic and musical characteristics of secular song, and into subtle manipulations of its generic assumptions.

LA COURT DE PARADIS

One manuscript of Gautier's *Les Miracles*, fr. 25532, a thirteenth-century copy that comes from St-Médard de Soissons, contains a range of extra pieces at the end, including a Psalm paraphrase, several saints' lives and Wace's *Conceptions Notre Dame*. After these, on fols. 331 v–335, is a copy of *La Court de paradis*. It is the only copy (of the work's surviving three) to contain musical notation for its inset refrains, and this notation (along with the text) appears to be written in the same hand as the music for the songs in the *Miracles*.[17] We have seen in the last chapter, through the analysis of a single migrating refrain, how *La Court de paradis* involves a range of parodic allusions to such genres as the motet and the *chanson de mal mariée*. Its most distinctive registral shift involves the recasting of secular refrains as expressions of religious sentiment. To take a typical example, the song of the Innocents:

> *Vrais Diex, la joie que j'ai*
> *Me vient de vos.*
> (318–19)

> *True God, the love I have comes to me from you.*

is a pious parody of

> *Amis dous,*
> *li malz que j'ai me vient de vos.*
> (vdB, refr. 127)

> *Sweet lover, the pain I have comes to me from you.*

In other cases, the words of the refrain are not altered but simply given a new meaning, so that 'amor' becomes *caritas*, as in this refrain sung by the Apostles:

> *Tout ainsi va qui d'amors vit*
> *Et qui bien aimme*
> (281–2)

> *Just like this goes the one who lives by love and who loves well.*

The author of *La Court de paradis* is able to make this kind of translation (both in the detail of the refrains and in the larger setting of the poem) with ease. It suggests his ready familiarity with the idea of the court scene with refrains (a topos which will be explored more fully in a later chapter). His bold appropriation of secular love motifs for the purpose of redefining heavenly pleasures as equivalent to earthly ones creates a strange meeting-ground between registers in which the refrains mark the points of interchange; it recalls Gautier's practice in the *Miracles*. Like Gautier's songs, *La Court de paradis* is not so much subverting the secular for the purposes of religion as allowing a powerfully secular framework to subvert its audience's view of the sacred. The topos of the court allows the poet to range across discrete social groups (the apostles, martyrs, confessors, holy innocents, virgins, loyally married women and widows). By drawing on different sources of generic expectation, the refrains underlie these differences.

There is more to associate *La Court de paradis* and the *Miracles* than is usually claimed. One point of connection is the refrain (also cited in Renart's *Rose*) which, as we noted above, occurs towards the end of Gautier's sermon on chastity:

> *Ne vos repentez mie*
> *de loiaument amer.*
> (see Ex. 2)

This is the third refrain in *La Court de paradis*, sung by all the apostles. Shortly afterwards come refrains sung by the virtuous women, including two (*Renvoisïement / i vois a mon ami* and *Einsi doit dame aler / a son ami*) which I discussed in the previous chapter (see Ex. 5 and Fig. 6(b)). This whole section of *La Court de paradis* not only gives emphasis to a community of saintly women, it includes descriptions of their clothing and their relationship with Christ which are close to similar descriptions in Gautier's sermon. For instance, Gautier addresses the nuns:

> Saichiez que Diex em paradys
> De vos fera ses flors de lis
> (1065–66)

> Know that God will make [of] you his lilies in paradise.

In *La Court de paradis* the heavenly dancers

> Par amor main a main se tienent
> Et sunt plus blanc que flors de lis
> De la joie de paradis
> (276–78)

> They hold hands for love, and are whiter than lilies through the joy of paradise.

Gautier goes on to talk of the way the earthly clothing of the nuns will become superseded by heavenly garments for their souls:

> Vos blanches fleurs, vos de Cistiaus,
> Qui affublez ces blans mantiaus,
> Qui les pliçons, qui les chemisez
> Pour blans buiriax avez jus misez,
> Ja sont ou ciel aparilliez
> Blanches chemises deliies
> Et les robes a or batues
> Dont vos ames seront vestues.
> (1067–74)

> You white flowers, you Cistercians, who dress in these white cloaks, who have put aside pelisses and chemises for white burrel-cloth, already in heaven are prepared fine white chemises and the robes of beaten gold in which your souls will be clothed.

Similarly, the married women in *La Court de paradis*:

> Mout tres richement atornees...
> Chascune eut vestu chainse blanche,
> Plus blanc que ne soit nois sor branche
> (351, 354–55)

> Very richly adorned ... each one was dressed in a white linen tunic, whiter than snow on a branch.

Many of these descriptions are of course biblical and mystical rather than 'original' to either work.[18] Nonetheless the particular conjunction of a female setting, a pious framework for the translation of earthly materiality into spiritual pleasure, and the citation of secular refrains makes it seem possible that Gautier's idiosyncratic sermon provided the impetus for the *Paradis*'s more extreme use of refrains within a sacred context. That the particular manuscript in which the two works are found together preserves the musical notation for each, and is also one of perhaps two manuscripts of the *Miracles* that may have been copied there directly from an authorised version, suggests that *La Court de paradis* is a locally produced offshoot. Again, however, the point is not so much whether there is evidence of direct borrowing, as to observe that sacred love poetry takes secular refrains as fundamental units of construction: the refrains are not incidental to the process of *contrafacta* but directly motivate and structure it.

L'ESTOIRE DE JOSEPH

One further example of a religious narrative that is given an unusual musical twist is a copy in n. a. fr. 10036 of *L'Estoire de Joseph*. This hexasyllabic version of the life of Joseph survives in three manuscripts. In the version in n. a. fr. 10036 (thirteenth century) four musical passages have been added in the lower margins by a separate scribe from that of the main narrative. In a variety of strophic forms, these musical interpolations partly substitute for and partly amplify passages of spoken dialogue between Joseph and members of his family. In the first, for example, which begins in alexandrines, Joseph is given four stanzas to sing, followed by three in reply from his father. Various brothers join in, their names indicated at the side: 'Judas cantands', Ruben, Levi and Nabulon. Dramatically, this musical passage has strong pastoral/*pastourelle* associations: it has a spring setting in which the brothers are cast as shepherds, one playing a horn and another a flute for their own rustic entertainment. The work's uncanny resemblance to a *bergerie* scene such as the one that occurs in the latter part of Adam de la Halle's *Le Jeu de Robin et Marion*, which is discussed in a later chapter, is then left to one side as the second and third interpolations shift into a more serious register. Jacob cries out in distress at the loss of Joseph and Benjamin, the musical phrase for the refrain-like 'Las, las, las' repeating mournfully throughout the song:

> Las las las, que ferai?
> Las las las, ja morrai.[19]

> Alas, alas, alas, what shall I do? Alas, alas, alas, I will certainly die.

Finally, the fourth passage, a song of praise, contains a recurrent refrain: 'Por joie avoir' [to have joy], which mutates twice (as is common, for instance, in *chansons de toile*) into 'Joseph veoir' [to see Joseph] and 'Sans joie avoir' [without having joy].

This unique copy seems to be part of a humble, probably personal devotional compilation. Alongside Gautier's chansons and *La Court de paradis* its idiosyncratic qualities gain more of a context: it looks to be another manifestation of an impulse (that becomes increasingly widespread throughout the thirteenth century) to overlay sacred narratives with secular textual and musical motifs drawn from lower style genres. The metonymic connections between biblical and historical peasant shepherds, as Elizabeth Salter reminds us, were a common iconographic preoccupation in fourteenth-century manuscripts:[20] it is interesting to discover a musical and verbal articulation of the same theme in this thirteenth-century story of Joseph.

ADAM DE LA BASSÉE, *LUDUS SUPER ANTICLAUDIANUM*

In the *Ludus super Anticlaudianum*, a Latin work written between 1279 and 1284–85, the parameters between sacred and secular are altered by the fact that Adam de la Bassée is not composing a straightforwardly devotional piece, but reworking a sophisticated philosophical narrative of a hundred years earlier, Alain de Lille's *Anticlaudianus*. Adam reduces and popularises Alain de Lille's original work, in part by recasting the metre and style of Alain's language, but most significantly, by dramatising its structure with the addition of thirty-eight musical pieces. The idea of music already plays an important part in the *Anticlaudianus*, particularly in the section of the work where Music helps to fashion one of the wheels of Prudence's chariot in which she makes her journey to Heaven. Alain's language is clearly Boethian in his description of music's binding power:

> showing what music may do, with what chains it binds all things together; by what manifestation of art it articulates the hours, orders the months and regulates the seasons of the year and their passing; by what means it binds the elements, joins the planets, moves the stars and directs their turning; by what means it arranges the parts of the human body, and the lesser world, and honours it for its image of a better.[21]

These ideas are amplified and illustrated by Adam's decision to give Music a practical as well as theoretical, a musical as well as verbal, role in the work.

His choice of music is highly eclectic. Many of the melodies are *contrafacta* of chansons by local trouvères such as Raoul de Soissons, Martin Béquin de Cambrai, and Lambert Ferri d'Arras. Two more songs are based on dance tunes (both unidentified), another is described as 'super pastoralem quae incipit: "L'autrier estoie montes sur mon palefroi amblant"', that is, set 'to [the tune of] the pastourelle which begins: "The other day I was passing on my horse"', by Henri III, duc de Brabant (No. 129).[22] There is also a two-part motet (No. 135) and some religious pieces: sequences, a responsory and an alleluia.

The work is difficult to place. As its title indicates, it is an elaborate example of clerical wit applied to an already elaborate, philosophically demanding twelfth-century clerical fantasy. In the context of the other works we have been considering, it is more diverse in range, and more musically ambitious. The limited dramatic potential of *La Court de paradis* or *L'Estoire de Joseph* is here given much fuller expression: using familiar local melodies that pass freely from secular dance to liturgical chant, Adam amplifies each stage of the metaphysical journey with a musical commentary, invocation or celebration. Various features of the *Ludus* imply that some care was taken by Adam to fit the method of performance of the various songs to the poetic context in which they occur, and to the particular character singing.[23] Other signs of the dramatic character of the *Ludus* are contained in the unique manuscript, Lille, Bibliothèque Municipale, MS 316, *olim* 397, which is not only fully notated musically but also, according to Bayart, revised, corrected and annotated by the author in his own hand.[24] The rubrication meticulously indicates the sequence of events, the name of the character or characters singing, and, where appropriate, the contrafacted melody.

The *Ludus*, while it has much in common with Gautier's treatment of the *Miracles* interpolations, is best understood in the context of late thirteenth-century northern French compositions such as Jacquemart Giélée's *Renart le Nouvel* and Adam de la Halle's *Jeu de Robin et de Marion*. A canon and priest of the collegiate church of St Pierre in Lille, where he died on 25 February 1286, Adam is likely to have had personal and literary connections with Jacquemart Gielée, a fellow Lillois. An unusually compendious instance of *contrafacta* composition, the *Ludus* indicates a characteristically thirteenth-century interest in crossing linguistic and generic barriers, in drawing eclectically on different registers to produce newly composite works. It reminds us that Latin and vernacular writing could at times touch each other closely, a coincidence brought out with startling generic virtuosity a few decades later in Gervès du Bus's version of the *Roman de Fauvel*, where Latin and French, sacred and secular verse interpolations are liberally juxtaposed.[25]

Contrafacta composition is an area of medieval creativity where at least two kinds of boundary are put under scrutiny: the relation between words and music and the sacred and the secular. The notion of a boundary is particularly delicate, as the above examples have shown, by being at once taken for granted and disputed. The cultural expectations attaching to a secular tune are harnessed in order to add value to words that set out precisely to condemn secular values. This process involves various genres of song and not just refrains. Yet the prevalence of refrain-citation in *contrafacta* pieces, especially in songs by Gautier de Coinci, indicates how exploitable they are. They are immediately recognisable as lower register forms which can be incorporated into an existing secular song, and newly married to religious words. Their nature as small, independent and culturally distinctive elements is used to redefine both kinds of boundary at once, to bolster the compositional structure of a song and motivate a reactionary text. Such creative potential is no small possession for these apparently ephemeral snippets of secular culture.

PART III

The location of culture

7

'Courtly' and 'popular' in the thirteenth century

This chapter turns more directly to the social circumstances within which works of mixed genre came to be written in the thirteenth century. It is not as straightforward an undertaking as one might wish, because the evidence connecting works to places and indeed specific people is sporadic, sometimes contradictory, and often elusive. Nonetheless, it is possible to find more evidentiary associations between one group of works of mixed genre than has hitherto been supposed, and the network that they form is both more intricate and culturally significant than has yet been acknowledged. This network radiates from Arras. Arras is a rich source of study because it turns out to be at the nexus of different kinds of poetic production. Under the joint fiefdom of the Comtes d'Artois and the King, by way of the bishop, it was a thriving urban centre where the courtly, the popular and the clerical mingled at every level. As the title of this section indicates, Arras is a model for the way in which the process of discovery between a piece of writing and its social location is mutual: the place does not simply explain a work, a work also helps to illuminate a place.

First, however, it may be helpful to comment explicitly on such terms as courtly, popular and clerical. I have used them several times in earlier chapters, usually with the protective hedging of inverted commas. Literary scholars usually describe them as types of register, but this term is itself subject to various usages. My interest is in the contrasts of perspective in works of mixed genre between higher and lower styles, more courtly, more urban or more rustic social circumstances, music and poetry, fiction and history. We need a suitable conceptual framework for understanding how these categories intersect, in particular, for connecting the formal and generic with the linguistic and social.

It is not easy to describe this sense of registral difference. For Zumthor, register is 'un réseau de relations pré-établies entre éléments relevant des divers niveaux de formalisation, ainsi qu'entre ces niveaux'.[1] Although this definition has been very influential, it remains a narrowly formalist view. 'Courtly', for example, includes many shades of meaning from the set of values that may be supposed to inhere to courtly experience, but which may be expressed purely as a style by someone far removed from a court, to the actualities of specific court circumstances. Pierre Bec's terms 'popularisant' and 'aristocratisant' better emphasise the way in which register bifurcates along broadly social categories. He is careful to present these as active rather than passive areas of definition, as directional tendencies rather than a hard and fast distinction; likewise, he retreats from attaching particular genres too closely to social groups.[2]

Bec's position is a more sophisticated version of notions of the courtly and the popular formulated by an earlier generation of critics, such as Wackernagel, Brakelmann, Bartsch, Jeanroy and Faral, who, in their efforts to discover the origin of medieval genres, conducted an intense debate about the chronology of courtly, popular and learned ingredients in surviving works. For the purposes of arguments about origins, romanticised ideas, especially about the primitive and folkloric nature of popular art, tended to dominate. Resisting this, Bec loosens the concepts until their social and historical specification is relatively weak. More nuanced reflection on what one might mean by 'popular culture' occurs in the work of the cultural critic Aron Gurevich. Rather than treat it as a bland, homogenising category, Gurevich points out some of the conflicting ways of thinking about it: for example, to see it as the culture of the lower, oppressed classes would not be equivalent to associating it with the *illiterati*, for the latter would include high-ranking groups. Alternatively one might consider it to have belonged to all people, but that among the élite it was usually concealed by official theology and learning, whereas among ordinary people it would come to the surface. Or perhaps popular culture was a creation of the people, or then again a culture created not *by* but *for* the people by other layers of society for the purposes of popularisation.[3]

It is not as if, in Gurevich's terms, any one of these views adequately does justice to the nature of medieval culture. Instead he takes up the idea of 'internal acculturation' (from Jacques Le Goff), that is, the mutual adaptation of different cultural traditions, in order to find a better means of expressing his sense of the competing cultural pressures of the period.[4] This leads him to talk of an 'oral, unrecorded layer of culture' as a key to written texts:[5]

> It is as if several layers of the genres of medieval literature overlapped and were in constant interaction, permeating each other . . . The pages of popularising medieval texts contain an ongoing hidden dialogue between official doctrine and folkloric consciousness, leading to their convergence but not to their fusion. (p. 5)

Gurevich introduces the important element of 'official' culture, by which he takes account of the kinds of clerical background that many of the authors of the surviving texts from the Middle Ages necessarily had. Placing this kind of cultural criticism alongside Bec's emphasis on 'interférences registrales' (*La Lyrique francaise*, I, p. 40) and 'réseaux typologiques' (I, p. 41) gives us a flexible means of reflecting on the 'courtly-popular' character of many thirteenth-century medieval works. It raises the possibility of connecting linguistic and formal features not only with literary traditions (both oral and learned), but also with the fluctuating processes of 'internal acculturation'. Thirteenth-century narrative, and in particular its relationship with inset refrains, invites such an approach. My aim in this chapter, revisiting issues broached in chapter 2, is to find newly specific ways of grasping the qualities of the 'courtly' and the 'popular' in the clerically diffused form in which it largely reaches us.[6] Through examining the social and literary expectations attached to refrains, and other instances of generic contrast, we can find precise and subtle ways of understanding registral shifts in medieval writing.

Both Zumthor and Bec imply that refrains play an important role in thirteenth-century genres. But Bec, in particular, as a coda to his survey of medieval lyric, talks of the function of the refrain as essentially disruptive:

> On voit donc que la fonction du refrain, comme dans la chanson traditionnelle, est d'actualiser un effet de rupture, à tous les niveaux: syntaxique, stylistique, lexical, prosodique, mélodique. (I, p. 43)

However, as we saw in the example of *Ainssi doit on aler*, a notion of rupture, while rightly describing certain features of refrain-citation, is only part of the issue. Heterogeneity, a favourite term of Zumthor's, is not the single or even most interesting result of the juxtapositions between genres in this period. As we saw with *contrafacta* composition, the very character of refrain-citation, the way in which refrains inhabit a wide plurality of contexts, suggests that we need to look harder at the kinds of expectation refrains carry with them from work to work. They carry some kind of registral charge, and are not just signs of discontinuity but a means of transferring or re-expressing meaning.

One reason why rupture proves an unreliable concept to attach to refrains is that it is not always clear what kind of split is being envisaged. This is illustrated in Bec's own account of the function of refrains, since it oscillates uneasily between two different views of them: that they are autonomous, and that they are fragments of *rondets de carole*. On the one hand, he takes his cue from van den Boogaard in emphasising – in quasi-scientific terms – the refrain's migratory character. Supplementing van den Boogaard's biological metaphor 'parasite',[7] Bec offers 'refrain *exogène*' (I, p. 43), which he defines as 'un ensemble [qui] tend à fonctionner d'une manière autonome' (I, p. 42). Yet elsewhere, as we saw in chapter 2, seemingly unable to detach himself fully from the modern consensus that refrains are fragments, Bec asserts, indecisively, that 'most refrains . . . are merely fragments (or are they generative elements?) of rondets' (I, p. 225).

In apparent recognition of a certain inconsistency in his position, he attempts a sketchy distinction between the 'refrain *exogène*' and the refrain that appears in dance-song, which Bec terms the 'refrain récurrent'. However, his definition collapses in on itself:

> En effet, à coté de ce refrain *récurrent*, plus ou moins intégré, sémantiquement et prosodiquement, au cursus strophique, comme dans le rondet de carole et dans la balette, existent des pièces à refrains *exogènes*, variables à chaque couplet, et correspondant visiblement à une autre couche textuelle que l'ensemble des couplets. (I, pp. 42–43)

His effort to maintain a firm distinction between the two types of refrain falters because even in the case of the 'refrain récurrent', he has to make allowance for the independent character of the refrain. The allowance is deliberately unspecific: the refrain has a linguistic signification which is 'assez variable'; it tends to function 'd'une manière autonome'; the refrain is integrated with the strophic sections 'plus ou moins'. But it is exactly at this level of specificity of how 'variable' a refrain's text is, in what 'manière' it is autonomous, and whether it is integrated 'moins' or 'plus', that any attempt to make a distinction between one kind of refrain and another must operate. In fact, as Bec implicitly acknowledges, there is no distinction to be made between refrains as they occur in *rondets de carole*, and as they occur outside *rondets*. To put it simply, they are often the same refrain.[8]

Trying to assign a different registral value to different types of refrain is thus a delicate task that has often been rendered more difficult by the way in which work on the function of refrains has tended to be confused with arguments about their origin. The characteristics of refrains in the form in which they have survived have been conflated with the characteristics of 'original' forms of dance-song, which refrains may be supposed to represent. Jeanroy, as we discussed in chapter 2, was the first to describe refrains in this way, as the detritus of 'un substrat autochtone', or in Bec's (after Zumthor's) paraphrase, as 'les débris d'une poésie archaïque et popularisante, des sortes d'épaves lyriques, conservées et valorisées par la poésie courtoise' (I, p. 43). Rather than associate refrains, in their thirteenth-century permutations, too rigidly with one particular form (*rondet*) or genre (dance-song), we need to try to take better account of the competing cultural currents in their citation. Refrains, perhaps more than any other medieval genre, would appear to express 'an ongoing hidden dialogue between official doctrine and folkloric consciousness'.

The complex relation between refrains and other thirteenth-century genres gains further insight from Mikhail Bakhtin's work on dialogic discourse.[9] Bakhtin's thinking is not explicitly societal,[10] but it does begin from an essentially socio-linguistic premiss: that utterance, by being inherently dialogic, always implies an audience. For him, this is a property of language itself, one voice implying another, both of which behave 'as if they actually hold a conversation with each other' (p. 46).[11] He extends the concept to talk of the 'dialogical contact' between distinct languages and genres, the supreme example of this generic play of communication taking place, as he sees it, in the novel.

Writing of Lensky's song in Pushkin's *Evgenij Onegin*, he argues that the song has no 'direct poetic significance at all'; instead it is 'characterizing itself, in its own language, in its own poetic manner' (p. 43). Simply by being quoted, a song (or other kind of quotation) begins to present an image of itself, 'the image of another's language' (p. 44). Yet Bakhtin insists that the author, even if he is not directly character-ising the quotation, still allows it to be 'permeated with [his] parodic and ironic accents'. Since it is *his* quotation, we see it in his light: it is as if he momentarily takes on this language, with 'intonational quota-tion marks'. He appropriates this form of speech, but with a constant attention to his distance from it. This gives the speech the ability to be 'simultaneously represented *and* representing' (p. 45): the author is always implicated in this language because he is speaking it. In describ-ing this relationship between the author and the image of speech he is reuttering, Bakhtin sees the possibility for a wide range of postures:

> the author is far from neutral . . . : to a certain extent he even polemi-cizes with this language, argues with it, agrees with it (although with conditions), interrogates it, eavesdrops on it, but also ridicules it, parodically exaggerates it and so forth. (p. 46)

Medieval compositions (especially in the thirteenth and fourteenth centuries) encompass a whole range of positions between the internally and the externally dialogic. The two-, three- or four-part motets rep-resent an example of explicitly external dialogue: their texts can vary so acutely that in some, a pious Latin text is juxtaposed with a secular French text.[12] Thus motets often provide not only an exchange of dis-tinct voices, but a literal 'interanimation' of distinct languages, French and Latin. In the *Chastelaine de Vergi*, as we saw, like Renart's *Roman de la rose* and the *Roman de la violette*, the author sets up a careful and explicit distance between his narration and the inset song ('Par Dieu, Amors . . .' by the Châtelain de Couci). This distance governs the role of the song as a commentary upon the story. However, Jakemés's *Le Roman du castelain de Couci* partially internalises this dialogic relation between song and narrative. Instead of an implied ironic (or respectful) distance between the subject of the narrative and the subject of the song, song and narrative (despite their formal difference) come close to sharing the same voice – although this is not the voice of the author. The songs simultaneously represent and are represented by the narrative. They ap-proach, then, an image of the trouvère's art, yet not in Bakhtin's fully internalised sense since they are created not within the narrator's own speech, but outside it.

Many other thirteenth-century works share this part-external, part-internal conversational conflict between types of utterance: in particular, between their exterior form (as *pastourelle, chanson d'amour, salut*) and the refrains. In its wandering existence as a recurrent citation, the refrain reflects a fluidity about generic definition which is at the heart of many types of compositional procedure in the thirteenth century. One of the reasons for this is that (in Bakhtinian terms) refrains are inherently difficult to perceive as being either internal or external to a work.

The involved nature of their ambiguous status constitutes one of the main lines of enquiry of this chapter. For the question of whether refrains are either on the margin or integral to the works in which they occur is related to the way in which a boundary of genre or register is formed. Is a refrain a factor causing discontinuity in a work, and hence a sign of generic difference, or might it be instead a point of reconciliation, and hence an agent of generic homogeneity?[13] These issues continue the debate of the first chapter over whether a refrain is autonomous or subsidiary, but here my concern is not so much with the connections between form and performance, as with those between form, register and social expectation. Again, Bakhtin's discussion of dialogism is pertinent. Bakhtin grounds his sense of the possible subtleties in the dialogic relationship in the presupposition that the two members of this relationship are distinct. But by not always allowing themselves to be seen as distinct from their context, refrains suggest that we need to consider the different kinds of tone that can be adopted towards a citation (from the pious to the highly disrespectful), and the degree of distance itself between the citation and the author. The difference here is between being able to describe the type of tone and being able to identify a tone at all. One reason for this may be the relation of the refrain to popular language. Like the *rondet de carole*, it represents a form of utterance which is anonymous and general: it belongs to no one since it belongs to everyone. The further direction of my discussion will therefore be to consider first, what relation refrains have to popular language, and second, what results from the interactive friction between 'popular' refrain registers and those of their (largely) 'courtly' contexts.

In an often-quoted phrase, Bakhtin describes speech genres as 'the drive belts from the history of society to the history of language'.[14] When we consider the relation of speech genres to literary language, we examine the process by which social and cultural practice passes into literary practice. Considering genres as forms of utterance encourages us to pay attention to a whole range of social factors: the status and position of the speakers, their network of social relations, the consequent familiarity or formality of their exchange, the relative social control each is able or attempting to exert over the other, their choice of linguistic register and so on. This is more than saying, with Todorov, that genre is a form of discourse: a 'codification de propriétés discursives'.[15] Instead, it is to understand generic distinctions as deeply indicative of the often sharply demarcated forms of social behaviour, expressed as a kind of collective perception. In part, then, this is a matter of understanding different genres to correspond to different social registers, but also of seeing genres pass between social groups, exposing yet also blurring social difference.

The material for this next chapter is drawn from the later part of the thirteenth century, and from a specific geographical location: the Artois. I begin with two kinds of link: that several of these works share various patterns of refrain usage, and that they were written at a similar date (as far as this can be discovered) in and around the famous literary centre of Arras. I explore the kinds of expectation carried by certain linguistic and musical registers and, in particular, how some of the patterns of shared citation connect, by means of a complexly interconnecting manuscript culture, with the specific social arena of Arras. This forms the basis of an attempt to approach more closely their processes of 'internal acculturation'. It leads, finally, to discussion of pastoral, one of the most prominent modes of thirteenth-century genres, where issues of formal, registral and social difference receive especially sharp expression, yet where the signals giving voice to social and poetic comment are notoriously difficult to interpret.[16]

8

Urban culture: Arras and the *puys*

Thirteenth-century Arras was the greatest urban literary centre in Europe.[1] It sometimes seems as if nearly every late thirteenth-century French work can be located within the Artois region of Northern France. Zumthor's claim that 180 Arrageois poets can be identified from this period is likely to be exaggerated;[2] nonetheless an enormous number of works can be traced to Arras, including dozens of songs and *jeux-partis*, *fabliaux*, *dits moraux*, *congés*, vernacular plays and *fatrasies*. These works attest to the way that the social conditions of vernacular writing shifted throughout the century, so that aspirations towards notions of courtliness were produced from within a self-consciously urban environment. This created a layered and ambiguous approach (or set of approaches) to the conventions and mannerisms of courtly writing, and a newly defined sense of the relation of the past to the present. The importance of this centre in defining a 'modern' French civic poetry cannot be overemphasised.

The cultural character of Arras was notoriously mixed. In trying to grasp the shifting relations between courtly, popular and clerical, their processes of 'internal acculturation', it may be helpful to consider the social structure of the town more closely. According to Berger, the character of Arras was formed from a central, historical division between la Cité and la Ville. These were two independent areas existing as such from 1100 or earlier until the major reorganisation of the town's bureaucracy in 1749. Each area had its own institutional focus: La Cité, smaller and more ancient, held the Cathedral, La Ville the Abbey. Each was owned and governed separately, La Cité by the bishop in lieu of the King of France, and La Ville by the Comte d'Artois and his representatives. The relation between aristocratic and ecclesiastical power was thus one that was fundamental to each area but realised differently, in a way that presumably gave the town a certain split identity and split perception of each type of jurisdiction.

The terms 'courtly' and 'popular' and 'clerical' must therefore have had a double valency within the town. This may cast light on the development of the town's two major poetic institutions, the *confrérie*, also known as the *Carité des ardents*, which was a large guild of *jongleurs* and bourgeois citizens who elected a yearly *maior*; and the *puy*, a more socially select organisation, which included poets from aristocratic families and elected a yearly *prince*.[3] The social composition of the poets and their audiences (in both societies?) was diverse, ranging from nobles and a sizeable class of wealthy patrician families, to clerics and humbler professionals and artisans. More information survives about the *confrérie* than the *puy*: thus while it is known that the former was part of the central guild structure of La Ville, the social context within which the *puy* was promoted is less clear. This makes it difficult to understand the impetus behind having two such institutions rather than one, and the kind of relation that existed between them. It does seem as if the *puy* had a social cachet that set it above the *confrérie* (if nothing else, the 'allure aristocratique', as Berger calls it, of the title of *prince* is clearly aiming high). The *Carité des ardents*, by contrast, began as a humble example of a professional guild – in this case that of 'des jogleors et des borgois' – comparable with other guilds such as that of the 'barbiers' or the 'tisserands'.[4] In this respect, the two institutions appear to confirm in a Northern context the Occitan distinction between troubadour and *joglar*, that is, between a poet-musician, often of high birth (Thibaut IV de Champagne was King of Navarre), and a usually itinerant professional instrumentalist, singer and entertainer. Yet just as this distinction holds only partially in Occitan, so the particular circumstances within Arras – the plural and in some sense competing economic and social structures of the town – caused various kinds of social distinction to become more fluid. It is probably more accurate to see the presence of two, socially distinct poetic gatherings in the same town as a sign of the complexity and multiplicity of social relations rather than as reinforcing a single courtly-bourgeois division.

Closer attention to the term 'bourgeois' in an Arras context reveals that it had a specific, economic meaning. It was not merely a generalised urban condition but a precisely defined status which it was possible to acquire either directly through birth or through a ceremonial process by which the prospective bourgeois was presented to the *échevins* (councillors), required to swear an oath and given a right of entry to La Ville. Townspeople were encouraged to become bourgeois by being offered various social advantages and fiscal privileges. An act of 17 January 1284 implies that all the inhabitants of La Ville who were not either of the nobility or the clergy were actually required to join the bourgeoisie:

> Comme jadiz fust atiré et ordené et commandé par les eschevins d'Arraz qui en ce tempz estoient, que tout cil qui n'estoient ou ne voloient estre de la bourgoiserie d'Arraz widassent la ville d'Arraz.[5]
>
> As it was formerly drawn up, arranged and commanded by the councillors of Arras who were at that time, all those who were not or did not want to belong to the bourgeoisie of Arras must leave the town of Arras.

This attempt (with a tinge of menace) to encourage civic inclusiveness gains further significance when we consider it alongside the situation of *les clercs*. Under the law of the Church they escaped the jurisdiction of the *échevins* which led in turn to their immunity from civil taxes.[6] Not surprisingly, various efforts were made to tax them by other means, but their distinct, marginal position succeeded in making them a continuing source of irritation to the town's bureaucracy. We have a glimpse here of one of the ways in which 'popular' (in the sense of majority civic status) and clerical were categories that came into daily economic collision.

Such details give a specific social framework to the often volatile and disconcerting juxtapositions between the courtly, urban and clerical that are characteristic of Arrageois productions. Adam de la Halle's *Jeu de la feuillée* is an extreme case of a work which ignores conventional poetic and social barriers by passing at dizzying speed from one perspective to another, and making the distinction between actor, audience and town inhabitant (and for that matter, stage, theatre and town) hard to sustain. Adam himself appears to have composed for both societies, showing that whatever the social distinction between them, it was not the sort that worked (in either case) to exclude a brilliant clerical poet.

The extraordinarily diverse social liaisons that seemed to be central to the experience of writing poetry in Arras are most evident in the *jeu-parti*, a quintessentially Arrageois genre. 114 pieces out of the surviving

182, that is, over three-quarters, were debated publicly in Arras by poets who either worked in Arras or had connections with those who did. The social standing of the participants ranges right across the structure of the whole town. Thus we have Thibaut de Champagne, King of Navarre debating with an anonymous cleric, Charles d'Anjou and the Duc de Brabant with the local trouvère Gillebert de Berneville, Dame Margot with Dame Marote, and Guillaume le Vinier (a married clerk) with his brother Gilles le Vinier (canon first of Lille then of Arras). The nobler participants and judges include Othon III, comte de Gueldre, the Comte de Bretagne (Geoffrey II), the Châtelain de Beaumetz, the King of Aragon (Pierre II) and Edward, prince of England (son of Henry III). Some of the judges were Arras bankers, such as Sire Ermenfroi, Pierre Wion and Audefroi Louchart (a proverbially rich financier). It is not clear how active a role such dignitaries played in deciding which songs should be crowned: no doubt naming someone as judge was part of the process of gaining patronage and the implied compliment to such a person's poetic skills may have been honorary rather than actual. The majority of chansons and *jeux-partis* are attributed to relatively humble, often unidentified *jongleurs* and bourgeois, including some women. Nonetheless, there is enough evidence to suggest that literary activities in Arras attracted the highest level of social interest as well as the involvement of a substantial professional class of poets. There was a local guild involvement, firmly attached to the social and economic concerns of the town, and a more international membership which established Arras as a major centre for vernacular writing. Arras attracted visits from many poets from neighbouring towns, especially during the large annual gatherings of the two poetic societies, when poetic festivals were organised with the *puys* of Gand, Douai, Tournai and Lille.

The activities of the *Confrérie des jongleurs et des bourgeois d'Arras*, otherwise known as the *Carité des ardents*, are reasonably well documented. Its regulations survive in a twelfth-century manuscript, BN fr. 8541, with thirteenth- and fourteenth-century additions. The opening forty folios of this manuscript also contain a list of the recorded deaths of its members from 1194 to 1357: this provides an invaluable (though inevitably often sketchy) source of information about the composition of the society.[7] Other sources preserve versions of the miraculous legend which inspired its original formation, in which it is recounted that two *jongleurs* were visited in the Cathedral of Arras by a vision of the Virgin who gave them a holy candle with powers to heal plague victims (those suffering from 'le mal des ardents'). The *carité* was founded in gratitude and apparently performed the double function of promoting charitable works in honour of the Virgin and regular feasts for its members. These were *jongleurs* divided at first into two professional groups, those who resided within the walls of La Ville and those who belonged outside ('de dehors'); from 1221 the *confrérie* came under the joint, though unequal, direction of bourgeois as well as *jongleurs*. The increasingly powerful bourgeois element introduced its own mayor, an entry fee and three annual meetings. The last of these in the week following Trinity was called 'le Grand Siège' and lasted three days from Thursday to Saturday. During this period the *jongleurs* met as a corporate assembly, elected three mayors, held a reception for new members, took out the Holy Candle in a solemn ceremony, and enjoyed a prolonged feast.[8]

It is difficult to believe that such an event was not also the occasion for musical and poetic entertainment, yet there is little specific evidence that poetic contests were part of the proceedings and, to my knowledge, no surviving poems mention the *confrérie*. Conversely, although documentary or archival information about the *puy* is fragmentary, there are several poetic references: various poems refer to the 'puy d'Arras' in the envoy, are addressed to the 'Prince du puy' (only two are known by name, Jehan Bretel and Robert Soumillon) or are described as 'couronnée'.[9] Records for other *puys*, such as the *Puy de Nostre-Dame* at Amiens, founded in 1388, or the London *puy* which flourished in the last quarter of the thirteenth century, are much more detailed.[10] At Amiens the main feast took place on the Day of the Purification of the Virgin (2 February) at which the new *maître* was elected. It was the duty of the old *maître* to preside over the feast (put on at his own expense), which was attended by previous *maîtres*, *rhétoriciens* involved in the judging of *chants royaux* and various dignitaries, including notable ecclesiastics. A play was performed during the dinner (a *jeu de mystère*), the performers rewarded with a *cappel vert* and a copy of the play; afterwards the judges retired to choose a winning *chant royal*. The eventual winner was given a silver crown.[11] By the fourteenth and fifteenth centuries such elaborate rituals are characteristic of a large number of northern *puys*, such as Rouen (founded 1072), Valenciennes (1229), Douai (1330), Abbeville (late four-teenth century), Dieppe (fifteenth century) and Caen (1527). *Puys* are also known to have existed at Lille, Tournai, Cambrai and Béthune; 'Princes des Sots' were elected in Ath, Bouchain, Denain and Condé.[12]

The mention in the Amiens records both of a play performance, and of the distribution of copies of the play is a tantalising indication (albeit of a later date) that *puys* provided an opportunity for works other than short songs to be publicly performed and collectively reproduced. It has proved surprisingly difficult to link surviving thirteenth-century manuscripts with specific *puys*. In several chansonniers certain songs are marked with a crown, presumably indicating that they were winning entries in *puy* contests, but the chansonniers themselves do not appear to be collections of *puy* repertories as such, but rather more wide-ranging attempts to collect songs by author or genre.[13] One compilation that stands out as a likely major exception is the 'Adam de la Halle' chansonnier fr. 25566: the effort to honour Adam with a 'complete works' edition of his writings coincides with, and was presumably motivated by his dominant role in the *puy* at Arras. The manuscript contains several longer narrative and dramatic works such as Adam's *Robin et Marion* and *Le Jeu de la feuillée*, and Jacquemart Giélée's *Renart le Nouvel*, all works known to have been performed locally.

In the case of *Renart le Nouvel*, van den Boogaard has made an at-tempt to link the work itself, the specific form in which it survives in manuscript, and another narrative, *Le Tournoi de Chauvency*, to the circumstances of *puy* production.[14] He argues that the manuscripts of *Renart le Nouvel* represent not different scribal copies of a single orig-inal work, but four *libretti* for four consecutive performances of the *roman* in 1288, 1289, 1290 and 1292 (the dates written respectively in each manuscript at verses 7753–54).[15] He also finds that a significant proportion of the refrains in *Renart le Nouvel* can be found firstly in *Le Tournoi de Chauvency*, and secondly in songs – mainly *ballettes* and *pastourelles* – contained in the Oxford chansonnier Douce 308. This is one of the manuscripts in which *Le Tournoi* is preserved. Since one of the *Renart le Nouvel* manuscripts (fr. 1581) makes reference to a *puy* at Lille (line 6964), he revives a suggestion made as early as 1886 by Schwan, that Douce 308 represents a collection of pieces for a *puy*.[16] De-spite several problems and lacunae in his argument, it remains the most suggestive study to date of the possible circumstances of performance of these various works.[17]

The patterns of refrain-citation can reveal further connections between authors, genres, copyists and literary motifs. Although the author of *Le Tournoi* refers to himself as Jacques Bretel, there remains a mystery as to his exact identity. His surname was well known in the minstrel circles of Arras in the mid-thirteenth century because of Jehan Bretel, a compatriot of Adam de la Halle, and a prolific composer of *jeux-partis*, who died in 1272. Jehan's grandfather, who died in 1230, was called Jacques; furthermore, in 1260, there was a 'maitre Jacques Bretel', related to Jehan, who was a canon at Notre-Dame in Arras. It is very possible, as Langlois thought, that the author of *Le Tournoi de Chauvency* came from the same family.[18] This can be no more than a conjecture, for Jacques Bretel shows such familiarity with the Lorraine area in his poem that Delbouille argues that he originated there.[19] But there is no reason why knowledge of the Lorraine area should preclude an association with Arras. Furthermore, *Le Tournoi de Chauvency* has such strong associations with works of a similar date produced at Arras or nearby at Lille in the same period, that Langlois's conjecture is worthy of more notice.

An examination of the refrains in *Le Tournoi de Chauvency* reveals that several are shared by other compositions which originate from nearby towns in Northern France. The work with the largest number of refrains in common with *Le Tournoi* is Jacquemart Giélée's *Renart le Nouvel*. These two works share more refrains – five – than any other two works in van den Boogaard's *roman* category. Jacquemart was from Lille, about thirty miles from Arras. His *roman*, the only member of the Renart corpus to contain refrains, employs them in scenes and situations which show a considerable resemblance not only to *Le Tournoi*, but also to *La Court de paradis* and the anonymous continuation of Mahieu le Poirier's *Le Court d'amours*. All these works share refrains in a complex pattern of liaisons.[20] Such patterns are particularly marked in the two manuscripts putatively connected with *puys*, Oxford, Bodleian Library, MS Douce 308 and the 'Adam de la Halle' manuscript (fr. 25566). Both Adam's dramatic *jeux*, *Le Jeu de la feuillée* and *Le Jeu de Robin et de Marion*, contain refrains, as does the later addition to *Robin et Marion*, *Li Jus du pelerin*. Again, refrain correspondences show a telling bias. First, no fewer than seven refrains in *Renart le Nouvel* occur in rondeaux by Adam.[21] Then there are some more spasmodic correspondences: one refrain in *Robin et Marion* appears in both *Renart le Nouvel* and *Le Tournoi de Chauvency*; and one of the three snatches of song in *Le Jeu de la feuillée* reappears in *Le Tournoi de Chauvency*.[22] Finally, a single anonymous *Salut d'amour* shares refrains in common with all of the following works, *Le Tournoi de Chauvency*, *Renart le Nouvel*, *Le Court d'amours (Suite)*, *Le Jeu de la feuillée*, and *Robin et Marion*, together with *Le Roman de la violette*, *Le Roman de la poire*, and *Le Roman de Fauvel*.[23]

It seems clear from these cross-references that the authors in this region were drawing upon a similar stock of refrains. The particular coincidences of citation suggest a common creative method, itself indicative of a wider interest in the cultural process of generic diffusion. I want now to review the evidence, work by work, of the kinds of further parallel that underlie this network of refrain connections. For example, nearly all these works share the topos of the court scene with refrains. Yet what particularly draws these works together, in the context of the social diversity of Arras, is a pleasure in combining sharply diverse registers. These registers question, indeed parody the courtly framework on which they ostensibly rest. The effect of parody is partly heightened by the centrality of performance: we find a common interest in public display, theatrical disguise and musical interlude that appears to correspond to *puy*-inspired circumstances of production.

Renart le Nouvel is perhaps the work with the most oddly (and comically) abrasive relationship between its different registers. It occurs in two parts, each of which recounts the enmity between Renart the Fox and Noble the Lion. Both parts end with a reconciliation which is celebrated with a feast. The final scene in the poem depicts the ceremonial entry of Noble's court into Renart's castle, Passe-Orgeuil. Groups of refrains are sung during these two feasts, and in love-scenes between Renart and his three paramours; but the largest concentration of songs (amounting to two-thirds of the total number of refrains) occurs in the final court procession. Here, as in *Le Tournoi*, miniature scenes are played out between pairs of lovers, such as Renart and Hersent the she-wolf and the monkeys Boursee and Symons. In many exchanges, the affair is complicated by a third party: thus when 'Cointeriaus' (another monkey) overhears Symons sing to Boursee (*'A ma dame servir / Ai mis mon cuer et moi'*

[*I have set my heart and myself to serving my lady*]), this is a cause for 'grant doel' (6780). The only Renart narrative to contain refrains, *Renart le Nouvel* cites them in a virtuosic display of reductive comedy.

Each time, Jacquemart exploits the shock of confrontation between the register of the refrain (sometimes 'aristocratisant', sometimes 'popularisant'), the speaker, and the context. The effect is particularly ambiguous in the long court scenes, where the quasi-grand, ceremonious setting, peopled by a noisy and often belligerent menagerie of animals, is punctuated by a series of song sketches that mark out the oddness of the relation between animal and court. The concentration of refrains in the final feast of reconciliation between Renart and Noble points to the function of the feast as a means of levelling social differences, the mobile register of the refrains serving to mediate between and hence defuse social antagonisms. In this role, their nature as melodies plays a further part: narrative is constantly shifted into song and back again, creating a rapid oscillation of media which enables each moment of social interaction to efface the last.[24] The result is a series of performances which are individually disparate but together form a means of reconciling the wayward narrative and satiric directions of the plot.

Perhaps surprisingly, *La Court de paradis* is one of the works that is closest in manner, if not in spirit, to *Renart le Nouvel*. As we noted in chapter 6, it belongs contextually (and physically in manuscript) with Gautier de Coinci's *Miracles* (although this gives no clue to its date). Yet it also, through the motif of the feast, shows itself to be a variation on a theme, something which could only exist if there were a theme strong enough to support variation. The device of giving a sequence of refrains to a large group of characters in a court setting links it with *Renart le Nouvel*, *Le Tournoi de Chauvency* (with which it shares two refrains) and *Le Court d'amours (Suite)*: its way of passing from secular to sacred through musical citations is reminiscent of the farce-like qualities of the *Renart* narrative.

One indication of truly popular genres, as Gurevich observes, concerns their relative 'immobility' over long periods.[25] The many links between the use of refrains in early and late thirteenth-century works suggest that authors were often dealing with genuinely popular material. Often the same refrains recur sixty years later, a length of time in which one might expect fashions, both social and literary, to change. Refrains from the early thirteenth-century *Roman de la poire* are quoted in the late thirteenth-century *Renart le Nouvel*, for example;[26] as is one refrain from the *Roman de la violette*.[27] In the case of the *unica*, it is not easy to tell whether they represent a genuinely traditional, or else a manufactured 'folkloric consciousness'. The transparency of popular language means that it is easy to generate, and fake archaism is characteristic of the thirteenth century.[28]

The narrative which perhaps illustrates some of the tensions between 'courtly' and 'popular' most directly is *Le Tournoi de Chauvency*. With the exception of the narrator himself, and the herald Bruiant, all the named characters are aristocratic. As I mentioned in chapter 2, on the Tuesday evening, towards midnight, two ladies, Agnès de Florenville and Jeannette de Boinville, perform 'la dance robardoise' or the game of the stolen kiss (2582) to the accompaniment of a *viele* played by Perrine d'Esch; during the Thursday evening, the Countess of Luxembourg is prevailed upon to perform the 'jeu du chapelet' or the game of the circlet of flowers.

If we consider the 'jeu du chapelet' from the point of view of its register, we can see that it has a strongly pastoral character, performed by a Countess who plays the rustic, dancing with her circlet of flowers, and referring in her refrains to the imaginary setting of a meadow by a river bank. The dialogue draws directly from the world of the *pastourelle*: her tart retort to the minstrel's question is like that of a shepherdess rejecting a knight's suit, although the courtly framework prevails by providing a twist in which she ends up with a knight after all, and of her choosing. The other game – the *robardel* – is also clearly pastoral, since the two aristocratic ladies play a shepherd and a shepherdess respectively. The pastoral edge to this game is indicated by several details: by the cross-dressing (shown in the illustration in the Oxford manuscript Douce 308 where they are clearly 'dressed up', see Fig. 4(a)) which causes some salacious comment among the audience, the exaggerated gestures of the performers, and the casually supercilious style of the narration (Bretel talks of 'la moquerie au robardel' [the playful contempt of the robber dance] (2562) and of the 'fin orguel' [noble pride] with which the 'shepherd' behaves like a king (2569–71)). To describe this scene as 'courtly-popular' is inadequate. The participants in this courtly entertainment are not appropriating popular culture in any simple way: they are relishing crossing barriers of decorum, class and gender and, if Bretel is an accurate register, savouring the tension between their real social role and their mimed behaviour.

Bretel's account of courtly pleasures differs from *pastourelle* and *bergerie* precisely in that the games are framed by narrative, and what is more, a narrative that makes such a large claim to social and historical accuracy. The referents that do not exist in *pastourelles*, and which, by their absence, allow the genre a certain symbolic potential, are here all clearly signalled: we know exactly who sings the refrains and who is in the audience, we even know how the audience reacts. Moreover, the members of the audience have a very clearly defined sense of themselves: the following rondeau (from the *Roman du castelain de Couci*) encapsulates their sense of self-referring courtly identity:

> *Toute vostre gent*
> *sont li plus joli*
> *du tournoiement.*
> S'eimment loiaument,
> *Toute vostre gent,*
> et pour ce li di
> qu'ils ont maintien gent.
> *Toute vostre gent*
> [*sont li plus joli*
> *du tournoiement*][29]
> (vdB, rond. 27, 1–10)

> *All your people are the most handsome of the tournament.* They love loyally, *all your people*, and for this reason I tell [them] they have a noble bearing. *All your people are the most handsome of the tournament.*

So tightly focused a notion of courtliness powerfully influences the kind of popular culture enjoyed by the aristocrats, to the extent that it is hard to know in what form it remains 'popular'. The 'popular', in this sense, seems as much defined by the 'courtly' as the 'courtly' is by the 'popular'.

Gurevich comments on the difficulty (normally) of trying to find traces of the popular culture of the Middle Ages in the overwhelmingly aristocratic and/or intellectual character of the written source material (p. xiv). Here, the wide currency of the inserted refrains means that we have a variety of kinds of source from which to assess their register.

The refrains in the 'Jeu du chapelet' yield a variety of clues. There are two types: the three that exist in other sources, and *unica*. The former all occur in other romances, and, in one case, a rondeau copied in another section of the same Oxford manuscript.[30] This set of contexts indicates that the process of aristocratic absorption of this cluster of refrains was complete by the last quarter of the thirteenth century. The rondeau recalls a *pastourelle* narrative in the way it presents a first-person speaker asserting his delight in conquest in the face of an unwilling partner:

> Je ne sai c'elle s'an plaint,
> mais j'an ris de joie.
> *Lai merci Deu, j'ai ataint*
> *lai ou je voloie.*
> (vdB rond. 147, 5–8)

> I do not know if she is complaining about it, but I am laughing with joy. *Thank God, I have attained what I wanted.*

Most of the refrains sung by the Countess are *unica*: possibly implying that they were newly composed by Jacques Bretel, or even by the participants in the 'Jeu'. Yet, even if they do not have precise correspondences elsewhere, several possess the register and diction of *rondets de carole*. This one, for example, belongs to the 'la gieus' type of *rondet*, of which there are many examples in Renart's *Roman de la rose*:

> *Biaus sire, et car le m'amenéz le jus en cel herbaige!*
> *Je m'en vois, vos m'i troverés seant sor le rivaige!*

> *Fine sir, lead him then for me over there by that tent! I am going now, you will find me there sitting by the riverbank!*

One might compare the following, in which the refrain is related semantically to *La merci Deu j'ai ataint – Se que je voloie*:

> C'est la gieus, en mi les prez
> *– j'ai amors a ma volenté–*
> dames i ont baus levez.
> Gari m'ont mi oel.
> *J'ai amors a ma volenté*
> *teles com ge voel.*
> (vdB rond. 16, 1–6)

It's over there, in the meadow – *I have love according to my desire* – ladies start dances there. They healed my eyes. *I have love according to my desire, just as I wish.*

Other *rondets* depict in their strophes the very scene that the Countess mimes (see Fig. 2).[31] See, for example, this 'Bele Aalis' *rondet* from a sermon by Stephen Langton:

> Belle Aalis mainz s'en leva,
> vesti son cors et para;
> en un vergier s'en entra,
> cinc florestes i trova,
> un chapelet fet en a
> [de] rose florie.
> (vdB rond. 42, 1–6)

Fair Aalis rose in the morning, she dressed and adorned herself; she went into an orchard and found five flowers there. She made of them a garland of flowering roses.

This parallel is matched, again, by a *rondet* copied into the Oxford manuscript:

> *Ancor un chaipelet ai*
> *ke fut m'amie;*
> doneiz me fut de cuer gai.
> *Ancor un chaipelet ai,*
> por s'amour lou garderai
> toute mai vie.
> *Ancor un chaipelet ai*
> *que fut m'amie.*
> (vdB rond. 142, 1–8)

I have another garland that was my lover's; it was given to me with a happy heart. *I have another garland,* for her love I will keep it all my life. *I have another garland that was my lover's.*

As a group, the collection of refrains in the 'jeu' seems to indicate a degree of 'internal acculturation' between older elements, drawn directly from the *rondets de carole*, and refrains which, whatever their original context, have acquired a new resonance from their association with romance. In Bakhtin's terms, the 'jeu du chapelet' takes on a dialogic relationship in which more than one accent can be heard, for the courtly tones of the Countess are pronouncing not only popular songs but also the kinds of song whose popular character is mediated through romance authors such as Bretel. *Le Tournoi*, to reiterate, is not a straightforward chronicle of popular pastimes,[32] but a self-conscious attempt – in which Bretel collaborates – to assert aristocratic superiority over popular culture.

Le Court d'amours, which occurs in a single early fourteenth-century manuscript (n. a. fr. 1731), concerns a court in more than one sense. For the aristocratic community which it describes has come together to form a court of law in order to try questions of love, and to hear love complaints.[33] The work is in two halves separated in the manuscript by a short piece called the *Ju de la capete Martinet*, which contains a single refrain (vdB, refr. 1418).[34] No music is given for either work. *Le Court d'amours (Suite)* bears a close resemblance to *Le Tournoi de Chauvency*. The parallels are numerous and include – apart from details of the action – the tournament, and the use of historical characters in the dancing scenes. Yet the series of thirty-three refrains in *Le Court d'amours (Suite)* form a longer complete sequence than any of the similar scenes in *Le Tournoi*. In this respect, then, it resembles more closely the long final processional scene in *Renart le Nouvel*, in which some thirty-five refrains are sung. From internal evidence the work appears to originate between 1277 and 1328 from Hainault, a region adjacent to Arras,[35] and the plausible suggestion by Hans Jauss that the three works formed a trilogy in performance, with the short *Ju de le capete Martinet* acting as an interlude between the two halves of the *Court d'amours*, draws attention to its potential character as a work of society entertainment.[36]

Dated after 1304, the *Suite* possesses signs of the developed formal interest in refrains that is characteristic of turn-of-the-century works such as some of the *Saluts d'amour* or the lyrics of Jehannot de Lescurel. It thus differs from *Le Tournoi* in its greater attention to poetic craft than to social verisimilitude; at the same time, it functions like *Le Tournoi* in its concise allusions to pastoral. For example, a king sings of a *pastourele* or shepherdess:

> conmencha li rois a canter
> .i. cant c'on dut bien escouter,

car il fu dis de volenté
  gaye et nouvele:
Triquedondele!
J'ai amé le pastourele.
(3457–62)

> The king began to sing a song that one ought to listen to well since it was happy and new, and performed in a happy, fresh spirit: *Triquedondele! I loved a shepherdess.*

Similarly, it finishes with a *treske*, a processional dance that is only rarely referred to, usually in *pastourelles*, and, most notably, in Adam de la Halle's dramatised *pastourelle, Robin et Marion*.[37] The mix of registers is swift and economic: the *pastourelle* references are thoroughly contained and absorbed by the courtly focus of the allegory.

The concordances between the refrains of *Le Tournoi de Chauvency, Renart le Nouvel, La Court de paradis*, and *Le Court d'amours*, are thus matched by a further pattern of rhetorical parallels. Just as *Renart le Nouvel* owes a great deal to *Le Tournoi*, so *Le Court d'amours* borrows from both *Le Tournoi* and *Renart le Nouvel* together. All four works perform a variation on the court scene with refrains, itself a development from Renart's *Rose*. The court setting provides a stable framework for various kinds of less stable device such as the juxtaposition of different types of social relationship, the repeated interruption of narrative with short pieces of song, and the replacement of familiar material in unfamiliar contexts.

A rewriting of register takes place throughout the thirteenth century in romance. Refrains play a key part in this gradual relocation of registral boundaries. Their inherent mobility of register (described wryly by Zumthor as 'un ensemble complexe de débris'),[38] allows them to create liaisons between the different worlds of the aristocrat and the peasant, the sacred and the secular, or the animal and the human. What characterises them is a variability of exchange: having not a single but a multiple frame of reference, each refrain sets up new connections in each of its citational appearances. Neither exactly external nor internal to a work in which they occur, refrains play out the polymorphous clerical procedures by which the courtly and the popular in the thirteenth century at once collide and are mutually absorbed.

I want to finish these reflections on works produced in Arras and its environs by considering the one which best exemplifies these shifts, collisions and absorptions: Adam de la Halle's *Le Jeu de la feuillée*. Set in the town of Arras, the *jeu* includes a range of local characters: a doctor, a monk, an innkeeper, a couple of half-wits, Douce Dame, and Adam himself, along with his father and several of his friends. The intensely local atmosphere is encouraged by the intimate and sarcastic way in which they speak to one another, combined with a constant stream of reference to local places and town notables. Adam, as a character in his own *jeu*, triggers this use of language by a huge speech near the start in which he reveals two kinds of personal fantasy in awkward opposition, his desire for an intellectual life in Paris and his desire for his wife. This is expressed in language which is strangely poised on the edge of parody, drawing on phrases and types of register from many genres of writing, *pastourelle, reverdie, congé, grand chant, sotte chanson*.[39]

That this semi-farcical eclecticism suggests a kind of creative dementia posing as sophistication (or vice versa) is further suggested by Adam's sparing but pointed use of song. The refrain '*Par chi va la mignotise, /Par chi ou je vois*' [*There goes kindness, there where I go*] (874–75), sung by the fairies, marks the moment where they vanish and the characters/spectators wake as if from sleep (see Ex. 9).

In this way, it occurs very precisely on the boundary between the play's contrasting yet disconcertingly interlocked worlds. At a later moment, when the company sings the refrain of a *chanson de toile* '*Ai[e] se siet en haute tour*' [*Ai sat in a high tower*] (1025), this turns into an occasion for satiric reference to the *puy*. The singers ask the innkeeper for praise ('Biaus ostes, est che bien canté?' [Fair host, was that well sung?] (1026)), but when they duly receive it, are interrupted by the fool ('Li Dervès') who angrily demands it for himself. This recalls an earlier scene where

Par chi va la mi - gno - ti - se par chi ou je vois

Ex. 9 'Par chi va la mignotise': refrain from *Le Jeu de la Feuillée* the fool, pretending to play the trumpet, pours scorn on the proceedings of the *puy* and its prince, Robert Soumillon (406–15). A similar moment occurs in *Le Jeu du Pelerin* when a line from the obscene *chanson de geste Audigier* is sung and praise is demanded. Adam appears to use these short sung citations to comment ironically, and no doubt self-mockingly, on the kind of public entertainment represented by the *puy*.

The role of Fortune in *Le Jeu de la feuillée* has a natural aptness in a work so full of movement and swift dramatic transitions. Fortune and her wheel are part of the fairies' entourage. She forms a dumb show to which the fairy actors provide a running commentary. Crokesos asks whether the people round the rim of Fortune's wheel are real. In the dialogue which follows, one of the fairies explains that it is an allegorical show in which the woman holding the wheel has been 'Muiele, sourde, et avulee' ('dumb, deaf and blind' (772)) since birth. She then comments that Fortune has begun to spin the wheel, which causes Crokesos to ask the identity of the people at the top who are now falling to the bottom and another fairy mischievously to start naming names among the Arras bourgeoisie. The centrality of the metaphor of Fortune in medieval culture hardly needs reiterating; yet Fortune has a special appropriateness here, in a work located so firmly in Arras, as a representation of mobility, of social levelling and of a bewildering process of subversion, elevation and reduction in quick succession.

This finds confirmation in the fact that full-page pictures of Fortune and her wheel are set at the end of two manuscripts of *Renart le Nouvel*. They are both elaborated by many smaller drawings of animals, including two figures on horseback holding scrolls. Comparing these with the description of the tableau in *Le Jeu de la feuillée* encourages the thought that these pictures are not merely conventional images of Fortune but possibly representations of the way in which the work was performed. The other miniatures in the *Renart le Nouvel* manuscripts give further support to the notion that the different animal parts in *Renart le Nouvel* were played by human actors. There are two types of miniature: those that depict real animals, and those which show animals in quasi-human postures and dress. These last have their closest parallel in the far more finely drawn miniatures of the *Roman de Fauvel* manuscript (fr. 146).[40] The presence of so many animal characters in these miniatures implies that they may be pictures of the final tableau of the performance in which all the actors participated. The kind of mimed representation of Fortune described in *Le Jeu de la feuillée* may have accompanied the scene towards the end of *Renart le Nouvel* in which Fortune is prominent.

Large-scale citation of refrains by poets composing in such circumstances is not surprising given the ability of these proverbial formulas to slide between registers, and to liaise between different generic strands. The context of the *puy* gives a much broader base of cultural cross-reference to our understanding of works such as *Le Tournoi* or *Renart le Nouvel* than an argument about narrower forms of allusion. Although the evidence linking the works I have referred to in this chapter with specific *puys* is largely circumstantial, it seems reasonable to infer that their production was influenced by the Arras-dominated *puy* culture of Northern France. Quoting refrains gives a poet access to a form of speech and melody with a broad spectrum of registral reference: he can, in a single deft manoeuvre, call on a whole structure of social and cultural expectation and then place it in such a way as either to confirm that expectation or redefine it. The *puy* provides a natural arena for such activity because it itself falls between the cultural and the social. Formed by specific guilds, often with a strictly religious motivation, *puys* in Northern French towns gradually mystified their origins by expressing their social function in these largely poetic annual rituals. Themselves a curious cultural compression of social function and poetic contest, they provoked works in which attention to the fine distinctions between social groupings, literary registers and genres is intense.[41]

9

The cultural contexts of Adam de la Halle:
Le Jeu de Robin et de Marion

Trouvère writing is characteristically a type of writing that does not stand on its own, but is always set into relief by other genres, other registers, other authors. Their world is one in which language, and particularly courtly language, is examined intensively by being juxtaposed with lower, more 'popular' styles. The genre of the *pastourelle* is a prime example. It is also a genre in which musical registers are set off against each other, perhaps even, as John Stevens has radically suggested, in which rhythmic styles are contrasted.[1] In this chapter I consider *pastourelle* from the many-faceted perspective of perhaps the most characteristically Arrageois work of all, Adam de la Halle's *Le Jeu de Robin et de Marion*. This work is a *tour de force* of *pastourelle* motifs, ingeniously played and replayed, in which the genre is so thoroughly scrutinised as to be almost reinvented, piece by piece.

We have discussed some of the ways in which the character of Arras and the surrounding regions is culturally ambiguous and fluid. Adam's own work illustrates this well. Some of the questions we find it hardest to answer of Adam – from where does Adam write? what is his cultural location? – precisely reveal the kinds of ambiguity thrown up by Arras itself. The *Jeu de la feuillée* addresses these issues by being about Paris as well as Arras, about Arras in relation to Paris, and how the aspiring bourgeois and the clever cleric looks from each other's perspective. Many uncertainties persist about Adam's patrons, about the source of production of the manuscripts of his works, and even about the context of his most celebrated work, *Le Jeu de Robin et de Marion*. *Robin et Marion* shows a different set of contrasting perspectives from *Le Jeu de la feuillée*, that is, the courtly–popular, or the aristocratic–villeinous. The questions prompted by *Robin et Marion* – which has a stronger prima facie connection with Naples than with Arras – are particularly difficult to settle: do we locate this work according to where it was composed, where it was copied, where the poet came from, where the poet's patrons were situated, or where it was performed? Framing these questions with a reconsideration of Adam's brilliant revision of pastoral may be one way of situating the work's elusive cultural context.

The *Jeu de Robin et de Marion* is a work both of transition and transposition. It is most commonly described as a dramatised *pastourelle*: yet in addition to transposing the genre of *pastourelle*, it presents many other kinds of formal, generic and social transition between *pastourelle* and *bergerie*, knight and peasant, male and female, narrative and lyric, spoken dialogue and song. *Pastourelles* lie close to the surface and may be uncovered by tracing the refrain concordances: of the ten refrains, four have a wide range of citation among two motets, four *romans à refrains* (*Renart le Nouvel*, *Le Tournoi de Chauvency*, and two *saluts d'amour*), and four *pastourelles*.[2] The three refrains with *pastourelle* contexts (Nos. 1, 8 and 10 from Table 9.1 below) act as pivots between the different texts in which they occur. *Robins m'aime, Robins m'a*, which Marion sings to begin the whole *Jeu*, holds three texts in concurrent relation: a five-stanza *pastourelle avec des refrains* 'Au tens nouvel' [In the new season], a four-stanza *pastourelle avec des refrains* 'A l'entrant de mai' [At the arrival of May], and the *Jeu* itself.

The two *pastourelles* which share the opening refrain of *Robin et Marion* form an excellent means of observing the relation of the *jeu* to the *pastourelle* genre. Both 'Au tens nouvel' (attributed to Perrin d'Angecourt) and 'A l'entrant de mai' (unattributed) supply implicit narrative models for the opening scene of the *Jeu*.[3] Here are the opening three stanzas of 'Au tens nouvel':

> Au tens nouvel   que cil oisel
> sont hetie et gai,
> en un boschel   sanz pastourel
> pastore trouvai,
> ou fesoit chapiau de flors
> et chantoit un son d'amors
> qui mult ert jolis:
> *'li pensers trop mi guerroie*
> *de vous, douz amis.'*

> Par grant revel   enz el prael
> dire li alai
> 's'il vous ert bel,   por vo chapel
> vostre devendrai,
> fins et loiaus a touz jors,
> sanz james penser aillors;
> et pour ce vous proi:
> *bergeronnete,*
> *fetes vostre ami de moi.'*
> 'Sire, alez ent,   c'est pour noient
> qu'estes ci assis;
> j'aim loiaument   Robin le gent
> et ferai touz dis.
> s'amie sui et serai,
> ne ja tant com ie vivrai
> autre n'en jorra.
> *Robin m'aime, Robin m'a,*
> *Robin m'a demandee, si m'avra.'*
> (1–27)

In the new season when the birds are high spirited and gay, I found a shepherdess in a wood without a shepherd, who was making a garland of flowers and singing a song of love that was very pretty: *thoughts of you, my sweet lover, make war on me!*

In great delight I went into the meadow, to say to her: if it seems good to you, in exchange for your garland, I will become yours, noble and loyal for ever, without ever thinking of anyone else; I thus beg you: '*Little shepherdess, make me your lover.*'

Sir, go away, you are sitting here for nothing; I love loyally Robin the fair and I always will. I am his lover and will be, and as long as I live, no one else will possess me. *Robin loves me, Robin has me; Robin has asked for me, and he will have me.*

'Au tens nouvel' is particularly close in detail to *Robin et Marion*: the shepherdess is making a headdress of flowers, singing one of the same songs, and rebuffing the chevalier with the same clarity. Her forthright behaviour is also a feature of 'A l'entrant de mai' (9–10, 28), along with references to the chevalier's attention to her singing (14–15, 20). Yet there are various shifts in their transposition from song to dramatic narrative. Adam is unlikely to be borrowing directly from any single *pastourelle*, but rather taking over a generic framework and then fragmenting it,

Table 9.1 *Refrain texts in the* Jeu de Robin et de Marion *with their concordances* [4]

---

1. *Robins m'aime, Robins m'a,*   vdB, refr. 1633
   Robins m'a demandee, si m'ara.
   [*Robin loves me, Robin has me; Robin has asked for me, and he will have me.*]
   (a) Rob. 1–2
   (b) R573. III 'Au tens nouvel'
   (c) R85. III 'A l'entrant de mai'
   (d) M298 déb / fin 'Mout me fu grief li departir / *Robin m'aime* / *Portare*'

2. *Je me repairoie du tournoiement,*
   Si trouvai Marote seulete au cors gent.
   [*I was coming back from a tournament, when I found pretty Marote all alone.*]
   (a) Rob. 9–10

3. *Hé! Robin, se tu m'aimes,*   vdB, refr. 871
   par amours maine-m'ent.
   [*Hey, Robin, if you love me, for love's sake, take me away.*]
   (a) Rob. 11–12, 18–19

4. *Vous perdés vo paine, sire Aubert,*   vdB, refr. 1869
   ja n'amerai autrui que Robert.
   [*You are wasting your time, Sir Aubert, I will never love anyone but Robert.*]
   (a) Rob. 83–84

5. *Bergeronnete sui, mais j'ai*   vdB, refr. 251
   ami bel et cointe et gai.
   [*I am only a little shepherdess, but I have a handsome, gracious and charming lover.*]
   (a) Rob. 90–91

6. *Trairi, deluriau, deluriau, deluriele,*
   Trairi, deluriau, deluriau, delurot
   (a) Rob. 95–6, 101–02

7. *Vous l'orrés bien dire,*   vdB, refr. 1860
   bele, vous l'orrés bien dire.
   [*You will certainly hear of it, darling, you will certainly hear of it.*]
   (a) Rob. 160–61

8. *Bergeronnete, douche baisselete,*   vdB, refr. 252
   donnés-le-moi vostre chapelet,
   donnés-le-moi vostre chapelet.

[*Little shepherdess, sweet little darling, give me your garland, give me your garland.*]
(a) Rob. 172–74
(b) R974 'L'autre jour je chevachoie'

9. *J'oi Robin flagoler, au flagol d'argent,*   vdB, refr. 1161
   au flagol d'argent.
   [*I hear Robin playing the flute, the silver flute, the silver flute.*]
   (a) Rob. 304

10. *Hé! resveille toi, Robin!*   vdB, refr. 870
    car on en maine Marot, car on en maine Marot.
    [*Hey, wake up Robin, for someone is taking Marot away, for someone is taking Marot away!*]
    (a) Rob. 342–43
    (b) R1700. IV 'Hier main quant je chevauchoie'
    (c) M870 T déb. 'En mai / L'autre jour/ *Hé! resveille toi*'
    (d) Sal. II, 8

11. *Aveuc tele compaignie*   vdB, refr. 200
    doit-on bien joie mener.
    [*With such company one really ought to enjoy oneself.*]
    (a) Rob. 421–22
    (b) Ren. 6632
    (c) Chauv. 3118
    (d) Sal. I, 8

12. *Venés apres moi, venés le sentele,*   vdB, refr. 1835
    le sentele, le sentele lés le bos.
    [*Come follow me, come follow the path, the path by the wood.*]
    (a) Rob. 762–63

reordering and restructuring its constituent parts in a way which partly parodies it, partly enables it to be used for parody. The most signal instance of this is the positioning of *Robin m'aime, Robin m'a* which comes at the start of the *Jeu*, but after the third stanza of both of the supporting *pastourelles*. In each *pastourelle* it marks a pivotal point in the narrative, but whereas in 'Au tens nouvel' it presages the rape of the shepherdess, in 'A l'entrant de mai' it introduces her successful rejection of the chevalier's advances. It is not necessary to assume that these two *pastourelles* are the specific models for Adam's compositional method to see that his relocation of the refrain makes a proleptic allusion to the *pastourelle* genre as a whole, and that this allusion takes the form of a sharply defined pair of alternatives: will she resist successfully or will she be raped?

The sense in the *Jeu* that a settled generic structure is being disturbed arises from a variety of details. For instance, in the first four exchanges (that are entirely in song) neither character directly addresses the other. Instead, the snatches of *pastourelle* material are juxtaposed in a manner that recalls a motet more than a *pastourelle* or a play. This condensed and implicit narrative in song indirectly poses the potential threat of the chevalier. The unsettling character of their self-enclosed singing surfaces in the chevalier's subsequent question to Marion about her refrain: *Hé! Robin, se tu m'aimes, / par amours maine-m'ent*, and in her reply which evasively gives a narrative paraphrase of her opening song *Robin m'aime, Robin m'a*. By having the chevalier comment on Marion's choice of song, Adam draws attention to the fact that the narrative has been fast-forwarded: Marion calls for Robin to take her away merely at the sight of the chevalier, before he has even greeted her, let alone made any advance.

Adam lays open his compositional method to scrutiny, for not only does his *Jeu* quote from *pastourelles*, it quotes itself, and does so within a few moments from the start. In this first scene, the citing of a refrain twice, first by Marion then by the chevalier, sets up a sequence of repetition in the dialogue, in which Marion punningly echoes each of the chevalier's questions in order to discomfit him with her apparent ignorance of his use of language (oisel, ane, hairon). Goaded into exclaiming that he is being mocked, the chevalier finds the tables turned on himself again as Marion starts to ask him questions and then makes fun of his replies in a further sequence which includes her refusal to acknowledge the term *chevalier*:

LI CHEVALIERS
Or dites, douche bergerete,
Ameriés-vous un chevalier?

MARIONS
Biaus sire, traiiés-vous arrier.
Je ne sai que chevalier sont.
(57–60)

THE KNIGHT: Now tell me, sweet little shepherdess, would you ever
   love a knight?
MARION: Fine sir, step back. I don't know what knights are.

The end of this section of dialogue is signalled by the next refrain, in
which Marion both mocks the chevalier's name (Aubert) by rhyming it
disadvantageously with Robert (Robin) and does so by mimicking the
tune of his earlier song (see Ex. 10):

Ex. 10 *Le Jeu de Robin et Marion*: comparison of two melodies '*Je me repairoie
du tournoiement*' and '*Vous perdés vo paine, sire Aubert*'

MARION, au chevalier,
Vous perdés vo paine, sire Aubert,
Je n'amerai autrui que Robert.
(83–84)
LI CHEVALIERS
Je me repairoie du tournoiement,
Si trouvai Marote seulete au cors gent.
(9–10)

MARION, to the knight: *You are wasting your efforts, Sir Aubert, I will never love anyone but Robert.*

THE KNIGHT: *I was returning from the tournament, when I found pretty Marote all alone.*

Their encounter finishes with a piece of more extended song that parallels the opening, so that the scene is framed by two sections of sung narrative drawn from the genre of *pastourelle*, each of which serves to epitomise the course of the drama first in prospect and then in retrospect. But this is only the start. Adam goes on to present two more versions of this scene, giving in total three re-runs of the fundamental *pastourelle* narrative, with three different types of narrative outcome: Marion discomfiting the chevalier, Marion straightforwardly rejecting the chevalier, and finally, the chevalier taking Marion off by force. These scenes are intersected by encounters between Marion and Robin that partially calque the chevalier scenes, for instance by means of songs which partially imitate songs from a previous scene (producing an effect similar to a half-rhyme), or in one case by Robin's appropriation of a refrain sung by the chevalier in another *pastourelle* analogue.[5] Adam brings the first half of the play to a close by comically drawing the two types of scene together. Robin is brought face to face with the chevalier only to receive a thorough beating (from which Marion rescues him) and unwittingly to spur his courtly rival into seizing Marion when the latter had been on the point of leaving her for good. Both these incidents invert conventional *pastourelle* motifs in which Marion usually calls on Robin to rescue her rather than the other way round, and in which the chevalier usually needs no external prompting to advance on Marion.

The refrain *Hé! resveille toi, Robin! / car on en maine Marot*, sung in this scene by Robin's cousin Gautier, occurs elsewhere in the *pastourelle avec des refrains* 'Hier main quant je chevauchoie' [Yesterday morning when I was riding] (attributed to Huitace de Fontaine).[6] This song provides an important subtext for this part of the *Jeu*. Its narrative belongs, once more, to the rape type, and a sense of threat is apparent even from the first stanza where it is stressed that the shepherdess is alone and in a remote place ('pres de bois et loing de gent' [near a wood and far from any people] (4)). Here she anxiously sings '*Dex, trop demeure; quant vendra? / loing est, entroubliee m'a'* ['*God he stays away too long; when will he return? He is far away, he has half-forgotten me*'] (9–10). In the *pastourelle* Robin's absence is frequently remarked: he is actually asleep with his club amongst his sheep, and does not awake even when Marion screams as loudly as she can: *Hé! resveille toi, Robin! / car on en maine Marot.* He only appears in the final strophe after the chevalier has raped Marion, in time to be taunted with the chevalier's insulting final refrain:

> '*a dieu conmant je mes amors,*
> *q'il les me gart.*'
> (49–50)

> '*I commend my loves to God, that he may guard them for me.*'

It is tempting to think that Adam is making a direct allusion to this *pastourelle*, for he highlights in the same way Robin's failure of timing. He illustrates this in his placing of the refrain not during the kidnapping scene, but after it. Here its very inappropriateness in the narrative sequence, along with the displacement of the singer from Marion to Gautier, enacts Gautier's mockery of Robin for missing his moment even though he was present (but hopelessly ineffective) throughout the whole scene.

This structure of repetition continues into the second half of the *Jeu*, where, following the final exit of the chevalier, the action models itself on *bergerie* rather than *pastourelle*, yet frequently recapitulates on the structural and dramatic patterns of the first half. [7] These are underpinned by the barely concealed presence of other *pastourelles*, which form a prior network of dramatic, narrative and linguistic expectations to which Adam's work makes constant allusion. The function of the refrains in the midst of the *Jeu* is to bring the network to the surface of the work: they act as individual points of contact and communication between the various elements in the verbal dialogue. Adam seems to gain impetus from established characteristics of refrain usage towards creating the larger formal structure of the *Jeu*, dependent as it is upon repetition, amplification, disjunction and allusion. Moreover, the kind of verbal generation motivated by the refrains applies equally to their melodies: as we have seen, processes of mocking half-repetition are enacted through the tunes as well as the words. [8]

The tracing of certain structural aspects of Adam's method of generic transposition identifies his concern with placing registers under scrutiny. His dismembering of the *pastourelle* genre causes its various constituent elements to gain a new visibility. At the same time, the subtlety of his method involves using one register to mask another; the result is a work that has a disarmingly simple exterior, but reveals some sharp oppositions just below the surface. Rosanna Brusegan has shown that the opening dialogue between Marion and the chevalier further contains a hidden erotic language: each term in this very short, concise exchange of words is loaded symbolically with an erotic code, so that *jüer* means 'jeu d'amor', *palefroi*, the male sex organ, *bosket* and *val*, the female, and so on.[9] By refusing to cooperate with the knight's use of language – as we saw, she systematically transposes each of his courtly metaphors (oisel, ane and so on) into a lower register – Marion simultaneously exposes his crudely amorous intentions and the impassable social gulf between knights and shepherdesses. The chevalier's smooth, apparently disingenuous opening gambits are repeatedly broken up by her deft unmasking of his subtext.

As Brusegan comments, however, the linguistic confrontation between Marion and the chevalier cannot be explained as a simple clash between two registers – courtly and peasant. The process of opposition here, and in the work as a whole, is more complex, and more confused (or confusing) than that. The strains in the *Jeu* include not just linguistic and formal, but also social and sexual tensions, and it is not necessarily clear how Adam differentiates between one kind of opposition and another. For instance, opinion is undecided over whether the central opposition in the *pastourelle* is social or sexual. Kathryn Gravdal has argued that 'the Old French *pastourelle*... presents rape as the inevitable encounter between the representatives of two different social classes',[10] and hence that 'the talk of social class, in the *pastourelle*, is (at least in part) a smokescreen' for the true battle of gender (p. 370). She seeks to overturn modern critical assumptions that social conflict is the prime issue in the *pastourelle* and to replace this with an argument asserting the primacy of rape. But her own qualification 'at least in part' weakens the force of this assertion.

Since the theoretical model of pastoral has been developed specifically to think through relations between the literary and the social, it may be helpful to recast the debate in these terms. Pastoral is a mode of writing in which questions of boundary are given a central theoretical focus, and not negotiated away. Its potency as a model derives from its capacity to illustrate the convolutions of the relationship so sharply. For while pastoral is clearly concerned with the social, it also mystifies it. Its relationship with the social is covert, or coded. William Empson, in a famous formulation, describes this with disarming offhandedness as 'the essential trick of the old pastoral', which is 'to imply a beautiful relation between rich and poor', a phrase which captures pastoral's aestheticisation of social differences.[11] The element of concealment (or mystification) in pastoral is important, because unless its social point is *successfully* covert (to at least part of its audience), it cannot function politically. What Empson seems to mean is less the notion of a political conspiracy (as if the rich were trying to trick the poor into thinking that their lives were noble and dignified) than a piece of magic (p. 69) or feigning (a word which, as he notes, puns between desire and pretence (p. 136)). Pastoral never has a straightforward relation to the encounter between rich and poor which it portrays: its actual social directions are obscured by the powerfully mystifying weight of its lengthy literary history.

Pastoral motifs in the Old French *pastourelle* follow the same twisting course: the knight and the shepherdess may seem to have their say in the genre, but the genre's highly conventional apparatus removes their encounter some distance from any genuine historical circumstance. More particularly, the *pastourelle* encounter sets up a whole spectrum of models of difference, not all of which cut the cloth in the same direction: for instance as well as knight/shepherdess, there are (to name only a few) courtly/peasant, male/female, high style/low style, beautiful/ugly, well dressed/torn dress, elegance of gesture/clumsiness or obscenity of gesture, clever/stupid, brave/cowardly. Part of the established satiric process of the *pastourelle*, and even more so of the *Jeu de Robin et de Marion*, is to overlay these distinctions in unexpected ways, so that Marion is both clever and brave and female, while the knight is stupid and obscene and male, even though she is a peasant and speaks in low style while he is an aristocrat and commands a high register.

The various ways of articulating these oppositions have the effect of blurring or confusing the distinctions. For example, the fact that the encounter between the knight and the shepherdess is narrated by the knight means that any perceptions of social and sexual difference that we read in a work are (apparently) being presented through male, aristocratic eyes. At the same time, any stability we might seek to find in this point of view is disrupted by the presentation of the peasants as using courtly language, or playing courtly games, and the knight as tiring of fine speech and behaving with rough and often violent aggression towards the shepherdess. It might be tempting to see such inversions as evidence of a carnivalesque mode in the genre, or the presentation of a world upside down, where knights ape peasants and peasants ape knights. The usual result of the carnivalesque, however, is to affirm the status quo rather than upset it, the disruptions acting as exceptions which prove the rule. But *pastourelles* also show more direct signs of contempt for the behaviour they portray, in some cases applied to the peasants (for looking vulgar, dirty, obscene and foolish) as much as to the knight (for behaving badly, angrily or violently). To that extent, if a central function of pastoral forms is 'the symbolic mediation of social relationships', then in the *pastourelle* the process of mediation is far from straightforward.[12]

One reason why the knight/shepherdess encounter carries so many potential readings concerns the complexity of the pastoral model itself. Located in an idealised rural landscape, the genre plays crucially on forms of displacement, in particular, on the character of the courtly *outside* the context of court so that the elaborate social encodings of the court are expressed in circumstances which allow them none of their usual kinds of social justification. It is as if the pastoral landscape works precisely to disrupt clear perceptions of difference: far from the court the knight becomes as much subject to new, threatening influences as the peasant does in encountering the knight. The crucial factor here is that the genre subjects *both* social strata to inversion: in this open idealised space outside the city walls all standards of normality become vulnerable.

If this is indeed the case, it is perhaps not surprising that we find ourselves in difficulties when we try to fit *pastourelles* into a single social or sexual frame of meaning. Critical thinking on the *pastourelle* has ranged widely from seeing it as a courtly genre to a non-courtly one: more recently, attention has been drawn to the urban, bourgeois context of large numbers of *pastourelles* from the third quarter of the thirteenth century.[13] Locating these works within the specific social context of late thirteenth-century Arras gives some basis for understanding the competing cultural pressures that they represent.

Adam's *Jeu de Robin et de Marion* is a particularly ambivalent example of social cross-breeding, since it is usually held to have been composed and first performed not in Arras, but in the Angevin court at Naples. Adam joined the service of Robert II, Count of Artois, in 1283, and on the strength of the short anonymous Prologue, *Li Jus du Pelerin*, is taken to have composed *Robin et Marion* in southern Italy before his death in about 1287. This does not mean, however, that the work was unknown in Arras. From the 'Adam de la Halle' manuscript (fr. 25566) it appears that a revised version of *Robin et Marion*, with the Prologue mentioned above and two pieces of interpolated dialogue, was put on in Arras around 1287. *Robin et Marion* displays a close continuity with the process of poetic activity in Arras; it is strikingly similar, in particular, to *Le Tournoi de Chauvency*, a work written just two years later. Those who have commented on the circumstances in which *Robin et Marion* was composed tend to say that Adam was writing to humour an aristocratic and military expatriate audience who wished to be reminded nostalgically of their French homeland.[14] And indeed *Robin et Marion* is usually described as a turning away from the whimsical, black comedy of *Le Jeu de la feuillée* towards a much more straightforwardly 'charming' piece of rusticity.[15]

Yet there are problems both with the description 'charming' and with the supposed nostalgic connection between *Robin et Marion* and its context. *Robin et Marion* is a far from merely 'charming' work. As for its hypothesised context, the Angevin court was in the midst of violence and rebellion: 30 March 1282 saw an uprising against the French inhabitants of Palermo in the notorious massacre known as the Sicilian Vespers. The court established by Charles, Roi de Sicile, in 1266, was a dazzling attempt at cultural colonisation in which French language, literature and administration were energetically asserted. All Charles's leading officials were Occitan or French.[16] Despite its unpopularity with Italians and Sicilians, he insisted on French as the language of government. Poets and musicians were brought over from France, including many from the Arras region such as Perrin d'Agincourt, Rutebeuf, Raoul de Soissons and Adam de la Halle himself, specifically to provide a highly visible cultural profile for the displaced court. That Adam contributed prominently to this process can be seen from his *chanson de geste Le Roi de Sicile*, a work that resounds with compliments to Charles.[17] By such means, Charles created an active and highly powered literary environment in which all the usual French displays of poetic skill took place in the form of prize-winning *jeux-partis*, and the exchange of *coblas*. He himself composed both verse and music.[18] The important collection of songs in the 'Chansonnier du Roi' has also been accredited to the Neapolitan court.[19]

Although Charles was a conscientious ruler, his policy of filling all major administrative posts with foreigners was resented, particularly in Sicily. The popular revolt in Palermo, seemingly a local affair, caused Charles's entire empire to fall. Adam's arrival in Naples was part of the response made to Charles's request to his two nephews, Robert d'Artois and Pierre d'Alençon, to raise military and financial support for him in France. If the *Jeu du Pelerin* is to be believed, *Robin et Marion* was composed against this background of impending disaster, of a powerful expatriate French court in the process of collapse through a single spark of popular discontent. The spark itself bears a remarkable similarity to the central dramatic event of the play, for the fighting was triggered by the over-familiarity of a group of drunk French soldiers with Sicilian women waiting in the crowd for the start of Vespers at the Church of the Holy Spirit on Easter Monday. One soldier, Drouet, dragged a young married woman from the crowd and began molesting her, so enraging her husband that he knifed him. Attempting to avenge their colleague's death, the other French soldiers were themselves immediately cut down by the Sicilian crowd, who, crying 'Death to the French!', proceeded to hunt out and kill every other French inhabitant of the city.

The extraordinary coincidence here of historical event and literary construction is worth pondering. Far from being a piece of light entertainment designed to amuse French soldiers and aristocrats by its very remoteness from local concerns, *Robin et Marion* stands out in relief against historical realities that underpin its generic structure with troubling precision: real peasants experienced genuine affront from real courtly oppressors, leading to an all too real disturbance whose ever-deepening consequences were still being played out as the play was first composed and performed. The scale of this unrest gives the historical encounter between oppressor and peasant girl a distinctly uncarnivalesque appearance: unlike, perhaps, the English revolt of 1381 which the boy-king Richard II ultimately managed to contain, the mechanism for rebellion in this Sicilian context seemed to go truly out of control.[20]

Although we may never know whether or not *Robin et Marion* emanates from Naples, how would the work speak to us from within this social matrix? It would be absurd, for example, to claim, as the nineteenth-century French critic O. Leroy did, that *Robin et Marion* actually caused the massacre,[21] neither would it make sense to claim that the massacre caused the play. The link between pastoral and history, as Empson observes, is aesthetic rather than literal or causal. At the same time, Adam's presence in Naples was not politically innocent: he was clearly brought over to play his part in the myth-making activities of cultural colonialism. The issue is not a matter of historical causality, but to seek an explanation for the forms which culture takes. It is possible to see various ways in which cultural forms, present in the generic make up of *Robin et Marion,* surface in the revolt: for instance, the Sicilians were reacting not just to soldiers as instruments of oppression, but to the soldiers as Frenchmen, and hence as representatives of a whole system of importation of French culture. Likewise, the offensive sexual form of the French–Sicilian encounter reflects a history of confrontation that is of central importance to the *pastourelle* genre.

As further illustration of the political form of this confrontation, the author of the anonymous *Suite de la 'Court d'amours'* chooses this very historical context for another rewriting of the *pastourelle* genre. The penultimate case brought before the Court of Love is that of a tearful shepherdess who has a complaint against the King of Sicily. He approached her one day, made love to her and promised that she should become queen, but then rode off and failed to return. The king is confronted in Naples with his feckless past, and summoned before the court. He publicly reaffirms his love, the shepherdess forgives him, and they marry. At the start of the case history, the narrative follows many details of the familiar *pastourelle* encounter: the king gets down from his 'palefroi' and utters the usual blandishments:

> et dist que j'avoie a tous jours
> trouvé ami, s'il me plaisoit
> (4408–09)

and said that I had found a lover for ever, if it pleased me.

There is even a scene where Bien Besongnant (an officer of the court), on his way to Naples to confront the king, meets a peasant who, like Marion in Adam's *jeu*, responds to questions with surly contrariness, turning phrases round and asserting incomprehension at every opportunity. Like a Shakespearean double plot in miniature, the scene replays the courtly/peasant confrontation between two new characters.

The legal case proceeds to turn the narrative conventions of *pastourelles* upside down: it enables the shepherdess to tell the encounter again, in her words, from her point of view, to a sympathetic public. Most startling of all is the final shift into romance. The king and girl are brought back together again, reunited in improbable fairy-tale permanence. This is the ending – a shocking levelling out of hierarchical and sexual difference – that is ruled out of every *pastourelle*, including Adam's *Robin et Marion*. Humorously, the author shows the French oppressor forced to marry a peasant: only through this extreme form of social humiliation would peace and political honour be restored. Again, the link between historical oppression and the core knight/peasant girl relationship in the literary form of the *pastourelle* is directly voiced: marriage makes good the political and the sexual affront.

All this combines to make *Robin et Marion* itself ripe for pastoral reading. It functions as a work not of simple sentimentality but of pointed displacement. Adam takes a genre already imbued with a long and delicate history of relating to history and transposes it from an urban, bourgeois context back into the kind of courtly arena from which the genre had only recently begun to be distanced. I spoke earlier of the way in which pastoral plays on the character of the courtly *outside* the context of court, so that the elaborate social encodings of the court are expressed in circumstances which allow them none of their usual kinds of social justification. *Robin et Marion* presents a new variation on this, since it is playing an urban tune outside its natural context within a court that is itself displaced. The result is a process of elaborate and multi-sided mystification, full of tensions glanced at but constantly displaced. Adam forgoes narrative closure, for example, in offering all three types of *pastourelle* encounter, but none conclusively. Rather than present a chevalier who is either straightforwardly successful, or else easily beaten off, he skates between the latent generic possibilities, allowing Marion to preserve her reputation and dignity, but giving the chevalier just enough grace to retreat on his own initiative. The abrupt shift into *bergerie*, in which the chevalier is then erased from the action, retrospectively undermines the importance of the encounter. In that sense, the peasants win the day, but they do so only by revealing their grosser aspects.

By not lending itself to a single political reading, *Le Jeu de Robin et de Marion* illustrates the cultural ambivalence of its author's position. The usefulness of the pastoral model to Adam in such a situation is precisely the degree to which it is at a remove from awkward historical circumstance. One might compare here Empson's characterisation of the pastoral relation as an experience of bafflement at the meeting of different worlds, and also Gurevich on the medieval perception of this life in relation to the next: individually they were taken for granted, 'it was the meeting of the two that struck a note of marvel: each of the worlds was made vicariously foreign to the other'.[22] At the same time, pastoral is capable of articulating a range of models of difference rather than a simple message or polarity, a characteristic which in fact does better justice to the complexity of motive in a work's social context. For instance, the very difficulty of deciding whether the social or the sexual encounter is of greater primary importance in the play is matched by the thorough conflation of the sexual and the social in the historical context. One sort of difference (social) is articulated by another (sexual) in such a way as to show the two kinds of confrontation to be mutually symptomatic.

Generic interaction, in the hands of Adam de la Halle, is shown to be a subtle, and to some extent covert means of negotiating different kinds of strain between genres and their literary pre-history, and between genre and history. A master of registral shifts, Adam locates the registral charge carried by individual generic allusions and uses it to create currents of tension in an outwardly smooth fictional surface. The mobility of refrains, as indicators of popular as well as courtly language, serves as a means of highlighting often awkward moments of transition between one register and another, between one genre and another, and hence between one social group and another. Refrains give formal expression to the failures of communication between the aristocrat and the 'vilein' through the formal anarchy of their migration between different styles and registers. They turn the transitional into an art form.

PART IV

Modes of inscription

10

Songs in writing: the evidence of the manuscripts

The later thirteenth century and early fourteenth is a period of fundamental change in the writing of words and music. Most strikingly, changes in genre coincide with changes in transcription and notation. To reflect further on this, I now turn from the cultural to the material form of songs in writing.

This book began by considering what manuscripts, in their necessarily literal way, reveal about the relations between text and performance. I have sought to show in successive chapters on the verbal, musical and cultural contexts of thirteenth-century song that medieval authors are greatly interested in the distinction between different kinds of writing. The physical evidence of manuscript layout also has much to tell us about a medieval understanding of categories of composition. Scribal differentiation between varieties of genre in the manuscripts of individual works is rife, and worth examining. The manuscripts also contain evidence about how a work was performed, and whether it was performed with music. The issues raised in the first section about the presence or absence of music for songs will now be considered over a broader range of evidence. It may also be possible, if not necessarily to discern reasons for change, then at least to identify some symptoms of it.

The experience of looking at manuscripts of works of mixed genre is to see genre rendered as a visual and spatial concept. In the sense that the physical attributes of manuscripts act as a visual correlative of scribal thinking, genre is one of the most marked features of these works' material appearance. While headings and glosses contribute significantly to this, many aspects of the *ordinatio* of the manuscripts are more widely involved: the organisation of material, the use and character of indices, a hierarchy of initials, borders and illuminations, different sizes and colours of script, the use of paraphs and underlining, practices of lineation, and the presence of musical notation, either directly or in the form of blank staves, or else spaces for staves.[1] On the basis of the study of some 230 manuscripts, including chansonniers, narratives, *dits*, sermons, translations and proverb collections, I attempt to summarise the various ways in which vernacular song is presented in writing during the thirteenth century and up to the mid-fourteenth century.[2] I proceed to two specific cases of works that shed special light on the relation between genre and *mise-en-page*: *Aucassin et Nicolette*, a celebrated thirteenth-century composition in prose and sung verse, and *Le Roman de Fauvel*, an early fourteenth-century witness to profound transition.

We may begin by noting the increasing preoccupation in the late thirteenth century with genre and generic terms in the organisation of manuscripts and in manuscript indices. The earliest chansonnier to group works generically in a systematic way is the 'Adam de la Halle' Manuscript (fr. 25566). The codex as a whole is unusual first in the prominence it gives to a single trouvère (this does not occur again before the compiling of the Machaut manuscripts),[3] and second, in the prominence it gives to genre within its organisation of that trouvère's works, in which the chansons (bound in separately), *jeux-partis*, rondeaux, motets and *jeux* are grouped. The original index also gives them in that order ('chansons, partures, rondiaus, motets'). A similar, though less author-based, principle is evident in the early fourteenth-century chansonnier Oxford, Bodleian Library, Douce 308, which, in the last section of the manuscript, groups its songs according to their genres (*gran chans, estampies* etc.), rather than by author, as in nearly all previous chansonniers.[4] Douce 308 also has an index (*l'abecelaire*) listing the song genres that are copied at the end of the manuscript.[5] As far as other indices are concerned, instead of the usual practice of listing works by their incipits, the index to one late thirteenth-century manuscript, a compilation that includes *L'Estoire de Joseph*, has indications of whether a piece is in prose or in verse.[6] The index to the *Fauvel* manuscript (fr. 146) takes the further step of listing all the different interpolations by genre, such as 'Rondeaux, Balades et Reffrez de Chancon'.[7] Such explicit attention to the genre of a work was no doubt stimulated (at least in part) by the sharply divergent copying requirements for different genres such as the motet, the monophonic chanson and the polyphonic chanson.

Polyphony, in particular, imposed radically new styles of manuscript lay-out which would naturally have caused scribes to consider very closely the category of work they were copying.

As Rebeccca Baltzer and Margaret Switten have argued, the history of the manuscript layout of music indicates how fundamentally the 'manuscript image' of a song conveys the kinds of perception held about song by medieval scribes and composers.[8] Baltzer has argued, of the thirteenth-century motet, that 'the achievement of a distinc-tive ... manuscript format was essential to the establishment – and in-deed to the definition – of the genre itself'.[9] To the extent that narratives with intercalated songs were analogous to chansonniers, the different song genres imposed special challenges of layout and presentation, es-pecially where musical notation was supplied.

The latter was, of course, one of the most obvious ways in which song was differentiated from narrative in French manuscripts. Was music present or anticipated in the written contexts for vernacular song in this period? An initial answer can be framed from some statistics (see the Appendix). Out of seventy-seven works (comprising 231 manuscripts), seventeen (in forty manuscripts) have notation. A further eleven (in thirty-nine manuscripts) are prepared for music with blank staves or spaces for staves. In total, just over a third of the works (twenty-eight) and their manuscripts (seventy-nine) have music or are prepared for music.[10] Of the rest, the majority gives some visual emphasis to the songs, by use of initials, paraphs, headings, coloured script and so on. Eighteen works, in some twenty-nine manuscripts, do not differentiate the songs in any way.

These figures need some comment. I have counted works and manuscripts separately because works survive in very varying numbers of copies, from *unica*, like Renart's *Rose*, to the eighty-odd copies of the *Miracles*. Each work moreover may be represented by its manuscripts in varying ways: among its sixteen copies the *Restor de paon* has notation for its rondeau in just one, spaces for staves in one other, while in a third the rondeau is underlined in red and written in long lines. None of the rest marks it out in any way. This means that care needs to be exercised in drawing conclusions on the basis of figures alone: the lack of musical notation in any unique manuscript cannot be regarded as an indication *in itself* that the songs were not intended to be sung. For example, if the first two copies of the *Restor* mentioned above had not survived, we might have been tempted to conclude that music was never projected for the work. Similarly, the *saluts d'amour* and *complaintes d'amour* appear to survive collectively without music; when one realises, however, that those with refrains are wholly represented by a single non-music manuscript (fr. 837), the grounds for thinking that music did not feature in these works may turn out to be somewhat restricted.

The survival of music is perhaps better approached by considering not how 'musical' or how 'literary' a work is, but where it was produced and by whom. It is important, I think, to try to capture a sense of the peculiar status of these secular music manuscripts. As we discussed in Chapter 2, they resemble chansonniers in anthologising songs, yet the earliest among them predate the chansonniers (which only started to be compiled in the mid-thirteenth century), and so represent some of the earliest surviving attempts to record vernacular songs in written form.[11] From this perspective, they represent all the uncertainty, flexibility and inventiveness of scribes using a new medium to attempt to record and transmit on the one hand vernacular song itself, and on the other a newly hybrid generic relationship – that between song and narrative.[12] Those which do possess notation range in quality of presentation from the hugely elaborate *Fauvel* manuscript at one extreme to the rough hand-ruled copy of *L'Estoire de Joseph* at the other. The first part of this account attempts to distinguish (however tentatively) between different kinds of context for their production.

The fifteen works that contain music reveal certain patterns of production. The most prominent is an association with Arras and the urban *puy*-culture of Northern France. This applies to the works by Adam de la Halle (*Robin et Marion, Le Jeu de la feuillée* and *Le Jeu du Pelerin*), *Renart le Nouvel, La Court de paradis* and the *Ludus super Anticlaudianum*. The case for connecting these works has been argued in the previous section: it is interesting to see how they are further connected through copying practices among the manuscripts.

The finest of these is the 'Adam de la Halle' manuscript, fr. 25566, which we may recall includes a copy of *Renart le Nouvel* (amongst other writings) throughcopied alongside Adam's complete works.[13] The placing of *Renart le Nouvel* in so generically conscious a compilation has a certain appropriateness: it points up the way in which both Adam and Jacquemart create new generic possibilities in their compositions through their wide and novel use of refrains.[14] It also makes clear the generic affinity between *Renart le Nouvel* and *Robin et Marion* by the similarities they share in layout, that is, in the interruption of columns of octosyllabic verse with musically notated songs on four-line red staves. The manuscript as a whole illustrates procedures of layout particularly well, ranging as it does from a diverse collection of independent song genres, to dramatic narratives with inset songs, to didactic prose ('Coument dieu fourma Adan').[15] It is not so much that each genre has its own layout, in a sense a self-evident observation, as that there are genres of layout. The scribe's work shows a careful modulation of one layout into another, as in the use of prose lineation for the three quite distinct purposes of presenting the second and subsequent stanzas of a chanson, a prose treatise, and the letters in *Renart le Nouvel*. A similar care is evident in the notation of refrains across rondeaux, motets, dramatic *jeux* and an animal satire, each of which demands quite different ways of allocating space for staves. The juxtaposition of these different genres shows a shifting emphasis in the written presentation of words and music from work to work, so that prose lineation, to take the same example, can range in signification from meaning words that are sung, to words that are very much spoken and written (in the case of the letters and treatises).

Seeing the music for the refrains in *Renart le Nouvel* alongside fully notated chansons[16] also points up the oddity (from the scribe's point of view), at least in a vernacular context, of having to set out music in the midst of copying a long narrative work.[17] Whereas normally the music sections of a vernacular manuscript would be set apart from narrative or didactic sections (indeed would usually be a separate manuscript), here a scribe has to plan for short musical interruptions right through the codex. In fr. 25566 the planning is evidently thorough, and in a sense facilitated by the decision to present Adam's work as an entirety, since that already sets up the need to make complex adjustments of *mise-en-page*. Some sense that he has to work out his principles of presentation as he goes along is shown by the various, but not entirely consistent distinctions of layout between the *jeux* and *Renart le Nouvel*. For example, whereas in Adam's *jeux* the names of the characters are written on a separate line in red immediately before each switch in speaker, the

Renart characters are not so identified, implying perhaps that the scribe thought the degree of dramatisation in the two kinds of work to be different. On the other hand, although flourished initials in *Renart le Nouvel* mark the return to narrative each time after a refrain, initials do not figure in the programme of *ordinatio* in *Robin et Marion*, whereas in the *Jeu de la Feuillée* they are very frequent, and seem to be used (largely) to mark the switches in dialogue.

Both *Renart le Nouvel* and *Robin et Marion* seem to have lent themselves to scribal improvisation in their layout. Three out of four copies of *Renart le Nouvel* (fr. 25566, fr. 372, fr. 1593) contain full musical notation for the refrains, and the fourth (fr. 1581), not quite completed, contains red staves above every refrain, and notation for just one song on fol. 48v (see Fig. 5). Such a consistent indication of music in all four manuscripts is rare amongst *romans* containing songs, and indicates the special status of the manuscripts of *Renart le Nouvel* as an unusually full transcription of performance practice.[18] In this respect, the third in date of these, fr. 1593, dated 1290, gives the most vivid (if obscure) impression. It is neither neat nor beautifully finished. Covered in annotations, and worked over by several different scribes, it strikes the modern reader very much as a well-thumbed, working copy. These annotations are particularly intriguing for the way in which they seem to turn the manuscript into something resembling a playbook. All the refrains have the name of the character (or characters) who sings them written in the margin, such as 'Pinte la geline' or 'Canteriaus le fils chaunticler' on fols. 52r ff. This is reminiscent of the *Ludus* where the names of the singers are written into the margins besides their respective songs. In addition, at the start of *Renart le Nouvel* on fols. 2v-3r, the names of nearly all the principal characters are written beside the lines which contain their names: Ysengrins, Hersenz, Pincars and so on. Further comparison may be drawn with the *Robin et Marion* manuscript fr. 1569, where the scribe gives a key to the names of all the characters in the play at the bottom of the first page. On this analogy, the scribe of fr. 1593 is giving a cast-list of all the principal characters in *Renart le Nouvel*.

Many aspects, as we have discussed, not just of this manuscript, but of the transmission of *Renart le Nouvel* as a whole are baffling: each manuscript contains a different number of refrains, in a different order, and in fr. 1593 there are no fewer than four music scribes who add layers of text and notation in the margins to the original layout. The difficulty (for which no fully satisfactory answer has yet been found) is in deciding what kind of performance logic this situation implies, how and why the refrains came to be written down in that order and chronology.[19] Perhaps the closest comparison with fr. 1593 is the unique copy in the Bibliothèque Municipale at Lille (MS 316, *olim* 397) of Adam de la Bassée's *Ludus super Anticlaudianum*.[20] Like fr. 1593 of *Renart le Nouvel*, much care has been expended on Lille 316 in terms of scribal corrections, additions and annotations. The manuscript has no illustrations and there is evidence of much rubbing and scraping in places. Yet it has clearly been carefully planned, with the Latin narrative in quatrains interrupted by sections of music, each in turn rubricated (where appropriate) with instructions on the source of the melody as well as the name of the character performing the song. The manuscript of the *Ludus* may be unpretentious overall yet the skill involved in its *mise-en-page* should not be underestimated given the work's novel, unique and generically complex character. Along with *Renart le Nouvel* itself, it is likely to have been a formative influence on the most visually elaborate manuscript (of either century), the huge *Roman de Fauvel* book, fr. 146.[21]

Despite their obscurities, these late thirteenth-century manuscripts share at least two important features: a scrupulous recording of music and an attention to precise details of performance. The value attached to production details is explicable within the kind of urban *puy*-dominated poetic culture I discussed in the last two chapters. A demand for publicly performed works, produced in a fast-moving, competitive and self-conscious atmosphere seems to have stimulated a particular kind of vernacular musical literacy. Although we do not know exactly who commissioned fr. 25566, or the manuscripts of *Renart le Nouvel*, the mixed urban culture of Arras and Lille evidently encouraged a wider use of clerical copying skills than seems to have been available elsewhere outside a monastic context.

The thirteen copies of Gautier's *Miracles* which contain notation offer emphatic – and unique – evidence (outside the chansonniers) of such monastic music copying skills being concentratedly applied to vernacular song. No other vernacular work of mixed genre was so widely disseminated, and in only three other cases (*Renart le Nouvel*, *Robin et Marion* and the prose *Tristan*) does music survive in more than one manuscript copy of a single work. No other surviving vernacular narrative work transmits music for a trouvère song:[22] the only other musical source for trouvère song is the *Ludus*. Presumably one reason for this is the greater technical difficulty of copying *grands chants* over short refrains. With the exception of certain isolated instances of accomplished clerical involvement with a work (as in the *Miracles*, the *Ludus* and *Fauvel*), the presence of music seems an unpredictable affair, and is largely confined, in any case, to refrains. The survival of just three notated refrains from the *Roman de la poire* (the first two damaged, the third complete) is a case in point: their highly contingent existence forms part of a series of fragmentary fourteenth-century remains of the narrative in fr. 24431. The two full copies of the poem (fr. 2186 and fr. 12786) respectively have empty staves for the refrains, and blank spaces for staves.[23] The precarious survival of music in these copies contrasts markedly with the care lavished on n. a. fr. 24541, (first half of the fourteenth century), one of the most important manuscripts of Gautier de Coinci's *Miracles*, a highly professional piece of work from scribes expert in music, text and illumination.[24]

The survival of high art song melodies in narrative in a sacred, and a Latin context, respectively, may have further implications. It seems to be an early indication of the shift in taste which had occurred by the early fourteenth century, in which aristocratic favour turned from *grands chants* towards the formerly lower register refrains and rondeaux. Both Gautier and Adam de la Bassée testify to the thirteenth-century fascination with creatively reworking trouvère song, but the very exclusiveness of their interest argues that the future lay with the humble refrain melody rather than the sophisticated musical patterns of the *chanson courtoise*.

In drawing a contrast between the urban culture of the Artois and the monastic environment of Gautier, it is important to recall that they are overlapping, rather than mutually exclusive contexts. This is best shown by fr. 25532, which contains both a thirteenth-century copy of the *Miracles* and *La Court de paradis*, the same musical (and textual) scribe copying both works.[25] The decision to add *La Court de paradis* to this copy of the *Miracles* by a musically competent scribe working in a rich and powerful abbey explains the accident of survival of music for the *Paradis* (of its three copies, one has notation, but the other two do not even have spaces for staves). *La Court de paradis* is a work that reveals the intersection between both cultures: within the ambit of production at the abbey, it also draws on the latest poetic and musical trends emanating from the nearby circle of Arras.[26]

This discussion has focused so far on the manuscripts with notation: those which contain blank staves, or spaces for staves, are naturally more difficult to interpret. Where works such as *Le Restor du paon*, *Robin et Marion* and the *Roman de la poire* have notation (or blank staves) in some copies and spaces for staves in others, it is clear that the latter are simply unfinished manuscripts, left for a musically literate scribe to complete.[27] Eight works, however, have no sign of actual music, only spaces left between the lines of each song.[28] The spaces in *Meliacin* are especially tantalising, for the songs include trouvère chansons.[29] It is possible, as in the eight manuscripts of *Cleomadés*, where the rondeaux are generally copied out with double- or sometimes triple-spacing between the lines, but not once with staves, that music was never provided for some works, even in the original exemplar. However, this may indicate more about the problems of writing music than performing it. The manuscripts of Jehan Acart de Hesdin's *La Prise amoureuse* present a different case again, because by this date (1332) one would expect the songs to be polyphonically notated, whereas the spaces left are sufficient only for monophonic music (see Fig. 7(b)).[30] Sometimes, as in the single surviving copy of *Le Court d'amours*, BN n. a. fr. 1731, such an erratic line spacing is given to the refrains that although it might conceivably represent a musically illiterate scribe's attempt to leave space for notation, some other explanation is probably to be sought.[31]

Examples like these suggest that the spaces may be a form of visual marker for the songs, but not necessarily a sign of music itself. It is possible that these particular copies testify to scribal uncertainty (perhaps owing to a failure of communication between compiler and scribe) about the character of the works being transcribed. Scribes who leave spaces between the lines of the refrains could in some cases be acting on their own initiative in assuming that the songs would be sung, and thus failing to transmit accurately works in which music was intended in a different form from the one they envisaged, or else not intended at all.

The moments of inconsistency in layout offer perhaps some of the most interesting glimpses of scribal thinking. In a few cases spaces for staves are given to the narrative and in the fr. 24391 copy of *La Prise amoureuse* where the normal layout for the rondeaux gives spaces for staves only to the refrains, the first two lines of the eighth rondeau are also quadruple-spaced.[32] Slips such as these attest to the strain on scribes caused by frequent shifts from song to narrative. The copies of *Cleomadés* show especial variation, one might say confusion, in layout. *Cleomadés* contains seven rondeaux in two separate groups (one of three, the other of four): fr. 1456 allocates double line-spacing to all except the first rondeau, and the first two lines of the second, whereas fr. 19165 gives double line-spacing for the last four rondeaux but not for the first three.[33] *Meliacin*, a reworking of the same romance as *Cleomadés*, has spaces for staves in three out of the four manuscripts I have been able to consult. The fourth has a double space left only above one of the refrains (fol. 37r), emphasising not only the structural importance of refrains (seen in fr. 24391 above), but perhaps also that the melody was more likely to be known of a refrain than a stanza of a chanson.

Scribal uncertainty may itself have acquired significance. To speculate further, the absence of music, however much it may have represented a simple lack of expertise in the art of writing (as opposed to performing) music, probably became an influential aspect of song layout in its own right. Thus although some manuscripts without music no doubt took that form because of a lack of copying skills, once a work was circulated without music for its song citations, it may have begun to create an audience who were prepared to consider the songs principally for their words. The copies of Baudouin's *Li Prison d'amours* are an interesting test case, since although one copy has blank staves, the other does not distinguish the refrains visually from the narrative in any way. The two manuscripts might indicate two different ways of responding to the *dit*: one presents it as a piece of purely verbal discourse, the other as a form of discourse that is divided between song and speech. The changing patterns of literacy in the thirteenth century make either possibility viable: what I want to emphasise here is that the issue is less a matter of trying to decide for one view as against another, than of recognising the extent to which thirteenth-century manuscripts are witnesses to a crisis of representation in the written medium.

Other aspects of song layout in the manuscripts may help to clarify our sense of the expectations attaching to song in these contexts. I want to consider the various types of *ordinatio* together, and how different features are planned to act in mutual support of an overall scribal interpretation of the work. My effort in reviewing these features is not necessarily to point out anything new: most, perhaps all, of them are familiar aspects of medieval manuscript layout. However, not all of them are familiar in the particular contexts I describe: and it is precisely the jar and shock of the juxtaposition, whether it be of music and narrative, or of a high courtly practice with a lower one, or of a liturgical and vernacular context, that I seek to grasp, in part by trying to uncover the very assumptions of familiarity that appear to inhere to one kind of layout or another.

Music certainly represents the most striking visual expression of the difference between song and narrative: the difference between melody and speech being given strong visual emphasis by means of the red staves and the notation itself. The Machaut manuscripts illustrate this superbly, with the abrupt use of the whole width of a page, red staves and notes possessing their own calligraphic features, longs, breves, and semi-breves. Both the Machaut and Froissart manuscripts emphatically single out the element of song, by music (in the case of Machaut only), by generic titles, by pictures of scrolls and performers, by large initials (see Figs. 12 and 14). All combine to give great visual prominence to the structural outline of each work and genre in the codex, including the *dits*, and the different lyric genres in the lyric sections. This kind of visual pointing is extended over the codex as a whole, thereby displaying it in turn as a single structurally complex entity. The vivid red headings, in particular, especially in the plainer copies, make explicit the shifts in genre from page to page, as the eye moves from ballade to verse narrative to rondeau, *lai, complainte* and prose letter.

In this sense, the presence of notation is as much a commentary on the distinction between two genres as it is a representation of musical sound. This is confirmed by the way in which the placing of staves is often made to coincide either with a separate miniature or with an initial of greater or lesser elaboration (ranging from the fully historiated down to simple alternating red and blue).[34] One of the finest examples of this collaboration between staves and initials occurs in the beautifully illuminated *Poire* manuscript, fr. 2186 (*c.* 1275): each refrain is written out with blank staves in red, usually at the head of a page, to the right-hand side of a detailed historiated initial (see Fig. 7(a)).[35] This format presumably derives from chansonnier layout, where it is standard to begin the first stanza of each song (usually the only stanza which is given notation) with a large initial (see Fig. 1 (b)): this can

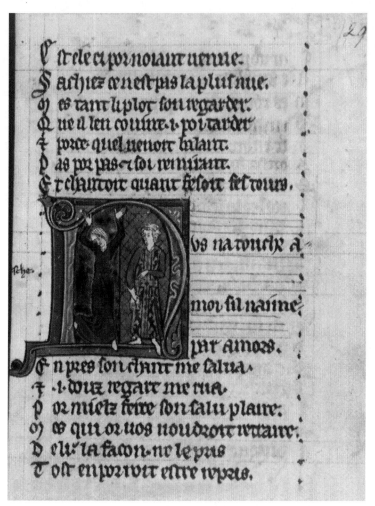

7 (a) Initial N of a refrain, showing a figure dancing (a 'performative marker'), with blank staves to the right, in Tibaut, *Le Roman de la Poire*, BN fr. 2186, fol. 29r.
(b) Ballade, with spaces left for staves in the first stanza, and refrain picked out with a paraph in the final stanza, in Jehan Acart de Hesdin, *La Prise amoureuse*, BN fr. 24391, fol. 138r.

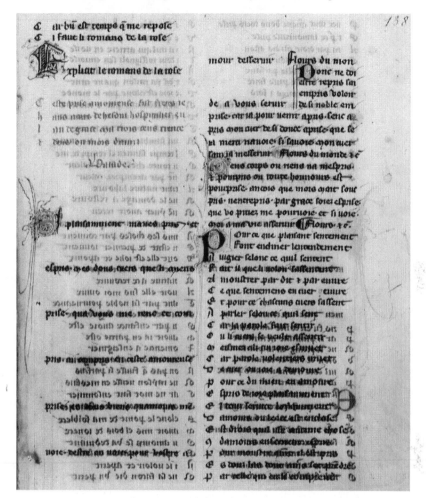

7 (cont.)

be seen, for instance, in the chansons that occur in copies of Gautier de Coinci's *Miracles*, such as Brussels, Bibliothèque Royale Albert 1 er, 10747 (see fols. 4v–5r or 103 v–104r), and in the Machaut manuscripts.[36] The more luxurious Machaut manuscripts, such as fr. 9221, 1584 and 1586, like the *Poire* copy in fr. 2186, interweave with the musical passages an elaborate scheme of miniatures, each with their own rubrics (see Figs. 12 and 14).

Initials thus play their part not merely in registering the presence of a song, but in emphasising a shift in performance. In the *Poire* manuscript each initial represents the speaker of the refrain: the initial thus becomes a performative marker (see Fig. 7(a)). Similarly, in the fr. 776 copy of the prose *Tristan*, a large initial on fol. 246r by a notated letter shows a lady standing with a piece of paper in her hand on which writing is clearly visible. Both examples may be compared with Aix-En-Provence, Bibliothèque de Méjanes, 572 of *Robin et Marion*, where the more obviously dramatic quality of the work is underscored by the same features of a large initial for the start of each song, often coinciding with a marginal miniature of the performers.[37] It is a short step from here to the fr. 15098 copy of *Le Roman du Castelain de Couci* which employs shorthand initials to mark the change of speaker in a conversation; they are similarly marked in the laisses of *Kanor* in fr. 1446.

The use of initials to register the presence of a song is perhaps the most consistent sign among the whole group of manuscripts. In several, this usage is supplemented by paraphs: if both visual signs are used then they are placed in a hierarchical relation. Thus three stanzaic works copied in fr. 837 – *La Chastelaine de Saint Gille*, *Li Confrere d'amours* and *Salut d'Amours (I)* – all have initials by every stanza and paraphs by every chanson and refrain; a fourth, the *fabliau Le Lai d'Aristote*, while it has paraphs for every refrain, less consistently has an initial for just one of its three *rondets*. Similarly, the copy of *La Prise amoureuse* in fr. 24391, which has initials for every stanza of its nine rondeaux and nine ballades, picks out the refrains within each ballade with paraphs (see Fig. 7(b)).[38] This kind of hierarchy demonstrates first, a desire to divide up songs (and narratives) stanzaically, and second, a particular focus on the unit of the refrain, even when it forms part of a larger song division.[39] Such textual pointing of refrains is given various other visual forms. For instance, the final word of a refrain may be followed by a tilde (~), or longer flourish (*Poire* fr. 2186, fols. 34v, 69 and 72 and the sermon in Vienna, Österreiches Nationalbibliothek 2621, fol. 52v), or else by a distinctive form of punctuation, such as an extended 'tick' (a form of *punctus elevatus*) in *Renart le Nouvel* and *Robin et Marion*, fr. 25566.[40] In a few instances the songs are highlighted by being written in red, as in fr. 1374 (*Violette*) (see Fig. 1 (a)), fr. 14968 (a *fatrasie* by Watriquet de Couvin), and Paris, Arsenal 3142 (a copy of a 'Bele Aelis' sermon), or else underlined in red (fr. 1455 (*Meliacin*) and fr. 1554 (*Restor de paon*)).[41] There are also manuscripts where song and 'narrative' are distinguished

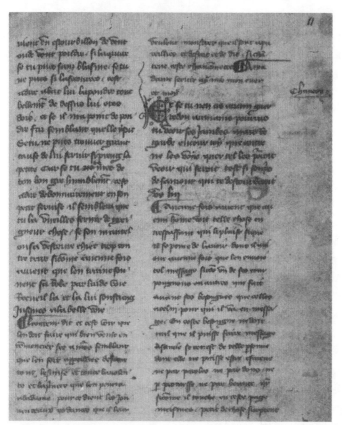

8 Text and gloss from the *Traduction et commentaire de l'Ars amatoria d'Ovide*, Paris, Bibliothèque de l'Arsenal 2741, fol. 11 r, showing different sizes of script (larger for the text, and smaller for the gloss). A refrain is cited in the far-right column, picked out by a paraph and signalled by the label *chancon* written in the margin.

by the size of the script, such as Paris, Bibliothèque de l'Arsenal 2741 of the *Traduction et commentaire de l'Ars amatoria d'Ovide* (see Fig. 8), and Besançon, Bibliothèque Municipale 551 of the *Miracles*.

Many of these features in the *ordinatio* of inset songs and refrains find their place in the larger history of the development of layout and punctuation in medieval academic books. As M. B. Parkes has argued, developments in the organisation of manuscripts from the twelfth century onwards work in harmony with developments in 'the structure of reasoning'.[42] The analogies between the layout of refrains and songs and that of scholastic texts are revealing about the assumptions scribes make about the role and function of embedded songs. Songs that are written or underlined in red recall the practice by which *lemmata* in the commentaries of Peter Lombard on the Psalter and Epistles of Paul were underlined in red, and where the *auctores* cited in the commentary were also marked out in red by name in the margin.[43] The latter in particular may be compared to the manuscript of Renart's *Rose* (Rome, Biblioteca Apostolica Vaticana, Reg. 1725) where, showing the same kind of academic impulse, the names of the authors of the chansons cited by Renart are written in the margin in a later (sixteenth-century?) hand by each song. Not surprisingly, the sermon contexts for *rondets* offer the closest analogy to scholastic practice: in Paris, Bibliothèque de l'Arsenal 3142 the 'Bele Aelis' *rondet* is first given in red at the start with a large initial, and then each line is written out singly in red as a *lemma* followed by individual commentary. The use of a hierarchy of script to which I have just alluded in copies of the *Traduction d'Ovide* and the *Miracles* is another standard means by which *lemmata* and commentary were distinguished in academic theological books:[44] in the *Traduction* 'Texte' and 'Glose' are laid out alternately with headings, the gloss (of which the refrains and other song and proverbial citations form a part) in a smaller script than the text (see Fig. 8).[45] In the Besançon copy of the *Miracles* the chansons are again in a smaller module than the text, but in a sermon copied in Rome, Biblioteca Apostolica Vaticana, Borghese 200 fol. 3 the rondeau is written in larger script than the following sermon. The direction of hierarchy is thus not always the same, for sometimes the refrains and songs are represented as commentary, sometimes as text; together these manuscripts offer interesting examples of vernacular appropriation of academic systems of textual organisation.

The whole practice of marking the start of songs with initials and paraphs again finds an analogy with the use of *litterae notabiliores* to indicate the beginnings of *sententiae* and the proliferation of paraphs in manuscripts from the thirteenth century onwards, 'used increasingly to indicate the beginning of a new *propositio*, or of a new stage in the development of an argument'.[46] In this context we see refrains and songs treated as authoritative texts, as an object and as a source of commentary. The ancient association of authoritative texts with special scripts which began with Anglo-Saxon scribes seems to pass into continental vernacular culture with these song-embedded texts: the particular form of their visual emphasis of the songs seems to indicate that many thirteenth- and fourteenth-century scribes saw the songs as representing special points of progress in the structural development of a work, and as examples of authoritative and sententious observation which demanded attention and comment.[47]

The ways in which scribes marked off the end of a song have a further implication. It would be a mistake to think of these designs, even in their more decorated versions, as mere 'space-fillers'. More likely, they are forms of *positurae* or 'end-of-section' marks that are used in the twelfth and thirteenth centuries to show the completion of a gloss at the end of a column. As Parkes notes, these appear 'sporadically throughout the later Middle Ages to indicate the end of a division (usually a Book) within a work' and can also be found 'at the ends of headings'.[48] In this light I suggest that we consider them alongside the very common practice in these manuscripts of giving initials to the section of narrative that immediately *follows* a song: in some cases these are the only parts of a work that are initialled (as in *Renart le Nouvel* fr. 372, fr. 1593; *Paradis* fr. 1802; *Poire*, fr. 24431) but more often they supplement the initials given to the songs themselves (as in *Cleomadés*, Brussels, Bibliothèque Royale, II 7444; *Couci*, fr. 15098; *Escanor*, fr. 24374 (see Fig. 9); *Violette*, fr. 1553; Hesdin, *La Prise amoureuse*, fr. 24432). Such emphasis both on the end of a song and on the start of the narrative suggests that the *positurae* and initials are functioning together as a generic marker. Like the shift between gloss and text, the end of a song is viewed as the end of one mode and the herald of another. In short, scribes are interested not only in the authoritative and sententious character of the songs but also in the way in which they create a disjunctive text, one that switches between modes of layout, modes of writing, and modes of performance.

The most obvious signs of scribal interest in genre occur in the headings themselves. These vary from marginal notes that simply comment informally on the presence of a song, such as BN lat. 11331 and Munich, Bayerische Staatsbibliothek, clm 4660 where in the former, a French refrain is written out in the margin next to a Latin song, and in the latter, 'refr' (for *refractus*) is written next to the refrain, to a more systematic allocation of generic headings.[49] It seems likely that the use of headings developed (at least in part) from the scribe's need to be conscious

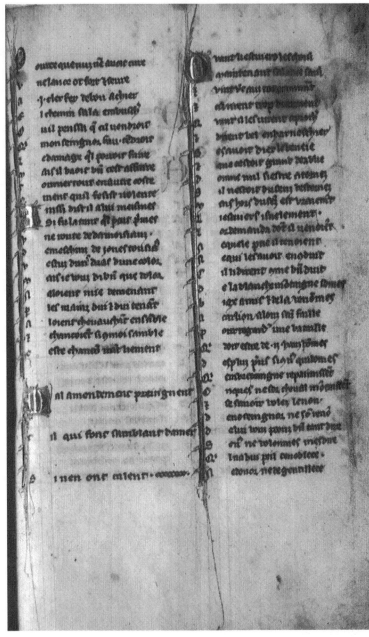

9 Refrain in Girart d'Amiens, *Escanor*, BN fr. 24374, fol. 68r, marked out by an enlarged initial, spaces left for staves, and an 'end of section' design filling in the last line of song in the left-hand column.

of when a change of layout was required. In one of the manuscripts of the *Roman du Castelain de Couci*, fr. 15098, 'chancon' is written in the extreme top margin of each page on which a song is copied, (see fol. 116r-v, for example)[50] in the same brown ink as the ruled lines (there is another instance in the fr. 24391 copy of Hesdin, *La Prise amoureuse*); similarly 'chant' occurs in black ink in the margin on fol. 3v in Brussels, Bibliothèque Royale, 10747, a copy of the *Miracles*. Otherwise, rubrics and headings for the songs (usually 'Canchon', sometimes, more specifically, 'balade', 'rondel' etc.) tend to be written into the body of the text as in manuscripts of the *Castelain de Couci, Cleomadés, Meliacin*, the prose *Violette, La Prise amoureuse* and *Le Parfait du paon*. The writing of 'chanson', 'prouerbe', and so on by the large number of interpolated refrains and proverbs in the glossing text of the *Traduction d'Ovide* has more of this labelling function. These forms of verbal recognition of refrains and other song genres act as examples not just of simple visual highlighting of the presence of a song but of an incipient kind of commentary, one that comes to be more fully articulated in the Machaut and Froissart manuscripts. It is characteristic of the latter to have frequent rubrics: lyrics (both those set into narrative and in separate groups) are given generic titles ('balade', 'rondeau', 'chanson royal'), usually set on a separate line within a column and sometimes in the margin as well (as in fr. 881), and there are frequent summarising headings in the narrative *dits*.[51]

The range of types of textual marker given to the songs in these manuscripts is remarkably extensive. Clearly, the physical activity of writing involved the scribes in many decisions about how to place the songs, which they carried out with recourse to various framing, signalling and labelling devices. The context for the type of sign chosen varies, presumably according to the training and background of the individual scribe and his perception of the kind of work he is copying, so that at times the decisions owe more to chansonnier layout, and at others to the writing of sermons or the production of chant books. Perhaps the strongest impression, however, is the flexibility of many of these forms of *mise-en-page*: in many we are seeing newly adapted copying procedures, as well as old signs given new meaning.

In conclusion, any attempt to understand the significance of music in these narrative contexts for song must take account of the specialist nature of music copying, and the patchiness of its survival. Enough survives, nonetheless, to suggest that music was widely expected to play a part in the performed and written character of a work. The dominance of Arras in encouraging new work with a strongly dramatic flavour and stimulating new ways of recording it in writing, may be singled out as an important factor in the changing trends of song, with the refrain provoking the greatest ingenuity of design. Further aspects of *mise-en-page* indicate that the expectations attaching to song were complex and various. There is a general desire to give visual emphasis to songs, to note their generic distinctiveness, and to assert their authoritative status. Different (though not mutually exclusive) traditions of copying – the monastic, urban, aristocratic and academic – leave their traces across the manuscripts: collectively they attest to the variety of processes by which a performed text acquires a written identity.[52] The manuscripts are not static witnesses to certain fixed and specifiable assumptions in the author or audience, but more like (arbitrarily chosen) snapshots of a continuous process. In that process, new forms of composition and interpretation are made possible and brought into being by new forms of *mise-en-page*. Manuscripts offer different views of a work, and perhaps, in their inconsistencies, different ways of realising it. The very instances of inconsistency and ambiguity reveal that the physical process of writing does not merely register perceptions of genre and sound passively, but it also materially alters them. Placing song in the midst of narrative prompts scribes and their audiences into rethinking how song and speech might be distinguished, and indeed whether they should be distinguished. Signs of this deliberation are evident across a whole spectrum of thirteenth- and early fourteenth-century manuscripts.

II

Chant/fable: *Aucassin et Nicolette*

The work with perhaps the highest claim to exclusivity in medieval French is the thirteenth-century *cantefable*, *Aucassin et Nicolette*. Even this felicitously appropriate term – *cantefable* – is a coinage private to the work, and however evocative, was not taken up (it seems) by any other writer. Later commentators have clung to the term as the only way to describe this short narrative, written in sections of alternating sung verse (*laisses*) and recited prose, in which two lovers eventually succeed in overcoming the obstacles (variously racial, religious, social and geographical) to their marriage. Nothing quite like it appears to exist. There is almost nothing else written in strictly alternating verse and prose in French in the thirteenth century, and the few examples in Latin do not form a straightforward parallel.[1] The musical notation for the verse *laisses* provided in the unique manuscript further contributes to the work's distinctiveness. Other French and Latin verse narratives have musical interludes, but none has any in the form of a *laisse*, and none with the same kind of melody. No other *laisse*-type melody precisely parallels the one in *Aucassin*. And again, while there are similarities between the plot elements of *Aucassin* and some other romances, *Aucassin* does not compare directly with them: its form, brevity and spare, irreverent tone set it apart.

The difficulty of locating *Aucassin et Nicolette* generically is compounded by its mode of survival. It exists in just one, fairly grubby late thirteenth-century manuscript (BN fr. 2168, fols. 70r–80v), without any illustrations or other signs of wealth. There are no direct clues as to its authorship, date or provenance: the dialect presents conflicting signals, and in any case there is no way of knowing if it represents the author's. Yet *Aucassin* evidently has much in common with some of the other contexts for song I have been examining in this book. I will be arguing here that it stands as paradigmatic of the kinds of issue raised by generically ambitious thirteenth-century writing. One reason for this is located in the manuscript, in the idiosyncrasies of its character and layout. The following account will review the work's hybrid features, reflecting in detail on the tantalisingly cryptic implications of its unique manuscript witness.

The most original characteristic of *Aucassin* – aside from its eclectic plot – concerns the disposition of the narrative into alternating prose and verse. There are forty-one sections altogether, and the work begins and ends with a *laisse*.[2] The sections vary considerably in length: from ten to forty-two lines in the *laisses* and from twelve to eighty-nine in prose. What kind of formal balance is struck between prose and verse, and how is it distinguished? Both verse and prose are constructed of monologues and dialogues as well as third-person narration: nonetheless, monologue is far more common in the *laisses* than in the prose sections (twelve *laisses* contain monologue compared to three prose sections), and conversely dialogue is a far greater element in the prose than in verse (sixteen prose sections compared to four *laisses*).[3] If this seems to imply that there is a 'lyric' concentration on the first person in the verse sections, then it is important also to notice that the *laisses* are far from irrelevant to the narrative: around ten contain narrative information not present in the prose, and hence are indispensable to the plot. Prose and verse, as Jean Trotin has shown, are tightly linked throughout, often reinforcing each other through partial repetition or parallel allusions.[4]

To understand the form of *Aucassin* we also need to take account of the music. The *laisses* are composed in seven-syllable lines, linked by assonance, and ending with a single short line of four (or five) syllables. Musically, this is itself a hybrid, in this case between epic and song. On the one hand *laisse* structures are normally only found in the *chansons de geste*, and in longer lines (ten or twelve syllables); on the other, lines of seven syllables occur widely in song, from *grands chants* to *pastourelles* and *lais*. There are further puzzles over the style of the music, and how the work might have been performed. Each prose is headed by the rubric 'or dient et content et fablent' [now they say, tell and narrate]; each *laisse* with 'or se cante' [now it is sung] is immediately followed in turn by

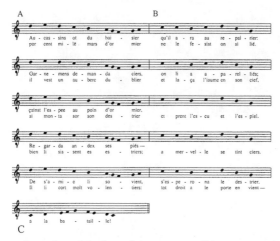

Ex. 11 *Aucassin et Nicolette, laisse* 9: a possible reconstruction.

three musical phrases, one for the final short line of each *laisse*, the first two (in an *ouvert–clos* pattern) for the other lines, (see Ex. 11).

The type of melody is not easy to place. Surviving examples of non-strophic narrative melody are so rare that it is hard to judge whether this one is typical of *laisse*-type melodies (that is, the kind of tune to which the *chansons de geste* were sung) or whether it is distinctive to *Aucassin*.[5] In fact, the closest parallels are with *lais*: the second phrase of the *Aucassin* melody is almost identical to one in the anonymous *Lai des Amants*, and several other *lais*, like *Aucassin*, have tri-partite melodies.[6] We have to imagine some flexibility in performance, however, since, in contrast to the *lais*, which unfold in a linear, sequential structure, many of the *Aucassin laisses* do not fit a single sequence of repetition in the melody. Thus although the simplest hypothesis about the musical structure is that phrase A and phrase B alternate up to the introduction of phrase C in the final short line, this does not necessarily fit the verbal structure of each *laisse*. Many have an odd number of seven-syllable lines, and, in addition, the syntax sometimes closes on what would be an 'open' phrase, or vice versa. A singer would have to tailor an individual pattern of repetition among the three phrases to each particular *laisse*.[7]

The physical transmission of the *cantefable* raises further intriguing questions (see Fig. 10). The rubrics are highly unusual examples of specific performance instructions: as Grace Frank pointed out long ago, they seem to act as cues to two kinds of performer, one reciting, and

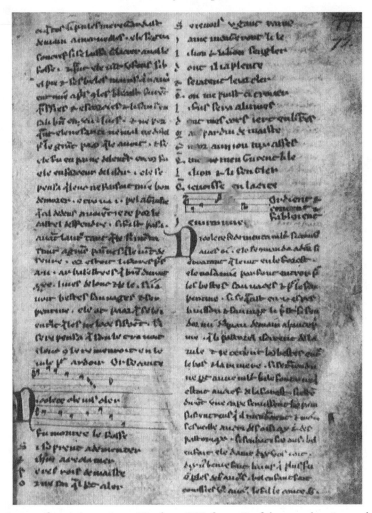

10 A page from *Aucassin et Nicolette*, BN fr. 2168, fol. 75 r, showing a *laisse* flanked by two prose sections. Three sections of music are provided, two at the start, and the third at the end of the *laisse*, together with the rubrics 'Or se cante' for the *laisse* and 'Or dient & content & fabloient' for the prose.

one singing.[8] The grammatical distinction in number between 'or se cante' and 'or dient et content et fablent' is ambiguous, especially as it is repeated through the entire work: it could mean that there was more than one performer of the prose sections, but only one singer. In fact, the passive form of 'or se cante' blurs this distinction. It is also surprising to find the music copied out for each *laisse*: music scribes in other contexts rarely write out musical repeats.

The presence of the rubrics may be one reason why *Aucassin* has attracted so much modern interest. No other vernacular narrative gives music so unambiguous a role, and therefore makes it so unavoidable a fact of the work's structure. Our reactions to all the other distinctive aspects of *Aucassin* cannot but include its character as a work half spoken and half sung, which gives it a kind of unique awkwardness for modern readers accustomed to think of narrative and music as mutually exclusive. Yet, as we have seen, narratives with musical interludes were well known in the thirteenth century, particularly in the Arras region. The date, character and layout of the manuscript, its lack of pretension, its neat but unglamorous staves and notation all align it with a work such as *Renart le Nouvel*. It would not be surprising if *Aucassin*, as well as *Renart le Nouvel*, were a *puy* production.[9] Comparison with the manuscripts of such narratives suggests that one reason for the almost pedantic music copying in fr. 2168 was the sheer novelty of combining words and music in this way: the pressure to invent new kinds of layout gives many of them, as I have discussed, an improvisatory or uncertain air. In this case, the scribe, conscious of the work's idiosyncratic character, may have felt that he could take no chances with his readers' expectations about how the *laisses* were to be performed.

Yet as ever, *Aucassin* fails to sit neatly within any one explanation. Other narratives with music, however important a context, throw up further aspects of its distinctiveness. One way in which *Aucassin* revises categories differently from other mixed verse–verse narratives is that it cuts the division between song and narrative differently. Despite its many links with both romance and song genres, and with works which combine romance and song, *Aucassin* is not a work in which song is set into narrative. Instead, it is structured around two different means of articulating narrative: through verse and prose, and through song and speech. The key principle in *Aucassin* is one not of hierarchy but strict alternation, in which an expectation is set up of a regular division of labours between one narrative mode and another. Structurally, the *romans à chansons* possess greater disturbance and irregularity than *Aucassin*. Songs are rarely set into thirteenth-century narratives at predictable intervals, and even though other kinds of ordering principle such as plot motivation and structure may apply, it is not possible to anticipate the degree and type of citation in any one work. By contrast, although the length of the verse and prose sections in *Aucassin* is irregular, the principle of alternation remains intact in a way that sanctions the disruptions of form and performance style.

Aucassin et Nicolette is recognisably part of a thirteenth-century predilection for questioning categories. The regular alternation between verse and prose causes each way of presenting the work to be examined through the other, particularly when one section reiterates or re-presents another. The result is not just that the work is full of internal structural patterns and connections, but also that the constant switch to a new mode imposes on the audience the need to consider the status of that mode. Narrative is no longer allowed to stand as a kind of neutral, all-embracing way of writing, but is constantly qualified by the presence of the verse *laisses*, which in their formal and aural difference reveal narrative as rhetoric, as merely one discourse among several.

The regular oscillation between performance styles is thus more than a superficial or decorative feature of the work; it marks a radical and reiterated sense of hiatus which causes the genre of the work to appear to be split in two. From this point of view, it should not perhaps surprise us that the performance rubrics in the manuscript are either so detailed or so prominent, for they are an effort to articulate *Aucassin*'s most crucial characteristic. Moreover, their very idiosyncrasy is a sign of the strains involved in presenting this fundamentally double text in writing.

As a work that sets narrative against narrative, it follows that the musical sections in *Aucassin* are a form not of 'lyric' but narrative melody. Narrative melody is a particularly volatile and hybrid form. Moreover, as I will shortly argue, narrative in the *Roman de Fauvel*, for example, is far from stable in its contrast with song. The wider implications of such formal tensions between narrative and song will be considered later in the book. In this respect, too, *Aucassin* belongs to a much broader process of cultural questioning about genre in the thirteenth century. Here I want to bring comparison back to an Arras work, Adam's *Le Jeu de Robin et de Marion*, and to the genre of the *pastourelle*, also a quintessentially Arras genre.

In *Robin et Marion*, as we saw, the contrast between narrative as a sung and as a spoken form is developed with astonishing originality to express the kinds of characteristic opposition that constitute the *pastourelle* model. These include many kinds of formal, generic and social differences between, for example, *pastourelle* and *bergerie*, knight and peasant, male and female, narrative and lyric, spoken dialogue and song. Like *Robin et Marion*, *Aucassin* is a work founded on a pattern of structural doubling.[10] *Aucassin* has a central group of verse and prose sections that draw on *pastourelle* motifs. There are two major encounters with shepherds, played out in the *cantefable* first with Nicolette and then with Aucassin as he goes in search of Nicolette in the forest. In *Aucassin*, as in *Robin et Marion*, the contrast between sung and spoken dialogue is subtly allied to issues of social and sexual rivalry. Nicolette's meeting with the shepherds effectively pre-empts Aucassin's, so that he is left looking rather foolish when he tries to engage them in conversation. One particular source of awkwardness concerns the medium of this conversation. The shepherds have been instructed by Nicolette to give Aucassin a message: they oblige when Aucassin happens to ride past, but insist on speaking rather than singing the message.

Their obstinacy draws attention to the way in which the author has chosen to articulate this pair of scenes through the verse and prose sections. At first sight, the choice is far from straightforward. For instance, one might expect the first allusion to *pastourelle* to be in verse, but in fact, it is conveyed in prose (Section XVLI). It is only at the start of the second encounter, with Aucassin, that we are given a kind of *pastourelle* song in verse (Section XXI).

> Or s'asanlent pastouret,
> Esmerés et Martinés,
> Früelins et Johanés,
> Robeçons et Aubriés.
> Li uns dist: 'Bel conpaignet,
> Dix aït Aucasinet,
> voire a foi! le bel vallet;
> et le mescine au corset
> qui avoit le poil blondet,
> cler le vis et l'oeul vairet,
> ki nos dona denerés
> dont acatrons gastelés,
> gaïnes et coutelés,

flaüsteles et cornés,
maçüeles et pipés,
Dix le garisse!'[11]

Now the shepherds are gathered together, Esmeret and Martinet,
Früelin and Johanet, Robeçon and Aubriet. One said: 'Fair friends,
may God aid young Aucassin, yes, indeed, the handsome youth; and
the girl with the fine figure who had blonde hair, bright face and
sparkling eyes, who gave us pennies to buy little cakes, sheaths and
penknives, flutes and horns, clubs and pipes, may God protect her!'

The *laisse* acts its part as a *pastourelle* with brilliant ease: crowded
with *pastourelle* names ('Robeçons et Aubriés') and objects ('flaüsteles
et cornés, / maçüeles et pipés'), it could pass for the first stanza of a
chanson. The irony is that when Aucassin asks them to repeat this song,
he is speaking in prose as part of the next section. The shepherds could
not comply with his request without breaking the formal pattern of the
work: in that sense he is asking the impossible. Their stubborn refusal to
sing ('chanter'), even though they are happy to narrate ('conter'), could
thus be regarded as a simple formal expedient. But it also refers to the
nature of their original promise to Nicolette, made in prose:

'Sire, les deniers prenderons nos, mais ce ne vos canterai mie, car j'en
ai juré; mais je le vos conterai, se vos volés.
De par Diu, fait Aucassins, encor aim je mix conter que nient.'
(Section XXII, 23–27)

'Lord, we will take the money, but I will never sing it for you, as I
have sworn not to; however I will tell you the story, if you wish'. 'For
God's sake', said Aucassin, 'I would rather hear it told than nothing.'

They did not swear to Nicolette that they would never sing her message;
they seem instead to show a kind of legalistic adherence to the fact
that they first heard the message in prose, and that to offer it in any
other form would be a kind of betrayal. The point is not the peasants'
psychology, but how insistently they introduce a debate which touches
on the central issues of the *cantefable*, its disposition into verse and
prose. There seems to be a kind of joke here – caught in the punning
word-play between *conterai* and *canterai* – about the hybrid form, about
the untranslatability of each medium into the other. Like many other

thirteenth-century authors, the author of *Aucassin* chooses pastoral, an intellectual model of displacement, to express a central theme of division by means of a divided mode of performance: prose and verse, speech and song.

Such explicit comment on the media through which *Aucassin* is performed brings us back full circle to Jean Renart, where the generic opposition between *chant* and *conte* is so prominently established.[12] I want to finish with one more passage which takes us to the heart of *Aucassin's* formal role in thirteenth-century 'mixed' genres. This is the scene where Nicolette plucks up courage to jump down from the castle walls rather than risk being caught and killed by the servants of Aucassin's father. The author greatly elaborates the fear and difficulty of her escape: she has a long monologue in Section XVII in which she gives vent to her fears about the wild animals known to frequent the forest, and the jump itself leaves her bleeding and bruised. The extent to which this transition is made to appear as difficult and momentous as possible could again be said to refer back to the fundamental topos of the *cantefable*: which is not just that it consists of two types of medium, but that its *raison d'être* is to make the transition, repeatedly and insistently, from one to the other. Nicolette's lingering on the boundary demonstrates with a symbolic potency the primary preoccupations of many thirteenth-century authors. Such authors are interested not just in creating hybrid genres, but in developing a keener recognition of the kinds of boundary that enable generic distinctions to be made, such as the sung and the spoken, verse and prose, forms, registers (popular, courtly, clerical), the visual and the aural. Reinforcing this perception is their determination to find out what takes place at these frontiers and what happens when they are crossed. Nicolette succeeds in going over the boundary; and there is a sense in which *Aucassin et Nicolette* also surpasses boundaries by being so resistant to comparison. Perhaps, after all, its most distinctive contribution to thirteenth-century writing is the clarity with which its author poses questions about what lies behind and beyond the crossing.

Writing music, writing poetry:
Le Roman de Fauvel in Paris BN fr. 146

Every text has its limits, every page its margins.[1] The celebrated Bibliothèque Nationale fr. 146 version of *Le Roman de Fauvel* at once revels in and confounds such boundaries. It represents the most remarkable attempt to combine poetry and music in any single manuscript of the thirteenth or fourteenth centuries, both in the sheer number and kind of song genres added to the narrative, and in its visual and conceptual virtuosity as a written artefact. The manuscript is extravagant in the most literal sense. In keeping with its topic of vicious excess, its production wanders from the path of honest moderation. Reading the book involves two contradictory sensations: that of a succession of pages crowded with notation, illumination and text, and of a *mise-en-page* which controls and contains all these elements. The supreme visual shock and power of the manuscript is achieved not by a brazen display of wealth and magnificence, but by a creative tension between the excesses of the material and the finesse of the design.

The original *roman* (written *c.* 1310–1314 in two books by the Parisian notary Gervès du Bus)[2] survives in thirteen manuscripts, and narrates the career of a fawn-coloured (*fauve*) horse, Fauvel, who represents acronymically the vices of *flaterie, avarice, vilanie, varieté, envie* and *lacheté*. Fauvel, flattered by all ranks and estates of people, religious and secular, rules the royal household in a reversal of God's order and justice. In this unique fourteenth version (*c.* 1316–18), the narrative is amplified both textually and musically by one Chaillou de Pesstain, possibly another notary working in the royal chancery.[3] The most substantial additions are made in Book 2, where Fauvel attempts to woo Fortune in an audacious bid to create stability for his wicked preeminence, is harshly rejected by her, and instead marries Vaine-Gloire.

Great set-pieces, elaborated by music, words and images, include a long description of the wedding feast, a wild charivari that takes place in the streets, a tournament between the Virtues and Vices, and a Fountain of Youth in which Fauvel and his brood of little fauvels seek to regenerate themselves in perpetuity.

The writing of the book draws attention to the book's own boundaries, to the physical limits imposed by the edges of a page or the outline of a drawing, and to the lines of demarcation between the written forms of word, music and image. To a remarkable degree, the work is directly constituted by its physical appearance.[4] Page openings are carefully planned around sections of original text, grouped in prominent positions at the top or bottom of a column or in a single column.[5] Chaillou de Pesstain appears to have conceived of his amplifications not, in general, as a matter of revising or expanding from line to line but as a series of blocks filling in spaces opened up in the original narrative. The musical expatiation is so thorough that no opening in *Fauvel* is without music, and two are exclusively given over to musical notation.

Such radical treatment of narrative, such questioning of its aural integrity, is symptomatic of the ambitious revision of categories that permeates the book. By making free play with its visual structure as a means of articulating so complex a structure of communication, fr. 146 examines the natural limits not only of what can be rendered in written signs, but also of how to represent the performable. The boundaries explored in *Fauvel* include aural time and comprehension, and visual space, dimension and proportion, as well as the verbal and musical boundaries of form, structure and scale. *Fauvel* in fr. 146 puts a discussion about genre and generic divisions into new terms. It stands out in the way it articulates such discussion through what one might call the texture of the book.

This may be better appreciated by recognising the importance of *Fauvel* in the history of change in French lyric. Boundaries can be determined only by being crossed, and a historical as well as literal characteristic of the interpolated *Fauvel* is that it moves, on every page, from one side of a boundary to another. This period sees a whole edifice of radical changes in which the fixing of new forms is superimposed on the old. The *grand chant courtois* of the trouvères is displaced from its former position of dominance by the kinds of genre that were formerly lower in style, the mobile dance-song forms of the *rondet de carole*, which gain new life as the *formes fixes* of rondeau, ballade and *chanson balladée* or virelai as it later comes to be known.[6] Underlying this shift are several profound innovations in musical compositional techniques that occur in the midst of a crucial period of transition between older (*ars antiqua*) and newer (*ars nova*) forms of musical notation. In brief, lyric genres (from the point of view of both music and text) undergo changes in form, in degree of linear complexity, in musical rhythm, in the relations between words and music, in their cultural register, and in the whole character of their musical transcription and hence their manuscript layout.[7]

In all these areas, fr. 146 provides crucial documentation. It is the only extant source of French polyphonic music (apart from a few short collections) to survive between the late thirteenth-century motet collections and the *ars nova* manuscripts of the 1360s and 1370s. Vital though this would make it on any reckoning, its character as a compendium of generic transformation gives it a symbolic status in this period of change. In its pages we see old pieces transformed from one genre to another, old texts given new verbal as well as new musical colouring, and old forms of notation given a new meaning and flexibility.[8] Over and above this, it presents this complex musical information in the form of an interpolated narrative rather than a conventional chansonnier. This embeds the topoi of transformation and transition within the structure of the overall compilation, so that we are drawn to consider the nature of generic change by the work's own shifts between narrative and song, speech and music. Thus Chaillou de Pesstain not only records in writing a historical moment of generic change, he enacts this process of change in the very pattern and disposition of the writing. This chapter seeks to unravel some of these signs of change by focusing on two specific moments of transition within *Fauvel*, the central semi-lyric ensembles. These hybrid pieces raise fundamental questions about the categorisation of verse and narrative in medieval French writing. Their *mise-en-page* articulates the transitional, hybrid character not only of these pieces, but also the *Fauvel* book itself.[9]

It may be helpful to begin by giving some sense of where the semi-lyric ensembles belong in the larger collection of inset material. The detail of interpolation in *Fauvel* is of immense complexity, and much remains still to be unravelled. Throughout, a process of inventive rewriting is evident. Among the extraordinarily large number of musical pieces, individual pieces are transformed from one genre to another; voice parts are added and removed; the rhythm of pieces changed; a strophic setting altered into a through-composed one and vice versa; texts parodied and 'fauvelised'; texts set to music which have no other surviving generic history of being set to music; and new genres recorded for the first time, such as the two so-called 'semi-lyric' pieces and the *sottes chansons* or *fatras*. Categorical revision occurs also in the rampant bilingualism, and in the sheer range and incongruity of the generic juxtapositions, such as the way the *Fauvel* author has chosen to place proses – a genre normally confined to a liturgical context – in the unexpected setting of a satiric romance, and alongside love songs and obscene expostulations. Visual hybridity is expressed repeatedly in the images of Fauvel himself, which veer from showing a horse's head on a human body (in nine pictures) to a human head on a horse's body (eighteen pictures). Disconcertingly, as Michael Camille has argued, these pictures of bestial reversal triumphantly occupy the central spaces of the page unlike many earlier books illustrating animal fables where the pictures of hybridity and monstrous shape shifting tend to be consigned to the margins.[10] This realignment of the central and the marginal is elemental to all aspects of the book.

Although the polyphony in fr. 146 has naturally claimed most attention from modern musicologists, the monophonic repertory is at least as rich a resource of information about generic change in this period. The forty-five monophonic French songs raise particularly acute questions of interpretation. With the exception of some of the refrains, all are unique to this manuscript (in contrast to the Latin-texted pieces which nearly all exist in other sources), and several are the earliest or even the only examples of their kind. In that sense, they appear to testify to a process of change which has already taken place by the time of the copying of the manuscript. Fr. 146 largely records only the new genres of the *formes fixes* and the *lai*, rather than the older *grands chants*, still present, for instance, in Nicole de Margival's early fourteenth-century (?) *Dit de la panthere*. However, certain pieces from fr. 146 are so anomalous in form that the moment of transition is still visible: these include two single-stanza songs, warily classified by modern editors as 'ballades', and the *sottes chançons* or *fatras* that pose several problems of form and structure.[11] The so-called 'semi-lyric' pieces, 'Amour dont tele est la puissance' [Love whose power is so great] and 'Han Diex ou pourrai je trouver' [Oh God, where could I find], constitute a third group. Both 'semi-lyrics' are characterised by their use of independent refrains.[12]

Before analysing these pieces, it is worth noting their location in the structure of the work and the manuscript. They occur in the mid-point of the interpolated narrative: a key structural position. They comprise the first of the 'addicions' announced by the following rubric in the lower half of the central column of fol. 23 v: 'Ci s'ensivent les addicions que mesire Chaillou de Pesstain ha mises en ce livre, oultre les choses dessus dites qui sont en chant' [Here follow the additions that mesire Chaillou de Pesstain has put in this book, not including the pieces already performed which have music]. This rubric has a pivotal role in the interpolated *Fauvel*. Eight lines newly set into the narrative immediately precede it, in which Gervès du Bus is named as the author of the first *roman* (vv. 41–48). The narrative exhibits here an extended moment of hiatus. It signals the point at which Chaillou de Pesstain began to execute his principal work of revision of the existing *roman*. His revision has two distinct stages: in the first book he adds musical pieces (mostly in Latin), but alters the text very little. Within the second book, he not only adds a large number of further pieces but also around 3,000 lines of extra narrative. The most substantial interpolations begin, as signalled by this rubric, with an expansion of Fauvel's attempt to woo Fortune.

At first sight, it is not clear why Chaillou should begin his 'addicions' where he does: he does not base his structural alterations, for instance, around the division between the two books at fol. 11 r. Where sections of text are repeatedly positioned strategically at the edges of a page, it seems especially curious to find so important a rubric buried relatively inconspicuously in the lower half of a central column.[13] However, on one reckoning of the final make-up of the *roman*, this rubric comes at its centre. Fol. 23 v marks the half-way point of the *roman*'s total number of forty-five folios, and the visual centre of this folio falls in the middle of the central column, which is where the lines naming Gervès begin.[14]

Medieval attention to the mid-point of a text is well attested:[15] what is notable here is the emphasis Chaillou gives to the physical form of the text over its conceptual structure, so that the spatial presence of the material book creates a counter structure to the narrative division into books of the original *roman*. The rubric signals various other kinds of division. The double authorial signature has the effect of marking the way in which one author is made to cede to the other: Chaillou, it seems, feels it appropriate to register his presence at this half-way point, perhaps because it draws eloquent attention to the kind of authorial changes he is making in the physical and material articulation of the satire. The transition between authors thus points to the difference between the old *roman* and the new, the former uninterrupted narrative shown to be literally displaced by 'addicions' on a grand scale. But the rubric also signals a change in Chaillou's own techniques of displacement: from a first half in which an existing narrative is (sometimes silently) broken up by musical interpolations that it was never intended to have, the *roman* passes to a second stage in which, by virtue of the added textual material, it is conceived from the outset as hybrid. In order to effect this, Chaillou alerts the reader to the fact that the narrative has itself undergone a generic change from being a satiric allegory to a love narrative with inset verse.

So emphatic an announcement of change and renewal arouses the reader's sense of anticipation about the nature of Chaillou's immediately subsequent 'addicions'. They turn out to comprise an extended ensemble at the centre of which are placed two pieces of seemingly inscrutable generic complexity. Attracting the term 'semi-lyric', neither piece has received much discussion in its own right.[16] Yet together they form part of a larger ensemble which the interpolator has placed at the very heart of the *roman*. As the following analysis argues, this monophonic ensemble, fixed at a key moment of transition within the *roman*, itself constitutes a model for a notion of transition that pervades the entire work.

The ensemble is itself elaborately symmetrical: at the centre is a ballade ('Se j'onques a mon vivant' [If I ever during my life] (fol. 26r)), and adjacent to this a sequence of six-line stanzas; either side of these are arranged the two semi-lyric compositions. These in turn are framed by the two formally anomalous single-stanza songs mentioned earlier; finally, at the outer edge of this widening circle of pieces, come another sequence of six-line stanzas and a group of *formes fixes*.

This great wave of interpolated material, rightly described by Nancy Regalado as a 'virtuoso display', creates a complex series of formal curves in which the categories of lyric and narrative constantly fluctuate and develop. *Formes fixes* provide fixed points at either edge of the ensemble; within it, however, few things are what they seem, so that on the one hand the narrative role of the octosyllabic couplets is both interrupted by refrains and usurped by long strings of *sixains*, and on the other lyric forms mutate and, in the case of the piece beginning 'Han Diex ou pourrai je trouver', fragment.

The role of the refrains is crucial to any understanding of transition in *Fauvel*. It is characteristic of the copious nature of *Fauvel* that it should contain so many varieties of refrain-citation. My catalogue, which numbers fifty-five refrains in total, demonstrates at a glance that refrains may represent, in different contexts, a repeated formal device within a lyric genre, a structural unit within a motet, an autonomous citation in narrative, a verbal or musical fragment, or a proverbial or visual motto. Unusually, *Fauvel* presents all these citational practices within a single work, sometimes, in a powerfully graphic manoeuvre, allowing the same refrain to be cited in more than one way ('Han Diex' is one of the most notable examples). Thus as well as a number of *formes fixes* in each of the major types – rondeau, ballade and 'virelai' – *Fauvel* includes thirty-six independent refrains set directly into the narrative. Among those that are interpolated into the first semi-lyric *dit*, six out of thirteen are widely attested in other contexts, with concordances among a range of further narratives, motets, chansons and rondeaux. This draws attention to a further idiosyncrasy of *Fauvel*, in the way that it includes a mixture of well-known refrains alongside *unica* and, in particular, *unica* which form a new sub-genre of refrain as *sotte chanson*. Altogether, *Fauvel* shows, in disconcerting juxtapositions, refrains working within narrative, within lyric, and within the semi-lyric and the semi-narrative.

The key areas of transition occur in the two extended pieces with inset refrains. The first, 'Amour dont tele est la puissance', described in the *roman* as a *dit*[17] is essentially a *dit à refrains*, on the model of Jacquemart Giélée's *Renart le Nouvel* (with which it has three refrains in common), Tibaut's *Roman de la poire* or Baudouin de Condé's *Li Prison d'amours*. All of these works, like *Fauvel*, survive with music for the refrains, yet all are far more lengthy narratives than this passage of some 540 lines. Analogues more comparable in length are the *saluts* and *complaintes*, though none of these occurs with music.[18] The *dit*, whose opening line is signalled by an enlarged initial, is divided into thirteen approximately equal sections of around forty lines, each of which concludes with a refrain. It is difficult to find a precise precedent for this: whereas many narratives have sections interrupted frequently by refrains, the spacing of the refrains is usually quite irregular; one of the few exceptions is in the opening court scene of the *Roman de la violette*, discussed in Chapter 2, where the narrative cues in between a series of seven refrains are each of five lines.[19] The *saluts* in which refrains occur at regular intervals are strophic rather than narrative. None of these types of piece, then, quite shares the mixture of regularity and irregularity of the *Fauvel dit* structure. On the other hand, the *saluts* provide instances of formal transpositions and of the setting of strophic songs alongside refrains which are close to the kinds of movement that take place across the whole ensemble in *Fauvel* from fol. 23v to fol. 27v.

Perhaps the closest formal analogy is provided by two pieces by Jehannot de Lescurel that are copied into a later section of the codex, the *diz entez sus refroiz de rondeaux* [dits grafted on refrains of rondeaux], as they are termed in the index. These, 'Gracieuse, faitisse et sage' [Gracious, delicate and wise] and 'Gracieux temps est quant rosier' [In the charming season when the rose bushes] consist of nine-line strophic sections, each terminating with a different refrain. The thirteen sections in the Fauvel *dit enté* are too irregular in length to be considered strophic, yet frequently enough divided by refrains to make their allegiance to narrative only slight. The piece thus falls directly between the strophic and the non-strophic, and in that sense between lyric and narrative. In addition, through the fact that, like the Lescurel *dits*, the refrains have musical notation but the intervening 'narrative' sections do not, the performing medium of the *dit* oscillates between the spoken and the sung. Semi-lyric, from this point of view, has two senses: a formal category that is located somewhere between lyric and narrative, and a hybrid character in performance that crosses between song and speech.

The second semi-lyric piece in *Fauvel*, 'Han Diex ou pourrai je trouver', functions quite differently from 'Amour dont tele est la puissance'. Briefly, it consists in a pre-existent fourteen-line motetus part that is split into consecutive fragments, each of which is used as a 'refrain' at the end of a six-line strophe that amplifies, purely textually, each so-called 'refrain'. This procedure may be compared to the complex shattering and recombining of narrative and lyric elements in Baude de la Quarière's *'Bele Aelis'*.[20]

> *Ainssi en moi choisist et prent*
> *Sanz parler a prevost n'a maire.*
> S'ainssi la bele sanz reprouche,
> Douce de vis, riant de bouche,
> En moi choisist et prent sanz bourde,
> Sanz parler, quar en riens ne touche
> A prevost n'a maire, et je couche
> Ma vie en li, que qui m'en sourde.[21]

> *Thus she takes and chooses me without speaking to a provost or mayor.* Thus the beautiful blameless one, sweet-faced, with a laughing mouth, chooses and takes me not in jest, without speaking (for it doesn't concern anyone) to a provost or mayor, and I lay my life next to hers, whatever blame may result from it.

A further curious feature of this dismembered voice part is that six of its lines, which then come to be turned into refrains, are identical with part of the fourth strophe of Nevelon Amion *Dit d'amour*.[22] This spiralling process of citation continues in fr. 146 itself, for one of these newly created refrain lines is in turn quoted in Jehannot de Lescurel's *dit enté* 'Gracieus temps est' [It is the charming season], just as the first line of the piece ('Han Diex ou pourrai je trouver') acts as the first line in the *enté* structure of a *sotte chanson* given later in the manuscript. The whole voice part, finally, is cited *in absentia* as it were by the motet *Ve qui gregi deficiunt / Trahunt in precipicia / Quasi non ministerium / Displicebat ei*, given here in a four-part version in which the French text is replaced by one in Latin.[23] This somewhat bewildering tissue of citations demonstrates the means by which several of the *Fauvel* interpolations are constructed.

These formal anomalies are expressed by means of a carefully conceived visual display. The ensemble begins with 'Providence, la senee' [Providence, the wise], a virelai (in form) described in the text as a 'balade'. This is followed by a formally anomalous single-stanza song, 'En chantant me veul complaindre' [In song I want to complain]. Halfway down the first column of fol. 24r, and introduced by a picture of Fauvel addressing Fortune, is placed the introduction to the first semi-lyric (see Fig. 11 (a)). The semi-lyric itself has pride of place on the page at the top of the centre column, with another picture and a large initial. Both picture and initial are unusual: this courtship episode is the only section of the manuscript in which musical interpolations are illustrated, and this size and type of initial occurs elsewhere only to mark the book divisions and the *lai* on fols. 28 *bis* and *ter*. The semi-lyric ('Amour dont tele est la puissance') extends over the next double page-opening and verso of fol. 25, where the last refrain serves as the lower boundary of one page and the upper boundary of the next (fol. 26r), crossing the border between one folio and another. It is worth remarking how the refrains also define the side margins of the semi-lyric, in the way that they frequently break out beyond the edge of the columns.

We have now reached the centre of the ensemble, and this is marked appositely by a true *forme fixe*, the ballade 'Se j'onques a mon vivant', and a frontal picture of Fauvel being crowned as king. From here the narrative octosyllabic couplets are transformed into seventeen *sixains*, each with a flourished initial, which fill the remaining two columns on the page. This allows the next page turning to uncover the second semi-lyric 'Han Diex ou pourrai je trouver' (see Fig. 11 (b)). This, like 'Amour dont tele est la puissance', is given visual prominence by its position on the page and the use of pictures, one at the start and another at the end to frame it. Again, the illumination is unusual, in this case because it is the only occasion in the manuscript where Fauvel is depicted with both his bestial and his human face on the same page. It would be difficult to imagine a more direct way of giving visual support to what must be the most intensely hybrid piece in the entire compilation. Even more so than in the first semi-lyric, the refrains break up the orderliness of the page: varying considerably in length, one dangles over the edge of a column and disturbs the layout of the following strophic text, two others are so brief that they do not fill the line.

Octosyllabic narrative is again suspended after 'Han Diex' in favour of a long sequence of *sixains*: visually the march of initials on the right-hand page matches the crowded array of initials for the semi-lyric on the left. Finally, the whole ensemble (in effect, a single utterance by Fauvel) is brought to an end on fol. 27v with a cluster of *formes fixes*: a second formally unique single-stanza song, two ballades, a 'virelai' and a rondeau, all of which fill the entire page.

11 (a) The first semi-lyric piece, 'Amour dont tele est la puissance', in *Le Roman de Fauvel*, BN fr. 146, fol. 24r, showing two notated refrains. It begins at the top of the middle column, with a picture and enlarged initial.

(b) The second, strophic semi-lyric piece, 'Han Diex ou pourrai je trouver', *Le Roman de Fauvel*, BN fr. 146, fol. 26v, with notated refrains, flanked by two converse pictures of Fauvel first with a horse's head and human body, and second, kneeling before Fortune, with human head and horse's hindquarters.

11 *(cont.)*

The suspension, even cessation, of narrative is characteristic of the ensemble: only twenty lines or so of narrative *rimes plates* occur (as the introduction to 'Amour dont tele est la puissance') in eight pages. The *roman* is effectively ceasing to function as a *roman*, and this takes place through a series of devices of interpolation which have been a characteristic of the *roman* genre for nearly a hundred years. Such a concatenation of interpolations leaves virtually no interstices of narrative to act as a frame for the inset pieces: in that sense the whole ensemble functions as a single lyric interpolation.

We could say, in other words, that lyric takes over as the dominant mode of the ensemble. This is clearly not a simple process, because the sequence offers such an improvisatory play of different and novel forms each merging into each other and yet at same time knocking abruptly against one another. The link between all these dissonant elements is the refrain, for it occurs both in the form of separate citations and as a structural component of the semi-lyrics and the *formes fixes*. Its status in 'Han Diex', in the work that Hoepffner wittily called a *motet farci*, is more difficult to describe. 'Han Diex' seems to turn the grafting procedure inside out. The refrains are not grafted into the work so much as created out of a process of splitting apart another work. The performance of this piece, a curious melée of the spoken and sung, would have a double disjointedness for anyone who knew the original motet, in the way that the original musical frame is broken up by speech. This piece, and 'Amour dont tele est la puissance', together form an extended exploration of the boundaries between song and speech, speech being used to interrupt, yet also to echo and reinforce song. Themselves a mixture of song and speech, the refrains generate a passage of strictly equivocal status at the centre of the *roman*.

Against the very full background of writing in mixed genres in the thirteenth century, Chaillou de Pesstain's version of *Fauvel* seems less singular but all the more hyperbolical. *Fauvel* is part of the large movement towards re-examining and realigning the categories of lyric and narrative that began early in the previous century. The high degree of self-consciousness in the layout of the manuscript, the use of initials, pictures, staves, notation and rubrics to create a complex commentary on the art of categorisation has a much earlier precedent in the *Roman de la poire*, and, as we have seen, is also recognisably part of a process of increasing attention to the mechanics of writing that is prominent among *puy*-inspired authors from the 1270s to 1290s. Similarly, the principle of formal diversity and disjunction is widely explored by thirteenth-century authors, especially through inventive forms of refrain-citation. In many manuscripts before fr. 146 we see scribes and authors working out the implications of setting one genre into another, or of creating liaisons between unlikely partners of text and melody.

At the same time, fr. 146 stands apart from precedent in the sheer density of its inclusiveness: it represents a kind of *summa* of all previous attempts to reflect on generic difference. For this reason, like *Aucassin et Nicolette*, it thus also alerts us to the ways in which writing in mixed genres during the thirteenth century cannot itself be neatly categorised. Any attempt to think of narratives with lyric insertions as a separate tradition has failed to learn, through *Fauvel*, how broad the base of generic experimentation is in the period, how wide a definition of 'narrative' and 'lyric' is reached, and how it includes melodies as well as poetic texts, and melodies and texts in many kinds of relation to each other.

The interpolated *Fauvel* is an archetype of transition. A catalogue of 'addicions' records multiple acts of transformation across the border from the *ars antiqua* to the *ars nova*. In the heart of the work, Chaillou sets down his signature to mark the place of an interpolation within an interpolation, a transition within a transition, in the form (or half-form) of the semi-lyric. The semi-lyrics are themselves structured around the key transitional element of the refrain, and even this element undergoes transition as it mutates from the first semi-lyric to the second.

Both semi-lyric compositions in *Fauvel* are marginal works that modern editors have found difficult to classify and even to print. Such an ensemble, at the heart of the *roman*, mimics in smaller compass the techniques of the whole, profoundly concerned as they are with scrutinising the nature of boundaries – musical, textual, visual and spatial. The refrain, at the heart of the ensemble, is a kind of synecdoche, in a double sense: it figures as a part for the whole precisely because it is also representing the whole for part. This is shown most clearly in 'Han Diex' where the sense of a song as a whole, through a process of deliberate fragmentation, creates many smaller units of song that each begin to function autonomously. In *Fauvel*, and especially in these central semi-lyric clusters, lyric turns into narrative and narrative turns into lyric quite literally before our eyes. Physical signs of the regeneration of lyric within narrative, and of the disorienting effect of lyric upon narrative are nowhere manifest more clearly than in the complexly balanced visual display in the pages of fr. 146. The crisis of genre represented in *Fauvel* shows the course of lyric and narrative writing to be changing irreversibly.

Fauvel offers tantalising suggestions about the radical changes in lyric form of the early fourteenth century. It represents a pattern for change in the sense of being both model and witness. Apart from this central

ensemble and the later group of *sottes chansons* (in many ways comparable
to the semi-lyrics), the corpus of French monophonic songs contained
within *Fauvel* is constituted by uniquely early attestations of the new
currency of fixed forms. In the centre of his book, Chaillou creates
space for a transitional passage in which the process of change in lyric
form is at once closely scrutinised and painstakingly manifested. He thus
registers, with extraordinary sensitivity, a moment of cultural transition.
Through its movement from one half-fixed genre to another, the semi-
lyric ensemble shows in miniature a gradual fixing of form. The wayward
progress of the refrain through the central interpolated sequence in
Fauvel finishes with it incorporated and contained within the *formes
fixes*: rondeau, virelai (at least in prototype) and ballade. Two decades
later, in Machaut's *Remede de Fortune*, the independent refrain is given
one last utterance (without music) as the final item in a list of newly
defined lyric forms. By this citation, Machaut recognises the historic
identity of the refrain, and yet by categorising it so consummately, sets
it in amber, as a dead letter. In *Fauvel*, by contrast, the refrain retains its
power to move, as a form of writing poised on the border.

PART V

Lyric and narrative

13

The two *Roses*: Machaut and
the thirteenth century

It is widely acknowledged that with Guillaume de Machaut vernacular song enters a new phase. His *lais*, rondeaux and ballades have an elaboration and artistic seriousness that sets them apart from thirteenth-century examples. As many have remarked, Machaut's works herald a new kind of relationship between lyric and narrative, a new kind of relationship between music and poetry, and a new vision of authorship and of writing.

So many claims to novelty need some clarification from both a musical and a literary perspective. It is not possible, for instance, to see Machaut as creating any of the genres in which he writes. The paucity of surviving music from the early decades of the fourteenth century makes Machaut's works stand out in isolated, brilliant prominence, but indicates (even in scattered and sketchy ways) that innovations were already well in train. The shadowy figure of Philippe de Vitry looms over these decades with a portentous spectrality as the composer most likely to have created a musical revolution.[1]

Nonetheless, by the time Machaut comes to compose his first mixed lyric-narrative work, the *Remede de Fortune* (*c.* 1340), change has been signalled and fresh claims made. The *Remede* makes such a statement more emphatically than any other of his works. Hoepffner was the first to point out that Machaut creates something like a *summa* of the love lyric by including one example each of a range of lyric types, carefully defined and presented (see Fig. 12).[2] The *Remede* could equally be called a catalogue of lyric citations, or even a bibliography of lyric. In this narrative the ability to define lyric is itself a feat of accomplishment; it gives the impression that a new kind of assertiveness about lyric is possible. The *Remede*'s act of citation functions as a revelation: here,

12 *Lay*, with notation, in Guillaume de Machaut, *Remede de Fortune*, BN fr. 1586, fol. 26r, with picture showing the Lover writing on a scroll.

Machaut seems to say, the *ars nova* has happened. Whether or not the *Remede* truly defines new forms of writing, the work is an act of definition and on these grounds alone, it creates a new status for lyric and narrative.

Yet it is not merely as an exemplary exemplifier that Machaut has so high a niche in fourteenth-century aesthetics. His most important role lies in his technical mastery of poetry and music together. Only Gautier de Coinci and Adam de la Halle approach his technical range, while yet falling far short of his musical versatility. This makes him a natural point of culmination for an argument about the ways poetry and music are combined in thirteenth- and fourteenth-century France; it also makes him a special, even disturbing case. Machaut's art creates a new set of relationships between poetry and music, yet, ironically, the new terms that Machaut defines prove hard to repeat.[3]

In the last part of this book I consider how changes between Renart's *Rose* and Machaut's *dits* might be characterised and explained. I investigate how song and narrative mutually influence and modify each other, and how close the connections are between music and text. Previous studies of the period have tended to blur formal categories and describe a trajectory of change in music or in literature, but not in both. Yet change takes place on a wide variety of fronts in song, in narrative and in musical style and technique. We need to appreciate the nature of change on a broader front than hitherto, and especially to consider together, rather than in separate categories, the interrelations between song and narrative, music and poetry. This will involve developing the discussion in earlier chapters on the kinds of distinction medieval authors make between one genre and another.

Jacqueline Cerquiglini distinguishes between two main kinds of relationship between lyric and narrative: where the lyric insertion functions as a citation (*collage*), and where it functions 'comme une matrice du texte' (*montage*).[4] Her prime example of *collage* is Renart's *Rose*; of *montage* Machaut's *Le Voir Dit*. If, however, we make the *Remede* the centre of comparison, then the contrast is less clear. For the *Remede* looks remarkably like a thirteenth-century romance. It is not, of course, an entirely simple matter to summarise the relation of the *Remede* to earlier narratives. One of Machaut's most widely acknowledged debts is to the *Roman de la rose* of Guillaume de Lorris and Jean de Meun.[5] However, compared to Nicole de Margival or Jehan Acart de Hesdin, Machaut uses allegory only lightly; instead, his *dits* have a more episodic structure, based around scenes of dancing, conversation and feasting that are highly reminiscent of the society romances of Renart, Gerbert de Montreuil, Jacques Bretel or Jakemés. Another instance of return to this kind of romance is his use of song: the *Remede*, especially, is structured around long, multi-strophic citations rather than clusters of short refrains creating, as in Renart, a broad boundary between lyric and narrative rather than a sequence of constant, brief interruptions and alternations.

Put crudely, the *Remede*, like Tibaut's *Roman de la poire*, is the product of two *Roses*. The *Remede* is a cross between allegorical clarity, didacticism, romance realism and formal variety. The *Voir Dit* takes up all these features but, more like *Fauvel* than Renart's *Rose* in its tendency towards rampant hybridity, casts new light on narrative and lyric again. In short, the *Remede* and the *Voir Dit* are not merely 'lyric insertion' narratives. Nor are they, in Huot's homogenising term 'lyrical narratives'. Each is a crucial defining point both for the nature of lyric and for the nature of narrative.

Any discussion of lyric and narrative in medieval vernacular poetry must therefore reckon with two *Romans de la rose*: one by Guillaume de Lorris and Jean de Meun and the other by Jean Renart. We may have learnt to read Machaut through Guillaume and Jean's *Rose*, but his relation to Renart's *Rose* remains relatively obscure. In particular, the relationship between these two narrative traditions still awaits detailed consideration. It has been persuasively argued that the authorial persona in Chaillou de Pesstain's version of *Fauvel* is modelled on Jean de Meun's radical revision of Guillaume de Lorris's *Rose*.[6] Yet the formal structure of the two works needs further comment. If *Fauvel* is indeed profoundly dependent on the *Rose*, why is it so different in form? The answer, I suggest, must lie in the legacy of the other *Rose*, Renart's *Rose*. Until this legacy is reassessed, the significance of *Fauvel* and, as a consequence, the course of vernacular secular writing in the fourteenth century will not be properly understood.

In regressing to the origins of the hybridisation of lyric and romance, we discover that both *Roses* are primary. Yet their roles are very different. For where in one *Rose* the distinction between lyric and romance is fundamental, and fundamentally explicit, in the other it is overridden. Where Guillaume's *Rose* makes a seamless union between lyric and narrative, Renart's *Rose* gives special prominence to the breaks and joins. Although the two works confront the same generic opposition, they diverge in their treatment of it. Moreover, it is Renart's work, rather than Guillaume's, which sets the pattern for the great majority of love narratives from the thirteenth and fourteenth centuries, in which formal distinctions between lyric and narrative are both consistently maintained and ceaselessly examined. By the fourteenth century, the traditions of editing and glossing the combined *Rose* indicate the influence of the Machaut generation on the reception of the combined *Rose* to be at least as important as the influence of this *Rose* on the Machaut generation.[7] One aim of this study, and a particular aim of this section, is to restore a sense of the importance of formal diversity and disjunction to medieval vernacular love writing, a perspective which Guillaume's, and later Jean de Meun's *Rose* – in its perceived position of dominance – has succeeded in obscuring.[8]

The changes in French song and narrative that take place across the border of the thirteenth and fourteenth centuries involve many factors. I have discussed some of these changes in relation to the fr. 146 version of *Fauvel*. Some are social as well as formal and musical. Lawrence Earp has remarked on a type of inversion that takes place in the cultural status of lyric genres: 'What was previously a lower-level popular genre associated with the dance is elevated, and what was previously the high-level genre is abased'.[9] As aristocratic taste turns to the former dance-song genres, so the direct formal descendant of the *grand chant*, the *chant royal*, is cultivated not by courts but by urban *puys*. In addition, whereas monophony was dominant in the music of the *grand chant courtois*, the new *formes fixes* are characteristically polyphonic. A further change takes place in the relation between words and music: single-note syllabic (where each syllable of text corresponds to a single note or short note group of music) gives way to the melismatic (where extensive note groups are used to perform a single syllable). This happens by degrees, since the very first polyphonic rondeaux (by Adam de la Halle) are syllabic, and the earliest melismatic rondeau (by Jehannot de Lescurel) is monophonic. All this, meanwhile, occurs in the midst of a crucial period of change in musical notation, one of the earliest attestations of which, as I have remarked, is the *Roman de Fauvel* manuscript fr. 146.

Such radical rethinking and regeneration in French song does not happen in isolation from narrative. On the contrary, the citation of lyric in fourteenth-century narrative turns out once again to include some of the earliest known instances of formal change. Just as the earliest recorded *rondets* occurred in narrative (in Renart's *Rose*), so do some of the earliest recorded rondeaux, virelais and ballades (in the epilogue to Nicole de Margival's *Le Dit de la panthère d'amours*).[10] That narratives should be among the first places in which the new lyric genres come to be copied down is worth pondering. It is of key importance in understanding both song and narrative. We must recognise that narrative and lyric each change in response to the other.

One reason for this is that innovations in musical techniques mutually interact with fundamental poetic and cultural shifts; another is that the new genres of song and narrative – notably the *formes fixes* and the first-person *dit* – are newly combined. *Fauvel* shows only too clearly how song and narrative are tightly – even intractably – enmeshed in the early fourteenth century. The next chapter revisits some of the evidence for change in pieces of writing that precede or are contemporary with *Fauvel*. Examples of song genres, narrative genres, and genres that combine song and narrative will all be brought into the discussion, finishing with Jehan Acart de Hesdin's *La Prise amoureuse*, a post-Fauvelian example, dated 1332, of a new-style *dit* inset with new-style rondeaux and ballades.

The final chapter of the section concerns the issue of citation and how it relates to authorship, which in turn is usually held to be one of the most significant defining factors in fourteenth-century lyric. Cerquiglini, among others, has not only stressed the importance of citation in Machaut, but also seen it as a decisive point of contrast between his work and the way in which lyric is set into earlier narratives. However, I would argue that citation and authorship are not opposed in thirteenth- and fourteenth-century writing so much as interlinked. The practice of citation not only leads inexorably into questions of authorship, it is always already caught up in the issue of how one distinguishes between one form of speech and another. To cite is thus already to pose the question of who is speaking, of who has the authority to speak.[11] Even Renart, although he labels the songs clearly as the productions of different well-known authors, makes a joking pretence at claiming authorship for himself: he has made their words fit his romance so well that people will think he is the author of the songs as well as the narrative. It is a typically subtle joke: he claims the rights of authorship even as he denies them, and in doing so shows how fragile the notion of authorship is and how vulnerable to being appropriated by a mere citer and compiler.

Machaut's works never lose that deep-rooted preoccupation with the process of citation (one that is also fundamental to the *Rose* of Guillaume de Lorris and Jean de Meun). The *Remede* may pass from citation to self-citation, but it betrays a keener absorption than ever in the boundaries between one kind of utterance and another. It is with the form of these utterances, and their history, that the next two chapters will be preoccupied.

Rewriting song: chanson, motet, *salut* and *dit*

The question of how lyric relates to narrative in the thirteenth and four-teenth centuries colours many strands of French vernacular composi-tion. Modern formulations of 'lyric' tend to be mutually hostile: they range across rigorous formal analyses, typologies of registers and conven-tions, the search for origins and influences, and efforts to dismantle its first-person position via notions of sincerity, autobiography and subjec-tivity. Although *narracion/narrative* and the verb *narrer* all occur in Old French, *lyrique* (as either adjective or noun) does not appear until 1495, and neither term becomes part of a descriptive rhetorical vocabulary until the sixteenth and seventeenth centuries.[1] Modern debate about medieval 'lyric' poetry has been influenced by Romantic associations of 'lyrical' and 'lyricism', referring to the personal and emotional, or to a loosely transferred metaphoric sense of 'high-flown sentiment', or to even looser notions of the 'musical' or 'song-like'. Such associations pre-vail as much among those who have vigorously denied its personal and subjective characteristics as among those who have insisted on them.[2]

It is often assumed that lyric and narrative define each other. Zumthor's emphasis on the 'circularity' of song has been influential in this regard, promoting an opposition between lyric stasis and atem-porality, on the one hand, and narrative linearity and resolution on the other.[3] Yet Guillaume de Lorris's *Rose* makes no formal distinction be-tween lyric and narrative. This has led to a rush to redefine narrative as lyric, and hence to call it, along with almost any work in the first person on the subject of love, 'lyrical narrative'.[4]

It is difficult to see that the term 'lyric' has much meaning once form has been abandoned. 'Lyrical narrative' is inadequate as a description of the majority of first-person love narratives because it blurs exactly those formal distinctions that characterise such works. The issue here is not one of quibbling over lifeless categories, but rather of how to grasp the ways in which categories change in this period. Unless we allow for the possibility of making careful distinctions between 'lyric' and 'narrative', a possibility denied by a portmanteau usage of 'lyric, lyrical, lyrical narrative, lyrico-narrative, lyricism', we will fail to notice the distinctions made by medieval authors and their interest in making them.

This chapter considers the different negotiations between narrative and lyric, the different formal and structural solutions to their competitive co-presence in a work, and the many instances of generic invention. The emphasis here is less on the cross-contextual character of lyric citation than on the formal effect of lyric citation within individual works. Many of the examples I discuss are formally or structurally unique, yet reveal a large and rapid process of revision of the terms, boundaries and functions of genre. It is to clarify this process that this section revisits some works from the thirteenth century as well as moves on to the fourteenth. Looking again at ideas of 'lyric' and 'narrative', I investigate a range of writings in which formal diversity, elaboration, amplification and repetition all serve to extend the usual (modern) definitions of song and narrative.

The concept of 'formal integrity' is an intriguingly delicate one in these instances. Although lyric – notably the *grand chant* – is fundamentally associated with form, formal integrity is not in fact an easy concept to apply to the *grand chant*. Large numbers of songs occur in widely varying forms from manuscript to manuscript, with differing numbers of stanzas, lines and syllables, and divergent melodies.[5] No simple equivalence exists between integrity and stability, a point that is of crucial importance in understanding the development of the lyric throughout the thirteenth century and into the fourteenth. A tension between stability of theme and irregularity of form is a persistent feature of lyric writing in this period, and it is not until Machaut that a fit between the two is fully manufactured.[6] The development of lyric and narrative is sometimes presented as a crumbling of lyric into narrative, in a process of either abandoning form altogether in favour of shapeless motifs and grammatical positions, or of fragmenting and truncating lyric in brief narrative citations. Yet in the formal structures of a wide range of 'transitional' works the seams and joins, the moments of fracture and discontinuity, show a keen sense of boundary, as well as an intense desire to redraw boundaries. The borderlines between 'lyric' and 'narrative' in motets, *chansons avec des refrains, saluts d'amour,* the *Roman de la Poire,* the *dits entés* of Jehan de Lescurel, and the *Roman de Fauvel* show that integrity is only fitfully perceived as a virtue among medieval authors.

I noted earlier in Chapter 10 that a preoccupation with genre and generic terms occurs in the organisation of manuscripts. Further evidence of the distinctions made by authors as well as scribes occurs in the works themselves. Terms for the inset genres proliferate within works. From Renart's *Roman de la rose* on, the introduction of a song or any kind of metrically or structurally distinct element into a narrative is usually signalled by formulaic phrases that often contain a reference to the kind of material that is about to be heard, and in this way draw attention to its difference from the narrative. In Renart's *Rose,* where there are no fewer than twelve *grands chants* by named authors set into the romance, the generic terms tend to be part of an authorial ascription ('La chanson Renaut de Baujieu (1451) . . . Des bon vers mon segnor Gasson' (3620)). 'Chanson' is the most frequent term, used largely for the high style song, with 'chançonete' for dance-song. Even this apparently loose terminology in Renart thus makes a specific registral distinction. In later works, especially those which contain only refrains, a whole spectrum of terms is employed, *refret d'amors,*[7] *reffrez de chancon,*[8] *refrait,*[9] *refrain,*[10] *mot, motet, pastorele, remembrance d'amor,*[11] *sonet,*[12] *chançon coronée,*[13] *canchon de sentement,*[14] *complainte, salut, lettre,*[15] *rondet,*[16] *canchon a carole,*[17] *rondet de carole*[18] as well as the ubiquitous *chant, chançon* and *chançonnette.*[19] The existence of so many terms should not, I think, be taken (as it often is) for mere inconsistency, vagueness, or lack of interest in the process of categorisation but rather, the reverse. They convey a strong sense of the way in which medieval authors draw attention not only to the practice of interpolation, but also, in the case of the refrain, to the latter's generic mobility: the refrain can be called all these things because it *is* all of them.[20] At the same time, the term 'refrain' itself has some currency, showing that its distinctness as a genre was also perceived. Certain phrases, such as *refret d'amors* from the *Poire,* and *remembrance d'amor* from *Salut II* succeed in characterising its independent qualities, and do not merely present it as a parasite on other genres.[21]

As well as individual terms for interpolated genres, works at the start of the tradition explicitly discuss the process of setting one genre into another. As we saw in earlier chapters, Jean Renart, Gerbert de Montreuil and Gautier de Coinci develop a vivid metaphorical language to describe the process, such as scattering fragrantly scented flowers throughout the book, adding costly scarlet dye to cloth to enhance its value, or comparing the songs to fine embroidery adding lustre to rich material. But all three authors also make plainer statements naming and apposing two distinct generic categories:

> einsi a il chans et sons mis / en cestui *Romans de la rose* (*Rose*, 10–11)
> in this way he has put songs and music in this *Romance of the Rose.*

> toz les moz des chans, / si afierent a ceuls del conte (*Rose*, 28–29)
> all the words of the songs belong so well to those of the story.

> Mainte courtoise chançonnete / Orrois, ains que li contes fine
> (*Violette*, 46–47)
> You will hear many courtly songs before the story ends.

> En cest livre volrai planter / De lius en lius chançons noveles
> (*Miracles*, I, Pr 2, p. 20, 18–19)
> In this book I will plant new songs here and there.

In each case the generic oppositions chan / roman, chan / conte and livre / chançons are prominently established. It is rare to find any attempt to define the mixed genre with a single term: one (tantalisingly unspecific) example occurs in the 1328 inventory of the deceased Queen Clémence of Hungary. Listed among her 'Livres de Chappelle, Roumans et autres Livres' is the following: 'Item, un roumans de chançons noté, présié 20s'.[22] Another is the term *cantefable* from *Aucassin et Nicolette*, a word which although highly apt to its own context seems not to occur anywhere else.[23] More common is the term *enté*, meaning grafted, which is most widely associated with the motet, but then comes to be applied to the curious semi-strophic *diz entés sus refroiz de rondeaux* by Jehannot de Lescurel.[24]

It is in this word *enté* that we probably come closest to a medieval conception of the making of hybrid works. As a horticultural metaphor, grafting refers to two kinds of process, splitting and joining. Thirteenth-century literary usage appears to understand it in a quite specific sense as a process of splitting apart refrains and then splicing the fragments to larger sections of text and/or melody. If we think of the refrain as itself fragmentary, it might seem surprising to realise that even this tiny element was itself broken up and recombined with further textual and melodic material, but this is a frequent occurrence in motets and is one way of understanding the structure of several other areas of refrain composition. I would like to concentrate in the following discussion on some of the means by which medieval authors both broke down poetic and musical structures and then sought to recombine them in explicitly patterned and formally intricate ways. The grafting or *enté* process is one of these; others can be linked to cento techniques or the structuring principle of the *chanson avec des refrains*. These are means of composing that are not restricted to particular genres so much as techniques that apply across seemingly high generic barriers, and are as much part of musical as of poetic practice. For this reason, they are all instrumental in loosening a sense of either lyric or narrative integrity.

Grafting in motets is still imperfectly understood: it is usually taken to refer to the splitting of a single two-line refrain to form the first and last line of a motet text and melody (see Bamberg No. 42, below), but in practice it is difficult to find any two examples which share exactly the same procedure. For a text and melody may be framed by two separate refrains, or else by a single refrain whose second half occurs in the middle (as opposed to the end) of the text.[25]

Often, as in Bamberg No. 43, the procedure is complicated by the presence of further refrains. In this motet with two upper voices from the Bamberg manuscript, the refrain '*Hé, amours! mourrai je sans avoir merci?*' is split across the text of the motetus and also inserted into the middle of the triplum. In fact it participates in a kind of double graft in the motetus alone, in that the final refrain line of the motetus (*sans avoir merci*) serves as a continuation of the opening refrain fragment (*Hé, amours, mourrai je*) and also of a second refrain inserted in the same voice part (*Dieus d'amours, vivrai je longuement enssi?*). *Sans avoir merci* can be grafted in seamlessly to the semantic structure of both refrain lines. More intratextual refrain-citation occurs between the voices in that *Dieus d'amours, vivrai je longuement enssi?* from the motetus is then taken up as the last two lines of the triplum.

Bamberg, No. 42:
Triplum

Haro! haro! je la voi la,
la riens del mont qui
plus m'a
mis en desconfort,
n'oncques n'en oi
deport;
mais adés en grant
doulour
sans séjour
m'a mis a tort.
Biau semblant sans
cuer amourous,
meschief et courrous
ai adés en la bele
trouvé;
et s'ai bone volenté
d'atendre le guerredon
cele qui m'a en sa prison.

*Halloo! Halloo! I see her
there*, the thing in the
world that has caused
me greatest
discomfort, nor have I
ever had joy from her;
but now she has put
me – wrongly –
in great pain without a
term to my suffering.
Fine seeming without
a loving heart,
mischievous and angry
I have now found [in]
the fair one; and yet I
with good will wait for
reward *from the one
who has me in her
prison.*

Bamberg, No. 43:
Triplum

*Amourousement mi
tient li maus que j'ai;*
pour ce chanterai:
'Ay mi!
*Hé, amours! mourrai
je sans avoir merci?'
Ay mi! las! ay mi!
je muir pour li,*
et nepourquant vuill je
chanter
pour moi deduire et
pour moi deporter;
*las! que porrai je
devenir?
nule riens tant ne desir;*
or me di,
*Dieus d'amours, vivrai
je longuement enssi?*

*The pain that I have
holds me in love*,
therefore I will sing:
'*Alas, Hey Love, will I
die without having
mercy?*' Oh, alas, oh, I
am dying for her, but
nevertheless I want to
sing to amuse and
distract myself; *Alas,
what will become of
me? there is nothing at
all that I desire so
much*; I now say to
myself, *God of Love,
will I live long like this?*

Bamberg, No. 43:
Motetus

Hé, amours, mourrai je
pour celi
cui j'ai trestout mon eage
de cuer et de cors servi?
Si fort m'a d'amours la
rage saisi
que riens ne feroit pour
mi
mes cuers fors penser a li.
Ay mi!
*Dieus d'amours, vivrai
je longuement enssi?*
Di pour les seins Dieu,
languirai
je sans avoir merci?

Hey, Love, will I die for
her whom I have served
with heart and body all
my life? So strongly has
the madness of love
seized me that my heart
would do nothing for
me except think of her.
Alas! *God of Love, will I
live long like this?* Tell
me, for God's saints'
sake, *will I languish
without having mercy?*

Ex. 12 Bamberg MS, Motet No. 43

As this example shows, the 'simple' grafting of refrains occurs along-side many other kinds of textual and musical duplication, inversion and cross-reference. The same refrain may be subject to different patterns of split-citation in separate motets;[26] and in some cases the motet voice-parts are themselves overlaid in different combinations, as in ['Celui de qui je me fi'] – 'La bele estoile de mer'–'La bele en cui je me fi'– 'IOHANNE', which exists in no fewer than five versions (with a du-plum, a triplum and a quadruplum, respectively, and in two Latin-texted forms that contrafact both the duplum and triplum).[27] Such intricate and ingenious methods of interweaving texts and music, as I have argued elsewhere, show that motets are far from seamless structures, but jointed and disjunct, their linearity artfully intersected by discrete units of text and melody.[28]

Grafting has many analogies with methods of narrative composi-tion, in particular with those used in the *saluts* and *complaintes*. One *complainte d'amour* from fr. 837, for instance, in octosyllabic rhyming couplets, is framed, like a *motet enté*, by a refrain at the start and at the end.[29] Another piece from the same manuscript, a *salut* in eleven five-line strophes, turns out to have borrowed three of its strophes from the *chanson de toile* 'Bele Ydoine' by Audefroi le Bâtard.[30] Each strophe has been stripped of its refrain but otherwise left formally unaltered, with the important difference that the gender of the first-person speaker is changed from feminine to masculine. The theft stands out because this particular strophic form is so rare in 'non-lyric' poetry: the result is a strange hybrid of narrative song and strophic narrative. The two *dits entés* of Jehannot de Lescurel, explicitly named as such in the manuscript, are also strophic 'narratives' in the first person, with inset refrains (supplied with music) after each nine-line strophe. In their strophic structure, these *dits entés*, 'Gracieuse, faitisse et sage' and 'Gracieus temps est', re-semble the strophic *saluts*; they are unique among these, however, in having music written in for the refrains, a feature which in turn recalls the *chanson avec des refrains*. Lescurel's pieces widen the sense of grafting from being a process of dividing refrains and enclosing the text within the fragments to one of dividing a text regularly *by* refrains. In this ex-tended sense, not only the strophic *saluts* but several of the longer *romans* and *dits à refrains*, including the semi-lyric pieces in *Fauvel*, could be held to share an analogous compositional procedure.

The *enté* technique confounds a notion of song as finite, circular or self-contained. Although often self-referential, motet texts and melodies are generated by refrain material that is extraneous and autonomous in character. Moreover, this material is not usually smoothed into its new setting: its differences of metre, rhyme and musical mode are allowed to stand out in ways that modern editors have found disconcerting. Motet texts have always resisted classification because of their formal irregularity; the stubborn alterity of refrains is largely responsible for this. They present a view of song as contingent and undefined. The element of arbitrary irregularity that the refrains provide stretches a sense of form to its limits, and beyond.

Cento composition works on this outer edge of formal possibilities. Some motets consist entirely of unbroken strings of up to thirteen refrains.[31] Like the *Kurzmotette* or *Refrain Motette* (tiny motets that consist of a single refrain over a tenor), an example of which we discussed in Chapter 5, *motets centons* show refrains taking over the compositional principle of the piece. They have no strophic core, but only pieces from the margins, redefined as the centre. The technique is Classical: a fourth-century cento that describes the creation of the world is made up entirely of lines and half-lines from Virgil.[32] A *salut d'amour* in the 'La Clayette' manuscript fits the Classical model reasonably well since it is a patchwork of fragmentary citations from *lais* set into the prose *Tristan*; here the citations come from a single type of source that has a specific identity.[33] However, the *motets centons* belong less naturally with this tradition, because the material on which they draw is not authorial but popular and anonymous. This marked change of register shows a concept of the authoritative that is divorced from the authorial. For this reason, centonisation in the motets is not quite part of the wittily maverick and self-enclosed high tradition of the Classical cento, but rather an extension *in extremis* of an intense thirteenth-century fascination with creating aggregate structures of small independent citations in a wide range of formal realisations.[34]

The motet is often regarded as a special case when it comes to formal irregularity, a characteristic of the texts which is usually blamed on the music (in fact one might as easily blame the musical structure of motets on their texts). However, formal realisation in the chanson is also subject to considerable tensions. Two main types of refrain song exist in the thirteenth century: those in which each strophe is followed by the same refrain (the *chansons à refrains*), and a much smaller group in which the refrain varies from strophe to strophe (the *chansons avec des refrains*). The two groups are distinguished by the formal character of the refrain. *Chansons avec des refrains* have the principle of irregularity built into them. Their refrains have a strangely double role: they occupy a formally regulating position, yet they disturb the song's overall structure by their unpredictability. The borderland between strophes in a chanson is a privileged area; it is a site of change and redefinition.[35]

A celebrated song from fr. 12615 (the Chansonnier de Noailles) by Baude de la Quarière (Kakerie), known as 'La Chanson de Bele Aelis', is a supreme illustration of this (see Fig. 13).[36] It is a *pastourelle avec des refrains* with a record number of refrains (fifteen) set into its five, irregular strophes. The music seems to confirm the sense of deliberate discontinuity that characterises the text, in the way that each strophe is not just concluded by refrains but broken up by them. This feature makes the song rare among chansons but comparable to motets and the quasi-lyric/quasi-narrative structures of the *saluts* and *dits*. In fact two kinds of grafting take place across the chanson, for, as well as the refrains, the opening strophic sections are partly made up of individual consecutive lines from the core narrative of 'Bele Aelis', splintered strophe by strophe into short fragments. These fragments can be pieced together to form a 'complete' narrative (see Table 14.1).

As we saw in Chapter 2, the 'Bele Aelis' narrative is a stock element of the *rondets de carole*, many of which are quoted in Jean Renart's *Roman de la rose*. It also occurs widely in other strophic chansons and motets, and even forms the basis of sermons.[37] Nearly every line from Baude de la Quarière's version can be paralleled, often several lines together.

Baude adds further narrative motifs, such as the nightingale who appears in every strophe to offer thoughts on love, and a flickering sense of dialogue between several voices – the nightingale herself, the first-person speaker, and Aelis – but all these elements are left tantalisingly brief and undeveloped. The effect of fragmenting the narrative in this way is to disturb the concept of 'chanson'. There is a degree of regularity, in that most strophes possess the same number of lines and the same structural pattern.[38] But within this there is considerable disunity. Metre, rhyme, line length and melodic mode are all varied, pronouns cut across

13 A page from the *chanson avec des refrains* 'Bele Aelis' by Baude de la Kakerie, BN fr. 12615, fol. 50v, showing a mixture of notated and unnotated lines, with refrains (and first lines of strophes) marked out by enlarged initials, including *Ne vos repentez mie de loiaument amer*.

Table 14.1 *The strophic incipits of 'La Chanson de Bele Aelis' in sequence*

Position (strophe and line)	Text	Textual concordances
I, 1	Main se leva la bien faite Aelis [Good-looking Aalis rose in the morning]	vdB, rond. 8
II, 1	Bel se para et plus bel se vesti [She prepared herself beautifully and dressed even more so]	vdB, rond. 8 cf. vdB, ronds. 2, 3, 7, 9, 42, 185
III, 1	Si prist l'aigue en un doré bacin [She took water in a golden bowl]	
IV, 1	Lava sa bouche et ses oex et son vis [Washed her mouth, eyes and face]	
V, 1	Si s'entre la bele en un gardin [Then the fair one went into the garden]	vdB, rond. 42
I, 12	Keudrai la violete au jour [I shall pick a violet in the daytime]	vdB, ronds. 43, 169, 8
I,13	Sour la raime [On the branch]	vdB, rond. 2

one another, unattributed and unattributable voices proliferate, and a stretched and discontinuous narrative is produced that succeeds not so much in shaping the song as in disrupting any possibility of sustained reflection. The most formally stable element of the piece (the first six lines of each strophe) is the result of an exercise in dismemberment.

The structural originality of Baude de la Quarière's chanson reminds us how flexible the concept of form becomes in the thirteenth century. Form is not abandoned, but pressure is placed on its boundaries by unpredictable, even improvisatory elements that create the central formal impetus of a piece through their irregularity. This type of song epitomises the tension in a refrain's function between its role as a regulating formal feature of a chanson, and as an irregularly cited, formally disruptive element in narrative. As a result, refrains represent a catalyst for change in both lyric and narrative. This occurs because refrains, by definition, work on the edge: on the margins of strophes, their presence in narrative creates pseudo-strophic boundaries that confuse the divisions between strophic and non-strophic, lyric and narrative, speech and melody.

The uncertainty in narrative when a song infiltrates its formal boundary is shown in the variety of types of formal liaison between the song genres and their narrative contexts. Sometimes the formal break between narrative and song is clean and absolute, as in the anonymous *Chastelaine de Vergi* which, as we saw in Chapter 2, cites a single strophe by Gui de Couci. In other cases, the narrative either colonises the song by adapting it to its own form and style, as in the treatment of refrains in Baudouin de Condé's *Li Prison d'amours*, or else allows itself to be imposed upon, by adapting its rhyme and occasionally metre to fit the song. A conspicuous example of the latter occurs in *Le Court d'amours (Suite)*. Here, the poet alters the normally octosyllabic narrative lines immediately preceding a refrain to match its metre and form a *rime croisée*:[39]

> 'si dist, car bien en fu maistresse,
> 'chest cant, pour chou c'on voie   (seven syllables)
> 'de sez pensés: (four syllables)
> '*Amés ! Pour avoir goie*   (seven syllables)
> '*mix en vaurés.*'   (four syllables)
> (3476–78b)

> and said this song, for she was truly the mistress, to show what she was thinking: *Love! You will be the more worthy for having joy.*

Rhyme is the most common kind of rapprochement between a song and its narrative context: this begins with some of the songs in Renart's *Rose* and continues in the majority of later thirteenth-century narratives. In general, there is a *vers de transition*: the line immediately before or after the citation bears the same rhyme as the first (or last) line of the song. This example is from the *Roman du Castelain de Couci*:

> En ce point a ce cant trouvé,
> Car adiés ses cancons faisoit
> Selonc cou ke son coer sentoit;
> Dont fu ceste tels li sons:
>   *Cancons.*

Quant li estés et la douce saisons...
(2587–91)

At this moment he found a song, for he then composed his songs according to what his heart was feeling; this is the melody of this one:
Song
When the summer and the sweet season...

In the case of refrains, as we saw with *Le Court d'amours*, the immediately preceding narrative line rhymes with the second line of a two-line refrain, or with the last two lines of a three-line refrain. In general, the narrative author either respects a song's formal difference, or else allows the formal status of his narrative to be compromised. Either way, as with the *chansons avec des refrains*, the friction between two distinct elements is taken as an opportunity for careful formal negotiation.[40]

The *saluts d'amour* are remarkable for the way in which they modulate between the categories of lyric and narrative. Their (largely anonymous) authors perform this not by some compromise compositional principle that removes any distinction between the two, but by taking two separate paths in which formal distinctions are differently articulated.

In his still standard discussion of the genre, Paul Meyer identifies twelve *saluts*.[41] Several more pieces may be added to this list, including some found only as narrative interpolations.[42] Many of these works are preserved in a single manuscript, the famous *fabliau* collection fr. 837 (which contains no fewer than fourteen *pièces à chansons*, including the *Lai d'Aristote*, *La Court de paradis* and *La Chastelaine de Vergi*).[43] Nearly all contain interpolated refrains or lyric strophes.[44] As a group they fall into two broad types: those that are written in 'narrative' octosyllabic *rimes plates*, and those that are strophic. The latter, in particular, show remarkable formal diversity.[45] Two (*Salut II* and *Li Confrere d'amours*) have quatrains of alexandrines, each quatrain ending in a different refrain; another (*Salut I*) has fourteen eleven-line strophes in octosyllabic *rimes plates*, ten of which end with rondeaux, the remaining four with refrains. In the case of *Salut III*, the form of the strophes even varies internally, since of the forty strophes, each ending in a different refrain, the first five are seven-line, the rest five-line.[46] The closest formal analogy to these strophic *saluts* is the *chanson avec des refrains*, although the number of strophes in the latter rarely rises above seven.

Complainte I, as we noted above, also recalls a song genre, since, like the *motet enté,* it is framed by a refrain at the start and at the end. Several end with strophic envoys; *La Complainte Douteuse* is interrupted by five strophic interludes before ending with a complete five-strophe song and envoy.

These greatly stretched chanson structures are complemented by the narrative *saluts* and *complaintes* which, conversely, are like abbreviated *dits à refrains. Salut Ia,* in *rimes plates,* has just one refrain in the middle; whereas *D'Amour et de jalousie* has twenty refrains in two sequences towards the end. Two illustrate considerable formal instability: 'Ma douce amie, salut, s'il vous agrée' [My sweet love, greetings, if it pleases you] (Meyer No. VIII) shifts from a seven-line ten-syllable opening (rhyming ababbab) to twenty monorhyming alexandrines, to a final group of eight ten-syllable lines rhyming ababbaab. All these moves are signalled in the explicit to the poem which reads: *Explicit requeste d'amors et complainte et regres.* Such formal variety recalls the *Roman de la poire,* which has further features in common with a *salut* structure. For example, the four messengers of Amour, named Beauté, Courtoisie, Noblesse and Franchise, all offer *saluts* (see lines 841, 862, 896, 950, 952, 1017). Textual uncertainty of a different kind occurs in *D'Amour et de jalousie* where the presence of refrains in the *rimes plates* structure is not always easy to detect. In some places 'deformities' in the couplets suggest that the scribe, not realising that a refrain is being cited, has tried (unsuccessfully) to regularise it into the octosyllabic pattern.[47]

Attempts to define the *saluts d'amour* have predictably (given this degree of formal variation) relied on poetic content rather than formal structure: thus according to Meyer, their distinguishing characteristic is 'la formule de salutation' with which they begin (for example, 'Salus vous manc, amie chiere' (Meyer No. I, line 9)). Other scholars have also stressed their epistolary connections, and in fact the term 'letre' is often used along with *salut* or *complainte* (see for example Meyer No. I, line 120; No. VIII, line 3).[48] Several fall into two halves, the formal address by the lover paired with a reply from the lady (for example Meyer No. III, *Salut III, D'Amour et de jalousie*) creating a dialogue structure. Through dialogue, they open up generic boundaries further by recalling *débats amoureux* in *Perceforest* and *Le Roman de Cassidorus.*[49] A neglected genre in modern terms, the formal instability of the *saluts* deserves to be reassessed in relation to larger trends in the thirteenth century, as an innovative attempt to revise the formal boundaries of lyric writing. Like the *complainte*, another genre with a wide range of formal realisation, the *salut* acts as a forum for the creative realignment of chanson and *dit*.[50]

I referred earlier to the use of the terms 'lyrical narrative' or 'lyrico-narrative' to describe works as formally disparate as Renart's *Rose*, Richard de Fournival's *Li Bestiaire d'amours* and Machaut's *Remede de Fortune*, that is, almost any kind of writing in the first person on the topic of love in either prose or verse from the thirteenth to the four-teenth centuries. Such terms testify once again to the discursive power of Guillaume's *Rose* and to the effort by modern readers to create a sin-gle generic category out of this formally distinctive poem in order to describe the plethora of works written in the wake of its influence. Yet, as this book seeks to show, narrative as well as lyric in the period pos-sesses all kinds of formal diversity, innovation and heterogeneity. None of these features is accounted for by the attempt to homogenise them within an all-embracing critical vocabulary.

To show the contrast between these instances of transition and vari-ability in the relations between lyric and narrative and a work from a few decades on, I want to turn to one final example. Here we see the categories of lyric and narrative given a newly sophisticated pattern of relation within a broadly narrative framework. Jehan Acart de Hesdin's *La Prise amoureuse* was written in 1332 approximately midway between the *Dit de la panthère* and Machaut's mature *dits*. The *dit* proper is a hunting allegory in which the lover is cast not as the hunter (as he is in the thirteenth-century *Dis dou cerf amoureus*) but as the prey. Jehan works out the allegory with a precision unusually close to the method of Guillaume de Lorris in his part of the *Roman de la rose* (other *dits* are in general only loosely allegorical). He was singled out for his subtlety by the commentator on *Les Echecs amoureux*, Evrart de Conty, who, dis-cussing the art of speaking 'plus subtilement, plus plaisamment et plus delectablement', mentions *La Prise amoureuse* as an example:

> sy comme on fait en la *Prise amoureuse* et en plusieurs autres traictiés d'amours pour la fainte maniere de parler soubtille et raisonnable soubz laquelle est enclose une sentence plaisant et delitable et moult souvent une moralité qui est de grant profit.[51]

just as is done in the *Prise amoureuse* and in several other treatises of love for the feigned manner of speaking subtly and with reason, beneath which is enclosed a pleasing and delightful sentence and very often a moral which is of great profit.

The poet casts Amours as the hunter, his lady's virtues and qualities as the hunting dogs, and his own senses as the prey. While in the wood of Jonece he is first attacked by Biauté. Subsequently, by describing his lady's appearance, Penser and Souvenir lure him away from his hiding place behind the bush of Enfance. Amours blows his horn and all the hounds leap up after him. He staggers as if all is lost, for he has indeed lost all his senses. Veering between anguish and joy, he tries to escape from the dogs, but runs into the net of Desir where he flounders, helpless as they tear him apart. Pursuing the logic of the allegory to the end, with an abrupt physicality reminiscent of the *coeur mangé* story (the basis of the *Roman du Castelain de Couci*), Jehan causes Amours to divide up the poet's remains: the body he keeps, the blood and the entrails are thrown to the dogs, and the heart is given to the lady.

This makes an intriguing and witty narrative, marked by rhythmic and syntactic variety in the ordinary verse couplets at appropriate moments in the drama.[52] Jehan adds a further layer of complexity to the composition in a direction that takes him away from Guillaume's *Rose*, by inserting nine ballades and nine rondeaux in an alternating sequence throughout the piece, beginning and ending with a ballade. He uses this lyric sequence to imply a secondary narrative running parallel with the allegory. The lyrics consist mainly of forms of direct address to his lady, in which Jehan switches out of the allegory and into a literal discussion of his own feelings towards her. The cleverness of this method lies in the timing of the lyrics in relation to the allegorical adventure: they act as sudden moments of translation.

We may take as an example the setting of the sixth ballade. The poet, trying to hide behind his bush, has just heard an enticing description of his lady's beauty. In emotional turmoil he complains in song:

> Bele et boinne entierement,
> Tresors de joie et d'amour,
> Or ne puis je longuement
> Fuïr contre vostre amour...

Si me renc pris et vaincus
En vo dous commandement...
Vostre grant biautés m'esprent...
(1098–1103, 1106)

Entirely beautiful and good, treasure of joy and love, I cannot now for
very long flee from your love ... it renders me captive and defeated,
in your sweet command ... Your great beauty has caught me...

Here the terms of the allegory – Biauté, Penser, his situation as a
trapped animal – are all turned back into their lyric metaphor equiva-
lents: he tells her that he does not know whether he can flee her love
since she has captured him through her 'grant Biautés'. By giving such
verve to the allegorical plot Jehan endows it with its own sense of reality,
especially at the moments of crisis, at which the tension in the chase becomes acute. The conventional appeals in the lyrics for his lady's mercy
gain dramatic emphasis by being placed in the midst of a rewriting of
the same situation. Jehan uses the contrasts in genre to redouble the
intensity of the lover's cry for mercy.

The structural sophistication of this poetic technique surpasses that
of the *dits à refrain*. Lyric and narrative in *La Prise amoureuse* are not
merely interdependent. The songs, as they echo the allegorical narrative,
turn it outwards and expose its true meaning. Jehan achieves this by
regularly alternating metaphor and allegory, the allegory giving life to
the dead metaphors of lyric. This recalls the *Castelain de Couci*, where the
romance plot breathes narrative life into – gives heart, one might say –
to the trouvère's chanson. The narrative action in *La Prise amoureuse*,
however, is all inner action. The songs do not so much comment on the
plot as represent it in another form.

Many of the pieces we have been considering in this chapter are on
the periphery of modern interests in thirteenth-century French writing. Dominated, in many respects rightly, by the *Roman de la rose* of
Guillaume de Lorris and Jean de Meun, these interests have tended to
overlook the widespread attention to form, to formal distinctions and
innovations of which these pieces are a symptom. Yet marginal genres
such as the *salut*, the *chanson avec des refrains* and the motet are revealing of the detailed, local revisions to the structure of song and narrative
which begin to precipitate the large changes in the character of French

song, and indeed narrative, that take place across the border of the thirteenth and fourteenth centuries. The pressures under which song and narrative are placed in all these works, brought about by allowing small units of text and melody to have a powerfully disrupting effect on form, metre, rhyme, and semantic continuity, create conditions by which the notion of category itself comes under renewed scrutiny. In *La Prise amoureuse* categorisation performs a changed role: fixed form and allegorical narrative are at once newly distinguished and newly integrated.

Citation and authorship from the thirteenth to the fourteenth century

That sense of a new fixity in form which we find in the first quarter of the fourteenth century is hard to locate in terms of a specific time, place or individual. In this chapter I want to consider the nature of change in song and narrative by way of the practice of citation. If the formal shifts and contrasts among the pieces that cite refrains are symptomatic of a profound attention to generic differences among thirteenth-century poets and composers, then the formal discontinuity of refrains is a symptom of their character as citations. They are distinct voices or perhaps, more precisely, a voice adopted by the speaker, 'the image of another's language', as Bakhtin puts it,[1] or 'comme des éléments d'un code particulier, intercalés à l'intérieur de messages échangés'.[2] As 'other' kinds of speech, they also act as a signal of difference: the moment of citation is the moment at which a sense of boundary between one form of speech and another is perceived. They mark out that these are someone else's words, not mine, or again, since refrains are a form of common language, that this is everybody's way of speaking, not just mine. Refrains both set up and break down barriers between different kinds of hold over speech: between mine and yours, ours and theirs, hers and his.

Yet refrains are difficult to understand as citations – in the way that proverbs are difficult – by being the kind of common currency that does not belong to a particular person but rather to a whole community. Refrains share many features with proverbs. In the analysis of A. J. Greimas, the twentieth-century structuralist and semiotician, these include a clear, closed structure with the dimensions of a phrase, proposition or a proposition without a verb, a certain archaic, atemporal character, a predominance of indicative present or imperative tenses and moods, and (although this is less frequent among refrains) a binary rhythmical structure which can be supported by means of rhyme or assonance. Despite these similarities, refrains do not fully lie under a proverbial description. Proverbs themselves resist neat classification: the sliding scale between idioms, sayings, sententious remarks, proverbial phrases and clichés has few fixed points.[3] Although some descriptions amongst these suit refrains, such as Greimas's comment on 'idiotismes' as 'une unité de signification saisie comme une totalité'[4] the looser, lighter construction of many refrains, their dominating (though not exclusive) topic of love, and in particular, their existence as forms of melody as well as of speech takes them out of the orbit of most proverbial analyses.

The difficulty with thinking of either refrains or proverbs as forms of citation is that it is hard to specify any one refrain-citation as a source for another. As we saw in Chapter 2, the attractions of thinking of refrains as 'primal' texts are acute, and were felt particularly strongly by scholars of the generation of Jeanroy and Bédier. Yet refrains pose seemingly insurmountable problems in the quest for their original contexts: such anonymous, inclusive forms of speech and melody do not easily admit a notion of original, authorial creation. We seem to be led towards an intertextual sense of refrains as part of a 'mirage' of citations, an unstable matrix of mutually determining textual traces, in which 'any text is constructed as a mosaic of quotations; any text is the absorption and transformation of another'.[5] In this perspective, the search for origins is itself a mirage: all discourse presupposes another discourse, and much of it has no origin as such. We are constantly speaking in words and phrases which have been set by generations of use, yet which have no possibility of being traced back to the moment when they were first coined.

To think of language as bound by the constraints of clichés is a salutary counter-argument to the notion that literary language is at the other extreme from cliché. An opposition is commonly set up between language as capable of being newly minted, coined, or created and a currency that is constantly devaluing itself through a process of endless circulation and exchange. Yet this distinction is not easy to maintain. Most literary language is dependent on ordinary speech. The view that literary language has special access to the new is cultivated through a very literate understanding of the processes of communication. It takes little account of oral culture, of a use of language that is dependent on common, anonymous phrases, and hence favours the proverbial over original forms of speech. Roland Barthes's remarks on the character of a text as made up of 'quotations that are anonymous, untraceable, and nevertheless *already read*' fit many *textes à refrains* in the Middle Ages with uncanny exactness.

Yet however important such insights are into the intertextual structure of language, questions remain. One of these is posed by refrain-citation itself. In certain contexts, refrains stand out clearly as citations; in others, refrains merge so closely into cliché that, especially in motets, they are hardly distinguishable.[6] One of the teasing characteristics of refrains is that they identify clichés as citations.[7] Frequently, a line has the function of a refrain in one context, but fades into the background in another. In its purer reaches intertextual theory effaces difference: it provides no way of saying why all language is not perceived in the same way. While it may be true in some sense that all language is formulaic, we still make distinctions between ordinary language, clichés, proverbs, famous sayings, quotations and allusions. These distinctions may be difficult to explain, but that does not alter the fact that we make them.

Refrains bear directly on these issues because they raise questions of how we ascribe identity to language, and how we demarcate this identity. Their relation to music introduces a further complication. Refrain melodies are generally light and easily memorable. A refrain's identity is thus formed by its character as a melody (if it survives with one) as well as a unit of speech. In common with other medieval song genres, however, the relation between a refrain's text and its tune is not simple. As we have seen in earlier chapters, a single text may be found in different contexts with several separate tunes; conversely a single refrain tune may be shared by more than one set of words.[8] There is a musical intertextuality among refrains which forms an archaeology of sound as deeply layered as the submerged clichés of their texts, but sometimes with rival structures of identity.

The new form of the first-person love narrative created by Guillaume de Lorris was recast as a lyric/narrative hybrid in one of its earliest imitations. *Le Roman de la poire*, the first work to combine autobiographical narrative with refrain songs, creates identity through love language with remarkable subtlety and emphasis. Sixteen of its twenty refrains form an acrostic from their initial letters which spells out the name of the lady, AN[G]NES, the name of the poet-lover, TIBAUT, and finally the word AMORS. Many allusions to the acrostic are made in the text: for example it is coyly pointed out that the lady's name and Love itself both begin and end with the same letters, 'A' and 'S', and that both lovers' names have six letters. The two names are spelt out again in riddling form in the narrative (lines 1795–1820 and 2724–43) ensuring that the acrostic exists both horizontally and vertically.

By this means, the refrains are literally (in the strict sense of the word) employed 'comme des éléments d'un code particulier, intercalés à l'intérieur de messages échangés'. Tibaut takes the process a stage further since the refrains are themselves messages, exchanged between allegorical representatives of Love and the lady such as Beauté and Loyauté, in such a way that the lover's greeting makes up the initials of *her* name, *her* messengers make up the initials of *his* name, and both together (appropriately enough) make 'AMORS'. The acrostic both generates and predetermines the whole work: once the lady completes the final 'S' of 'AMORS', in the refrain *Soutenez moi, li max d'amors m'ocit* [*Sustain me, the pains of love are killing me*], the book comes to a swift conclusion.

Attention to letters is carried right through the work, from the first line 'Amors, qui par A se commence' [Amors, which begins with A] to the play on the graphic forms of i/j and u/v (interpreted vertically in the acrostic as vowels and horizontally as consonants), and the Latin retrograde pun on Tibaut (*tua sit*) where, as the poet explains, the small letter 'b' forms a long '∫' when it is written backwards (2746–43). The encoding of the refrains permeates not only the entire verbal structure of the work, but also its material construction: Tibaut makes their articulation a matter of the meticulous physical drawing of signs, as well as of more abstract, emotional utterance.

The manuscript presentation of the poem contributes prominently to the sense of graphic difference created by and for each refrain. The most celebrated copy, as we noted earlier, is fr. 2186, which, along with a series of nine large paintings at the start that accompany the alexandrine monologues, decorates the initial letter of each refrain with exquisitely historiated scenes.[9] These are accompanied at the right-hand side of each initial by the triple-spaced text of the refrain, the spaces mostly filled in with blank red staves (see Fig. 7(a)). No other thirteenth-century manuscript in the lyric-narrative tradition (though the fourteenth-century *Roman de Fauvel* manuscript fr. 146 surpasses even this) makes so clear and triply emphatic a distinction (in word, picture and music) between refrain and context. Fr. 12786 has the same layout but it has been left in an unfinished state without any illumination or staves.

Through text, music and illumination, the *Roman de la poire* makes visible the process of constructing clichés. There is a paradox in the way that Tibaut, through the device of the acrostic, confects authorial identity out of quintessential commonplaces that, by their nature, resist authorial appropriation. In their horizontal meaning the refrains function as one sort of code; in their vertical meaning as another, Tibaut wittily turning common language into a means of forming signatures. The double signature, crowned by Love itself, poses the question of how language is possessed by those who utter it. The gradual accretion of letters as each name is put together is created by acts of exchange between the two lovers in which each tries to convince the other of the truth and loyalty of their love. Refrains become proof texts, partly by virtue of being involved in the hidden exercise in naming, partly by the extent to which each lover can successfully take on their voices. An example is the *mal mariée* refrain that Pitié sings on behalf of the lady:

> *Vos avrois la seignorie,*
> *amis, sur moi,*
> *ce que mes mariz n'a mie.*
> (2568–70)

> *You would have the lordship, beloved, over me, which my husband does not have at all.*

This is a well-known refrain (it occurs in a rondeau in one of the *Poire* manuscripts and in *Renart le Nouvel*) from an easily identifiable topos (the unhappily married woman). The lady is acting a role in trying to utter it as her own, and indeed the lover is not fully convinced until she has sent further proofs. In this kind of citation, the distance between the speaker and the cited voice is open to doubt, each lover struggling to gain control over the formulas, both in communicating and in receiving them.

The intransigent character of refrains, even in so carefully controlled a work as the *Poire*, is shown in the four refrains that lie outside the acrostic: one is cited in a short, distinctively versified passage in the midst of the introductory monologues, the second starts the 'dit' proper, the third occurs in between the words TIBAUT and AMORS, and the fourth is an afterword written in at the end (without any visual differentiation) in just one of the manuscripts. Each refrain raises different issues: for instance, the fourth, *Qui bien aime a tart oblie* [*He who loves well forgets slowly*], one of the most widely cited refrains from either the thirteenth or fourteenth century, looks like a scribal continuation, and attests to the way in which refrains had a living social existence among the lettered community of authors, readers and scribes.[10] The other three are more puzzling in relation to the work's overall conception, for it seems odd that Tibaut should be content to leave loose ends in an otherwise tight construction. The third loose refrain is given an initial only in fr. 12786; the otherwise meticulously drawn fr. 2186 does not mark it out in any way.[11] Another mystery is provided by *An, Diex! Li maus d'amer m'ocit* [*Ah God, the pains of love are killing me*] (284; vdB, refr. 784) which does have an historiated initial but appears to be extraneous to the activity of naming that begins with the subsequent refrain *A mon voloir ont choisi mi eill* [*My eyes have chosen according to my desire*] (837; vdB, refr. 138). Finally, the first refrain in the work:

> *Unques n'amai tant com ge fui amee*
> *Cuer desleaus, a tart vos ai veincu*
> (250–1; vdB, refr. 1427)
>
> *I have never loved as much as I was loved; disloyal heart, I have conquered you too late*

although in a prominent position, again seems to lie rather randomly outside the acrostic pattern.

Although part of Tibaut's purpose is evidently to impose an order over such stubbornly anonymous citations, there is no reason to assume that the acrostic is the only source of structural interest in the poem. One way of interpreting the place of *An, Diex, li maus d'amer m'ocit* in the poem is to note that it parallels the last refrain, *Soutenez moi, li max d'amors m'ocit* [*Sustain me, the pains of love are killing me*] (the 'S' of AMORS). This produces a kind of *enté* structure, in which the '*dit*' is framed by a slightly varied repetition of the same refrain. The conceit is created of a single refrain both beginning and ending the acrostic, but with different letters. In addition, the phrase *li maus d'amer*, one of the most widespread common places of French love poetry, infiltrates the poem to an unusual degree.[12] *An, Diex, li maus d'amer m'ocit* prefaces a long passage on the nature of the poet-lover's suffering in love, in which the poet-lover, in conversation with his anonymous questioner, repeats and examines the phrase many times.[13] Several more refrains take up the same theme (see, for example, 1151–52; vdB, refr. 70)), and the lady's repetition of these words near the end of the work, in order to assure her lover that she shares his pains, creates symmetry:

> *Or sai ge bien qu'est **maus d'amours**,*
> *Bien l'ai apris*
> (2864–65; vdB, refr. 1457)[14]

> *Now I know well what the pain of love is, I have learnt it well.*

Her singing, finally, of *Soutenez moi, li max d'amors m'ocit* therefore marks a culminating, and suitably echoing reply to the lover's opening declaration through *An, Diex* of his experience in love.

Another kind of *enté* principle is at work in *Unques n'amai*. Here, the principle seems to work in reverse so that rather than the refrain's being split and grafted around an intervening text, the refrain is itself created through a grafting process. It has been formed out of the first line of the first strophe and the last line of the last strophe of a song by Richard de Fournival.[15] It is not possible to be certain that the borrowing takes place in this direction, since Richard's dates (1201–1259 or 1260) overlap with the *Poire*. However, the likelihood seems strong for several reasons. First, this procedure is quite common in the creation of refrains (see, for instance, the eleventh refrain in the *Poire*); second, it is interesting to discover that a *salut d'amour* (*Sal. II*) makes a similar kind of theft from the same song, this time by combining the first and last lines of the first strophe:

> *Onques n'amai tant comme je fu amée,*
> *Par mon orgueil ai mon ami perdu.*
> (*Sal. II*, strophe IV)

> *I never loved as much as I was loved. Through my pride I have lost my lover.*

This latter combination recurs in the anonymous continuation of Mahieu le Poirier's *Le Court d'amours* (3522).[16] Another refrain in the *Poire* is also shared by the same *salut*, and a third by *Sal. I*: this network of connections confirms the generic similarities between *saluts* and the *Poire* and in the case of the song by Richard de Fournival even suggests a possible compositional link. If this is right, then unlike many of the other refrains *Unques n'amai* is thus a traceable citation, a specific song rather than a proverbial tag, but then also a specific song which is being turned into a proverbial tag. It shows how Tibaut is working with two models of citation: the attributable being turned into the proverbial, and the proverbial into the attributable. Both illustrate the boundary between one kind of utterance and another, the very moment at which types of utterance gain or lose their authorial signature.[17] The peculiar fascination of compositions built around refrains is that they show the line of demarcation between cliché and citation to be so variable: they are full of clichés turning into citations, clichés masquerading as citations, citations being forgotten back into clichés. Tibaut, above all, seems to delight in finding this margin between cliché and citation an opportunity for creative realignments.

Since the chanson by Richard de Fournival survives with music, we have some trace of the melody of the citation in the *Poire* (even though it is not one of the refrains that survives with notation). Musically, the grafting works successfully (and is of course equivalent whether the last line of the first strophe or the last line of the last strophe is used), since Richard crafts the beginning and end of the strophe to form a coherent unit, even recapitulating on the closing few notes of the first line as a means of introducing the last line:

Ex. 13 Richard de Fournival, 'Onques n'amai', lines 1–2, 8–9

If these are indeed the origins of the refrain, then the melody, a haunting, controlled phrase from an elevated musical register (see Ex. 13), stands out from other refrain melodies, which often have a more abrupt, light and dance-like character (see Ex. 1). The music would thus support the words in giving this opening refrain-citation in the *Poire* a more emphatic authorial presence than many of the subsequent refrains. Like the exemplary narratives of Cligès and Fenice, Tristan and Iseut, and Paris and Helen in which it is embedded, this may be a way of giving an authoritative context to the work that is to follow.

The apparent dichotomy between a view of language as 'original' and as 'déjà dit' goes some way towards being bridged by refrain-citation. Tibaut's *Roman de la poire* is a brilliant attempt to reinscribe the 'déjà dit' within an autobiographical frame. The authorising of the refrains, their acrostic production of Tibaut's name, is the only form in which the authorship of the *Poire* survives. Following Guillaume's *Rose*, but choosing a divergent formal route, Tibaut turns the sense of difference provided by refrains into a means of making visible boundaries that are usually hidden.

It is remarkable to find this kind of verbal play with refrains in a poem whose author makes such a point of presenting them as songs, sung by a character within the narrative. In the *Roman de la violette* or *Le Tournoi de Chauvency*, the circumstances of performance constitute a large part of the meaning of the refrains. The words of the song gain their importance from the social nuance suggested by who is singing them, and to whom. Tibaut, however, carries the verbal significance of the refrains much further. Not only do they play their part in the hidden verbal pattern of the acrostic, they also have a proverbial meaning, by means of which the personified characters epitomise, or if necessary defend, their point of view. None of this appears to diminish the musical performance of the refrains in the *Roman de la poire*. This is suggested both by the way in which they take up narrative time, characters are presented as dancing (946–49)[18] and, more directly, by the fact that all three surviving manuscripts either contain music, or indications that it was intended.[19] The role of music in the *Poire* contributes to the distinctiveness of the refrains: music helps to characterise their difference from the rest of the language of the poem.

BAUDOUIN DE CONDÉ, *LI PRISON D'AMOURS*

Baudouin de Condé takes an even greater verbal interest in refrains than Tibaut. His *Prison d'amours* was written at some time between 1240 and 1280.[20] In James Wimsatt's terms it is a psychological allegory rather than an episodic *dit* like the *Poire*, and thus resembles works such as Philippe de Remi's *Salut à refrains* and Jehan Acart de Hesdin's *La Prise amoureuse*.[21] Baudouin's own description of the poem is as a *traitié*, and the scholastic implication of this term is borne out by the rigorous method by which he applies each stage of the allegory to his 'own' experiences of love. The *matere* of the work is entirely built around its central metaphor of the Prison of Love; its argumentative structure, especially in the earlier part, is built around the forty-nine refrains.

In contrast to the *Roman de la poire*, the refrains are rarely framed with the introductory formula 'En chantant' and the closing 'Quant ot chanté'. Instead they are often slipped almost imperceptibly into the narrative, unobtrusively contained within the syntax:

> Et tous les haus solas del monde
> Covient d'amors naistre et movoir.
> Qui dire vous en veut le voir,

Cuers qui par amours n'aime
Ne doit mie grant joie avoir.
(580–84)

And all the great pleasures in the world ought to originate with
and live by love. Whoever wants to tell you the truth of the matter, *the heart who does not love through Love should never have great
joy.*

The connection between text and refrain is so smooth in this example
that van den Boogaard and Scheler disagree as to whether the line 'Qui
dire vous en veut le voir' should be regarded as part of the refrain.

By a variety of methods, Baudouin creates a sophisticated interplay
between narrative and refrain. Sometimes the impending quotation of
a refrain is suggested in advance, at others the timing of a refrain enables a point to be made more forcefully, to be summarised, or capped
with an epithet.[22] From being messages containing significant meanings
in the *Roman de la poire*, the refrains in the *Prison d'amours* have become an integral part of the work's argumentative structure. Not only
do they provide a gloss upon the narrative, they also provide *matere*
for it; subjects and points of view which in turn require commentary and interpretation. All of these effects are so thoroughly textual
that it may come as a surprise to recall that music was apparently intended for the refrains. Musical evidence is scarce in this case; nevertheless, two refrains out of forty-nine have been notated in the Vienna,
Österreiches Nationalbibliothek 2621,[23] and a further one (*Jamais
amours n'oublierai, / n'onques ne fis* [*I will never forget love, nor have I ever*])
appears with notation in *Renart le Nouvel*, line 1746.[24] These indications
of music, together with the sharp visual distinction between narrative
and refrain created in the manuscript by the blank staves drawn in over
each refrain, show that no easy assumptions can be made about the relative unimportance of music to the refrain in this context.[25] It does seem
in this manuscript that the refrains were intended to be accompanied
by music, even though the refrains are rarely described or presented as
songs.[26]

Dialogue, as we have seen, is integral to the structure of the *Roman
de la poire*, and in the *Prison d'amours* Baudouin often engages conver-
sationally in his narrative with his chosen refrains. The same technique

is set by the *Salut* poets within a more rigorously formal framework, so that the fluid, prospective and retrospective technique of commentary in the *Prison d'amours* occurs in the strophic *Saluts* as a tight, rhetorical patterning of concatenation:

> *J'ai, j'ai* **amoretes** *au* **cuer**
> *qui* **me tienent gay.**
> **Gay me tient amors** *et joli*
> *et tout mon* **cuer** *a si saisi. . .*
> (*Sal. III*, 8–11)

> *I, I have* **love** *in my* **heart** *which* **keeps me happy.** **Love keeps me happy** *and pretty and has thus seized my whole* **heart. . .**

This *Salut* contains several exchanges between the lover and the *dame*: in the second part, under the rubric 'Ci respont la damoisele', the lover's *dame* returns to reply in the second strophe (lines 8–14). She resumes for the next ten strophes, but he has the final word in the form of the last refrain:

> *Douce dame, granz merciz!*
> *et je plus ne demant.*
> (*Sal. III*, 91–92)

> *Sweet lady, be merciful! and I ask nothing more.*

This pattern of response and counter-response is matched by the relation between the strophes and their answering refrains. The concatenation implicitly demonstrates the dominance of the refrains within this structure (a characteristic of the strophic *Saluts*), since it suggests that the function of the strophes is simply to echo the refrains. The refrains are the central skeleton of the poem. They represent the most succinct and condensed version of what each character is trying to express; the strophes have the complementary role of providing the forward momentum of the argument. Strophes are in the pivotal position of both commenting on the refrain of the previous strophe, and of being summarised in turn by a new refrain.

In the *Saluts* which particularly emphasise the refrains as songs (such as *Sal. I* and *Sal. II*), refrains are picked out as a distinct genre. In *Sal. II*, for example, the refrains are even described under a wide array of generic terms: *refrait, pastorele, motet, chançon* and *mot.*[27] But neither the refrain nor the rest of the poem has the same kind of independent role which each possesses in a *roman à refrains*. Even in the *Prison d'amours*, the central allegory has its own autonomy to which the refrains are seen to be contributing. The *Saluts* (with the possible exception of *D'Amour et de jalousie*), by contrast, present us with a juxtaposition not so much between narrative and lyric as between two kinds of lyric genre.

The *Saluts à refrains*, as we have seen, are works that occupy a formal area between 'narrative' and 'lyric'. Refrains create in them a method of composition that runs counter to other trends in medieval poetry. By encouraging an attention to their autonomy, refrains resist the common medieval practice of creative plagiarism. Rather than being simply absorbed into the larger structure of the *Saluts* the verbal, formal and musical integrity of the refrains is respected. The kind of authority that the refrains represent, is not the kind of 'old matere' which is learnt and then reproduced in new phrasing, and with a new context. Their authority is inseparable from the condensed, gnomic form in which it is expressed. And yet many of the refrains are quite ordinary snippets of conversation or exclamations:

> Bele, de fin cuer amée, merci.
> (*Sal. II*: I, 5)
>
> Beautiful lady, loved with a pure heart, have mercy.

In the poetic context of a *dit* or 'saying' about love, the refrain gains currency as an authoritative saying on love; or as one *Salut* poet puts it, a 'remembrance d'amor'.

We noticed this in one of the very earliest examples of a love *dit* with refrains, the *Roman de la poire*, where the refrains are imbued with a special sort of significance. In the *Prison d'amours*, Baudouin uses the word 'authority' quite explicitly:

> Ains lor de fine verité,
> Si le proeve d'auctorité
> D'un rondet dont c'est ci li dis:
> *Sa biele boucete, par un très douc ris*
> *A mon cuer en sa prizon mis.*
> (123–27)

Rather then with pure truth, I prove it authoritatively by means of a rondet, whose words are as follows: *Her pretty little mouth, with a very sweet laugh, has put my heart in her prison.*

He caps his appeal with another refrain:

> La sentensce le retiesmoingne
> Au recort de ceste cançon:
> *Sa boucete vermillete m'a mis en prizon.*
> (210–12)

The sentence bears witness to it with the witness of this song: *Her little red mouth has put me in prison.*

Like Tibaut, Baudouin seems to be making the often slight differences between refrains work to his own advantage. The idea of *auctoritas* in such a context has a certain comic fragility. The refrains supposedly verify the truth of his *dit*: yet if he has invented (or reformulated) them himself (as seems likely), what is the value of their authority as independent witnesses?[28] The love discourse in his *dit* seems to define itself circularly from within.

TRADUCTION ET COMMENTAIRE DE L'ARS AMATORIA D'OVIDE

One further work, probably close in date to the *Saluts d'amours*, takes up each of these elements explored in the *Saluts* and in the *Prison d'amours*: the use of dialogue and patterned exchange between strophe and refrain, and the issue of authority. It belongs at first sight to a quite distinct literary category, as it is a vernacular prose translation (the first complete in French) of Ovid's *Ars amatoria*.[29] The translation alternates with passages of gloss, each clearly marked as such in the manuscripts. The 'glose' in turn is augmented with a range of citations and allusions, including French and Latin proverbs, references to French poetry and romance, one *pastourelle*, two rondeaux, six separate strophes from six different songs, and over sixty refrains.[30]

In these glosses the translator wanders far from Ovid. They represent not so much a commentary on the Latin text as an excuse to discuss current practices of the 'Art of Love'. They are a strange mixture of personal comment, social description and literary allusion:

> C'est chose prouvee et congueüe que les dames vont volentiers aus karoles et aus dances, et que ceste maniere de deduit ne fust trouvee pour autre raison fors pour monstrer leurs jolivetés et envoiseüres des cuers. Et illuec sont faiz les bons commencemens d'amours par les merveilleuses contenances et par les beaux dis que on y dist, si comme nous avons dit et dirons. Et quant elles en sont plus blasmees, et plus volentiers y vont, et chantent en despit de ceulx qui les en blasment, et dient:

> 'Vous le lairés, le baler, le jouer,
> Mais nous ne le lairons mie'.
> (*Traduction d'Ovide*, I, 512–21)

> It is something proved and generally admitted that women like going to caroles and dances, and that this manner of enjoyment was not invented for any other reason than to show their liveliness and the amusement of their hearts. And there fine overtures to love are made by the wonderful looks and elegant words which people utter there, just as we have said and will say. And the more they are blamed, the more eagerly they go there, and sing in spite of those who blame them, and say: *You may abandon it, the dancing and playing, but we will never abandon it.*

The structure of this gloss bears a remarkable resemblance to the structure of the *Saluts* or of the *Prison d'amours*. A refrain nearly always ends a paragraph of gloss (which may in fact contain two or three refrains): the whole paragraph acts to introduce the refrain and to give it an amorous and social context. In this way, as in a strophic *Salut*, the refrains appear to crown each paragraph. Seen in the light of such a commentary, the work undergoes a change in function and perspective. Overtly, it may begin as a translation, but the final impression is more of a love *dit à refrains*. The process of interpolation appears to have a momentum of its own in which the original Ovid is left to recede into the distance.

Refrains in this translation are directly involved in the process of commentary and gloss.[31] Although the 'glose' is ostensibly commenting on Ovid, it would be more accurate to describe it as a commentary on the refrains. The translator explains an Ovidian remark by providing analogies which in turn gradually metamorphose into an explanation of why and in what circumstances ladies decide to sing such and such a refrain. The fact that Ovid is the spur to this kind of discussion shows how closely refrains were associated with the 'Art of Love' in all its literary as well as social circumstances.[32] For this translator, the refrain, and more generally the *carole*, are the supreme modern illustrations of the *Ars amatoria*. He has translated the old *auctoritas* of love into its modern counterpart.

This group of thirteenth-century pieces offers a preview of fourteenth-century concerns. We have seen the citation of refrains develop into a quasi-scholastic activity in which they are credited with textual authority. In the strophic *Saluts d'amour*, the process of interpolation is articulate in both senses of the word: it provides a form of internal commentary, and creates regular structural division. We have also seen, in the *Traduction d'Ovide*, a close connection made between the textual and social authority of song and the 'Art of Love'. It is not difficult to see how continuous these practices are with earlier thirteenth-century refrain usage. The same principle of alternation between two kinds of voice – one individual, one communal – in a *rondet de carole* comes into play with the practice of citation. More broadly, especially in the *dits à refrains*, the citation of refrains provides a means of switching between a first-person voice and another, distinct voice. The author creates a movement between the individual and the common voice.

For Baudouin this movement – between narrative and refrain – is enough to stimulate a discussion of authority. The ascription of authority to a refrain is provoked by several factors. One of these concerns repetition itself. Like proverbs, refrain sayings become more true the more they are repeated: they acquire an increasing weight of popular assent through repetition. Another concerns their structural potential as elements that can both divide (divide a work in two or else, in the grafting process, be themselves divided in two) and repeat. The combination of both features is a powerful means of generating authority. When used as a device to divide up a text strophically the refrain gains the privileged position of becoming the last word, to the strophe and thence to the whole piece.

NICOLE DE MARGIVAL, *LE DIT DE LA PANTHERE D'AMOURS*

One of the most significant developments in the nature of song citation towards the beginning of the fourteenth century is that poets begin to draw more attention to their own processes of composition. If we keep a close eye on the practice of citation some of the minutiae of change in the perception of authorship become apparent. Written about 1300, probably within the same decade as the *Roman du Castelain de Couci*, the poems and *dits entés* of Lescurel and perhaps also *Le Court d'amours*, Nicole de Margival's *Dit de la panthère d'amours* could almost be described as the sum of all their characteristics.[33] Like Jakemés, Nicole looks back to a celebrated poet from a previous generation, in his case Adam de la Halle; yet he places Adam's chansons not in a romance plot, but in his own first-person narrated dream. They are quoted, not by a romance hero, but by a personified character, Venus, in a setting which consists not in the active pursuit of love, but in a debate discussing this pursuit at one remove. The dream itself is framed with an address to his lady that borrows all the opening formulas of the *Saluts*:

> A dame bele et bone et sage,
> Noble de cuer et de lignage,
> Cilz qui son dous non n'ose escrire...
> En lieu de salu li envoie
> Son cuer et toute sa pensee
> Avec ceste oevre...
> (1–3, 6–8)

> To a beautiful, good and wise lady, noble of heart and lineage, the one who does not dare write her sweet name... instead of a salut [or greeting] sends her his heart and all his thoughts with this work

Nicole, however, turns the formulas round: wanting to address his lady, but not daring to do it directly, he offers a *dit* instead of a *Salut* (line 6), together with his heart and all his thoughts.

For the first time in a *dit amoureux*, Nicole, alongside the chansons by Adam de la Halle, encloses songs of his own.[34] The dream proper contains three 'dits', as they are termed in the narrative – one in decasyllabic couplets, one in heptasyllabic couplets, and the other in five twelve-line stanzas.[35] The poem is concluded by an epilogue, in which Nicole arranges a series of songs connected by narrative links which explain the origin of each song in successive events in the love affair. This epilogue is in some ways the most interesting part of the poem. Neither *dit* exactly, nor dream, it functions as a gloss upon the art of writing lyric poetry. As in Dante's *Vita Nuova*, the origin of the composition of each song is described and explained as if for its own sake. In marked contrast to Dante, however, this section has an almost apologetic air, as if Nicole felt in need of an excuse for collecting this group of his own lyrics.[36]

The way in which the *Dit de la panthère* resembles on the one hand the *Castelain de Couci* and on the other the *Saluts d'amours* is evident when we examine Nicole's manner of quotation from Adam de la Halle in detail. I discussed in Chapter 2 how Jakemés' decision to quote exclusively from the Châtelain de Couci's lyric output implies respect for the trouvère's reputation, and an intention to honour him further. The romance setting lends an ideal context to the songs, and the two elements combine to produce an ideal representation of love. Taking the poetic authority of the chansons for granted, Jakemés gives them experiential validity in the action of romance.

Nicole attributes poetic authority to Adam in more explicit terms. Adam's verse is adduced by Venus when she is trying to find ways of reasoning the cowardly first-person narrator into a bolder attitude towards love:

> Car s'Amors te veult essaier,
> Tu ne t'en dois pas esmoier.
> Entent qu'Adam au cuer loial
> En dit en .i. sien chant royal:[37]
>   Qui a droit veut Amors servir. . .
> (1539–43)

> For if Love wants to try you, you must not be dismayed. Listen to what Adam with a loyal heart says in one of his chant royals: 'He who wishes to serve Love properly. . .'

Venus quotes Adam's lyric verse in tones of ringing authority to fortify and at the same time rebuke the would-be lover.

As in *D'Amour et de jalousie*, Nicole casts this sequence of quotation from Adam into a debate structure. Venus, by quoting this stanza,[38] is

responding to an earlier argument proposed by the narrator in defence of
his timidity in which he has quoted stanzas from three separate songs by
Adam (1067–1107). He, in turn, makes a further reply to Venus with all
five stanzas of 'Grant deduit a et savoureuse vie' [He has great delight and
a pleasurable life].³⁹ In this way, Nicole changes Jakemés' emphasis. His
concern is not to give the chansons experiential validity, but conversely to
claim validity from them for his narrator's experience. Adam's chansons,
unlike the Châtelain's, are held up as *exempla* not merely of sentiment,
but of the authoritative expression of sentiment in poetry.

One of the hybrid characteristics of the *Dit de la panthère* is that
Nicole uses chansons to conduct a love debate after the style of a *dit
à refrains*. Like Tibaut in the *Roman de la poire*, Nicole refers to the
sentence of the songs:

> Encor dist il allors, sans doute,
> .I. ver dont maint amant se doute,
> Quant li souvient de la sentence
> Du ver, liquelz ainsi commence:
>   Folz est qui trop en son cuidier se fie. . .
> (1096–1100)

> Again he then says, without a doubt, one stanza which many lovers
> fear, when they recall the sentence of the stanza which begins: 'He is
> foolish who trusts too much in his hopes'. . .

We also find the technique employed by Baudouin de Condé of
glossing a song in advance. Venus describes Adam's point of view in the
following manner before quoting the song itself:

> Adam en l'autre ver raconte,
> Dont Amor vient et comment monte
> Sa puissance. . .
> . . .ce dit en ceste guise
> Li vers que cy après dita
> Adam d'Arras; maint bon dit a.
>   Par rire et par biaus dis oÿr. . .
> (1561–63, 1568–71)

> Adam in another stanza relates where Love comes from and how his
> power increases . . . the stanza which Adam of Arras afterwards wrote
> says this in this way (he has many good poems): 'By laughing and by
> hearing fine words' . . . .

Venus has already given us what she considers to be the 'matere' of the chanson, and the chanson now puts it 'en ceste guise'. The inserted chansons thus draw attention to their own difference in form and metre from the narrative octosyllabic couplets of the *dit*. The implication is that song-form itself constitutes grounds for the songs' authority, and that Venus' comments gain new force once they are repeated in a lyric stanza.

The *Dit de la panthère* presents two models of authorship. Nicole sets up Adam as an *auctor*; he also sets up himself. One thing that refrain-citation helps us to see is that this is a convoluted, even contradictory process. For an *auctor* is always someone else: he has authority precisely by being other than oneself, by being already known (*déjà dit*). To claim authorship for oneself is then a difficult matter. One way of doing it, as Baudouin does, is to claim possession of a text that is already known though not authored, that is, a piece of common currency like a refrain or proverb. The author's role is to claim that language as his own, either simply by repeating it, or by agreeing with it, or by taking on its terms as his (by allowing the words of the refrains to infiltrate his first-person narrative). Tibaut's even more implicit route is to take possession of the refrains through the device of an acrostic.

In asserting himself as an author, Nicole, too, is implicit. He does not name himself directly as author of his own songs.[40] Yet his songs mark a radical change in form and style from those he cites by Adam and thus – implicitly – draw attention to their novelty. The difference that Nicole makes to the art of song can be seen when we compare him to Baudouin. Where Baudouin cites refrains, Nicole cites rondeaux and other *formes fixes*. This is one of the great shifts in song composition in medieval France: from a 'popular', semi-oral form to a high art 'fixed' form. In Earp's terms, this is where dance-lyrics become exalted poetry. It is plain that the connection with dance here is remote. What we are witnessing in the *Dit de la panthère* is common language becoming authorised language. If the refrain, and hence the *rondet* is a commonplace form, then the rondeau is an authored form.

The fact that Nicole, unlike Adam, is still not named as an author attests to the faint but subtle distinction between 'authoring' and 'authorising'. To be an author, one has to be recognised as such. The harder Nicole works to credit Adam with authorship, the more silent he appears to be on his own account. He shows that the effort to authorise language involves making claims. The author has to lay claim to the language he uses and elicit from his audience their sense of his right to make that claim. What we see in the *Panthère* is a demonstration of how to create an idea of authorship carried out at one remove: Nicole creates a paradigm of authorship on behalf of Adam but hesitates from applying it directly to himself.

Perhaps the most significant lesson in the *Panthère* concerns Nicole's attribution of authority to the songs. Like Tibaut, and like Baudouin, he treats the songs (Adam's in particular) as separable and distinct forms of language from his own first-person narrative. It is the fact of difference, the sense of a boundary between his language and theirs that enables him first to ascribe an identity to them and second, grant them an authoritative voice. We might call this difference a generic boundary between lyric and narrative. The kinds of narrative we have been considering throughout this chapter offer several definitions of this boundary. For example, citational distance may be supported by the presence of music; other factors include the delineation of distinct voices – male and female, first person and third person, narrator and interlocutor – and changes of verse form. In all of these ways authorship depends on the ability to make distinctions between different forms of language. This is an insight that Guillaume de Machaut was ready to possess for himself.

GUILLAUME DE MACHAUT, *REMEDE DE FORTUNE* AND *LE VOIR DIT*

I want to compare, finally, the use of refrain-citation in two works by Machaut, one written towards the start of his career (the *Remede*), the other at the end (the *Voir Dit*).[41] The first refrain in the *Remede* functions as an archetypal citation – it is the only non-authorial song citation in the *Remede* – summing up the history of refrain-citation in romance. Because Machaut does not set it to music its presence has received little comment.[42] It bears all the characteristics of the thirteenth-century type. It occurs straight after the virelai that the lover has been asked to sing during his turn in a *carole*:

> Aprés ma chançon commença
> Une dame qui la dança,

14 (a) Carole in Guillaume de Machaut, *Remede de Fortune*, BN fr. 1586, fol. 51r, with notated virelai below.
(b) 'La karole d'amours', *Le Roman de la Rose*, BL Royal MS 20. A. XVII, fol. 9r.

14 *(cont.)*

Qui moult me sembla envoisie,
Car elle estoit cointe et jolie,
Si prist a chanter sans demeure:
'Dieus, quant venra li temps et l'eure
Que je voie ce que j'aim si ?'
Et sa chanson fina einsi.
(3497–3504)[43]

After my song a lady, who had been dancing there and who seemed to
me very charming, gracious and pretty, began at once to sing: *'Dear
God, when will the time and hour come that I may see the one I love?'*
And she finished her song with this refrain.[44]

No refrain appears in precisely this form in van den Boogaard's bibliography (which does not, of course, extend this far in date), but several
resemble it.[45] It is striking that Machaut should give the refrain so firm an
association with dance-song. This whole scene in the *Remede*, exquisitely
illustrated in fr. 1586 (see Fig. 14(a)),[46] undoubtedly re-creates the *querole*
described in the *Roman de la rose* of Guillaume de Lorris (see Fig. 14(b))
where Leesce starts up the singing of refrains:

Bien sot chanter et plesanment,
ne nule plus avenanment

265

ne plus bel ses refrez feïst.
(729–31)⁴⁷

She knew how to sing well and pleasingly, no one could do it more
attractively or perform refrains more beautifully.

It is important to recognise that, in its direct citation of dance-
songs and refrains, the scene equally recalls Renart's *Rose* (see especially
lines 286–333, discussed in Chapter 2). Machaut's inclusion of a refrain
amongst all the other lyric genres suggests that he regarded the refrain
as a distinct genre, a status which, as we saw in Chapter 2, scholars
have often been reluctant to grant it. Machaut emphasises the typ-
icality of the setting at least as much as the song, by implying that a
refrain is an intrinsic element of the tradition of reporting such scenes in
romance.⁴⁸

But dance-song is not the only context for refrains in romance. Like
Tibaut, Baudouin de Condé and the *Salut* poets, Machaut also employed
refrains as amorous epithets. A favourite of his was one of the most
current refrains of the period, *Qui bien aimme, a tart oublie* [*He who
loves well forgets slowly*] (4258) which he quotes as the last line of the
Remede (before the brief epilogue) in a way that partially recalls its flyleaf
citation in the fr. 2186 copy of the *Roman de la poire*.⁴⁹ It is the first line
of his *Lai de Plour*, and occurs in the triplum of Motet 3, and repeatedly
in the *Voir Dit*.⁵⁰ Another epithet, which also recalls refrains used in the
Poire, occurs in the *complainte* set into *La Fonteinne amoureuse*:

Dont vient cils maus? Il vient d'outre la mer,
Si m'ocirra...
(493–94)

Where do these pains come from? They come from beyond the sea,
and will kill me...⁵¹

In his last great work, the *Voir Dit*, Machaut reverts to the large-scale
refrain-citation of *Renart le Nouvel*, Baudouin de Condé's *Li Prisons
d'amours,* and *Fauvel*. The work as a whole is deeply discontinuous (to
use Jacqueline Cerquiglini's apt designation).⁵² The plot is divided between two characters, Guillaume, the aged poet, and a young girl, Toute
Belle, who writes to him, seeking friendship because she is so admiring

of his poetic reputation. They exchange forty-six prose letters, and over sixty lyrics; the narrative couplets that describe the progress of their relationship are also gradually exchanged, so that the writing down of the love affair becomes indistinguishable from the affair itself. In contrast to the *Remede*, Machaut moves away from the single, inclusive perspective of the lover towards a split narrative. The lady, silent and passive in the structure of the *Remede*, becomes active and articulate in the structure of the *Voir Dit*: language and music are no longer the unassailable possession of the author but a shared commodity between two authors.[53] It is not clear whether Toute Belle represents a real female author; but even if we were to understand her as a fictional character, Machaut has ensured a genuine sense of rupture in the narrating voice. The uncertainty among modern readers of the *Voir Dit* over Toute Belle's historical status testifies to her success as a rival author figure in the narrative.

This ambiguous notion of authority fractures the narrative mode of the *Voir Dit*. Narrative verse and lyric verse do not merely alternate (though this is not a simple process even in the *Remede*), but rather, as in *Fauvel*, pass between all kinds of verse and between verse and prose. The effect of these formal shifts is that narrative is subjected to frequent disruption: the same event is told several times in lyric, in verse narrative and in prose letters which causes narrative time to keep restarting, pausing, partially recapitulating, partially amplifying. Divided as it is between two characters, a further change in perspective arises as one and then the other narrates and comments. At first, when the relationship is blossoming, the formal discontinuities tend to work in a similar emotional direction and hence towards a convergence of view. However, later in the story when distrust begins to breed, the issue of veracity becomes more pressing, and it is no longer clear whose narrative, at any one time, has better claim to truth. The last part of the *Voir Dit* places greatest strain on 'true speaking', and the formal breaks, changes and reduplications stretch the tension to breaking point.

Such a complex structure makes citation a subtle and unstable process in the *Voir Dit*. Our view of how citation works depends in part on our view of Toute Belle. For some, she is a separate historical figure who wrote a large collection of letters to the poet and sent him several of her own lyrics; for others, she – and the writing attributed to her – is a fictional

construct created by the poet.[54] The puzzle of Toute Belle raises the same
questions as the *razos* and *vidas* of the lives of the troubadours, poised
between the life of the author and the life as author, the life as composed
of the lyrics in the narrative, and the life as lived while composing these
same lyrics. Machaut's title – *Le Voir Dit* – is an understated but pointed
declaration of this punning, double-voiced relationship between veracity
and verisimilitude, fictionality and authenticity.[55]

It comes as no surprise, given his far-reaching exploration of the border between language and history, that Machaut should weave refrains
into the *Voir Dit* with such purpose.[56] Machaut makes creative use of
refrains in three major ways: by quoting common refrains as if they were
proverbs (as in *Qui bien aimme*); by requoting refrains from his inset
lyrics within the narrative or the letters; and finally, by linking together
pairs of lyrics with the same refrain, a practice fairly common in his
Louange des dames.[57]

The importance of these procedures, as Cerquiglini demonstrates, is
that it creates a close interlinking ('l'enchaïnement') between lyric and
narrative, in which themes and phrases from the inset lyrics provoke
repetition and amplification in the form of narrative.[58] In the light of
the study of refrains in this book, and of their use in a wide number of
narrative, motet and chanson texts reaching back to the early thirteenth
century, these interesting observations can be augmented in several directions. We see in Machaut's frequent requotation of them, refrains in
the act of being created. What starts as the refrain of a ballade becomes,
through the course of several citations throughout the work, a newly
independent phrase which may itself become the subject of narrative
discussion. One precedent for this technique in Machaut is *Li Prison
d'amours*. The difference is that Machaut now makes explicit what in
Baudouin was only implicit: where Baudouin had to seek for variants of
refrains to create an accretion of authority for his case, Machaut indulges
in self-quotation.

The case of *Qu'assez reuve qui se va complaignant* [[*That*] *he asks
enough who complains*] shows the relation between Machaut's technique
and Baudouin's particularly clearly. The narrator and Toute Belle are
together for the first time and meeting each other every day in the
vergier. Guillaume performs to her the ballade 'Le plus grant bien
qui me viengne d'amer' [The greatest benefit that comes from loving]

(L-W & P, lines 2641–64), in which he complains at not being completely cured from love's pains. This prompts a conversation between them in which he amplifies the message of the ballade at length. Finally, he concludes:

> Je weil ci finer mon sermon
> Que trop longuement vous sermon
> Et say bien prouvé par mon plaint
> *Quassez rueve qui se complaint*
> (2801–04)

> I mean to finish my sermon at this point, having lectured you too long; In my complaint, I've proved well '*That he asks enough who complains.*'

In reply, Toute Belle quotes the same refrain back at him:

> Par quoy vo conclusion prueve
> *Que qui se complaint assez rueve*
> Si quamis ie responderay...
> (2823–25)

> And all this supports your conclusion '*that he asks enough who complains*'. And so, darling, I intend to respond...

Just as in the *Prison d'amours* the refrain is used to conclude the argument, here it is taken as representing the essence of the ballade, and also as a proof or testimony of Guillaume's feelings. In this we see a change from Baudouin: in the *Prison d'amours* the refrains bolster the poet's allegorical analogy, whereas here they are supposed to guarantee the 'truth' of the poet's sentiments.[59]

We considered in the last chapter how the *salut*, the *chanson avec des refrains* and the motet are all examples of genres in which small elements of text and melody are used to open up generic categories, creating structures which cause us to redefine our notions of lyric and narrative. Machaut continues this process, by using different forms of lyric, and different forms of narrative (verse and prose), and by treating lyric as narrative (in the 'operatic' sequences) and narrative as lyric (in the repetition and discussion of refrains). He grafts and interweaves, using refrains as ways of liaising between the different forms of writing. He even uses them to liaise between his different works, a practice we have seen to be characteristic of the compiler(s) of the *Fauvel* MS fr. 146, and will shortly investigate in Adam de la Halle. The result is that composition – as a procedure – looks increasingly like creative compilation and recategorisation. By the time he puts together the *Voir Dit*, Machaut seems to turn authorship into something both fractured and distinctive. He looks, as an author, not for seamless control, but for an increasingly intense ability to distinguish between different types of language, different modes of utterance. The refrains, as ever, break out from formal boundaries – in this case the examples of *formes fixes* – to work as independent units. Even the *formes fixes* are used by Machaut as a means of rethinking and representing narrative, producing a work that leaps imaginatively into a new kind of citational art.

I have argued that vernacular authors were acutely sensitive to the differences between one voice and another and to the challenges of turning a common, 'popular' language into something more personally authoritative. Machaut's obsession with citation links him with much earlier explorations of the limits of genre. The relation between song and narrative offers a means for authors to articulate new versions of authority.

The link between formal revision in various song and narrative genres and an increasingly prominent use of refrain citation is worth emphasising. It is unlikely to provide us with a single key towards understanding the processes of compositional change across the thirteenth and fourteenth centuries. Change, even of a very marked and deep-seated kind, does not always yield to attempts to find a specific cause or impetus, but rather reveals itself as arising out of a complex nexus of small and larger factors. This is especially true of the extraordinarily emphatic way in which the *forme fixe* takes over from *grand chant* as the dominant mode of medieval song, and reigns as such for two centuries. We need to find a way of grasping this change as a process that was both dynamic and volatile. The last chapter will now turn to the *formes fixes* themselves in the hope of discerning further aspects of their transformation into a new art.

PART VI

Envoy: The new art

The *formes fixes*: from Adam de la Halle
to Guillaume de Machaut

The experience of listening to a rondeau by Adam de la Halle does little to prepare one for the experience of listening to one by Guillaume de Machaut. Despite the fact that both songs are described by the same term – rondeau – the soundworld in each is markedly different. Machaut's rhythmical complexity is not only of a different order, but the scope, balance and relation of the musical and textual components have changed. One might compare Adam's rondeau 'Diex, comment porroie' (see Fig. 15) with Machaut's 'Quand je ne voy'. The difference in length is obvious and paramount. In the kind of statistic made available by modern recordings, Adam's rondeau takes 1'20 to sing, Machaut's 5'20.[1] The refrain in 'Quand je ne voy' lasts as long as the entire performance of Adam's rondeau (see Ex. 14). The last syllable ('n'oy') of the fourteenth-century piece is temporally equivalent (28 seconds) to four lines of the thirteenth-century song (the full three-line refrain and the first strophic line).

We are largely registering the difference between a syllabic and melismatic relation between the words and the music. The verbal and musical elements coincide in Adam's song to form an uncomplicated, though multiple set of sounds. In Machaut, however, the melismas break up the verbal line, stretching the syllables into sounds which lose their connection with verbal meaning. The repetitions of the refrain in Adam underscore it semantically; in Machaut the refrain becomes so dominant a musical experience that it becomes harder to hear the sense for the sound. Another kind of discontinuity is introduced alongside the formal repetition of the refrain line: with almost comic ingenuity the melismas on 'n'oy' keep tantalising the listener with the prospect of a line ending that is repeatedly denied by another phrase. Machaut makes

15 Adam de la Halle, polyphonic rondeaux, BN fr. 25566, fol. 34r.

Ex. 14 Comparison of Adam de la Halle, rondeau 'Diex, comment porroie'
(refrain) and Guillaume de Machaut, rondeau 'Quant je ne voy' (refrain)

Adam de la Halle

Guillaume de Machaut

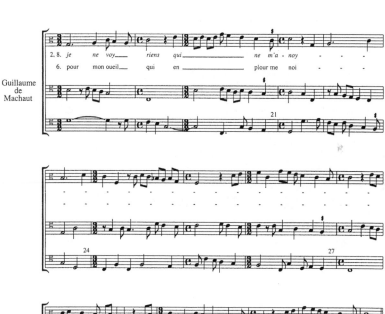

the aural experience not just a matter of hearing a verbal line extended musically, but of a series of false line endings, resolving only after the fourth interruption into silence.

The points of connection between the two songs are almost more difficult to explain. It would be easier if we could posit a notion of complete change between the song forms of the late thirteenth century and those of the central decades of the fourteenth. The language of re-birth, or renaissance is often used (after the term *ars nova* introduced by Johannes de Muris and Philippe de Vitry) to describe the atmosphere of radical musical innovation that must have come into existence at the turn of the century (or so it is assumed) in order to produce such an experience of difference. Such language is attractive perhaps partly because it appears to make the need for much explanation redundant: a fresh start implies a hiatus of some sort, and hence is explanation enough for the awkward gap in the surviving musical repertories between Adam and Guillaume de Machaut. Material evidence of transition is notori-ously difficult to locate. Apart from fr. 146 (*c.* 1316–18?), the complex character of which provokes more questions than answers, we have only a group of non-musical manuscripts, the collection of lyrics in Oxford, Bodleian Library, MS Douce 308 (*c.* 1300), Nicole de Margival's *Le Dit de la panthère d'amours* (composed between 1290 and 1328?), Jehan Acart de Hesdin's *La Prise amoureuse* (1332) and Jehan de la Mote's *Li Regret Guillaume Comte de Hainaut* (1339).[2]

But the problem with the language of rebirth is that it can mislead. It conceals the fact that despite the evidence of so much change having taken place, we cannot readily find the instances themselves of change. Moreover, we are still far from clear about how to describe the state of af-fairs in lyric composition prior to this period of posited change. Instead, as recent accounts emphasise, 'the early history of these forms and of their interrelationships presents a confused and confusing picture'.[3] Such con-fusion is glossed over by the following typical historical summary:

> [The forms] did not, in fact, become 'fixed' until late in the thirteenth century, when the activity of the trouvères was drawing to a close. This establishment of the fixed forms coincides with their transformation from simple dance tunes into polyphonic songs. Once that transfor-mation had been accomplished, the three distinctively different forms

> dominated French lyric poetry almost to the end of the fifteenth cen-
> tury. (Hoppin, p. 296)

There are several problems here. First, it is difficult to see how 'the fixed
forms' could be described as already fixed by the end of the thirteenth
century. Hoppin is presumably referring to the polyphonic rondeaux by
Adam, of which sixteen survive. These are a fascinating phenomenon,
but hardly 'establish' either the rondeau in particular or the fixed forms
in general. Christopher Page has argued that the *ars nova* ballade did
not exist before 1300, but was developed in Paris sometime between
the date of Johannes de Grocheio's treatise of that date and fr. 146.[4] A
word like 'coincides' begs in its very precision the question of how that
transformation from 'simple dance tunes' to 'polyphonic songs' took
place.

Second, the notion of fixity itself needs careful examination. As we
have seen, it tends to be applied retrospectively, both historically and formally. The clarity of structure in later fourteenth- and fifteenth-century
examples appears from that vantage-point to have an independent pre-
existent character, so that our historical task is taken to be a matter
of locating the moment of crystallisation, the critical hardening of a
prior state of flux. From the perspective of the thirteenth century, however, the task looks rather different. It is important to recall that the
defining characteristic of the *formes fixes* (itself a retrospective term that
metaphorically predefines its object) is determined by the refrain, more
precisely by the relation between the refrain and its strophic context.
When we further consider that the refrain is a mobile element throughout a whole spectrum of thirteenth-century compositions then its role
as a fixer of form seems paradoxical rather than inevitable. The purpose
of this final chapter is to make steps towards investigating how the broad
context for refrain-citation in the thirteenth century relates to the role
of the refrain in fourteenth-century compositional practice.

My approach differs in certain respects from the stimulating attempt by Lawrence Earp (alluded to in Chapter 12) to account for
the changes in lyric composition between Adam de la Halle and Guillaume de Machaut.[5] Earp's general thesis – his contrasting of the generic
affiliations of measured and unmeasured song – is not under dispute
here. Drawing on pioneering work by John Stevens on the rhythmic

differences between the *grand chant* and the dance-song traditions, Earp, and also Page, outline the important argument that the development of the *formes fixes* results from the application of fourteenth-century musical rhythmic innovations first to the motet and then to dance-song. Earp discusses the lyrics of Nicole de Margival and Jehan Acart de Hesdin to consider what these examples indicate (even without music) of the intervening stages of lyric composition. He concludes that they show a gradual and linear dislocation from dance towards 'more exalted' poetic ends.

As a broad-brush narrative this has a certain schematic accuracy. However, in the light of more detailed work on thirteenth- and fourteenth-century refrain-citation in earlier chapters of this book, a more nuanced outline of some of the generic shifts that take place across the turn of the century may be attempted. The blanket description of lyrics that predate Machaut as 'dance-songs' must be corrected. It is an obviously inappropriate term for the group of thirty elegiac ballades set into Jehan de la Mote's *Regret Guillaume*, a work commissioned by Philippa of Hainault as a funerary commemoration of her father, Guillaume Ier. More generally, fuller knowledge of refrain-citation in the period shows that the range and variety of roles played by refrains in motets, chansons, strophic and non-strophic narratives and *saluts d'amour* has passed well beyond the limiting scope implied by dance. Recognising this helps us to appreciate how the construction of rondeaux, ballades and later, virelais in the fourteenth century takes place within the context of a fundamentally continuous, and broad-based practice of refrain-citation.

The following examples consider not only how the refrain functions structurally in any one piece, but also how it functions as a citation. Not every song that survives between Adam and Machaut contains a refrain-citation, of course, though the presence of refrains is indeed ubiquitous, but the extent to which pieces draw on the same constructional material perhaps deserves greater emphasis. Examining this practice is, I suggest, one way of gaining a more flexible understanding of early fourteenth-century lyric structures.

Adam's polyphonic rondeaux, the natural starting point for this discussion, present a fascinating case of multiple citation. Of the sixteen, eleven are based on refrains that occur in at least one other context. In seven cases, there is a cross-reference to Jacquemart Giélée's *Renart le Nouvel.*[6] Other refrain contexts include eight motets, a *chanson avec des refrains* and the following narratives: *Le Roman de la poire, Le Tournoi de Chauvency, Le Roman de la violette* and *Le Roman de Fauvel.* Adam's compositions are remarkable for their generic range: as well as the rondeaux, he composed thirty-six *grands chants*, eighteen *jeux-partis*, eleven motets, two celebrated *jeux, Le Jeu de Robin et Marion* and *Le Jeu de la feuillée,* and a diverse collection of narrative pieces, *Les Vers de la mort,* the *Congés,* a *Dit d'amour* and a *chanson de geste, Le Roi de Sicile.* He is likely to have composed some *lais* (which have not survived), and perhaps also *Le Jeu du pelerin,* though this may be the posthumous work of another trouvère. One constant factor in all this variety is Adam's recurrent interest in creating larger compositional structures out of small, widely current verbal and musical formulas, many of which circulate within his own corpus.

Before concentrating on the rondeaux, it may be illuminating to note some instances of these internally re-cited formulas. Not unexpectedly, Adam's motets are especially rich in these. Motet No. 2, 'De ma dame vient / Diex, comment porroie / Omnes', has four refrains built into the two upper voice-parts:

1. *De ma dame vient*
   la grant joie que j'ai. (vdB, refr. 477); four contexts

   From my lady comes the great joy that I have.

2. *Fui toi, gaite, fai moi voie;*
   par ci passent gens de joie. (vdB, refr. 765); four contexts

   Flee, watchman, make way for me; joyful people pass through here.

3. *Mais lasse! [Diex] comment porroie*
   sans cheli durer
   qui me tient en joie? (vdB, refr. 496);[7] three contexts

   But alas, [God] how could I live longer without the one who keeps me joyful?

4. *Par ci va la mignotise,*
   par ci ou je vois. (vdB, refr. 1473); seven contexts

   Along here goes graciousness, along here where I go.

Although the grafting processes are particularly interesting in all four cases, there is no space to comment further here beyond pointing out that *Diex, comment porroie* and *Par ci va la mignotise* both occur elsewhere in Adam's oeuvre. *Diex, comment porroie* is the refrain of his twelfth polyphonic rondeau, (cited at the start of this chapter) and *Par chi va la mignotise* is sung mockingly by the spirits in *Le Jeu de la feuillée* (Ex. 9). Two of the motets cite refrains that are part of *Le Jeu de Robin et Marion*; two more (Nos. 9 (triplum) and 10 (motetus)) each cite the refrain *Hé Dieus, quant verrai / cele que j'aim?* [*Oh God, when will I see the one I love?*] which is the root of his eleventh rondeau. These instances of formulaic exchange between different pieces are not confined to motets and rondeaux. Amongst its collection of pastourelle and quasi-pastourelle song motifs, *Robin et Marion*, as we discussed in Chapter 9, is a tour de force of cyclical and symmetrical repetitions.

The transferability of these refrain-citations helps us to see that the late thirteenth-century refrain cannot be given a narrow generic designation, beyond that of 'refrain', and certainly not one that confines it to dance-song. This is not to say that individual contexts might not be associated with dance. Clearly *Robin et Marion* is precisely (in certain sections) a context for performed dance. However, even here, the complex forms of allusion to *pastourelles* take the dramatic narrative into a new relation with song: the sung exchanges between Marion and Le Chevalier are dramatic song, not *caroles*. Once individual refrains from this *pastourelle* setting are quoted in motets, then drama retreats further. Other refrains, that take the form of an exclamation, question or statement about love, are versatile in their generic reference. They can pass readily between higher and lower registers, between exclusively verbal contexts – such as a *dit* – and the intricately musical conversation of a three-part motet.

In musical terms, and in Earp's discussion, dance-song implies measured rhythm. While the assumption that dance-song should be measured is eminently reasonable, the assumption works less easily in reverse. It has yet to be shown that all refrains derive from dance-song. I would rather argue, by the late thirteenth century, that in a creative atmosphere of intense reworking and re-presenting of formulaic material, refrains have carried their rhythmic charge into all kinds of genre. The result is that many contexts remote from dance come into creative friction with snippets of measured rhythm, a process that has an irrevocable effect on the rhythmic character of the whole composition.

It follows that this gives us a less restricted view of the relation between refrains and the short monophonic forms that are usually retrospectively seen as the precursors to the *formes fixes*. Adam's work, in its extraordinary generic diversity, and its deployment of refrains right across its generic range, shows refrains functioning as free agents, insinuating their way into satiric narratives as easily as into chansons, motets or rondeaux.

I want now to pause over the connections between Adam's motets and his rondeaux. It is instructive to compare them as pieces of polyphony. Is giving a polyphonic realisation to a rondeau a different procedure, for Adam, from grafting a refrain into a motet? As a direct result of Adam's working practice, the same refrain can be observed in both types of generic realisation. I make a few tentative initial observations. One characteristic of Adam's citational practice, in which his work varies from many others, is that he tends to cite exactly: there is not that margin of variability from context to context in the refrain's textual and musical definition. This suggests already the creative importance to Adam of a refrain's rhythmic (as well as verbal and melodic) stability. Moreover, it is striking how the rondeaux refrains and the motet refrain are often placed with similar melodic lines (see Exx. 15 and 16).[8]

Ex. 15 Adam de la Halle, Motet No. 6 (opening) and rondeau No. 6

Ex. 16 Adam de la Halle, Motet No. 10 (ending) and rondeau No. 11

The tenor of a rondeau is often a lightly expanded version of the corresponding motet (see Ex. 17)[9].

One possible conclusion is that Adam's polyphonic rondeaux are not simply *rondets de caroles* given a three-part conductus texture, but rather

Ex. 17 Adam del la Halle, Motet No. 1 (opening) and rondeau No. 5

that they function for Adam as a means of sharpening the rhythmic focus of refrains. From this point of view, he is able to combine the generative structural function of refrains (at its clearest in a circular, repeated form) with the multiple texture of a motet, using polyphony as a means of adding gravitas and aural complexity to the powerfully measured character of the citation. I suggest that we see his polyphonic rondeaux as a response to experiments with refrains in polyphony in the genre of the motet, and not – in an unhelpfully limiting sense – as forms of dance-song.[10]

Looked at as a group, the rondeaux themselves exhibit many signs of formal experimentation. Perhaps the most extreme case is the song that begins with the refrain *Fines amouretes ai, Dieus, si ne sai quant les verrai* [*I have noble lovers, God, but I don't know when I will see them*]. This has been variously classified by modern scholars with mutual disregard as a chanson, ballade, virelai *and* rondeau: and is copied under the headings respectively of 'rondeaux et motets' (fr. 25566) and 'motets' (Cambrai, Bibliothèque Municipale, 1328).[11] Another, beginning *Dieus soit en cheste maison* [*God be in this house*], has a ballade rather than a rondeau structure, with a five-line through-composed strophe followed by a two-line refrain. Without giving a full survey of the formal variety of the 'rondeaux', they are perhaps best described as miniature essays in amplification. The central generating cell of the refrain can be two, three or four lines in length, each of which becomes the trigger for various kinds of repetition, from the highly condensed *Bone amourete me tient gai* [*Good love keeps me happy*] (which takes all of twenty-nine seconds to perform, twice through) to the slightly more extended *Diex comment porroie* or *Je muir, je muir d'amourete* [*I will die, I will die of love*]. Collectively, the impression they give is of an author trying out different kinds of balance between the length of line, the number of textual and musical repetitions and the pace and momentum achieved by means of these variables from line to line.

Adam quickly becomes a major *auctor* figure for subsequent poets and composers, notably Nicole de Margival, as we have seen in the last chapter, and Guillaume de Machaut. Nicole's *Dit de la panthère d'amours*, as we recall, quotes from nine of Adam's chansons; lines from Adam's rondeaux are set into certain of Machaut's ballades.[12] Another chanson by Adam (reduced to three stanzas) finds its way into the *balette* section of Douce 308.[13] All three poets are associated in the final section of Nicole's *Dit*, which, alongside citations from Adam, incorporates seven of his own lyric compositions. These comprise a range of lyric types connected by a brief autobiographical narrative, a mixed structure which acts as a precedent for Machaut's *Remède de Fortune*. One connection between Adam and Nicole which appears to have been overlooked is that the rondeau 'Soyez liez et menez joie' [Be happy and keep joyful] (*Panthère*, 2515–26) has the same distinctive formal structure as Adam's rondeau 'Je muir, je muir d'amourete'. Both have a four-line refrain of which only one line is repeated internally, resulting in an overall structure of fourteen lines rather than the (retrospectively) more common sixteen.[14] To discover that 'Soyez liez' is not an original rondeau structure but one already anticipated by Adam confirms Adam's importance for Nicole. Such links direct us away from trying to find originary moments for a new genre, and instead towards acknowledging Adam's mastery, not as an originator himself so much as a celebrated practitioner of the art of regenerating pre-existent material.

That this compositional procedure was not only common but also valued in the late thirteenth and early fourteenth centuries is suggested by the numerous examples of citation, allusion and cross-reference amongst contemporary poets and composers. For instance, in addition to the examples mentioned above, refrains are shared between a ballade by Jehannot de Lescurel and two ballettes in Douce 308, and between Lescurel's *dits entés* and *Le Roman de Fauvel*.[15] The 'chançonete' 'Biautez, bontez, douce chiere' [Beauty, goodness, sweet face] in the *Dit de la panthère* also occurs in Douce 308 (No. 153). The first line of Machaut's ballade from *La Louange des dames* ('On ne porroit penser ne souhaidier' [One could not think or wish] (Wilkins, No. 151)) is identical to that of the first ballade of Jehan de la Mote's *Regret Guillaume* (597–617). Machaut's twelfth ballade 'Pour ce que tous mes chans' shares material with a song in Douce 308,[16] a motet in the Montpellier manuscript (Motet 277) and a *chace* ('Se je chant mains') in the Ivrea codex.[17] Many other examples of poetic and musical exchange could be adduced, especially later into the fourteenth century when the practice of producing ballades competitively, using an existing form or refrain, became widespread.[18] It is worth noting how far the surviving lyric repertory between Adam and Machaut is drawn together by these connecting threads. The process of

Ex. 18 Jehan de Lescurel, 'A vous, douce debonnaire' (polyphonic version)

generic change in this period is not a single evolutionary route between dance-songs and *formes fixes*. It takes place in an atmosphere in which authors increasingly saw composition as a mutual, collaborative exercise, in which the boundaries of cross-reference were constantly explored and stretched.

Lescurel's compositions are traditionally hailed as 'the earliest extant dance lyrics set to a dramatically new musical style'.[19] The key characteristic of this new musical style is his use of melismas, whereby he instantly gives greater linear space to the text. Only one piece is polyphonic, 'A vous, douce debonnaire'; by listening to this we can hear both kinds of musical effect simultaneously (see Ex. 18).

The comparison with Adam is interesting: Adam explores the consequences of creating polyphony with the monophonic genre of the refrain far more inventively than Lescurel; yet this lone piece by Lescurel is *the* potent combination of melisma and polyphony which appears to create singlehandedly the soundworld of the fourteenth century.[20]

Like Adam, Lescurel's work is laced with self-citation. 'A vous, douce debonnaire' comes in a monophonic as well as a polyphonic version; and the two *dits entés*, 'Gracïeuse, faitisse et sage', and 'Gracieus temps est, quant rosier' employ refrains cited in three of the shorter songs as well as sharing *Je l'amerai mon vivant*. Since music survives in all these cases, we have the rare opportunity to see whether the melody of each duplicated refrain remains the same, or whether Lescurel varies them in any way. The melodies are not changed, although in each case they are transposed. Again, as with Adam, one has the sense that Lescurel saw the refrain as the fundamental constructional element of his work. The two *dits entés*, rarely discussed in the same context as the short songs, illustrate how Lescurel saw the refrain as a means of generating a principle of formal division which could be applied just as much to spoken narrative couplets as to strophic song. The opening sequence of refrains in 'Gracieus temps est' could be strung together to form a single *chanson reverdie*, a process that mirrors Baude de la Quarière's 'La Chanson de bele Aelis' and is reversed in the second semi-lyric 'Han Diex ou pourrai je trouver' of *Fauvel*.

The relation between refrain and narrative text in the *dits entés* is close and supple. Very often, in a technique that goes back to *Le Roman de la violette* and *Le Tournoi de Chauvency*, the refrain simply completes a sentence begun in the narrative:

> Quant le voir savoir pourrai,
> *Bien croi que de duel mourrai.*
> ('Gracïeuse, faitisse et sage', str. 13)

> When I can know the truth, *I imagine I will truly die of grief.*

This may be compared with narrative and song in the *Dit de la panthère*: Nicole anticipates the exact words of a refrain in the narrative, so that when the refrain finally appears, we meet it with a sense of recognition. An example occurs near the start of the epilogue. The poet has just woken from his dream and is thinking over all it contained. His thoughts turn immediately to his *dame*, to whom he reaffirms his present loyalty despite the suffering this may entail:

> Et si n'en puis ne veil retraire
> Mon cuer por mal ne por contraire
> Qu'aye souffert dusques a ore,
> Ne que j'aie a soffrir encore
> (2210–13)

> And so I neither can nor wish to withdraw my heart either for any ill or adversity I have suffered up to now, or for what I may yet suffer.

In this state of mind he composes a rondeau, with rhyme words borrowed from the narrative:

> *Pour ennuy ne por contraire*
> *Ne pour mal souffrir*
> *Ne me puis d'amer tenir.*
> Mes cuers ne m'en lait retraire,
> *Por ennui ne por contraire...*
> (2226–30)

> *Not for trouble, or adversity, or for any ill I undergo, can I prevent myself*
> *from loving.* My heart will not let me withdraw from it. *Not for trouble,*
> *or adversity...*

Although it might be tempting to describe Nicole's technique as one appropriate to a non-musical approach to the *formes fixes*, it cannot be said of Lescurel's. Both authors are making use of the potential of refrains to stimulate new generic relationships, to create a dynamic formal dialogue between two opposing kinds of utterance, whether this be a musical *ouvert–clos* or statement–respond axis, or speech and song, narrative and lyric, monophony and polyphony, or the syllabic and the melismatic.

In turning finally to Machaut, such reflections bear upon the way in which the majority of surviving lyrics between Adam and Machaut occur in a narrative context. We might well wonder why the surviving evidence for change in the character of lyric composition in this period should largely be contained by a group of narrative poems.

I will take an indirect route towards this question by considering Machaut's approach to 'fixed form' more closely. His formal structures vary markedly: some basic patterns emerge, but differences in line length, the number of repeated sections, the length of the refrain and the degree of polyphonic elaboration create multiple possibilities of pace, balance and texture. Daniel Leech-Wilkinson has drawn attention to Machaut's reuse of elements from one piece in another, in this case, the way in which Rondeau 17, 'Dix et sept, cinq, trese, quatorse et quinse' [Ten and seven, five, thirteen, fourteen and fifteen], 'is a patchwork of near-quotations from Ballades 32 and 33'.[21] Machaut shows remarkable flexibility in exchanging material from one form to another. Fixity, from this point of view, is not a hard and fast process, but a matter of inventively recombining and juxtaposing textual and musical elements within specific (but subtly redefined) structures of repetition.

Leech-Wilkinson finds the start of 'Dix et sept' (the only passage that does not contain material from the ballades) strange and unconventional, but that a sense of its compositional logic is created through the repetitive structure of the rondeau. A refrain's role in a rondeau, ballade or *chanson balladée*/virelai is characterised by contradiction. The structure of repetition creates fixed points or one could say circularity. As material continuously unfolds, it is regularly interrupted and halted by the refrain. Yet the repetition, apparently a means for asserting the same, univocal text and melody, also creates a kind of openness. The more we hear the same phrase, each time in a slightly different context, the more it offers up a plurality of meanings. This is the creative heart of refrain-citation, in both narrative and lyric composition, and the so-called fixed forms do no more (in a sense) than devise further strategies for liberating this contradictory potential.

I want to elaborate on this, in conclusion, by way of the author, perhaps Jerome of Moravia, of a unique coda (in lat. 16663) appended to Johannes de Garlandia's *De mensurabili musica*. He has some remarkable comments linking the notion of *color* to refrain-citation:

> Repetitio eiusdem vocis est color faciens ignotum sonum esse notum, per quam notitiam auditus recipit placentiam. Et isto modo utimur in rondellis et cantilenis vulgaribus. Repetitio diversae vocis est idem sonus repetitus in tempore diverso a diversis vocibus. Et iste modus reperitur in triplicibus, quadruplicibus et conductis et multis aliis

> Repetition of the same voice is a *color* that causes an inconspicuous musical phrase to be conspicuous; the ear takes pleasure in that recognition. We use this manner [of *color*] in rondeaux and in vernacular songs. Repetition of diverse voice is the same musical phrase repeated at different times by different voices. This manner [of repetition] is found in tripla, quadrupla and in conducti and in many other kinds of music

> Tertia regula est: pone colores loco sonorum proportionator[um] ignotorum, et quanto magis colores, tanto sonus erit notus, et si fuerit notus, erit placens. Item loco coloris in regione cuiuslibet pone

cantilenam notam, copulam, vel punctum vel descensum vel ascensum alicuius instrumenti, vel clausam lay.

> The third rule is: put *colores* in the place of inconspicuous [literally: unknown] sounds; the more *colores* there are, so much the more will the sound be more clearly noticed, and if it will be noticeable, it will be pleasing. Again, in the place of a *color* put a known song [a refrain?] in that area, a hocket, a punctum or an ascending or descending figure upon an instrument, or a secular song.[22]

The practices he describes of causing 'an inconspicuous musical phrase to be conspicuous' (which he glosses in the second passage as putting 'a known song [a refrain?] in that area') and the repetition of the 'same musical phrase...at different times by different voices', corresponds strikingly with the kinds of intricate cross-referencing we have just been discussing.[23]

The remarks are also apt, perhaps surprisingly, to the technique I described earlier employed by Nicole de Margival and Lescurel in creating echoing links between sections of narrative and inset refrains. What we find in Jerome of Moravia as part of a description of musical practice, turns out to resonate with examples of contemporary poetic practice. Common to both musical and poetic contexts is the same pleasure in playing off repeated phrases, in turning sounds and words into a structure of recognition.

In conclusion, I would like to suggest that the consistent framing of *formes fixes* in narrative is not incidental to the generic shifts in the composition of song in this period of transition. Reflecting on aspects of the change in song that has taken place between the work of Jean Renart and that of Guillaume de Machaut, we have seen that the practice of citation is a key factor connecting thirteenth-century and fourteenth-century compositions. It is misleading to think of the *ars nova* as a break in musical history: the *formes fixes* are the culminating result of a century of creative exploration of the relations between one genre and another, and between poetry and music. The refrain consistently emerges as a fundamental constructional element in all kinds of work: moreover, the creative energies inherent in refrain-citation are as central to narrative as to song genres. We can see this in works as diverse as motets by Adam and the *Voir Dit* by Machaut. The working out of these changes in the context of narrative means that the smaller, subtle adjustments in the relation between refrain and strophe are embedded within the larger generic dialogue between song and narrative text. It is perhaps this dialogue that most contributes, in the *longue durée*, to the eventual disjunction between text and melody in the *formes fixes*, since it is a disjunction that has been displayed, explored, contradicted and yet sustained throughout the history of vernacular song.

Epilogue

O flour des flours de toute melodie,
Tres doulz maistres qui tant fuestes adrois,
Guillaume, mondain diex d'armonie,
Après vos fais, qui obtendra le choys
Sur tous fayseurs?
(1–5)

O flower of flowers of all melody, very dear master who was so skilful,
Guillaume, worldly god of harmony, after your achievements, who
will be pre-eminent above every poet?[1]

There is much to observe in this celebrated remark. One feature is the
way Deschamps draws attention first to Machaut's music rather than his
poetry. Deschamps does famously use *poète* of Machaut elsewhere, in so
doing applying the word for the first time in French literary history to a
contemporary (as opposed to a Classical) author.[2] Here he chooses the
more common *fayseur*. This term has a useful neutrality that can apply to
his music as well as to his poetry.[3] It draws out a retrospective pun on *fais*,
which can mean not only 'achievements' or 'deeds' but 'compositions'.
In other references to Machaut, Deschamps talks of 'l'art de musique et
le gay sentement', as well as 'le noble rethouryque'. Deschamps appears
able to find the terms to do justice to Machaut's achievements in both
music and poetry. Perhaps this is because he does not make any hard-
fought distinction between them; the skills of rhetoric and of music
meet together in Machaut to create a *maistre*. Machaut is not, or at
least not quite, at this stage in the fourteenth century, either a poet
or a musician, but a craftsman with a range of accomplishments. It is
possible, moreover, that even *poète* means author, rather than necessarily

the more modern meaning of poet; given this ambiguity, what we are reading in Deschamps's eulogies amounts to a comment less about music and poetry than about music and authorial status.

The plausibility of this reading is strengthened by Machaut's own comments about music and poetry. I want briefly to consider the Prologue, written, it seems, especially to introduce his collected works in fr. 1584 (MS A), dated to the 1370s. Placed at the front of the manuscript, and not included in the index, the Prologue appears to be a remarkable aesthetic statement written by Machaut at the end of his career as a way of epitomising his entire artistic production. This work takes the form of four ballades, in pairs, followed by 184 lines of narrative. In the first pair of ballades, Nature commands him to make 'nouviaus dis amoureus'. For advice and encouragement, she offers him three of her children: 'Scens, Retorique et Musique'. The second ballade takes the form of the poet's reply in which he duly accepts her charge with appropriate gratitude, humility and commitment. In the next pair, Amours offers three more of her children: Dous Penser, Plaisance and Esperance as 'matere' for his compositions. He responds again accordingly. As in the *Remede*, Machaut makes a three-fold classification.[4] He is a rhetorician and a musician, employing rhyme and melody, whose *sens* is derived from the *matere* of Amours.

The Prologue as a whole has been much discussed and debated. Some have argued, via the terms *musique artificiele* and *musique naturele* used in Deschamps's *L'Art de Dictier*, that music has so encompassing a meaning in Machaut that we should 'assume that he defines poetry as music'.[5] This is to ignore the plain and unambiguous way Machaut talks of rhetoric and music. Music is not subsumed under rhetoric, neither is rhetoric equivalent to poetry. They are separate skills working towards a similar goal, the praise of ladies and the Art of Love. There is a danger in so overreading the term *musique* in Machaut that one loses sight of the pragmatic, technical meaning of the word to any composer. Music and poetry have a professional rather than sentimental relationship in Machaut. His rather academic, unglamorous remarks especially in the *Voir Dit* on his musical settings are of a piece with the fact that he sets relatively few of his poems to music. This was not, I suspect, because he thought it all music in any case, but because (on the evidence of the *Voir Dit*) he found the technicalities of musical composition more

time-consuming than those of poetry. The more mystifying views of
music found in Deschamps and Froissart, it must be remembered, are
those of non-musicians.

The manuscript presentation of this Prologue, as Earp points out, is
intriguing: two later manuscripts (fr. 9221 and fr. 881) start with the
four ballades only, which introduce, in turn, Machaut's lyrical poems
as the start of his complete works.[6] Other, earlier manuscripts (fr. 1584,
fr. 22545, and New York, Pierpont Morgan Library, MS M. 396) include the narrative section of the Prologue as well as the ballades, and
start with Machaut's narrative poems. The logic of these arrangements
appears to point towards a desire to match up the generic order of the
codex with the generic structure of the Prologue. If a choice is made in
the works as a whole to begin with lyric, then they are given a lyric introduction, but if the choice falls to narrative, then narrative introduces
the works.[7] Whether or not it was Machaut himself in every case who
made this decision, it indicates how thoroughly generic issues dominate
the manner in which Machaut's compositions were presented.

Machaut's Prologue is deeply interesting for the sense it gives of
Machaut's looking over his complete works and pondering an appropriate way to introduce them. We gain an immediate insight into the
balance and order of his codices, and a strong impression of a single
individual seeking to control the public image of his writings. Fr. 146,
the *Fauvel* manuscript, comes closest to this impression, but in that
case, the energy behind the careful plotting of design, juxtaposition and
interpolation is driven by a political polemic, rather than by a single,
and highly personal aesthetic aspiration. Three author collections predate Machaut's: those of Adam de la Halle in fr. 25566, the chansons
of Thibaut, Roi de Navarre which introduce so many of the chansonniers, and Gautier's *Miracles*. Each varies in the kind and degree of unity
they manage to impose on the writing. Thibaut's has unity in the first
instance of genre, for the notion of authorship is added on to an already cohesive group of high art *grands chants*. In Adam's works the
notion of authorship pulls against that of genre. Authorship wins out
but by acknowledging the extreme generic diversity of the compilation.
Generic diversity is also a feature of Gautier's collections, but his poetic
authority is subsumed to the authority of the Virgin. She is the single,
cohesive topic that justifies and indeed impels his work.[8] Adam's oeuvre

does not have this kind of cohesion: its justification – a newly exposed position – is Adam himself.

Adam's works in fr. 25566 are usually taken as the most important immediate precedent for Machaut's oeuvre. Nonetheless, fr. 25566 was compiled for Adam rather than by him, which leaves Gautier in splendid early isolation as a vernacular author who tried to exert unusual control over the manuscript presentation of his own work. Machaut's efforts connect in this way with the earliest bold gestures of the thirteenth century. As I have argued, continuity exists in the issues concerning music and poetry throughout the 150 years that this book spans. The traditional view of a linear change 'from song to book' relies too straightforwardly on the obvious point that authors in the period partake in a climate of increasing literacy, in which books survive in greater numbers. Music, as well as poetry, becomes a more literate activity, but this does not result in a decline in performed music. Both poets and composers of music adapt with enormous creative energy to the changing stimulus of writing song. It sometimes seems as if we are being told that books gradually replace the art of performance: on the contrary, books become all the more important to the pragmatics of performance. The more literate music becomes, the more it participates in the bookish cultural circumstances of poetry, the more, ironically enough, it becomes a distinct performance art. We are privileged that in the *Fauvel* manuscript and the Machaut manuscripts survive examples of *mise-en-page* that are an extraordinarily sophisticated coordination of both kinds of performance.

A major concern of this book has been to trace the role of narrative in the writing down of song. Narrative is a permanent presence in the absorption of vernacular song into a literate world, and an influential one. We have seen how its influence consists partly in form, in the stretching and abbreviating of song into semi-lyric and semi-narrative. This fascination with creating and examining the differences between genre, between music and poetry, between languages, registers, and cultures is symptomatic of deep tendencies towards hybridity in the creative practice of thirteenth-century composers, from motet to romance. Much of this is enabled by the refrain, by its fundamentally double characteristic of being on the one hand an element that creates stability in a song structure by its pattern of repetition, and on the other, an element that creates division by introducing boundaries between one genre and another. In the transition from anonymity to authorship, refrains offer an illuminating perspective on the means by which formulas become part of the process of exerting greater types of control over language, over language in writing, over musical language and musical writing.

Above all, the presence of narrative shows us the importance of context to the way that song is presented in thirteenth- and fourteenth-century works and their manuscripts. It reminds us that song is never abstracted from its social form, but is mirrored, invented and reproduced by means of narrative throughout this period of its history. We might wish to avoid, in conclusion, the retrospective literary hegemony that sees the relationship between music and poetry as doomed to end in the middle of the fourteenth century. This suppresses the contribution of music to poetry as well as of poetry to music in medieval writing. Rather than finish (as so often) with the thought that this period ends with divorce and dissolution, we might seek instead to celebrate the superlatively inventive set of relationships between the two arts that it contains, and which continues to find new forms throughout the fifteenth century and beyond.

Glossary

Additamenta (pl.), used by Johannes de Grocheio to refer to strophic elements of a rondeau

Alleluia, in Gregorian chant, the third item of the Proper of the Mass (i.e. the variable rather than set liturgy of the Roman rite)

Aristocratisant, from Bec, a socio-poetic term, describing courtly register (see *popularisant*)

Ars Antiqua, the era and compositional practices of thirteenth-century French polyphony

Ars Nova, from Philippe de Vitry's treatise, *Ars nova*, the term describes the stylistic, rhythmic and theoretical characteristics of fourteenth-century polyphony

Ballade, used in fourteenth century to describe one of the three principal *formes fixes* (*see* rondeau and virelai)

Ballette, used in Douce 308 for collection of song texts with refrains, distinct from *grands chants*. They have no set form

Bergerie, a pastoral poem or dramatic scene

Canso, Occitan song of *fin'amor*

Cantefable, term uniquely used in *Aucassin et Nicolette*, which aptly describes the work's unique sung and spoken form in alternating prose and verse

Cantilena, song (Lat.), both sacred and secular

Cantilena entatam, *insertum*, used by Johannes de Grocheio to describe a type of *cantilena*, see *enté*

Carnivalesque, from carnival: festive culture of social reversal described by Bakhtin

Carole, general term for dance-song, characterised by use of refrain and

296

alternation between soloist and chorus. Does not imply a particular form

Cento (Lat. 'patchwork'), a work created from a collection of pre-existing elements

Chançon Coronée, (i) term used by Grocheio for a kind of trouvère chanson; (ii) also refers to a prize-winning song in a *puy*

Chanson à Refrain, Refrain Song, strophic song with the same refrain after each strophe

Chanson avec des Refrains, strophic song with a different (variable) refrain after each strophe

Chanson Balladée, *see* virelai

Chanson Courtoise, the principal genre of the trouvères, see *grand chant courtois*

Chanson Dramatique, term used by Lecoy for unique example of narrative song in Renart's *Rose*

Chanson d'Eloge, song praising a patron

Chanson d'Histoire, a song telling a story

Chanson de Mal Mariée, song expressing the grievances of an unhappily married woman

Chansonniers, manuscript collections of French and Occitan song, compiled from the mid-thirteenth century

Chanson Pieuse, sacred vernacular song, on a secular model

Chanson Reverdie, song on theme of renewal of the earth, and feelings of love, in the spring

Chanson de Toile, thirteenth-century narrative song on disappointed love, supposedly sung by women while spinning or weaving.

Chant Royal, early fourteenth-century fixed form, standardised by the *puys*, of five stanzas with refrain, and envoy

Clausula, a section of twelfth- and thirteenth-century polyphonic chant in discant (two-voice) style; basis for the thirteenth-century motet

Cobla, stanza in troubadour poem

Color, a melodic pattern in the isorhythmic motet, a type of motet which is structured on the repetition of a rhythmic pattern throughout a voice-part.

Complainte, Complainte d'amour, general term for a love lament; also specific, extended verse form developed by Machaut, and imitated by Froissart

Conductus, a song with Latin text, for one, two or three voices in note-against-note counterpoint

Confréries, religious, charitable associations formed in Northern French towns, *see puys*

Congé, a poem of farewell

Conte, a tale

Contrafactum, Contrafacere, Contrefaire, a song, or vocal part to which a new set of words has been fitted

Dance-Song, *see carole*

Débats Amoureux, versified love debates that may take a variety of forms

Déjà Dit, term coined by Roland Barthes to describe cliché

Discantus, discant, a second voice-part composed to a cantus (song, normally plainsong)

Dit, synonymous with poem, usually narrative or didactic

Dit à refrains, a *dit* inset with or structured around refrains

Diz Enté, term used in fr. 146 to describe two hybrid pieces by Jehan de Lescurel

Duplum, in polyphony, the voice above the tenor (also called *motetus* in thirteenth-century motet)

Enté, 'grafted', term used in fr. 845 of motet, in fr. 146 of *dit,* and elsewhere, usually to describe pieces with inset refrains; precise formal meaning is now debated

Estampie, type of instrumental dance, or a poem derived from it

Fabliau, short comic narrative, often sexually explicit or scatological

Fatras, burlesque genre derived from *fatrasies,* short nonsense poems fashionable in Picardy and Artois in the thirteenth century

Formalism, term associated with a literary movement in Russia from 1917 that concentrated on form to the exclusion of other considerations. Through the influence of Roman Jakobson, formalist aesthetics influenced later structuralist developments in linguistics, such as the work of A. J. Greimas

Forme Fixe, modern term for fourteenth-century songs in 'fixed forms', principally rondeau, ballade and virelai (*chanson balladée*)

Gran(t/d) Chan(t) Courtois, used by trouvère-chansonnier scribes and others to refer to the courtly chanson (e.g. in Douce 308). It differs from the *ballette* and the ballade in having five stanzas, normally, and no refrain.

Hoquet, breaking of melody into single notes or very short phrases by means of rests, often shared between two voices

Jeu-parti, a debate-song, usually on an erotic or courtly theme, shared between two real or fictional troubadours or trouvères

Jongleur, a professional entertainer

Lai, (i) extended song composition with sequential structure; (ii) Arthurian *lai*, type of song found only in thirteenth- and fourteenth-century Arthurian prose romances

Laisse, verse unit, of varying length, of the Old French *chanson de geste*

Lemma, *lemmata* (pl.), a passage from the text embedded in a commentary as a point of departure for the discussion

Litterae notabiliores, letters highlighted to indicate the beginnings of *sententiae* or sections of prose and verse

Measured, music consisting of notes of different lengths in fixed proportions

Melisma, melismatic, a large group of notes to a single syllable of text

Mensural notation, a type of musical notation in which the symbols clearly distinguish between notes of different durations in fixed proportions

Mode, (i) melodic: the scale (usually eight-note) in which a piece is written; (ii) rhythmic: a recurrent metrical pattern of long and short notes; (iii) literary: kind of or approach to writing

Monophony, music consisting in a single line of melody without accompaniment

Mot (Fr. 'word'), *see* motet

Motet, (i) composition for two, three, or four voices in which the tenor, drawn from chant, serves as foundation for upper voice(s) sung with French or Latin texts; (ii) one of the texted upper voices (*motetus*, from *mot*). The third voice is called *triplum*, the fourth, *quadruplum*

Motet Centon, see *cento*

Motet Enté, see *enté*

Organum, medieval polyphony

Ouvert–Clos Phrase, 'open–shut': describes cadences or ends of phrase, where 'ouvert' is a phrase that implies continuation, and 'clos' a closed ending

Pastoral, a mode of writing (originating in ancient Greece) that idealises shepherd life, often associated with satire

Pastourel(l)e, pastourelle avec des refrains, a type of stanzaic narrative song, in Latin or a vernacular, which tells of an encounter between a knight on horseback and a shepherdess. *Pastourelles* commonly have refrains; a number have the form of a *'chanson avec des refrains'*

Plainsong, monophonic Christian liturgical chant

Plica, notational symbol representing two pitches

Polyphony, music that simultaneously combines several lines

Popularisant, from Bec, a socio-poetic term, describing popular register (*see aristocratisant*)

Positura, a punctuation symbol which indicated the end of a section of text; *positurae*, a general term for punctuation signs

Premensural Notation, thirteenth-century notation (and earlier) which does not make mensural distinctions

Probationes Pennae, pen exercises, usually carried out by a scribe on a flyleaf to test his pen

Prosimetrum, a work that combines prose and verse

Punctus Elevatus, one of the *positurae*: used to indicate a pause

Puys, poetic societies that flourished in Northern French towns from the eleventh century onwards

Quadruplum, see motet

Razos, see *vidas*

Refractus, see refrain

Refrain, short, usually one- or two-line verse or melody (or both) that can appear: (i) (in usual modern sense) as a recurring element after each stanza of a song; or (ii) as an autonomous element in all kinds of musical and poetic genres of the thirteenth and early fourteenth century. Since a single refrain can have both functions, I make no typological distinction between the terms. Medieval terms include: *refractus*, (Lat. broken); also (Fr.) *refrait, reffrez* and *refret d'amors*

Refrain Exogène, term used by Bec to describe function (ii) of refrain

Refrain Récurrent, term used by Bec to describe function (i) of refrain

Responsory, type of liturgical chant

Reverdie, Reverdie Pieuse, see *chanson reverdie, chanson pieuse*

Rime Croisée, alternating rhymes (abab cdcd)

Rime Plate, rhyming couplets (aabbcc)

Roman, originally 'vernacular', translated from Latin; general term for narrative

Rondeau, a type of song, often in the thirteenth century associated with dance, with a repeated refrain mid-stanza; in the fourteenth century, one of the principal *formes fixes*

Rondellus, a rondeau with Latin text

Rondet de carole, a dance-song, first recorded in the thirteenth century, of variable form, but always with refrain

Salut, Salut d'amour, literally a 'greeting', love poem of variable form

Signifiant ('signifier'), term from Saussure meaning sound-image

Signifié ('signified'), term from Saussure meaning concept

Sotte chanson, see *fatras*

Source, (i) musical: manuscript; (ii) literary: textual origin

Stave, also staff, the set of lines (and spaces between them) each representing a pitch, on which music is written

Strophe, originally Greek (first part of a choral ode in drama), now used synonymously with stanza

Syllabic, of a song, either (i) having a relationship of one note to a syllable; or (ii) comprised of a mixture of single notes and short note-groups each of which is attached to a single syllable of text

Te Deum (laudamus), a song of praise to God sung in Roman rite at end of Matins. Often sung at religious and secular ceremonies, such as coronations

Tençon, from Occitan *tenso* (dispute), genre in which two voices engage in dialogue, usually in alternating stanzas

Tenor, from Latin *tenere* 'to hold': the lowest part in a polyphonic composition; often a borrowed melody (usually a segment of chant, sometimes a vernacular refrain), it is the foundational element in the musical composition

Through-composed, a song, set to music, which does not use the device of repetition.

Triplum, see motet

Trope, (i) musical: a newly composed interpolation of text or music or both, in official liturgical chant; (ii) literary: a figure of speech

Troubadours, poets and poet-composers of song in the *langue d'oc*

Trouvères, poets and poet-composers of song in the *langue d'oil* and also of narrative

Unicum, unique example

Vidas, short prose biographies of troubadours; *razos* explain circumstances of composition of songs

Viele, bowed, stringed instrument

Virelai, one of the three principal *formes fixes*, less current than the rondeau or ballade. Machaut also used the term *chanson balladée*.

Appendix

Manuscript sources of song in narrative and didactic texts of the thirteenth and fourteenth centuries from Jean Renart to Guillaume de Machaut: an annotated catalogue

Arsenal   Bibliothèque de l'Arsenal
BL   British Library
BM   Bibliothèque Municipale
BN   Bibliothèque Nationale
BR   Bibliothèque Royale

This catalogue, prepared in its earlier stages in collaboration with Mark Everist, whose work I gratefully acknowledge, is based on vdB's 'Liste des textes narratifs et didactiques contenant des refrains' IV. I have retained his sometimes idiosyncratic titles for ease of reference. However, this catalogue has been expanded to include: (1) other inset pieces in addition to refrains, and (2) works which contain other inset pieces but no refrains. In each case, the total number of inset pieces is given, together with an indication of whether each manuscript has music, blank staves or spaces for staves.[1] It is hard to give exact numbers for the inset pieces: some works are not edited, or only partially so, others, such as Machaut's *Voir Dit*, await further research: figures given must therefore be understood as provisional, and part of work in progress. This catalogue is presented (as in the bibliography) according to alphabetical order of first name of author (or title where author is unknown). For convenience, I have given the vdB title (where appropriate) as a cross-reference in square brackets. The chronological range overlaps with vdB, but is extended to include the works of Guillaume de Machaut.[2]

Legend:

* = MS not viewed
Double-spaced = one line left blank by scribe
Triple-spaced = two lines left blank etc.

L'*Abeïe dou chastel amoureus* [Abeïe]   **15 refrains**
Angers, BM 403 fols. 90v–91 v

Adam de la Bassée: *Ludus super Anticlaudianum* [c. lat. 2]   **38 Latin**
pieces (including 1 French refrain)[3]
Lille, BM 316 (*olim* 397) fols. 2–41 (music)

French Translation of *Ludus super Anticlaudianum* [Tr. Lud]
approx. 18 pieces (including 2 rondeaux[4])
Paris, BN fr. 1149 fol. 124–
Paris, BN fr. 1634 fols. 1–52
Paris, BN n. a. fr. 10047 fols. 2–41 (space before and after each refrain)

Adam de la Halle: *Jeu de la feuillée* [Feuillée][5]   **1 refrain**
Paris, BN fr. 25566 fols. 49–59 (music)

Adam de la Halle: *Le Jeu de Robin et Marion* [Rob.]
11 refrains, 5 further songs
Aix-en-Provence, Bibl. Méjanes 166(572) fols. 1–11 v (music)
Paris, BN fr. 1569 fols. 140–144v (double-spaced)
Paris, BN fr. 25566 fols. 39–48v (music)

Adam de la Halle: *Li Jus du pelerin* [Pelerin]   **2 refrains**
Paris, BN fr. 25566 fols. 37–39 (music)

Adenet le Roi: *Cleomadés* [Cleom.]   **7 rondeaux**
Berne, Stadt- und Universitätsbibliothek 238 fols. 1–150v (triple-spaced)
Brussels, BR II 7444 fols. 1–183 (triple-spaced)[6]
Paris, Arsenal 3142 fols. 1–72 (double-spaced)
Paris, BN fr. 1456 fols. 1–150 (double-spaced, except for first rondeau and
first two lines of second rondeau)
Paris, BN fr. 19165 fols. 38–389 (double-spaced for last four rondeaux only,
although rondeau 3 has double space before 1st line)
Paris, BN fr. 24404 fols. 1–168 (double-spaced)
Paris, BN fr. 24405 fols. 26–132v (triple-spaced)
Paris, BN fr. 24430 fols. 1–58v (double-spaced)
Paris, Institut de France 636 fols. 1–156 (1st three songs have double-spacing
before and after each whole song)

D'*Amors et de jalousie* [Jal.]   **20 refrains**
Paris, BN fr. 19152 fols. 110r–112v

Aucassin et Nicolette   **21 laisses**
Paris, BN fr. 2168 fols. 70–80v (music)[7]

Baudouin de Condé: *Le Conte de la rose* [Rose]   1 refrain
Brussels, BR 9411–9426 fols. 130–132
Dijon, BM 526 fols. 158–160
Paris, Arsenal 3142 fols. 314v–
Paris, Arsenal 3524 fols. 13–
Paris, BN fr. 1446 fols. 119–121 v
Turin, Biblioteca Nazionale Universitaria, L. V. 32 fols. 89–91*

Baudouin de Condé: *Prison d'amours* [Pris.]   54 refrains[8]
Dijon, BM 526 fols. 157–158
Turin, Biblioteca Nazionale Universitaria, L. V. 32*
Vienna, Österreiches Nationalbibliothek 2621 fols. 21–45 (music for two
    refrains; blank stave lines for the remainder)

Chansons latines [c. lat.]
    (1) Paris, BN lat. 15131 fols. 177–190   **17 refrains**
    (2) Paris, BN lat. 11331 fol. 12[9]   **1 refrain**
    (3) Paris, BN lat. 11331 fol. 12   **1 refrain**
    (4) München, Bayerische Staatsbibliothek, clm 4660 fol. 49v   **1 refrain**

La Chastelaine de Saint Gille [ChSG]   **35 refrains**
Paris, BN fr. 837 fols. 114v–116

La Chastelaine de Vergi   **1 chanson stanza**[10]
Berlin, Staatsbibliothek, Hamilton 25 fols. 37c–42b
Brussels, BR 9574–75 fols. 138c–144a
Paris, BN fr. 375 fols. 331 v–333 v
Paris, BN fr. 837 fols. 6b–11 a
Paris, BN fr. 1555, fols. 82v–96v
Paris, BN fr. 2136 fols. 139r–152v
Paris, BN fr. 25545 fols. 84a–89c
Paris, BN n. a. fr. 4531 fols. 88b–94d[11]

Citations latines concernant l'amour . . . [cit. am.]   **1 refrain**
Dijon, BM 526 fol. 3 v

Complainte d'amours [Compl. I]   **2 refrains**
Paris, BN fr. 837 fols. 267–268

Complainte d'amours [Compl. II]   **1 chanson (incl. 1 refrain)**
Paris, BN fr. 837 fols. 355–362v

Li Confrere d'amours [Confr.]   **12 refrains**
Paris, BN fr. 837 fol. 275

Correspondance amoureuse [corr. am.]   1 chanson (incl. 1 refrain)
Cambridge, Gonville and Caius College MS 54/31, fol. 146r (flyleaf)[12]

Le Court d'amours [suite anonyme] [Cour d'Am.]   33 refrains
Paris, BN n. a. fr. 1731 fols. 36–72 (refrains differentiated by double-spacing variously: (1) before the refrain; (2) after the refrain; (3) both before and after the refrain; and (4) in the middle of the refrain)

La Court de paradis [Par.]   20 pieces: 19 refrains[13] and 1 Latin liturgical incipit
Paris, BN fr. 837 fols. 57–60v
Paris, BN fr. 1802 fols. 95–106v (refrains underlined in lead)
Paris, BN fr. 25532 fols. 331v–335 (music; except for refrain vdB 1786)

L'Estoire de Joseph   4 songs[14]
Paris, BN fr. 24429 fols. 94v–105r
Paris, BN n. a. fr. 10036 fols. 105–124v (music; marginal additions to text)
Rome, Biblioteca Apostolica-Vaticana Reg. Lat. 1682 fols. 81–92

Galeran de Bretagne [Galeran]   1 refrain
Paris, BN fr. 24042 fols. 1–105

Gautier de Coinci: *Les Miracles de Notre Dame* [Mir.] 22 chansons pieuses, incl. 14 refrains (+27 apocryphal songs in French, 16 in Latin)[15]
(a) MSS with music:
Brussels, BR 10747 fols. 1–228 (music; some blank staves)
Leningrad, Bibl. Publ. Fr. F. v. XIV 9 fols. 1–285 (music)
London, BL Egerton 274 fols. 98–99 (music)
London, BL Harley 4401 fols. 1–189 (music)
Paris, Arsenal 3517–3518 fols. 1–186, 1–221 (music)
Paris, BN fr. 986 fols. 1–210 (music)
Paris, BN fr. 1530 fols. 1–257 (music)
Paris, BN fr. 1536 fols. 1–256 (music)
Paris, BN fr. 2163 fols. 1–226 (music)
Paris, BN fr. 22928 fols. 36–299 (music)
Paris, BN fr. 25532 fols. 4–221v (music)
Paris, BN n. a. fr. 24541 fols. 2–243v (music)
(b) MSS with blank staves or spaces for staves:
Besançon, BM 551 fols. 1–180 (double-spaced)
Paris, Arsenal 3527 fols. 100–154 (quadruple-spaced)
Paris, BN fr. 1533 fols. 37–263v (first stanza quadruple-spaced)
Paris, BN fr. 2193 fols. 1–148 (music on a two-line stave)[16]

Paris, BN n. a. fr. 6295 fols. 104v–167 (1st stanza only of each chanson triple-spaced)

Rome, Biblioteca Apostolica-Vaticana Pal. lat. 1969 fols. 1–220v (double-spaced; some blank staves)

(c) MSS without music:

Blois, BM 34 fols. 1–273

Florence, Biblioteca Medicea Laurenziana, 45, Ashburnham 53*

Neuchâtel, BM 4816 (B.P. 4816) fols. 285–371

Paris, BN fr. 817 fols. 1–190

Paris, BN fr. 1613 fols. 1–183

Paris, BN fr. 23111 fols. 64–332 (with additions)

Paris, BN fr. 24300 fols. 83–end

Tours, BM 948 fols. 1–130

Gérard de Liège: ***Quinque incitamenta ad Deum amandum ardenter*** **[Quinque]   9 refrains**

Brussels, BR 2475–81 fols. 72–94v

Rome, Biblioteca Apostolica Vaticana Reg. 71 fols. 43v–62

Troyes, BM 1890 fols. 197–226v

Gerbert de Montreuil: *Le Roman de la violette ou de Gerart de Nevers* **[Viol.]   44 pieces:**[17] **10 chansons, 3 Occitan cansos, 29 refrains, 1 chanson de toile, 1 laisse from a chanson de geste**

New York, Pierpoint Morgan Library 36 fols. 1–111

Paris, BN fr. 1374 fols. 133–172v + 183 (songs written in red)

Paris, BN fr. 1553 fols. 288–325

PROSE VERSION

Brussels, BR 9631 fols. 1–127

Paris, BN fr. 24378 fols. 1–348

Gervès du Bus: *Le Roman de Fauvel* **[Fauv.]   169 pieces: 53 settings of Latin prose, 36 refrains (including 2 'semi-lyrics'), 4 rondeaux, 6 ballades, 2 virelais,**[18] **1 single stanza song, 2 fatras, 4 French lais, 5 Latin lais, 1 motet enté, 21 conductus, 34 polyphonic motets**

Paris, BN fr. 146 fols. 3–45 (music)[19]

Girart d'Amiens: *Escanor* **[Escanor]   4 refrains**

Paris, BN fr. 24374 fols. 1–218 (triple-spaced)

Girart d'Amiens: *Meliacin / Le Conte du Cheval de fust* **[Mel.]   24 pieces: 13 chanson extracts, 1 complete chanson, 7 motet texts, 2 rondeaux, 1 further refrain**

Brussels, BR IV 319 fols. 15–129v*

Florence, Biblioteca Riccardiana 2757 fols. 2–173 (triple-spaced)
Paris, BN fr. 1455 fols. 1–129v (songs underlined in red; double space above refrain 8)[20]
Paris, BN fr. 1589 fols. 1–166 (triple-spaced)
Paris, BN fr. 1633 fols. 1–157 (triple-spaced; [identical to fr. 1589])

Guillaume de Machaut: *Remède de Fortune*   **9 pieces: 1 lai, 1 complainte, 1 chant royal, 1 baladelle, 1 ballade, 1 prière, 1 virelai, 1 refrain, 1 rondeau**
Aberystwyth, National Library of Wales, 5010 C fols. 30r–41v (fragment; music lost)
Berne, Burgerbibliothek MS 218 fols. 43r–47r; 50r–60r (music for *En amer* (baladelle) and *Dame, de qui* (ballade) only)[21]
Cambridge, Magdalene College, Pepysian Library 1594 fols. 1r–36v (music)
New York, Pierpont Morgan Library, M. 396 fols. 47v–73v (text only)
New York, Wildenstein Collection (no shelfmark) fols. 90r–121r (music)
Paris, Arsenal 5203 fols. 47r–76r (text only)
Paris, BN fr. 843 fols. 50r–77r (text only)
Paris, BN fr. 1584 fols. 49v–80r (music)
Paris, BN fr. 1585 fols. 107r–138r (music) (except for *chanson roial*)
Paris, BN fr. 1586 fols. 23r–58v (music)
Paris, BN fr. 9221 fols. 22r–36v (music)
Paris, BN fr. 22545 fols. 40r–63v (music)

Guillaume de Machaut: *La Fonteinne amoureuse*   **3 pieces: 1 complainte, 1 confort, 1 rondel**
Berne, Burgerbibliothek MS 218 fols. 108r–114r; 116r–123r
New York, Pierpont Morgan MS M. 396 fols. 102r–117v
New York, Wildenstein Collection (no shelfmark) fols. 197r–216r
Paris, Arsenal 5203 fols. 118r–137v
Paris BN fr. 843 fols. 146r–164r
Paris BN fr. 1584 fols. 154r–173v
Paris BN fr. 1585 fols. 204r–217v
Paris BN fr. 9221 fols. 83r–91r
Paris BN fr. 22545 fols. 119v–134v

Guillaume de Machaut: *Le Livre dou Voir Dit*   **105 pieces and refrains: 1 lai, 3 complaintes, 19 ballades, 31 rondeaux, 9 chansons balladées, refrains[22], 46 prose letters, 1 prière, 5 circles of Fortune**
Berne, Burgerbibliothek MS 218 fols. 133r–135r
New York, Pierpont Morgan MS M. 396 fols. 122r–182v
Paris, Arsenal 5203 fols. 147v–151v
Paris, BN fr. 1584 fols. 221r–306r

Paris, BN fr. 9221 fols. 171r–210r (music for eight songs)
Paris, BN fr. 22545 fols. 137v–198v

Guiron le Courtois[23] **various pieces including lais, verse letters, epitaphs**
London, BL, Additional 36673 fols. 1–216v[24]
Paris, BN fr. 350 fols. 1–438v[25]

Henri d'Andeli: *Lai d'Aristote* [Arist.]   5 pieces: 3 rondeaux, 1 chanson de toile stanza, 1 refrain
Paris, Arsenal 3516 fols. 344v–347
Paris, BN fr. 837 fols. 80v–83
Paris, BN fr. 1593 fols. 154–156
Paris, BN fr. 19152 fols. 71v–73v
Paris, BN n. a. fr. 1104 fols. 69v–72 (triple-spaced[26])

Jacquemart Giélée: *Renart le Nouvel* [Ren.]   118 pieces: 111 refrains,[27] 2 Latin liturgical incipits,[28] 5 prose letters
Paris, BN fr. 372 fols. 1–60 (music)
Paris, BN fr. 1581 fols. 1–57 (music for one refrain, the rest blank staves)
Paris, BN fr. 1593 fols. 2–58v (music)
Paris, BN fr. 25566 fols. 119–179 (music)

Jacques Bretel: *Le Tournoi de Chauvency* [Chauv.]   35 refrains
Florence, Biblioteca Medicea Laurenziana, Palatinus CXVII*[29]
Mons, BM 330–215 fols. 82–105v
Oxford, Bodleian Library, Douce 308 fols. 114–147v

Jakemès: *Le Roman du castelain de Couci et de la dame de Fayel* [Couci] 10 pieces: 7 chansons (incl. 1 in virelai form), 3 rondeaux
Paris, BN fr. 15098 fols. 1–159v
Paris, BN n. a. fr. 7514 fols. 34–91v

Jean de Condé: *Lays dou blanc chevalier* [Blanc Ch.]   1 refrain
Turin, Biblioteca Nazionale, 1626 fols. 22–27v L.I.13 *[30]

Jean le Court, dit Brisebarre: *Le Restor de paon* [Rest.]   1 rondeau
Copenhagen, BR Thott 414*
London, BL Additional 16888 fols. 142–161
New York, Pierpoint Morgan Library, William D. Glazer Coll. G.24 = Donaueschingen, Fürstlich Füstenbergerische Bibliothek 168 fols. 102v–141v*
Oxford, Bodleian Library, Bodley 264 fols. 165–182v (music for first six lines of eight-line rondeau)
Oxford, Bodleian Library, Douce 165 fols. 138–182v
Paris, Arsenal 2776 fols. 135–153

Paris, BN fr. 790 fols. 192–199v
Paris, BN fr. 1375 fols. 538–554v
Paris, BN fr. 1554 fols. 139v–160v (rondeau underlined in red)
Paris, BN fr. 2166 fols. 32v–63v
Paris, BN fr. 12565 fols. 189–233v (quadruple-spaced)
Paris, BN fr. 12567 fols. 194–205v
Paris, BN fr. 20045 fols. 139–159
Paris, BN fr. 24386 fols. 164–183v
Paris, BN fr. 25521 fols. 151–172* (refrain is missing and ms apparently lost)
Rouen, BM 1057 (O. 8) fols. 131–148

Jean Renart: *Le Roman de la rose ou de Guillaume de Dole* [Guill.]
48 pieces: 13 chansons françaises (extracts), 3 chansons occitanes (extracts), 3 chansons de toile, 1 chanson d'histoire, 2 chansons dramatiques, 2 pastourelles, 1 chanson d'éloge, 1 tornoi de dames, 17 rondets de carole, 3 refrains, 1 Latin liturgical incipit,[31] 1 laisse from a chanson de geste
Rome, Biblioteca Apostolica Vaticana Reg. 1725 fols. 68v–98v

Jehan Acart de Hesdin: *La Prise amoureuse* [Acart]   18 pieces: 9 ballades, 9 rondeaux
Arras, BM 897 fols. 141–152
Berne, Stadt- und Universitätsbibliothek A. 95. I fols. 1–4v
Paris, BN fr. 24391 fols. 138–150v (quadruple-spacing for first stanza of each balade and refrain of each rondeau; rondeaux 7 and 9 have quadruple-spacing throughout; in rondeau 8, 1st 2 lines of strophe also quadruple-spaced)
Paris, BN fr. 24432 fols. 396v–412

Jehan de la Mote, *Le Parfait du paon*   8 ballades
Paris, BN fr. 12565 fols. 233–297
Oxford, Bodleian Library, Douce 165 fols. 200v–206

Jehan de la Mote, *Li Regret Guillaume comte de Hainault*   30 ballades
Paris, BN n. a. fr. 7514 fols. 1–33v

Jehannot de Le scurel: *Diz entez sus Refroiz de Rondeaux* [Esc.]
52 refrains[32]
'Gracieuse faitisse et sage', dit enté, 24 refrains
'Gracieus temps est', dit enté, 28 refrains
Paris, BN fr. 146 fols. 57–62v (music)

***Ju de le capete Martinet* [Cap.]   1 refrain**
Paris, BN n. a. fr. 1731 fols. 32–36

Manuscrit [ms]
    Paris, Arsenal 2776 fol. 153 v   **1 refrain**
    Paris, BN fr. 14968 fol. 169   **1 refrain**
    Tours, BM 136 fol. 196v   **1 refrain**

Le Mariage des sept arts (version anonyme) [Mar.]   **5 pieces: 4 refrains, 1 chanson**
    Reims, BM 1275 fols. 64–66[33]

Nevelon Amion: *Vers d'amours* [Nevelon]   **2 refrains**
    Paris, BN fr. 25566 fols. 278–280
    Rome, Biblioteca Apostolica Vaticana Reg. Lat. 1490 fols. 129v–130v

Nicole de Margival: *Le Dit de la panthère d'amors* [Panth.]   **19 pieces: 3 dits, 3 rondeaux, 1 baladelle, 1 ballade, 11 citations from 8 chansons (4 in full)**[34]
    Paris, BN fr. 24432 fols. 152v–170

Perceforest   **20 pieces: 8 lais, 1 prière, 1 réponse, 1 oraison, 1 inscription, 3 débats amoureux, 5 chansons**[35]
    London, BL Royal 15 E V, fols. 1–333; London, BL Royal 19 E III–19 E II, fols. 1–300, 1–315
    Paris, BN fr. 106–109
    Paris, BN fr. 345–348
    Paris, Arsenal 3483–3494

Philippe de Novare: *Mémoires* [Mém.]   **1 refrain**
    Verzuolo, Bibl. C. Perrin*

Philippe de Rémi: *Salut á refrains* [Beaum.]   **8 refrains**
    Paris, BN fr. 1588 fol. 114v

Proverbs [Prov. H]   **5 refrains**
    Hereford, Cathedral Library P. 3. 3. fols. 164–167

Proverbs [Prov. T]   **4 refrains**
    Tours, BM 468 fols. 178–186

Resverie [Resverie]   **1 refrain**
    Paris, BN fr. 837 fols. 174–175

Richard de Fournival: *Li Bestiaires d'amours* [Best.]   **1 refrain**
    Oxford, Bodleian Library, Douce 308 fols. 86v–107v
    Paris, BN fr. 412 fols. 228–236

Richard de Fournival?: *Li Commens d'amours* [Comm. d'am.]   **1 refrain**
    Dijon, BM 526 fols. 4–10 (triple spacing for refrains on fol. 6v)

Robert de Blois, *Le Chastoiement des dames*³⁶   1 complainte
Paris, Arsenal 3516 fols. 296v–298v
Paris, Arsenal 5201 fols. 8–19
Paris BN fr. 837 fols. 129v–133v
Paris BN fr. 24301 fols. 550–560

Le Roman de Cassidorus (continuation of Le Roman des sept sages)
1 débat (incl. 6-strophe verse letter)³⁷
Brussels, BR 9245 fols. 184v–296*
Brussels, BR 9401 fols. 1–166v*
London, BL Harley 4903 fols. 1–16
Paris BN fr. 93 fols. 186–294v*
Paris BN fr. 17000 fols. 147v–
Paris BN fr. 22548 fols. 172–206v
Paris BN fr. 22549 fols. 1–74
Turin, Biblioteca Nazionale Universitaria 1650 fols. 1–76v*

Le Romans de la dame a la licorne et du biau chevalier   **29 pieces:**
15 ballades, 1 balette, 7 rondeaux, 1 chanson stanza, 1 dit, 1 complainte,
1 refrain, 1 prose letter, 1 prière
Paris, BN fr. 12562 fols. 1–68v (all ballades and all except 2 rondeaux triple-spaced)

Le Roman de Kanor (continuation of Le Roman des sept sages)   **3 pieces:**
1 refrain, 2 rondeaux
London, BL Harley 4903 fols. 135–231r^b (triple-spaced)
Paris, BN fr. 1446 fols. 1–70v
Paris, BN fr. 22550 fols. 112–163 (triple-spaced)

Le Roman de Laurin (continuation of Le Roman des sept sages)
3 rondeaux
Paris, BN fr. 17000 fols. 39–147 (double-spaced)
Paris, BN fr. 22548 fols. 56–172 (double-spaced)³⁸

Le Roman de Peliarmanus (continuation of Le Roman des sept sages)
3 pieces: 1 refrain, 1 rondeau, 1 verse letter
London, BL Harley 4903 fols. 16–134r^b (triple-spaced)
Paris, BN fr. 22550 fols. 1–112 (triple-spaced)³⁹

Le Roman de Tristan en prose⁴⁰   17 lais⁴¹
Paris, BN fr. 776 (music for 3 lais, fols. 181, 246, 271v)
Paris, BN fr. 12599 fols. 39– (all lais double-spaced)
Vienna, Österreiches Nationalbibliothek 2542 (music)

***Salut d'amours* [Sal. I]   14 pieces: 10 rondeaux, 4 refrains**
Paris, BN fr. 837 fols. 253v–255

Salut d'amours [Sal. Ia]   1 refrain
Paris, BN fr. 837 fol. 182

Salut d'amours [Sal. II]   29 refrains
Paris, BN fr. 837 fols. 269–271

Salut d'amours [Sal. III]   40 refrains
Paris, BN fr. 837 fols. 271–272v

Sermons [Serm.]
(a) 1 rondeau (vdB, rond. 42)
Cambridge, Gonville and Caius College MS 136/76 p. 235
Cambridge, Trinity College B. 14. 39 fol. 34
London, BL Arundel 292 fol. 38
Poitiers BM 97 fols. 32v–33
Rome, Vaticana Borghese 200 fol. 3

(b) 2 rondeaux (vdB, ronds. 42, 43)
Paris, BN lat. 16497 fol. 128v

(c) 1 rondeau (vdB, rond. 44)
Paris, BN fr. 12467 fol. 53v (rondeau written in red at the beginning of
the Moralités)
Paris, Arsenal 3142 fol. 284v (rondeau written in red at beginning; each
line written in red and individually glossed on subsequent folios)
Vienna, Österreiches Nationalbibliothek 2621 fol. 52v

Sone de Nansay [Sone]   2 rondeaux
Turin, Biblioteca Nazionale Universitaria 1626 fols. 35v–108

Tibaut: *Le Roman de la poire* [Poire]   20 refrains
Paris, BN fr. 2186 fols. 1–83v (refrains given historiated initial at head of
page with blank staves to the right; staves not drawn in occasionally; see
notes to vdB 1427, and Fig. 7(a))
Paris, BN fr. 12786 fols. 1–24 (triple-spaced)
Paris, BN fr. 24431 fols. 180–189 (fragmentary; music for three refrains)

Traduction de l'Ars amandi d'Ovide en prose avec commentaire [Ovide]
72 pieces: 1 pastourelle stanza, 2 rondeaux, 6 chanson stanzas,[42]
63 refrains[43]
Modena, Biblioteca Estense, γ.G.3.20(=Campori 42)
Paris, Arsenal 2741 fols. 1–61
Paris, BN fr. 881 fols. 49–96v
Brussels, BR 10988, fols. 1–94v*

Watriquet de Couvin: *Fatrasie* [Fatr.]   30 refrains and 1 Latin refrain
Paris, BN fr. 14968 fols. 162–269 (refrains written in red)

Watriquet de Couvin: *Trois dames de Paris* [Tr. D.]   2 refrains
Paris, Arsenal 3525 fols. 88v–94

Notes

PROLOGUE

1 For example, Page, *The Owl and the Nightingale*.
2 In the sense of both a stemma and a literary source.
3 Huot, *From Song to Book*; Butterfield, 'Interpolated Lyric'; Boulton, *The Song in the Story*; Gregory B. Stone, *The Death of the Troubadour: The Late Medieval Resistance to the Renaissance* (Philadelphia, 1994).
4 Zink, *Roman rose et rose rouge*.
5 *OED*, REFRAIN.
6 Switten, *Music and Poetry*, 131.
7 Stevens, *Words and Music*, 162, 175 and *passim*.
8 Homi K. Bhabha, *The Location of Culture* (London and New York, 1994).
9 Among musicologists, Bent, Stevens, Baltzer, and Roesner *et al.*, eds., *Le Roman de Fauvel*, in the introduction to the facsimile of *Le Roman de Fauvel* found in Paris, BN, français 146; among literary scholars, notably Huot and Switten.
10 For a survey, see Green, 'Orality and Reading'; Coleman, *Public Reading*.

CHAPTER I

1 A full bibliography on this large set of issues cannot be given here; for a broad-ranging discussion and references see Switten, *Music and Poetry*, 'Introduction'. For further, more recent comments, see Bent, 'Editing Early Music' and 'The Grammar of Early Music'.
2 Stevens, *Words and Music*, 458–59; and Switten, *Music and Poetry*, 3–20.
3 Clanchy, *From Memory to Written Record*, 248–57.
4 Zumthor, *La Poésie et la Voix*, 68.
5 Jameson, *Political Unconscious*, 106.
6 Bakhtin, *Speech Genres*; Kristeva, 'Word, Dialogue and Novel'.
7 Bec, *La lyrique française*, I, 17–53. See Ch. 7 below.
8 Zink, *Roman rose et rose rouge*, 26–29; Hult, *Self-Fulfilling Prophecies*, 202–04; Stevens, *Words and Music*, 168–69; Butterfield, 'Interpolated Lyric', 8–12; Page, *The Owl and the Nightingale*, 107–08, Boulton, *The Song in the Story*, 9–15, and Durling, ed., *Jean Renart*. The date of the *roman* remains uncertain. It has been conjectured to be as early as 1200–01 (Servois), or as late as 1228 (Lecoy and Zink), with some scholars arguing for 1208–10 (Lejeune, Mattioli). For the most recent detailed discussion and references, see Psaki, ed., *Jean Renart*, and John W. Baldwin, '"Once there was an emperor ...": A Political Reading of the Romances of Jean Renart', in Durling, ed., *Jean Renart*, 45–82,

who argues for a date between 1202 and 1218. My own preference is for a date before the second recension of Gautier de Coinci's *Miracles*, to allow for the possibility that Gautier was reacting directly to Renart's work. Given that the dates of composition of the *Miracles* are themselves insecure, I incline towards *c.* 1210 or perhaps even earlier.

9 'mist...en romans' in the first line can also mean 'translated into French'. I cite from Lecoy's edition, unless otherwise indicated.

10 Also Page, *Owl and Nightingale*, 107.

11 'Suspension and Fall', in Durling, ed., *Jean Renart*, 108.

12 Hunt, 'The Prologue'; also his 'Rhetorical Background'.

13 Compare *Le Comte de Poitiers*, a probable source for the *Violette*. This does not contain any songs but begins straightaway with the story.

14 Psaki, ed., *Jean Renart*, xxvii–xxviii. The translator's word 'scores' is unfortunately misleading, as its modern meaning is far removed from thirteenth-century musical monody.

15 He cites just one reference, from Froissart, which is far from clear-cut (*L'Espinette amoureuse*, 1046–47), 'Suspension and Fall', 107. Two examples from motet texts are instructive: 'Une pucele...si notoit: O,o,o,o,o,o' [A girl...sang: O,o,o,o,o,o'] (M764, duplum), see Ch. 6 below, where 'noter' does plainly mean 'sing'; and 'car il convient que je de ce chant et not' ['for it is fitting that I should sing and make notes'] (M262, duplum), where 'chanter' and 'noter' are distinguished. (For M in the motet references, see the List of Abbreviations.) There are many more references for both meanings in Tobler-Lommatsch (who, incidentally, cite lines 1–3 of Renart's *Rose* as an example of *noter* meaning 'aufzeichnen').

16 All citations from the *Violette* are taken from Buffum, ed., *Le Roman de la violette*.

17 Huot regards Gautier as irrelevant to court poetry (*From Song to Book*, 40). In my view, however, he has great significance for our understanding of thirteenth- and fourteenth-century secular poetry.

18 See *Les Chansons à la Vierge*, ed. Chailley.

19 Citations from the *Miracles* are taken from Koenig, ed., *Les Miracles de Nostre Dame*, unless otherwise indicated.

20 Of the twenty-six manuscripts with songs, twelve have music, six have blank staves and eight no signs of music. See the Appendix.

21 See also the related discussion in Page, *The Owl and the Nightingale*, 107–08, who speculates that a written tradition of trouvère monody may well have existed before 1220. My view – in partial support – is that this is implied in any case by the Gautier de Coinci manuscripts (not mentioned by Page). However, the fact that surviving written records of trouvère song are no earlier than the thirteenth century seems to me to be of a piece with the kinds of emphasis placed on song in that period.

22 Roques, ed., *Aucassin et Nicolette*.

23 Butterfield, 'Aucassin'.

CHAPTER 2

1 See the debate occasioned by Page, *Discarding Images*, notably Bent, 'Reflections'; Page, 'A Reply'; and Strohm, 'How to Make Medieval Music Our Own'.

2 For two representative instances of debate on this issue, see Leech-Wilkinson, 'Machaut's "Rose, Lis"' and Bent, 'Editing Early Music'.

3 Switten, *Music and Poetry*, 4–5. For other early citations of troubadour song in Catalan treatises, see Aubrey. *Music of the Troubadours*, 72–73.

4 Buffum, ed., *Roman de la violette*, vii–ix.

5 The standard bibliography of refrains is van den Boogaard, *Rondeaux et refrains* (hereafter vdB). As vdB remarks, refrains as repeated elements in a strophic song must be as old as song composition itself. His earliest refrain is of this kind, from the oldest known French song, datable 1147–48 (see vdB, 10–11).

6 See Maillard, 'Lais avec notation'; and Baumgartner, 'Remarques'.

7 In the thirteenth century, *lais* also occur in *Guiron le Courtois*. In the fourteenth, two further Arthurian romances resemble the prose *Tristan* in their use of song: *Le Roman de Perceforest* and Froissart's *Meliador*. For the songs in *Perceforest*, see Lods, ed., *Les pièces lyriques*.

8 A fascinating source of song, the Arthurian prose romances have still not been fully edited. Their special generic features make it preferable for them to be treated separately.

9 Scholars of trouvère song, principally Van der Werf, Tischler and Stevens, have largely been occupied with necessary primary issues of editing and transmission; see Switten, *Music and Poetry*, 'Introduction'; Doss-Quinby, *The Lyrics of the Trouvères*. For discussion of chansonniers from a literary perspective, see Huot, *From Song to Book*, Ch. 2.

10 Boulton, *The Story in the Song*, 80–119; Huot, *From Song to Book*, 108–10. Recent studies have been more adventurous in connecting the presence of songs to issues of gender, see Kay, *Subjectivity*, and the essays in Durling, ed., *Jean Renart*.

11 See the Appendix.

12 It is the main precedent for the *Cantigas de Santa Maria*, compiled at the Spanish court of Alfonso the Wise (1252–84).

13 The lengthiest bibliography of French narratives containing lyrics is that of Boulton, *The Story in the Song*, 295–97. Considerable caution should be exercised, however, over the numbers given for the inset pieces as these rely uncritically on normalising modern editions and are frequently either inaccurate or misleading (for instance, *Le Roman de Fauvel* is listed as containing one refrain). Shorter, but more reliable published listings are given in vdB, Part III, Section IV; and Ludwig, 'Die Quellen'. My Appendix revises and extends Boulton's as far as Guillaume de Machaut (but excluding Froissart).

14 See Chs. 8–9 below.

15 See Ch. 6 below.

16 On this complex genre, see vdB and Doss-Quinby, *Les Refrains* (discussion of texts only); Clark, 'Refrain'; Butterfield, 'Repetition', 'The Refrain' and 'Catalogue of Refrains' (texts and melodies). Work on refrain melodies still has to rely on Gennrich, *Rondeaux, Virelais und Balladen*, but see Apel, 'Rondeaux, Virelais and Ballades', and vdB, 18, on its inadequacies.

17 Out of twenty-two authentically attributed songs (and twenty-seven apocrypha), there are just two two-voice chansons in the *Miracles*, Nos. 10 and 15 in Chailley, ed., *Les Chansons*. An impromptu *discantus* has been added to one of the refrains in the fr. 1593 copy of *Renart le Nouvel*, fol. 18r (see Fig. 5).

18 This statistic is based on examination of some 231 manuscripts of 'narratives' containing inset verse from the early thirteenth century to the mid-fourteenth. See the Appendix. Approximately one-tenth of troubadour and two-thirds of trouvère songs survive with music.

19 For R in the Chanson references (e.g. R787), see the List of Abbreviations.

20 Of thirteen sources, five have music (Linker, *A Bibliography*, No. 65–51).

21 Fols. 94r–109v.

22 This practice is not so consistent later in the manuscript.

23 A further instance of interconnection is that some chansonniers, like the *Miracles*, include collections of chansons to the Virgin.

24 Compare the red ink used in sermon manuscripts: see Ch. 10.

25 Psaki's comments (see Ch. 1, n. 14 above) are representative of this kind of view.

26 It would qualify, for example, the argument of Huot, *From Song to Book*, whose tracing of the progress 'from song to book' leaves out the complicating factor of musical transmission.

27 The chanson in *Meliacin* is actually by Gace Brulé; see Lerond, ed., *Chansons*, No. XXXI.

28 *Ibid.*, No. I.

29 *Ibid.*, No. V.

30 This can also be seen from the way in which Gerbert reworks the plot of *Le Comte de Poitiers*, a probable source for the *Violette*, by cavalierly splicing in the songs and opportunities to sing them.

31 *Vergi* cannot be dated more precisely than between 1203 and 1288 (Whitehead, ed., *La Chastelaine*, ix); for the dating of *Couci*, see Delbouille, ed., *Le Roman*, lxxiv.

32 *La Prison*, ed. Fourrier.

33 de Montaiglon, ed., *Chansons, ballades et rondeaux*, 260.

34 Deschamps, *Oeuvres*, ed. le Marquis de Queux de Saint-Hilaire and Raynaud, X, xlix, Ballade XLII.

35 *Débats de deux amants*, in *Oeuvres poétiques*, ed. Roy, II, 72.

36 This is the same stanza that is cited in the *Violette*. Whitehead, ed., *La Chastelaine*, xi–xii, deduces from this and from the fact that the two romances share the character of the Chastelaine that the *Violette* is a possible source for the *Vergi*.

37 Zumthor, 'De la chanson au récit'.

38 Whitehead, ed., *La Chastelaine*.

39 See Boutière, Schutz and Cluzel, eds., *Biographies des troubadours*.

40 *Ibid.*, No. XCIV, 530–55.

41 Williams, *Culture* and *The Politics of Modernism*; and Davis, *Society and Culture*.

42 Jeanroy, *Les Origines*; Bédier, 'Les plus anciennes danses'.

43 *Les Origines*, 102–26, 387–401, 406–26.

44 For a fuller discussion of the history of modern scholarship on the refrain, see Butterfield, 'Interpolated Lyric', 30–46.

45 Doss-Quinby, *Les Refrains*.

46 See Jeanroy, *Les Origines*, 111 ff., and Sahlin, *Etude*.

47 Bec, *La Lyrique française*, I, 225.

48 Doss-Quinby does not address this problem in her own discussion of the role of the *refrain* in the rondeau (*Les Refrains*, 62–70).

49 This in itself is enough to show that any historical development of the refrain out of the *rondet*, or vice versa (we cannot know which), must have taken place prior to this romance.

50 Jeanroy uses the three separate terms *rondet*, *rondel* and rondeau in order to differentiate between different periods of the development of the form from the thirteenth to the fifteenth century (*Les Origines*, 112, 406–26 and 426–38). For the sake of clarity, and in common with scholars such as Delbouille, Maillard and Bec, I use the single term *rondet de carole* (sometimes abbreviated to *rondet*) to designate those lyrics of this genre particularly associated with the *carole* which occur in thirteenth-century *romans*. It should be noted that vdB uses rondeau as a collective term for the purposes of his bibliography. But see his 'Jacquemart Giélée' for his specific use of *rondet de carole*.

51 For descriptions of *rondets de carole*, see Jeanroy, *Les Origines*, 392, 406–08 and *passim*; Sahlin, *Etude*; Doss-Quinby, *Les Refrains*, 69–70; and Page, *The Owl and the Nightingale*, 110–33.

52 I give the text from vdB.

53 Page, 'Johannes de Grocheio', 27–28. See also Rohloff, ed., *Die Quellenhandschriften*, 74–75, 132.

54 Text from vdB.

55 'Bele Aelis' and 'C'est la jus' form two principal topoi in the *rondets de carole*. From vdB, it can be seen that apart from the sixteen *rondets* in Renart's *Rose*, one or other of the two types also occurs in the *Lai d'Aristote* (vdB, rond. 17); sermons (vdB, ronds. 42–44); *Sone de Nansai* (vdB, rond. 45); *Meliacin* (vdB, rond. 47); *rondeaux* by Guillaume d'Amiens (vdB, ronds. 92–93); vdB, rond. 111 (from the Montpellier MS); vdB, ronds. 159–62 and 164–65 (from fr. 12615), and vdB, ronds. 180 and 185 (from fr. 12786). That makes 33 out of the 198 *rondeaux* printed by vdB. See also Bartsch (excluding some duplications), *Altfranzösische Romanzen*, II, Nos. 80, 85, 87, 88, 90, 93, 102. On the 'types-cadres' of the *rondets de carole*, see Zumthor, *Essai*, 253, 289–306; and Delbouille, 'Sur les traces'.

56 The following examples from Renart are quoted from the diplomatic edition by Psaki, who imitates manuscript layout in her positioning of the first initial of each line. Translations are mine.

57 Bédier, 'Les plus anciennes danses', 399.

58 Doss-Quinby's independent discussion of this *rondet* comes to the same conclusion (*Les Refrains*, 66).

59 For a different reconstruction, see Françon, 'Sur la structure du rondeau', 147–49. On the general problem of scribal abbreviation of the refrains, see further his 'La structure du rondeau', 54–9. See also Bec, *La Lyrique française*, I, 226–27. Interestingly, this particular song seems to have caused problems of layout for the scribe: the line of narrative that follows is squeezed awkwardly into the last line of the song (Rome, Biblioteca Apostolica Vaticana MS Reg. 1725, fol. 97r).

60 As, for example, in the *rondets* by Adam de la Halle. See Maillard, *Adam de la Halle*, 85–112. Note also the last part of Grocheio's definition of the rondeau: 'Nos autem solum illam rotundam vel rotundellum dicimus cuius partes non habent diversum cantum a cantu responsorii vel refractus' ('However, I only call the kind of song a 'rotunda' or 'rotundellus' whose parts have the 'same music as the music of the response or refrain', ed. and trans. Page, 'Johannes de Grocheio', 24–26).

61 Rome, Biblioteca Apostolica Vaticana MS Reg. Lat. 1490 contains ten rondeaux by Guillaume d'Amiens with music written out in full. For transcriptions, see Stevens, *Words and Music*, 186–90.

62 *La Lyrique française*, I, 223–28, 228–33, 234–240. Bec also argues that both the *vireli/virelai* and the *ballette* are based in turn on the *rondet*.

63 For full references, see vdB, refr. 1375, and Ch. 4 below.

64 This comparison was completed in draft some years before I encountered Zink's interesting essay 'Suspension and Fall' in Durling, ed., *Jean Renart*, 105–21, which comments on the same passages. Our different interpretations indicate the complexity of the material under discussion.

65 Chailley, 'La nature musicale', 111–17 (esp. 116), and more recently, Zink, 'Suspension and Fall'. This ignores the fact that isolated refrains first appear in Renart's *Rose*, alongside the *rondets*. In addition, the occurrence of refrains in so many other thirteenth-century genres apart from romance shows the assumption that the refrain was 'born' in romance to be facile. Furthermore, scribal laziness can be ruled out as a reason for the brevity of the refrains in the *Roman de la violette*, because they are consistently attached to the narrative by rhyme (see below).

66 For another reference to 'tour', see the description of carolling in Guillaume de Lorris,

Le Roman de la rose, ed. Lecoy, I, 727ff.; further examples of 'recommencer' used in a dance context occur in *Le Tournoi de Chauvency*, ed. Delbouille, 3115–17, and in *Le Roman du castelain de Couci*, ed. Delbouille, 3877–80.

67 I'm trying to avoid implying that 'oral' necessarily means 'unstructured', see Finnegan, *Oral Poetry*.

68 This is common in later thirteenth-century narratives: see, for example, *Renart le Nouvel* and *Le Court d'amours (suite)*.

69 Huot, *From Song to Book*, *passim*.

70 For references to *probationes pennae*, see vdB, 331, 326 and 316 (*cit. am*).

71 Barber, *The Knight*, 137; Barker, *The Tournament*, 102–04, 110.

72 Lecoy, ed., *Le Roman de la rose*, I, 553–55. Oiseuse is also wearing a chaplet of fresh roses.

CHAPTER 3

1 Baumgartner, 'Les citations lyriques'. For other discussions of the lyrics in this romance, see Jung, 'L' Empereur Conrad'; Huot, *From Song to Book*, 108–16; and Psaki, 'Jean Renart's Expanded Text' in Durling, ed., *Jean Renart*, 122–41.

2 For these and subsequent citations from Renart's *Rose*, I return to Lecoy, ed., *Roman de la rose*.

3 Compare the use of the *Te Deum* in *Renart le Nouvel*, line 2469 (Roussel, ed., *Renart le Nouvel*, 106).

CHAPTER 4

1 *OED*, REFRAIN.

2 See Ch. 2, 45–47 and n. 59.

3 Doss-Quinby, *Les Refrains*, 96–111; and Stevens, *Words and Music*, 466–68; 468–71.

4 The two still standard editions of the texts of the motets are by Raynaud, *Recueil de motets* and Stimming, *Die altfranzösischen Motette*. For the music see Rokseth, *Polyphonies*; Tischler, *The Montpellier Codex*, and *The Earliest Motets*; Anderson, *Motets of the Manuscript La Clayette* and *Compositions of the Bamberg Manuscript*.

5 See Everist, 'The Refrain Cento', who argues for a tighter and considerably reduced view of the *motet centon* than previous scholars.

6 Many questions remain about how to interpret motets, on behalf of modern and medieval audiences: see Page, *The Owl and the Nightingale*, 134–54, and *Discarding Images*, Ch. 3, 65–111; and Pesce, *Hearing the Motet*.

7 But note the half-lyric, half-*dit* structure of the *Saluts d'amour*, discussed below, Ch. 14.

8 vdB's collective term 'roman' stands for a loose assortment of longer works from *romans*, *dits*, *contes*, *fatrasies* and *fabliaux*, to sermons, plays, and even two proverb collections. French refrains also appear in a late thirteenth-century collection of Latin *rondelli* (see vdB, 316). The Latin *rondellus* is analogous in many respects to the French *rondet de carole*. See Spanke, 'Das lateinische Rondeau'; and Stevens, *Words and Music*, 178–86.

9 Full references are cited in vdB. For R in the chanson references (e.g. R1323) and M in the motet references (e.g. M764), see the List of Abbreviations. The eight contexts of this refrain are discussed by Doss-Quinby, *Les Refrains*, 193–215.

10 The thirteen refrains are vdB, refrs. 65, 387, 662, 824, 935, 1127, 1322, 1375, 1402, 1473, 1781, 1840, 1872.

11 See vdB, 10.

12 On the relation of the origin of the motet to the use of troped material in liturgical music, see Everist, *French Motets*, Ch. 2.

13 See the Appendix.

14 Gennrich, *Rondeaux, Virelais und Balladen*. See Ch. 2, n. 16 above. Gennrich gives some 500 tunes for nearly 1,300 texts. For a new catalogue of the refrain texts and melodies in *Le Roman de Fauvel*, see Butterfield, 'Catalogue of Refrains'.

15 These and subsequent transcriptions of refrains, unless otherwise stated, are taken from M. V. Fowler, 'Musical Interpolations', II. I have adapted her sigla as follows:

Roi	Paris BN fr. 844 (Le Manuscrit du Roi)
Noailles	Paris BN f. fr. 12615 (Le Chansonnier de Noailles)
Miracles (Soissons)	Paris BN n. a. fr. 24541
Miracles (Leningrad)	Leningrad, Saltykov-Chtchédrine Library, MS fr. F. v. XIV. 9
Mo	Montpellier, Bibliothèque de l'école de Médicine, MS H 196
Munich	Munich, Bayerische Staatsbibliothek, Frag. mus. 4775
Miracles (fr. 25532)/*Paradis*	Paris BN fr. 25532

As some sources are mensurally notated while others are not, I have confined my remarks to melodic characteristics.

16 Van den Boogaard, 'Jacquemart Giélée', and Maillard, 'Les Refrains de caroles', 277–93.

17 Van der Werf, *The Chansons of the Troubadours and Trouvères*, 26–34; Karp, 'Borrowed Material' and 'Troubadours, trouvères', in *New Grove*, §III. Music: 1. MS sources, 807–10.

18 Van der Werf, ed., *Trouvères-Melodien*; Tischler, ed., *Trouvère Lyrics. Li nouviaus tanz* is also in Rosenberg and Tischler, *Chansons des trouvères: Chanter m'estuet*, rev. edn, 388–92.

19 For an example, see Butterfield, 'The Language of Medieval Music', 10–11.

20 See Ch. 6.

21 Butterfield, 'Repetition'.

CHAPTER 5

1 In both tables I use the editions cited in vdB, with the exception of Marchello-Nizia, ed., *Le Roman de la poire* (which replaces that cited in vdB). vdB, rond. 1 =Renart's *Rose*, 295 indicates that vdB rond. 1 occurs in Renart's *Rose*, line 295.

2 Butterfield, 'Repetition'.

3 This version of the refrain comes from Oxford, Bodleian Library, MS Douce 308; the version printed by Delbouille here from his base text, Mons, Bibliothèque de la Ville, MS 330–215, is *Ainsi doit on aler a son ami*, which turns out to be identical to the rondeau and motet citations.

4 Renart, *Rose*, lines 295 ff. and 2514ff. (vdB, rond. 1). Compare vdB, rond. 51 =Jean le Court, dite Brisebarre, *Le Restor du Paon*, 2531, which is cited at the high point of a feast.

5 Since the *Lai* is earlier in date than *Le Tournoi*, it seems to me clear that this wider generic expectation about *Ainsi doit* predates both works.

6 The manuscripts of the *Lai d'Aristote* give several variants for this rondeau (see vdB, 32–33 who prints 'maint' in error). Compare vdB, rond. 47 (*Meliacin*).

7 See Everist, 'The Polyphonic Rondeau'.

8 Ed. Rosenberg and Tischler, *Chanter M'Estuet*, No. 119, 279–82; Occitan version ed. Newcombe, *Les Poésies*, 91–104.

9 See Table 5.1. context (b).

10 Interestingly, the fr. 1802 copy of *Paradis* has a further variant of *Ainsi doit* at line 304: *Ainsi va qui d'amors vit / et qui bien aime.*

11 For a thoughtful account of *Paradis* and its connections with motet texts, see Huot, *Allegorical Play*, 77–84. As Everist has shown, M1143a and M435 are part of a family of motets with Artesian links that shares tenors drawn from an Assumption alleluia, *French Motets*, 122–25.

12 Of course, these particular examples of motets are not necessarily typical of motet treatments of refrains in general.

13 Butterfield, 'Repetition', 23.

CHAPTER 6

1 Falck, 'Parody and Contrafactum'. In the strictest cases, a *contrafactum* employs not only the melody but also the rhythm and metrical scheme of its model, and adapts the meaning of its text.

2 See also Falck, 'Contrafactum', *New Grove*, §I, 367–68.

3 Bec, *La Lyrique française*, I, 142–43 (who cites Frappier).

4 For some related comments, see Aubrey, 'The Dialectic', 4–6.

5 See Hunt, 'De la chanson au sermon'. One of Langton's sermons is edited from Cambridge, Trinity College, MS B. 14. 39 by Reichl, *Religiöse Dichtung*. On other sermon material relating to caroles, see Page, *The Owl and the Nightingale*, ch. 5, 110–33.

6 See Page, *The Owl and the Nightingale*, 172, on the term *literatus*.

7 It is tempting to see this as a further religious parody of Renart's use of the rose symbol.

8 See Zink, *Roman rose*.

9 Gautier de Coinci, *Les Chansons à la Vierge*.

10 As Drzewicka, 'La Fonction', asserts.

11 See also Huot, *Allegorical Play*, 64–66. I am grateful to Suzannah Clark for discussing these songs with me.

12 The two Blondel songs which Gautier uses as models occur in sequence in fr. 1613.

13 Their main reasons are that there is no preparation for music, and that the piece is not formally in quatrains: Chailley, *Les Chansons à la Vierge*, 37, and Koenig, 'Sur une prétendue reverdie'.

14 See the Appendix, Sermons for examples, and n. 5 above.

15 See Ch. 2, 46 and n. 55, and ch. 5, 92.

16 The frequent references to the Virgin as rose, and even as violet ('C'est la fleurs, la violete, la rose espanie', 'Hui matin', 22–23), standard as they are in devotional Latin poetry, could be seen as an explicit effort by Gautier to reclaim them for the vernacular as sacred metaphors.

17 The staves are more narrowly drawn than in the *Miracles* songs because the text scribe has left only one line free for them, unlike in the *Miracles* where two lines are skipped each time (compare the refrains on fol. 109). But the practice with initials is consistent between the two works.

18 Compare Revelation 15. I am grateful to Stephen Medcalf for his help with this point.

19 Compare the opening of one of Gautier's St Léocade songs: 'Las! las! las! las! par grant delit' (I Ch 45, Koenig).

20 Salter, 'The Annunciation'.

21 My translation; for text, see Alain de Lille, *Anticlaudianus*, ed. Bossuat.
22 Bayart, ed., *Ludus super Anticlaudianum*.
23 Hughes, 'The *Ludus*'.
24 The annotations seem to be of two kinds – one similar to the main text, the other (occurring in the later part of the volume) more cursive and informal. The glosses are of many types: interlinear, marginal, boxed. Bayart disputes the catalogue date of fourteenth century in favour of the last quarter of the thirteenth (*Ludus*, vii).
25 Adam's work was itself translated into French (though without music): see Adam de la Bassée, *Ludus*, ed. Bayart, cv, and Bossuat, 'Une prétendue traduction'. For details of the manuscripts, see Bayart, ed., *Ludus* lxxix–lxxx, and Bossuat, 'Une prétendue traduction', 272.

CHAPTER 7

1 Zumthor, *Essai*, 232.
2 Bec, *La Lyrique française*, I, 17–53.
3 Gurevich, *Medieval Popular Culture*, xv–xvi.
4 For his reference to Le Goff, see *Medieval Popular Culture*, xvi.
5 Gurevich (*Medieval Popular Culture*, 5) is here quoting from Iu. M. Lotman and B. A. Uspenskii, 'Novye aspekty izucheniia kul'tury Drevnei Rusi' ['New Aspects for the Study of the Culture of Old Russia'], *Voprosy literatury*, 3 (1977), 150.
6 See Page's conspectus of sources in *The Owl and the Nightingale*, 187–207.
7 vdB, 17.
8 Bec does at least make an effort to characterise more than one type of refrain usage. With the exception of Doss-Quinby, most recent scholars have taken for granted the more obvious fallacy that refrains are fragments of *rondets*. Jean Maillard, for instance, in his study of the music of Adam de la Halle, discusses the refrains in Adam's compositions not in their own right, but under the chapter heading 'Les Rondets de caroles', ch. V. But while some of the refrains do occur in *rondets* by Adam, many have no immediate connection with *rondets de caroles*. Maillard also states of the refrains in *Renart le Nouvel*, that 'ces insertions lyriques consistent principalement en refrains de rondets' ('Les Refrains de caroles', 277). Even vdB makes the same supposition about the refrains in *Renart le Nouvel*, despite his own formidable demonstration of the numerous range of sources in which they occur ('Jacquemart Giélée', 333–53).
9 Bakhtin, *Dialogic Imagination*, especially 'From the Prehistory of Novelistic Discourse', 41–83, and 'Discourse in the Novel', 259–422. Although it has become something of a cliché to refer to 'dialogism', it seems to me that Bakhtin's comments have a particularly interesting bearing on refrain citation.
10 Todorov, *Mikhail Bakhtin*, tries to set Bakhtin's theory of genre into a historical framework but occasionally admits (for example, 90–91) that this is not easy.
11 See also Kristeva, 'Word, Dialogue and Novel', 67–68.
12 See, for example, Tischler, *The Montpellier Codex*, III, fascicle 7, No. 272, 98–100: '*Triplum*: Tres joliement me voell / *Motetus*: Imperatrix supernorum / *Tenor*: Cis, a cui je sui amie', where a pious prayer to the Virgin is sandwiched between a French refrain in the tenor and a lover's intimate description of his mistress. For a full study of textual juxtapositions in the thirteenth-century motet, see Huot, *Allegorical Play*.
13 For a related discussion, see Camille, *Image on the Edge*.
14 Bakhtin, *Speech Genres*, 65.

15 Todorov, *Les Genres du discours*, 49.
16 On pastoral as a 'mode', see Fowler, *Kinds of Literature*, 106–11 (here 109–10).

' CHAPTER 8

1 Berger, ed., *Le Nécrologe*, 309. On the social and literary context of Arras, see Ungureanu, *La Bourgeoisie*, and Berger, *Littérature et société arrageoises*.
2 According to Berger, *Le Nécrologe*, 309.
3 There is no single wide-ranging account of the *puys*, although Wilkins, *The Lyric Art*, 8–35, gives a useful account. On Arras, see Cavrois, *Cartulaire*, summarised by Richardson, 'The Confrérie'; on other Northern towns see de Beauvillé, *Recueil de documents*, 139–54 and Breuil, 'La Confrérie'.
4 Berger (*Littérature et société*, 80) points out that of the six hospitals run by charitable institutions in La Ville, the smallest was that of the *Confrérie des jongleurs et des bourgeois* which had only three beds. However, the charity grew into a thriving concern: the large and prosperous membership in due course had their own hall and, in 1200, erected a tower in the Petit Marché (86).
5 Berger, *Littérature et société*, 75, n. 428.
6 The row over *impots* is prominent in the satiric poems in fr. 12615.
7 See Berger, ed., *Le Nécrologe*.
8 Berger, *Littérature et société*, 86.
9 E.g. Dinaux, *Trouvères*, III, 16, 76, 70. Robert de le Piere talks in one of his songs of his 'kanchon courounee'.
10 Riley, ed., 'Regulations of the Feste de Pui', 216–28. See Sutton, 'Merchants, Music and Social Harmony'.
11 Breuil, 'La Confrérie', 490–575, 609–13, 627–28, and Beauvillé, *Recueil de documents*.
12 On Flemish 'Chambres de Rhétoriques', see Slocum, 'Confrérie'.
13 See the detailed discussion of fr. 12615 in Berger, *Littérature et société*.
14 vdB, 'Jacquemart Giélée', 333–53.
15 According to vdB, every time a refrain is displaced among the four manuscripts, it is given to a different character to sing. He also observes that refrains tend to be quoted in the *roman* to herald some kind of action, such as the start of a new scene, or the entrance of a new character.
16 Schwan, *Altfranzösischen Liederhandschriften*, 263. For other descriptions of this manuscript, see Meyer, 'Troisième rapport'; and Långfors, 'Mélanges'. The lyric pieces have all been diplomatically transcribed by Steffens, *Altfranzösischen Liederhandschriften*. Many similarities exist (as is noted below) between refrains in *Le Tournoi* and songs from this chansonnier; moreover, it contains twelve refrains from *Renart le Nouvel* and eleven from *La Court de paradis*.
17 For a more detailed discussion, see my 'Interpolated Lyric', 76–78.
18 C.-V. Langlois, *La Vie en France*, I, 228.
19 Delbouille, ed., *Le Tournoi*, lvi.
20 Refrains shared as follows: *Le Tournoi* and *Le Court d'amours*: vdB, refrs. 765, 777, 936; *Renart le Nouvel* and *Le Court d'amours*: vdB, refrs. 485, 936, 955 and 969; *La Court de paradis* and *Le Tournoi*: vdB, refrs. 65 and 936. Note that No. 936 (see Fig. 5) is shared by all four works. See also Vilamo-Pentti, ed., *La Court de paradis*, 43 and 54–78.
21 vdB, refrs. 156, 289, 430, 496, 746, 784 and 1074.
22 vdB, refr. 200 occurs in *Robin et Marion*, *Renart le Nouvel*, *Le Tournoi* and *Salut d'amour* I; refr. 1473 in *Feuillée* and *Le Tournoi*.

23 Edited by Jubinal, *Nouveau recueil*, II, 235–41. It has the form of an extended *chanson avec des refrains*, with twenty-nine stanzas (varying from four to eight lines), each ending with a separate refrain. It is interesting for the variety of terms it uses to describe the refrain: 'mot', 'motet', 'pastourelle', 'chanson' and 'refrait'. See Ch. 14 below. We know little about the provenance and date of the *Saluts d'amour*, but this one at least, by virtue of its refrains, shows that it is likely to be another work from the Lille–Arras region.

24 For further comment, see Peraino, 'Et pui conmencha a canter'.

25 Gurevich, *Medieval Popular Culture*, 10–11.

26 *Le Roman de la poire* and *Renart le Nouvel* share two refrains: vdB, refrs. 784 and 1853.

27 vdB, refr. 1004 is shared by *Violette* and *Renart le Nouvel*.

28 An argument first put forward by Faral in 'Les Chansons de toile'. See also Lecoy, ed., *Le Roman de la rose*, xxv; Zink, *Belle: Essai sur les chansons de toile*, 9–19; and I. Frank, 'Mélanges', for whom the song 'Tuit cil qui sunt enamourat' is not an 'original' dance-song but a thirteenth-century pastiche, a view supported more recently by Aubrey, 'The Dialectic', 15–16.

29 The other manuscript of the poem (n. a. fr. 7514) records 'nostre' for 'vostre', giving an even more self-enclosed sense to the rondeau.

30 vdB, rond. 147. Refrain correspondences: *J'aim miex mon chapelet de flors que malvais mariaige!* (4250, vdB, refr. 960); *Diex, trop demoure! Quant venra ? – Sa demoree m'ocirra!* (4282, vdB, refr. 577); *La merci Deu j'ai ataint – Se que je voloie.* (4296, vdB, refr. 1191). See also Ch. 2 above.

31 Compare the narrative expansions of *Ainssi doit en aler*, discussed in Ch. 5.

32 It is, of course, still used as a source for such pastimes: see Opie, *The Singing Game*, 10.

33 Poems concerning 'questions d'amor' are common: two of the earliest in Latin are the twelfth-century *Concilium Romarici Montis*, and the *Altercatio Phyllidis et Florae*, which gave rise to several works in French. For references to courts of love, see Neilson, *Origins and Sources*. A related debate genre is the sung *jeu-parti* discussed above.

34 Refrains occur in the anonymous continuation of *Le Court d'amours*. This begins without a rubric immediately after the *Ju*, and has no scribal identification apart from the final rubric 'Explicit de le court d'amours'.

35 Scully, ed., *Le Court d'amours*, xxii.

36 Jauss, 'Entstehung', 240.

37 Schwam-Baird, ed., *Le Jeu de Robin et Marion*, line 209.

38 Zumthor, *Essai*, 254.

39 See, for example, line 9 where, as Dufournet points out (*Le Jeu de la feuillée*, 124), there are comparisons with Chanson XXX, *jeu-parti* XI and the Congé, stanza 5; and lines 54–74, particularly line 66. Parallels exist with *Robin et Marion* at 544–45; and at 578 with *Renart le Nouvel* and *Fauvel*.

40 Compare also the marginal illuminations in the *Roman d'Alexandre*: Oxford, Bodleian Library, MS Bodley 264.

41 The social form of the *puy* meetings merits further discussion, for instance the aristocratic terminology of the structure of contests (in which the winner is crowned 'Prince' etc.). Davis, *Society and Culture*, 'The Reasons of Misrule', 97–123, is illuminating on the related 'Abbeys of Misrule', who elected a 'Prince des Sots'.

CHAPTER 9

1 See Stevens, *Words and Music*, Ch. 14 'Rhythm and Genre', especially 466–68, and 471–76 (here 475).

2 The other six are *unica* (vdB, refrs. 871, 1869, 251, 1860, 1161 and 1835).

3 'Au tens nouvel', ed. Bartsch, *Altfranzösische Romanzen*, 295–96; 'A l'entrant de mai', ed. Rivière, *Pastourelles*, II, 123–26. The latter survives in one manuscript (Chansonnier de l'Arsenal, Paris, Ars. 5198) with music.

4 Text of refrains (and line numbers) are taken from Varty, ed., *Le Jeu de Robin et de Marion*. Translations are mine. It is not clear to me why vdB omits '*Trairi, deluriau, deluriau, deluriele, / Trairi, deluriau, deluriau, delurot*', which is the refrain of the *pastourelle* stanza sung by the chevalier (lines 101–02), anticipated by Marion (lines 95–96).

5 R974 'L'autre jour je chevachoie', ed. Rivière, *Pastourelles*, I, 75–77, No. I.

6 In fr. 847, R1700. The refrain is also cited in the tenor of a motet (M870) and *Salut d'amours* (II), ed. A. Jubinal.

7 See Dufournet, 'Complexité et ambiguïté'; Brusegan, 'Le *Jeu de Robin et Marion*'; and Brownlee, 'Transformations'.

8 As well as the example discussed above of '*Vous perdés vo paine, sire Aubert*' (83–84), see also (i) lines 95–96 and 101–02, where Marion anticipates the chevalier's refrain *Trairi, deluriau*'; and (ii) '*Vous l'orrés bien dire*' (160–61) which has the same tune as the B section of the dialogue song '*Robin par l'ame ten pere*' (187–210). The music of this song seems to have been particularly well known: it occurs in *Renart le Nouvel* (line 6876) with the words '*Ne me mokiés mie biele ne me mokiés mie*' (see Gennrich, *Rondeaux, Virelais und Balladen*, II, 126), and in a hitherto unnoticed correspondence, in the motet '*En non Dieu, que que nus die / Quant voi la rose espanie / Nobis*', with the words '*Marion, laisse Robin pour moi amer!*' (see Butterfield, 'The Language of Medieval Music', 10–11). The line '*Ne vous hastez mie, bele, ne vous hastez mie*' in M22 has a similar tune. For a general discussion of the music in *Robin et Marion*, see Chailley, 'La Nature musicale'. For a richly detailed discussion of the use of 'Robin m'aime' in a motet context, see Pesce, 'Beyond Glossing'.

9 Brusegan, 'Le *Jeu de Robin et Marion*', 121–24.

10 Gravdal, 'Camouflaging Rape', 365. See Paden's reply, 'Rape in the Pastourelle'. Gravdal's *Ravishing Maidens* presents a wider framework for her discussion of *pastourelles* and rape.

11 Empson, *Some Versions of Pastoral*, 11.

12 The phrase is Montrose's, ' "Eliza" ', 153.

13 Ungureanu, *La Bourgeoisie*. See also Zink, *La Pastourelle*.

14 See, for instance, Guy, *Essai*, 514–15.

15 Guy, *Essai*, 516; Zumthor, *Essai*, 446.

16 Runciman, *Sicilian Vespers*, 147. This account also draws on Léonard, *Les Angevins*, Sabatini, *Napoli angioina*, and Dunbabin, *Charles I of Anjou*.

17 There is some debate as to whether the work is unfinished, and hence whether it was written before or after Charles's death. Other poetic tributes to Charles include Jean de Meun's remarks in the *Rose* (Lecoy, ed., *Le Roman de la Rose*, I, 203–06, lines 6607–6710) and numerous references in Arrageois chansons and *jeux-partis* (see Maillard, *Charles d'Anjou*).

18 Maillard, *Charles d'Anjou*.

19 J.-B. and L. Beck's (in my view plausible) suggestion that it was copied for Charles d'Anjou remains unsubstantiated, see Aubrey, *New Grove*, 'Sources', MS §III, 4, 853.

20 Compare Crane, 'The Writing Lesson', 201–21.

21 O. Leroy, *Epoques de l'histoire de France en rapport avec le théâtre français* (Paris, 1843), cited and discussed in Guy, *Essai*, 511–16.

22 Taking *1 Henry IV* as his example, Empson describes how its three worlds ('rebel camp, tavern, and court') 'tend to separate . . . making us sympathise with all three sides so that

we are baffled when they meet' (*Some Versions*, 43); Gurevich, *Medieval Popular Culture*, 183.

CHAPTER 10

1 I use the term *ordinatio* after Parkes, in his seminal essay 'The Influence of the Concepts of *Ordinatio* and *Compilatio* on the Development of the Book'.

2 See the Appendix. Although some reference will be made to chansonniers, this chapter is primarily concerned with surveying other, less well-studied types of manuscript context for song.

3 Adam was not the first author to have his works separately collected since an author collection, now lost, must have existed for Thibaut de Champagne (Wallensköld, ed., *Les Chansons*, xxviii–xxxviii and xli). Gautier de Coinci's *Miracles* are a further example.

4 Nearly all chansonniers are arranged by author, the occasional one alphabetically. Certain genres, such as *motets entés*, are, however, regularly grouped, as in n. a. fr. 1050, fr. 845 and Rome, Biblioteca Apostolica Vaticana Reg. 1490). Vat. Regina 1490 is comparable to Douce 308 in its grouping of anonymous *pastourelles*, *jeux-partis* and chansons Nostre Dame, although it also has some authorial organisation. Arrangement by genre also takes place in the Las Huelgas MS (*c.* 1300–*c.* 1325). See Ch. 2.

5 On the *balettes* in Douce 308, see Page, 'Tradition and Innovation'.

6 fr. 24429. Its contents consist of various devotional treatises (e.g. history of saints and apostles, sermons of St Gregory) in prose and verse.

7 See Roesner, Avril and Regalado, eds., *Le Roman de Fauvel*, fol. Bva.

8 Switten, *Music and Poetry*, 4.

9 Cited by Switten, *ibid.*, 12.

10 See the Appendix. Musical transcriptions for a selected number of romances are given in Fowler, 'Musical Interpolations'.

11 Whole genres of song are first (and in some cases, uniquely) recorded in these kinds of source. See Ch. 2, p. 26.

12 A song can have a prominent, independent, structuring role in a narrative yet not be at all visually emphasised, as for instance, in the romance *Galeran de Bretagne*, which contains just one two-line refrain among some 7,800 lines of narrative.

13 Although there is more than one textual hand in *Renart le Nouvel*.

14 No fewer than seven refrains in *Renart le Nouvel* occur in rondeaux by Adam (see Ch. 8, n. 21).

15 For a brief discussion, see Huot, *From Song to Book*, 73.

16 A few songs have blank staves.

17 It has not been possible, in the space of this study, to include proper comparison of copying practices in religious as well as secular books (although some reference has been made to the Gautier de Coinci manuscripts). An obvious starting point would be the fr. 146 copy of *Fauvel*, in which a substantial repertory of chant is interpolated within the secular narrative and songs (see Rankin, 'The Divine Truth' and 'The Alleluyes, antenes, respons, ygnes et verssez' in BN fr. 146: A Catalogue Raisonné', in Bent and Wathey, eds., *Fauvel Studies*, 421–66).

18 See Ch. 8 above.

19 See Ch. 8 above. Comparable problems exist in the transmission of *chansons avec des refrains* (see Butterfield, 'Medieval Genres', 197).

20 See Ch. 6 above.

21 See Ch. 12 below. The two works are comparable in that they handle opposing aspects of their moralising subject matter: the *Ludus* (after the *Anticlaudianus*) treating of the Arts and Virtues, *Fauvel* of the Vices. Both draw widely on sacred and secular genres, mixing sequences and hymns with love-song melodies and, in the case of *Fauvel*, obscene expostulations.

22 I am excepting here the Arthurian *lais* in the prose *Tristan*. Spaces for staves are left in *Meliacin* for trouvère songs, as I discuss below.

23 A fourth fragment of the poem (without music) was discovered in 1982: see Marchello-Nizia, *Le Roman de la poire*, lxix–lxx.

24 It belonged to Jean le Bon, who lost it after Poitiers. Charles V bought it back from the English, and subsequently gave it to Jean, duc de Berri (Chailley, *Les Chansons*, p. 33).

25 Vilamo-Pentti, ed., *La Court de Paradis*, 22. See Ch. 6, p. 115 and n. 17.

26 Compare the juxtaposition of works by Adenet le Roi, Baudouin de Condé and sermons in the late thirteenth-century Ars. 3142.

27 In two instances, fr. 1581 of *Renart le Nouvel* and Vienna, Österreiches Nationalbibliothek. 2621 of Baudouin de Condé's *Li Prison d'Amours*, the otherwise empty staves have notation for just one (in the latter, two) refrains, implying perhaps that a scribe, and/or casual reader, could not resist filling in one that he happened to know. From a microfilm examination of the Vienna manuscript it appears that these two refrain melodies (fols. 27v and 31v) are in different hands: the second, in small, rushed notes looks like a later addition to the manuscript.

28 *Acart, Aristote, Cleomadés, Li Commens d'amours, Le Court d'amours, Escanor, Meliacin, Kanor, Laurin, Peliarmanus* and *Licorne*.

29 See the Appendix.

30 For an analogous argument, see Earp, 'Scribal Practice', 166.

31 All the refrains have some kind of spacing, but it is inconsistent, along with the lineation: thus some are cramped into one long line, whereas others are set into two lines, but with only one line left blank before the refrain.

32 In fr. 1455, fol. 42r of *Meliacin*, the scribe mistakenly writes out the first line of the song 'Bonne auenture' as part of the text, and then repeats it with a coloured initial and red underlining.

33 The last four also have spaces for initials, unlike the first three.

34 Initials coincide with spaces left for staves in fr. 24391 (*La Prise amoureuse*); several manuscripts of *Cleomadés, Meliacin,* and the *Miracles*; fr. 24374 (*Escanor*); fr. 2186 and 12786 (*Poire*); and Dijon, Bibliothèque Municipale 526 (*Li Commens d'amours*).

35 Staves are not drawn in every time.

36 The refrains in fr. 25532 (*La Court de paradis*) are another example of such initialling.

37 The use of author portraits in the opening initial of chansonnier fascicles is presumably the basis of this practice; some show the trouvère with a musical instrument (e.g. Perrin d'Angecourt's songs are introduced by a figure holding a portative organ in Rome, Biblioteca Apostolica Vaticana, Reg. 1490, and Adenet le Roi is consistently shown as a minstrel).

38 fr. 817 and 1533 (Gautier de Coinci, *Miracles*) has large initials for the start of a chanson, smaller ones for the stanzas.

39 Doss-Quinby (after Spanke) has pointed out that upper-case initials are regularly given to refrains in the manuscripts of *chansons avec des refrains*; *Les refrains*, 107–08 and n. 18. Page also reports that *litterae notabiliores* are sometimes used in fr. 1591, fols. 41r–76r to signal in the text of a song the AB AB X structure of its music ('Tradition', in Bent and Wathey, eds., *Fauvel Studies*, 369, n. 51). See also Fig. 13.

40 Line decoration at the end of songs also occurs in Rome, Biblioteca Apostolica Vaticana, Reg. 1725 (Renart's *Rose*) (see Fig. 3) and fr. 24378 (*Roman de la violette* (prose version)). It is particularly common in the Arthurian romance manuscripts.

41 fr. 1802 (*Paradis*) has pencil/faint pen underlining (of an uncertain date) for the refrains.

42 Parkes, 'The Influence', 121. See also Parkes, *Pause and Effect*.

43 Parkes, 'The Influence', 116.

44 Parkes, *Pause and Effect*, 27.

45 Paris, Arsenal 2741.

46 Parkes, *Pause and Effect*, 43–44.

47 Cf. *Le Roman de la poire*, 2793–96, in which a refrain is described as the *sentence* of a song:

> Dites moi del chant la sentence!
> – Si vos volez, tres bien le vueill:
> *Amors ai a ma volenté*
> *teles con ge veill.*

48 Parkes, *Pause and Effect*, 43, 103–04. As he also notes, *positurae* occur in eleventh- and twelfth-century liturgical manuscripts to indicate the use of melodic formulas in the delivery of the text: since these 'formulae inevitably fell at the end of sense units, [these] signs could come to be used as punctuation to mark pauses', *ibid.*, 36.

49 See the Appendix, 'Chansons latines'.

50 The n. a. fr. 7514 copy of Couci has 'Cancon' headings for Songs II (fol. 39v) and IV (fol. 52r).

51 Butterfield, '*Mise en page*', 65–71.

52 The inclusion of letters becomes a further factor in the layout of certain *romans à chansons* (such as *Renart le Nouvel* and the *Roman du Castelain de Couci*), and gains especial importance in Machaut's *Voir Dit*.

CHAPTER II

1 The only instances of prose and verse in French are an early thirteenth-century hagiographic compilation translated from Latin (Szkilnik), Arthurian prose romance, and narratives with prose letters, (Ch. 2, p. 26 and nn. 6 and 7 above). Prose-verse translations of Boethius, *De consolatione philosophiae* did not appear until the fourteenth century. See Dwyer, *Boethian Fictions*.

2 This contrasts with Boethius, *De consolatione*, which begins with verse and ends with prose.

3 Roques, ed., *Aucassin et Nicolette*, iii.

4 Trotin, 'Vers et Prose'.

5 Hardly any melodies for the *chanson de geste* survive: the best known is the line from *Audigier* (a scatological parody of a *chanson de geste*) cited in Adam de la Halle's *Robin et Marion*. See Stevens, *Words and Music*, 222–34.

6 T. Gérold, *La Musique au Moyen Age* (Paris, 1932), Ch. IX, 79–90 (esp. 85–86), and Stevens, *Words and Music*, 227.

7 For a possible reconstruction, see Stevens, *Words and Music*, 226.

8 Frank, 'The Cues'. Other examples of performance instructions are discussed in Ch. 10. One might compare stage directions in medieval French drama which, according to Noomen, 'Passages narratifs', are normally in prose and in the present tense.

9 As Gaston Paris long ago wondered, see Roques, ed., *Aucassin et Nicolette*, xv.
10 The phrase 'a pattern of structural doubling' is Brownlee's, 'Discourse as *Proueces*', 170.
11 Roques, ed., *Aucassin et Nicolette*.
12 See Ch. 1 above.

CHAPTER 12

1 The discussion of boundaries and margins which follows has been illuminated by Derrida, 'Living On: Borderlines'.
2 Some debate exists about whether Gervès wrote both books: according to one school of thought, the first book is anonymous. See Bent and Wathey, eds., *Fauvel Studies*, 12–13.
3 The precise relationship between the work of Gervès du Bus and of Chaillou de Pesstain is still subject to debate. See Bent and Wathey, eds., *Fauvel Studies*, 'Introduction', 12–15. For a recent attempt to identify Chaillou, see Elizabeth Lalou, 'La chancellerie royale à la fin du règne de Philippe IV le Bel', in Bent and Wathey, eds., *Fauvel Studies*, 307–19, with further discussion in Richard and Mary Rouse, *Manuscripts*, 227, n. 201.
4 Roesner *et al.*, in eds., *Le Roman de Fauvel*, 27–28.
5 Roesner *et al.*, eds., *Le Roman de Fauvel*, 9–10, 28–29.
6 Earp, 'Lyrics for Reading', 101–31.
7 For detailed discussion of the complex issues of notation in *Fauvel*, see Roesner *et al.*, eds., *Fauvel*, 'Introduction'.
8 Roesner *et al.*, eds., *Le Roman de Fauvel*, 24.
9 The important work of Roesner, *et al.*, eds., *Le Roman de Fauvel*, and Morin ('The Genesis' and 'Jehannot de Lescurel's Chansons') on the overall design of the codex, including the *dits* by Geffroy de Paris, the pieces by Jehan de Lescurel, and the metrical chronicle, has shown that not only the *Fauvel* folios, but the codex as a whole was subject to careful, unifying planning. The codicological arguments have found support in Dunbabin, 'The Metrical Chronicle Traditionally Ascribed to Geffroy de Paris', in Bent and Wathey, eds., *Fauvel Studies*, 233–46. On the production history of fr. 146, see recent work by Richard and Mary Rouse, *Manuscripts*, I, ch. 8, 225–33.
10 Camille, 'Hybridity, Monstrosity and Bestiality in the *Roman de Fauvel*', in Bent and Wathey, eds., *Fauvel Studies*, 161–74.
11 On the latter see Uhl, 'Les "Sotes Chançons"'.
12 Butterfield, 'The Refrain' and 'Catalogue of Refrains'.
13 See the puzzlement expressed by Roesner *et al.*, eds., *Le Roman de Fauvel*, 29.
14 Claims about where the precise mid-point of the narrative lies require caution: in this case, it might well be objected that the codicological extent of the interpolated *Fauvel* cannot have been known so precisely in advance, since there is spare ruling at the end of the final folio. It is also not clear at what stage in the preparation of the volume the bifolium making up fols. 28 *bis* and *ter* was added: it would have to be assumed here that it was added retrospectively in order to move this rubric into a more central position. But it is not necessary for the rubric to be the precise geometrical or arithmetical mid-point of the book for its mid-way position to be significant.
15 Uitti, 'From Clerc to Poète'; Huot, *From Song to Book*, 69, 72–73, 90.
16 I am grateful to Nancy Regalado for allowing me to read her unpublished papers 'Description of the Semi-Lyric Ensemble in BN MS f. fr. 146, fols. 24r–28ter v', presented to the Medieval Academy of America, Toronto, April 1987 and 'The Place of the

Lescurel and *Fauvel* Semi-Lyric Pieces in the Design of fr. 146', presented with Elizabeth A. R. Brown at Oxford University, 20 November 1992.

17 Dahnk, *L' Hérésie de Fauvel*, line 78.

18 See Ch. 14 below.

19 Lines 104–53.

20 Discussed in Ch. 14 below.

21 Rosenberg and Tischler, eds., *Monophonic Songs*, R.6.2, strophe 11, p. 100.

22 Strophe IV, lines 43–48; line 45 ('Fui de ci! De toi n'ai que faire') is very close to Adam de la Halle, *Dit d'amour*, ed. Jeanroy, 'Trois dits d'amour' strophe IV, line 48 ('Tu li respons: "Fui! va te voie!"').

23 For full references, see Butterfield, 'Catalogue of Refrains', refrain nos. 25–35.

CHAPTER 13

1 Vitry's importance as composer, poet and *ars nova* theorist is qualified only by the relatively small number of surviving works that can be confidently attributed to him. For the suggestion that Vitry may be associated with the creation of the *ars nova* ballade, see Page, 'Tradition'; see also Leech-Wilkinson, 'The Emergence of *Ars Nova*'; Wathey, 'The Motets' and 'Myth and Mythography'.

2 Hoepffner, Introduction to the *Remède de Fortune*, II, xiv.

3 There has not been space to include Froissart and other later fourteenth-century authors in this book: they will be discussed in a forthcoming study.

4 Cerquiglini, *'Un Engin si Soutil'*, 24. She also refers to a combination of the two (*collage-montage*). For a refinement and further discussion of this distinction, see Taylor, 'The Lyric Insertion'.

5 Amongst others, Badel, *Le Roman*, and Brownlee and Huot, eds., *Rethinking the Romance of the Rose*.

6 Brownlee, 'Authorial Self-Representation and Literary Models in the *Roman de Fauvel*', in Bent and Wathey, eds., *Fauvel Studies*, 73–103.

7 Badel, *Le Roman de la Rose*; Brownlee and Huot, eds., *Rethinking*; and Huot, *The Romance of the Rose*.

8 Discussion of Guillaume's *Rose* in relation to lyric and romance models includes Uitti, 'From Clerc to Poète'; Hult, *Self-Fulfilling Prophecies*, 186–262; Huot, *From Song to Book*, 84–85.

9 Earp, 'Lyrics for Reading'.

10 The date of the *Panthère* is uncertain: Todd, ed., *Le Dit de la panthère d'amours*, dates it between 1290 and 1328. Other early citations of *formes fixes* occur in Oxford, Bodleian Library, MS Douce 308, and fr. 146 in the *Roman de Fauvel* and the songs of Jehan de Lescurel.

11 Kristeva, *Le Texte du roman*, 139–76.

CHAPTER 14

1 See the references in Tobler-Lommatzsch under *narracion*, *narrative* and *narrer*; also *Le Grand Robert*, which gives 1190 as the first reference for *narration*, 1680 as the date of its rhetorical sense, 1388 for *narrer*, 1440 for *narratif, ive* and 1500 for *narrateur*. *Lyrique* does not occur in Tobler-Lommatzsch (although cf. *lire* (lyre) in the prologue to Gautier de Coinci's *Miracles*).

2 Some of the most influential formalist writing on the medieval lyric, produced in reaction to an earlier generation's emphasis on autobiography, includes Guiette, *D'une poésie formelle*; Dragonetti, *La Technique poétique*; Zumthor, *Essai*; Bec, *La Lyrique française*.

3 Zumthor, 'De la circularité du chant'.

4 Huot, *From Song to Book*, 1–2, deliberately defines her terms (such as 'lyrico-narrative', 'lyrical', 'lyrical narrative') loosely. Ironically, however, in confining the term 'lyric' itself to the *chanson courtoise*, she rules out for discussion most of the songs set into narrative in this period, few of which are *chansons courtoises*.

5 See Marshall's groundbreaking articles, 'Textual Transmission' and 'Une versification lyrique popularisante'.

6 *Contrafacta* confirm the point in reverse by showing thematic irregularity and formal regularity.

7 *Poire*, 1149. The following references (unless otherwise noted) are to works cited in vdB. They are not intended to be fully inclusive.

8 Index to the *Fauvel* manuscript (fr. 146).

9 Guillaume de Lorris, *Rose*, 731; *Sal. II*, ed. Jubinal, str. 6; R1192 (Guillaume le Vinier, 'En mi mai quant s'est la saisons partie', 9).

10 *Le Court d'amours*, 3416.

11 *Sal. II*, ed. Jubinal, str. 25. For *motet*, see also *Renart le Nouvel*, 2409, 6776 etc.

12 *Poire*, 2411.

13 *La Complainte douteuse*, ed. Jubinal, 60.

14 *Le Court d'amours*, 3339; *Couci*, 3856.

15 Meyer, ed., 'Le Salut d'amour', No. VII, str. 15; VIII, 3.

16 *Renart le Nouvel*, 2555, 6768 etc.

17 *Renart le Nouvel*, 4410.

18 *Renart le Nouvel*, 6884.

19 Compare 'carmen' in Gérard de Liège, *Quinque*, ed. Wilmart, 211, 217 etc.

20 On the designation of refrains, see also Doss-Quinby, *Les Refrains*, 160–80. It seems generally accepted that the motet was named after the refrain and not vice versa, see *ibid.*, 165–66.

21 The term 'parasite' is vdB's (17). See Ch. 7, p. 128 and n. 7. For the abbreviation *Salut II*, see vdB and n. 41 below.

22 Douët-d'Arcq, *Nouveau recueil*, 64. Unfortunately, this *roman* has not been identified.

23 For an attempt to link *chantefable* with the punning, ambiguous title of Machaut's 'Voir Dit' see Cerquiglini, 'Le Clerc et l'écriture'.

24 This is the manuscript rubric. As a classificatory term, *motet enté* occurs as a rubric in two medieval manuscript lyric collections, Paris, BN, fr. 845 and fr. 146. The genre is also defined in the musical treatise *De musica* (*c.* 1300) by Johannes de Grocheio: 'Est etiam alius modus cantilenarum, quem *cantum insertum* vel *cantilenam entatam* vocant, qui ad modum cantilenarum incipit et earum fine clauditur vel finitur' (There is also another kind of *cantilena* which they [i.e. the Parisians] call 'ornamented song' or 'grafted song'. It begins in the manner of *cantilene* and ends or comes to a close in their fashion), Page, 'Johannes de Grocheio', 27 and n. 41. *Enté* itself is much more widespread.

25 Anderson, ed., *Compositions of the Bamberg Manuscript*, Nos. 42 and 43. Translations are mine.

26 As, for instance, the refrain *En non Dieu* in Tischler, ed., *The Montpellier Codex* (*Mo*), Nos. 96 and 24. See Butterfield, 'The Language of Medieval Music'.

27 Anderson, ed., *Compositions of the Bamberg Manuscript*, No. 55 (*Mo* 8,345 and 2,20).

28 Butterfield, 'The Language of Medieval Music'.

29 *Complainte I*, fols. 267b–268a. For the title *Complainte I*, see vdB and n. 41 below.

30 Eloranta, 'Couplets d'une romance d'Audefroi'.

31 True cento composition is comparatively rare (in its strict sense) among the motets: Everist, 'Refrain Cento', 183. He argues that there are just three: *La bele m'ocit, Dieus! – In Seculum* (M166), *Cele m'a s'amour donée – Alleluia, Hodie* (M433) and *Cis a cui je sui amie* (M880T).

32 Everist, 'Refrain Cento', 167, n. 9.

33 O'Gorman, 'The Salut d'Amour'; the *Salut* is edited by Monfrin.

34 On comparable compositional procedures in chant, see Treitler, 'Homer and Gregory' and 'Centonate Chant'.

35 Doss-Quinby, *Les Refrains*, 96–111.

36 See Zink, *Les Chansons de toile*, 42–45; Huot, *Allegorical Play*, 57–59.

37 See Ch. 2, n. 55 above.

38 Meyer *et al.* eds., *La Chanson*, exaggerate the regularity: their edition irons out most of the textual and musical disturbance caused by the refrains. Perhaps the most extreme instance is their removal of a line from the second refrain of strophe III.

39 In the process he gives a specificity to the metre and line length of refrains that is normally (owing to the inconsistencies of scribal lineation) hard to define.

40 Doss-Quinby, *Les Refrains*, 180–215. Occasionally, as well as the metre and rhyme, the melody is also shaped to introduce the refrains occurring at the end of each stanza: see Rosenberg and Tischler, *Chansons des trouvères: Chanter m'estuet*, rev. edn, nos. 25, 27, 33, 128, although note the disparate metrical and melodic schemas between stanzas and refrains in no. 25.

41 'Le Salut d'amour'. For the numbering of the *Saluts* and *Complaintes*, I follow vdB where appropriate. It is difficult to date these pieces, but correspondences of refrains suggest that *Salut II*, at least, is late thirteenth century (see Ch. 8, n. 23). See also Bec, 'Pour un essai'.

42 *D'Amour et de jalousie*; *Li Confrere d'amours*; *La Flour d'amours*; *Le Débat du clerc et de la damoiselle*; Nevelon Amiot, *Dit d'amour*. In addition, one of the *dits* in Nicole de Margival's *Panthère d'amours* is described as a *salut* in the text (line 1750). See also the *salut* preserved in the 'La Clayette' Manuscript (n. 33 above).

43 Omont, *Fabliaux*.

44 For the latter, see *La Complainte douteuse*, ed. Jubinal, II, 243–56, and Meyer, 'Le Salut d'amour', No. III, 147.

45 Twenty occitan *saluts* also date from the thirteenth century, of which four present strophic divisions. See Bec, 'Pour un essai', 199.

46 *Salut II* shows similar formal variability, since it has a single odd strophe of eight lines plus a one-line refrain amongst a sequence of four- or five-line strophes.

47 See lines 362–64; 374–76, Faral, *D'Amour et de jalousie*, 348 and note.

48 On *saluts*, see Melli, 'l "Salut"', and Camargo, 'The Verse Love Epistle'. References to *salutz* as love-letters can be found in the Provençal romance *Flamenca*, for example lines 7067–69, 7075–76 and 7084–88. Letters in the form of lyrics are also found in the prose *Tristan*: they are of two kinds, described as 'lettres en semblance de lai' and 'lettres en vers'. The first letter begins with the salutation formula described by Meyer ('Le Salut d'amour') as characteristic of the *saluts* ('Amis Amanz ... saluz voz mande'). Music survives for three of the 'lettres en semblance de lai' in Vienna MS 2542. Verse letters are common in Arthurian prose romance.

49 Bossuat, 'Un débat d'amour', 63–75. *Cassidorus* also contains a six-line *salut d'amours* (see Palermo, ed., *Le Roman de Cassidorus*, I, 193).

50 Compare *La Chastelaine de Saint Gille*, another thirteenth-century poem with an extended *chanson avec des refrains* structure.

51 This passage is quoted by Badel, *Le Roman*, 344. For an edition of the commentary, see Guichard-Tesson and B. Roy, eds., *Le Livre des eschez amoureux moralisés*. On the identification of the commentator as Evrart, see liii-lvi.

52 See lines 544–45, 1575–80.

CHAPTER 15

1 Bakhtin, *The Dialogic Imagination*, 44.

2 Greimas, 'Idiotismes', 57.

3 On proverbs, see the contrasting approaches of Whiting, 'The Nature of the Proverb', and 'Proverbial Material'; and *Rhétorique du proverbe*: Special Issue, especially J. et B. Cerquiglini, 'L'Ecriture proverbiale'.

4 Greimas, 'Idiotismes', 50.

5 Kristeva, 'Word, Dialogue and Novel', 66 (adapting Bakhtin).

6 Doss-Quinby, *Les Refrains*, 55.

7 For further discussion, see Butterfield, 'Repetition'.

8 For examples, see Chs. 4, 6 and 9 above.

9 Reproductions of the major illuminations in this manuscript are included by Marchello-Nizia, ed., *Le Roman*, Plates I–XVIII, 159–78. For further discussion, see Huot, *From Song to Book*, 174–93.

10 For discussion of *Qui bien aime* in an Anglo-French context, see Butterfield, 'French Culture', 102–05. See also nn. 49–50 below.

11 Huot has argued that the extra 'E' could be worked into the acrostic to spell TIBAUTE, which is an anagram of BIAUTET, the first messenger (*From Song to Book*, 191–92).

12 Butterfield, 'Repetition'.

13 See lines 311, **333**, 350, 355, **548, 588**, 607, 608, 609, 613, 614, 630, **695, 698, 700, 712, 758** (those with the exact phrasing noted in bold).

14 Compare: *Bien doi endurer **le mal** / puis que j'ai ami leal* [*I must endure well the pain since I have a loyal lover*] (2484–85; vdB, refr. 259) and *Tel dit qu'il se muert d'amour, Qui ne sent **mal** ne doulour* [*Such a one says that he is dying of love who does not feel pain or grief*] (2606–07; vdB, refr. 1768).

15 The song occurs in two manuscripts as a chanson, and in four as a motet, over the tenor *Sancte Germane*. For an edition, see Gennrich, ed., *Altfranzösische Lieder*, II, 40–42.

16 Marchello-Nizia's phrasing here is ambiguous, but should not be mistaken for meaning that *Le Court d'amours* cites the first two lines of the first strophe (*Le Roman*, xxxvii).

17 This may be compared with the way in which the two authorial signatures of Gervès du Bus and Chaillou de Pesstain are announced on fol. 23v of *Fauvel* (see Ch. 12 above).

18 Compare this scene with the description of the 'Jeu du Chapelet' in *Le Tournoi de Chauvency*, 4190–4300.

19 See the Appendix.

20 Scheler, ed., *Li Prisons*, I, xiii.

21 Wimsatt, *Chaucer and the French Love Poets*, 39.

22 Refrains are similarly used in the conclusions of motets (Rokseth, ed., *Polyphonie*, IV, 247).

23 See Ch. 10, n. 27 above.

24 vdB, refr. 991.

25 For example, both Boulton (*The Song in the Story*, 280 and 282) and Fowler ('Musical

333

Interpolations', 27) assert without evidence that the more proverbial the function of a refrain, the less likely that it was sung.

26 For further discussion of this in relation to the other surviving manuscript of the *Prisons*, see Ch. 10, 180.

27 Compare Ch. 14, nn. 7–19 and the similarly wide range of terms given to the refrains in the *Traduction d'Ovide*, discussed below: *chançon, motet, pastourelle, chançonette* and *karole*.

28 Of the two refrains quoted above, the first is unique to *Li Prisons d'amours*, but the second appears after the fourth strophe of a *chanson avec des refrains* (R150). The second also has a parallel in the refrain of R1646: *Li debonnaires Diex m'a mis en sa prison* [*The gracious God has put me in his prison*]. As none of these songs can be dated precisely, we cannot tell the direction of the borrowing, or indeed whether these are independent citations.

29 An inconclusive attempt to date the work (to before 1240) by an analysis of the refrains it contains has been made by vdB, 'L'*Art d'aimer*'.

30 Roy, ed., *Traduction*, 45–49.

31 Refrains are also supplied with commentary in the Hereford proverb collection, Hereford Cathedral Library, MS P. 3. 3, fols. 164–167.

32 The mid-thirteenth-century *Chastoiement des dames* by Robert de Blois is also based on the *Ars amatoria*, and includes a *chanson d'amours* as a sample of what a lover might sing.

33 One of its manuscripts (Leningrad, Bibl.publ.fr.F.v.XIV), also contains *Le Roman de la violette*: it provides an example of the way in which *roumans de chançons notés* were often collected together in the same manuscript.

34 The twelve songs at the beginning of the *Roman de la poire* could be seen as an exception, but they are not integrated into the narrative.

35 These *dits* are often left out in discussions of the lyrics in the *Panthère* (for instance, in Reaney, 'The Development of the Rondeau'). However, they are all in distinct metres, the second (in twelve-line stanzas, rhyming aabaab / bbabba) having the same form as the poem to the Virgin interpolated into Guillaume de Deguileville's *Le Pelerinage de la vie humaine* (composed 1330–32).

36 One *rondel* of his ('Soyez liez et menez goye') occurs with musical settings in two manuscripts, and also without music in the Pennsylvania MS French 15 discussed by Wimsatt, *Chaucer and the Poems of 'Ch'*.

37 As Hoepffner points out ('Les Poésies lyriques', 217), this is probably the earliest reference to the term *chant royal*.

38 Stanza 1 from *Chanson* No. 20, Marshall, ed., *The Chansons*.

39 *Chanson* No. 25, Marshall, ed., *The Chansons*.

40 The anagram at the end makes less of an authorial pitch for the songs than Tibaut's acrostic keyed in to the refrain initials. On the treatment of female authority in the *Poire* and the *Panthère*, see Solterer, *Minerva*, ch. 2, 61–78.

41 Recent work on citation, mainly on the ballades and the later fourteenth century, includes Plumley, Boogaart, and Leach. See also Günther, 'Zitate', and Arlt, 'Aspekte'.

42 Hoepffner mentions the refrain in passing, along with the *priere*; however, with the exception of Earp, *Guide*, 212 and 238, modern accounts of the work's inset pieces (such as Huot, 249, Wimsatt and Kibler, eds., *Guillaume de Machaut*, 39 and Boulton, *The Song in the Story*, 188) have ignored it.

43 All citations from the *Remede* are taken from Wimsatt and Kibler, eds., *Guillaume de Machaut*.

44 Wimsatt and Kibler's translation of line 3504 is more specific than the original.

45 For example, vdB, refrs. 823, 822, 575, 576, 577 and 1811.

46 Avril, *Manuscript Painting*, Plate 24, and p. 86.

47 Ed. Lecoy, *Le Roman de la rose*.

48 Page, *The Owl and the Nightingale*, Ch. 5, also his 'Court and City in France, 1100–1300', in McKinnon, ed., *Antiquity*, 197–217.

49 See vdB, refr. 1585; Morawski, ed., *Proverbes*, no. 1835; Hassell, *Middle French Proverbs*, A63; Ludwig, ed., *Musikalische Werke*, II, 33*–34*. On its circulation in England, see Butterfield, 'French Culture', 103–07.

50 Leech-Wilkinson and Palmer, ed., *Le Livre* [hereafter L-W & P], Letter 10, p. 122; Letter 30, p. 394; line 7372, p. 506. Deschamps also uses it as the refrain of a ballade (No. 1345 in *Oeuvres complètes*, VII, 124–25).

51 Ed. Hoepffner, *Guillaume de Machaut*, III. This is a close variant of: 'Don[t] vient li maus d'amer qui m'ocirra?' [Where do the pains of love come from that will kill me?] (vdB, refr. 595), Butterfield, 'Repetition'.

52 Cerquiglini, 'Le Clerc et l'écriture', 158. Taking the *Voir Dit* as exemplary in its discontinuities of form, narrative sequence and time, Cerquiglini further argues that discontinuity is a defining and polemical characteristic of the *dit*: 'le dit est une genre qui travaille sur le discontinu' (158).

53 The sharing of authorship characterises both the *Rose* of Lorris and Jean de Meun, and the revised fr. 146 version of *Fauvel*.

54 The issue of the historical 'truth' of the *Voir Dit* has been thoroughly re-examined by Leech-Wilkinson, '*Le Voir Dit* and *La Messe de Nostre Dame*', '*Le Voir Dit*: a Reconstruction', and *Le Livre dou Voir Dit*, 'Introduction'. On the identification of Toute Belle as Peronne d'Armentières, and full references to the differing interpretations of Machaut's anagrams and riddles see 'Introduction', xxxviii–xl, nn. 4 and 5.

55 Cerquiglini, 'Le Clerc et l'écriture'.

56 The far from satisfactory 1875 edition by Paris has now been superseded by L-W & P, cited here, and Cerquiglini-Toulet and Imbs, ed. and trans., *Le Livre*.

57 Some poems share the same refrain (e.g. Wilkins, ed. *La Louange*, Nos. 148 & 155), or the first line of one becomes the refrain of another (e.g. Nos. 32 & 149). Lines from No. 188 are used as the refrains of the next four ballades in the manuscripts (Wilkins, *ibid.*, Nos. 206, 12, 34, 49). See his note to No. 188, 177; Earp, *Guide*, 349–50.

58 Cerquiglini, '*Un Engin*', 37–38.

59 A further two citations of this refrain occur still later in the work, in Letters XVII (232) and XXXVII (456).

CHAPTER 16

1 In the following performances: Sequentia: *Trouvères: Höfische Liebeslieder aus Nordfrankreich um 1175–1300*, Harmonia mundi, CD: RD 77155, disc 1, track 19; Gothic Voices: *Lancaster and Valois*, Hyperion, CDA66588, track 6.

2 To this may be added the group of thirty-five rondeaux in fr. 12786, ruled for three-voice polyphony but with the music not filled in, see Everist, 'The Polyphonic Rondeau'. Comparative research is needed on the relations between the song forms in these manuscripts and the Montpellier codex.

3 Hoppin, *Medieval Music*, 296.

4 Page, 'Tradition', 353–94 (here 388).

5 Earp, 'Lyrics for Reading'.

6 See Ch. 8, n. 21 above.
7 This refrain is not italicised in Wilkins's edition of Adam's *Lyric Works*.
8 For another example, see Motet No. 10, rond. 11.
9 For example, compare Motet No. 1 and rond. 5.
10 My chronological supposition that the rondeaux respond compositionally to the motet may, of course, be disputed. I make it on the grounds that the motet is the older genre, and by comparing the use of tenors.
11 Maillard, *Adam de la Halle*, 124, and vdB, refr. 747, note.
12 *Tant que je vivrai / N'amerai / Autrui que vous* (Adam, rondeau No. 15); *Tant com je vivray, sans meffaire* (refrain of 'Tres douce dame que j'aour', Machaut, Ballade no. 24, ed. Schrade, IV, 37–38); *Tant com je vivray* (refrain of 'N'en fait n'en dit', Machaut, Ballade no. 11, ed. Schrade, IV, 15).
13 Marshall, ed., *The Chansons*, No. 31.
14 *Pace* Earp, 'Lyrics for Reading', 108.
15 Ballade No. 16 ed. Wilkins, and Douce 308 Nos. 11 and 115. For cross-references between Lescurel and *Fauvel*, see Butterfield, 'Catalogue', Nos. 6, 33 and 38.
16 Gennrich, *Rondeaux, Virelais und Balladen*, I, No. 171, and II, p. 113.
17 Kügle, *The Manuscript Ivrea*, 162; Plumley, 'Citation and Allusion', 287–88.
18 Günther, 'Zitate'; Plumley, 'Citation and Allusion'.
19 Earp, 'Lyrics for Reading', 103.
20 Arlt, 'Aspekte' and 'Jehannot de Lescurel'.
21 *PMM*, 2 (1993), 43–73, (here 55). On other interrelationships in Machaut's ballades, see Leach, 'Fortune's Demesne' and Boogaart, 'Love's Unstable Balance'.
22 E. Reimer, ed., *Johannes de Garlandia: De mensurabili musica*, 2 vols. (Wiesbaden, 1972), I, 95. I am grateful to Christopher Page for originally drawing my attention to this intriguing passage. The translation cited is his. He also discusses it in 'Tradition', 387.
23 The comments on repetition cover such disparate genres (organum, conducti, hocket, secular song) that any reference to refrain-citation must be understood within broad terms.

EPILOGUE

1 From the double ballade 'Armes, Amours, Dames, Chevalerie' that Deschamps wrote to lament the death of Machaut, set to music by Andrieu. Cited and translated in Wimsatt, *Chaucer and his French Contemporaries*, 246–47.
2 Brownlee, *Poetic Identity*, 9–12.
3 Compare the opening stanza of this ballade (line 2) and also the often quoted lines of Gilles li Muisis, writing of Jehan de la Mote: 'Or ye rest Jehans de le Mote / Qui bien le lettre et le notte / Troève, et fait de moult biaus dis, / Dont maint signeur a resbaudis, / Si k'a honneur en est venus / Et des milleurs faiseurs tenus' (Now there remains Jean de le Mote, who composes both words and music well, making very lovely poems, from which many lords take pleasure, so that he has come to honour because of them and is accounted among the best poets); Wimsatt, *Chaucer and his French Contemporaries*, 51.
4 Lines 2099–100.
5 Lukitsch, 'The Poetics', 264, cited approvingly by Wimsatt, *Chaucer and his French Contemporaries*, 5, n. 5.
6 Earp, *Guide*, 205.
7 The question of which, and how many of the surviving 'complete works' manuscripts

were supervised in their copying arrangements by Machaut has not been fully settled: fr. 1586 and 1584 are generally agreed to be the likeliest candidates. See Earp, 'Scribal Practice', and Huot, *From Song to Book*, 246–48 and 274–75.

8 Gautier's role in presenting his own work deserves a separate and more extended account than I can give here.

APPENDIX

1 Unfortunately, space does not permit me to include other details of *mise-en-page*, such as the use of initials, illumination, marginal annotation etc. I hope to publish this information at a future stage.

2 Consistent with the chronological limits of the book, Froissart, however, is omitted.

3 For a list of genres on which the sacred songs are based, see Bayart, ed., *Ludus*, 219. They include chansons, hymns, one antiphon, one conductus, proses, motets, one refrain, one *pastourelle*, one response, one alleluia, one rondeau.

4 This remains unedited, though see Bayart's outline, *Ludus*, lxxix–cvi. Since the translator sometimes gives the songs in indirect speech, or merely announces them, exact numbers are hard to ascertain.

5 Two further manuscripts that preserve the beginning of the poem do not contain the refrain: Rome, Biblioteca Apostolica-Vaticana Reg. Lat. 1490 and Paris, BN fr. 837.

6 Two more composite manuscripts have an abbreviated version of *Cleomadès* at the start followed by *Meliacin:* Brussels BR IV 319 and Paris BN fr. 1455.

7 On fol. 65r of this manuscript, in the same hand as *Aucassin*, begins the *Lai de Graelant*, provided with a single blank stave (col. 6). I am indebted to John Haines for kindly drawing my attention to this.

8 Including variants (see vdB, 330–31).

9 The refrain is written out twice in the margin.

10 Châtelain de Couci, 'A vos, amant', Stanza III.

11 Also Paris, BN Moreau 1719 fols. 221–250, an eighteenth-century copy of a now lost thirteenth- to fourteenth-century manuscript (not viewed).

12 See M. Camargo's corrections to the foliation of M. R. James in the College copy of James's catalogue.

13 Including two variants (see Vilamo-Pentti, ed., *La Court de paradis*, 54–78 (60) and 63–4 (vdB, refr. 1788).

14 In varying strophic forms, the fourth with a refrain '*Por joie avoir*' (not in vdB). See Steuer, '*Histoire de Joseph*', 248–50.

15 See Chailley, ed., *Les Chansons*, 6–10. Only the manuscripts containing songs are listed here. For further details, see Chailley, ed., *Les Chansons*.

16 The notation is meaningless: written by 'un ignorant prétentieux', in Chailley's withering phrase, *Les Chansons*, 34.

17 Including four in the variants.

18 One is introduced as a 'balade', but is in virelai form (see Page, 'Tradition', 373).

19 The thirteen manuscripts of the 'original' version of the *roman* do not contain any songs.

20 See vdB, notes on refrs. 290 and 1077.

21 The surviving manuscript has only 103 folios; several folios are missing and others re-numbered.

22 The refrains have not yet been catalogued.

23 This unedited work survives in thirty manuscripts, see Lathuillère, *Guiron le Courtois*, 36–96.

24 Inset pieces may be found on fol. 151r, 159v–160r, 160r–v, 161r–v, 197r–v etc.

25 Inset pieces may be found on fol. 44r, 89r, 95v–96r, 96r, 97r, 110r, 124r, 125v and 138v.

26 See the commentary on refr. 149 in vdB, 105.

27 Including variants.

28 'Asperges me' and 'Te Deum laudamus'.

29 According to Delbouille, ed., the Florence MS is a copy of the Mons MS; a further fragmentary copy, Rheims BM 1007, does not contain the refrains.

30 These folios are missing in the copy of this manuscript consulted in the Institut de recherche et d'histoire des textes (IRHT).

31 'Te Deum laudamus'.

32 vdB lists 81 refrains in total, but this includes the ballades and rondeaux.

33 One other copy, BN fr. 837, does not include the refrains.

34 Three citations are from the same song ('Qui a droit veult amors servir').

35 Figures from Lods, ed., *Les Pièces lyriques*. There are many more inscriptions, letters etc. in the vast bulk of the work, which, until editing is complete, await to be catalogued. Book VI additionally has four ballades, see Taylor, ed., *Le Roman de Perceforest*, 'Introduction.'

36 This work is followed in three manuscripts by a *chanson d'amour*, which also occurs separately in Paris Arsenal 5201 and fr. 2236.

37 See Bossuat, 'Un débat'. The work includes many other letters.

38 According to Thorpe, *Roman de Laurin*, the work survives in a further six manuscripts: Brussels, BR 9245; Brussels, BR 9433–4; Fitzw. McCl. 179; Florence, Bibl. Laur. Ashb. 49; Paris, Arsenal 3355 and Paris, BN fr. 93.

39 The letter (fol. 61r^c) is in the form of a rondeau.

40 The work survives in two versions: one in a unique manuscript (fr. 757); the other in eighty-two manuscripts. Some twenty-four manuscripts contain lais, in varying numbers. I give only the manuscripts which have music, or spaces, from Fotitch and Steiner, eds., *Les Lais du roman de Tristan*.

41 Five are 'lettres en semblances de lais'. There are many more inscriptions, *dévinailles*, enigmas etc. in the work as a whole.

42 Roy, ed., *Traduction*, omits the stanza at 2430 in his list of 'passages lyriques' on p. 47.

43 See Roy, ed., *Traduction*, 47, n. 1 for corrections to vdB. vdB's figure of 67 includes repeated refrains.

Bibliography

Facsimile editions cited

Aubry, P. and A. Jeanroy, eds., *Le Chansonnier de l'Arsenal: reproduction phototypique du MS 5198 de la Bibliothèque de l'Arsenal* (Paris, 1913)

Beck, J.-B., ed., *Les Chansonniers des troubadours et des trouvères publiés en facsimilé et transcrits en notation moderne: I. Le Chansonnier Cangé, Paris BN MS fr. 846*, Corpus cantilenarum medii aevi, first series, No. 1, 2 vols. (Paris and Philadelphia, 1927)

Beck, J.-B. and L. Beck, eds., *Les Chansonniers des troubadours et des trouvères publiés en facsimilé et transcrits en notation moderne: II. Le Manuscrit du Roi (f. fr. 844 de la BN)*, Corpus cantilenarum medii aevi, first series, No. 2, 2 vols. (London and Philadelphia, 1938)

Gervès du Bus and Chaillou de Pesstain, [facsimile] *Le Roman de Fauvel*, ed. L. F. P. Aubry (Paris, 1907)

[facsimile] *Le Roman de Fauvel in the Edition of Messire Chaillou de Pesstain, A Reproduction in Facsimile of the Complete Manuscript Paris Bibliothèque Nationale, Fonds Français 146*, ed. Edward H. Roesner, François Avril and Nancy Freeman Regalado (New York, 1990)

Jeanroy, Alfred, ed., *Le Chansonnier d'Arras, reproduction en phototype*, SATF (Paris, 1925)

Meyer, Paul and G. Raynaud, eds., *Le Chansonnier français de Saint-Germain-des-Prés (BN fr. 20050)*, SATF, facs. edn (Paris, 1892)

Omont, Henri, ed., *Fabliaux, dits et contes en vers français du XIIIe siècle, facsimilé du MS fr. 837 du BN* (Paris, 1932; repr. Geneva, 1973)

The Romance of Alexander: A Collotype Facsimile of MS Bodley 264, ed. M. R. James (Oxford, 1933)

Primary sources

Adam de la Bassée, *Ludus super Anticlaudianum*, ed. Paul Bayart (Tourcoing, 1930)

Adam de la Halle, *Le Jeu de Robin et de Marion, précédé du Jeu du Pèlerin*, ed. K. Varty (London, 1960)

The Lyric Works of Adam de la Hale: Chansons, Jeux Partis, Rondeaux, Motets, CMM 44, ed. Nigel Wilkins (Rome, 1967)

Bibliography

The Chansons of Adam de la Halle, ed. J. H. Marshall (Manchester, 1971)
Le Jeu de la feuillée, ed. J. Dufournet (Gand, 1977)
The Lyrics and Melodies of Adam de la Halle, lyrics trans. and ed. D. Nelson; melodies ed. H. van der Werf, GLML 24 (New York, 1985)
Le Jeu de Robin et Marion, ed. and trans. J. Dufournet (Paris, 1989)
Le Jeu de Robin et Marion, ed. and trans. Shira I. Schwam-Baird, music ed. Milton G. Scheuermann, Jr., GLML 94A (New York, 1994)
Adenet le Roi, *Cleomadés*, ed. Albert Henry, *Les Oeuvres d'Adenet le Roi, Volume V*, Université de Bruxelles, Travaux de la Faculté de Philosophie et Lettres 46, 2 vols. (Brussels, 1971)
Alain de Lille, *Anticlaudianus*, ed. R. Bossuat (Paris, 1955)
D'Amour et de jalousie: complainte d'amour du XIIIe siècle, ed. E. Faral, *Romania*, 59 (1933), 333–50
Anderson, Gordon A., ed., *Motets of the Manuscript La Clayette: Paris Bibliothèque Nationale, nouv.acq.f.fr.13521*, CMM 68 (American Institute of Musicology, 1975)
Compositions of the Bamberg Manuscript: Bamberg, Staatsbibliothek, Lit.115 (olim Ed.IV.6), CMM 75 (American Institute of Musicology, 1977)
Andreas Capellanus, *Andreas Capellanus on Love*, ed. and trans. P. G. Walsh (London, 1982)
Aucassin et Nicolette: chantefable du XIIIe siècle, ed. M. Roques, CFMA 41 (Paris, 1967)
Aucassin et Nicolette: chantefable du XIIIe siècle, ed. and trans. Jean Dufournet (Paris, 1973)
Babb, W., trans., and C. Palisca, ed., *Hucbald, Guido and John on Music: Three Medieval Treatises*, Music Theory Translation Series 3 (New Haven and London, 1978)
Bartsch, Karl, ed., *Altfranzösische Romanzen und Pastorellen des 12. und 13. Jahrhunderts* (Leipzig, 1870)
Baude de la Quarière, *La Chanson de bele Aalis*, ed. R. Meyer, J. Bédier and P. Aubry (Paris, 1904)
Baudouin de Condé, *Li Contes de la rose*, ed. A. Scheler, *Dits et contes de Baudouin de Condé et de son fils Jean de Condé*, 3 vols. (Brussels, 1866–67), I, 133–46
Li Prisons d'amours, Dits, ed. Scheler, I, 267–377
Beauvillé, V. de, *Recueil de documents concernant la Picardie*, I (Paris, 1860), 139–54
Berger, R., ed., *Le Nécrologe de la confrérie des jongleurs et des bourgeois d'Arras (1194–1361)*, Mémoires de la Commission Départementale des Monuments historiques du Pas-de-Calais 11² and 13² (Arras, 1963 and 1970)
Littérature et société arrageoises au XIIIe siècle: Les chansons et dits artésiens, Mémoires de la Commission Départmentale des Monuments Historiques du Pas-de-Calais 31 (Arras, 1981)
Birnbaum, S. H., trans., *Johannes de Garlandia: Concerning Measured Music* (Colorado Springs, 1978)
Boogaard, Nico H. J. van den, ed., *Rondeaux et refrains du XIIe siècle au début du XIVe* (Paris, 1969)
Boutière, Jean and A.-H. Schutz, eds., *Biographies des troubadours: textes provençaux des XIIIe et XIVe siècles*, rev. edn by Jean Boutière and D'I.-M. Cluzel (Paris, 1964)

Bibliography

Bretel, *see* Jacques Bretel

Breuil, August, 'La Confrérie de Notre-Dame du Puy d'Amiens', *Mémoires de la Société des antiquaires de Picardie*, 2nd series 3 (1854), 485–680

Cavrois, Louis, ed., *Cartulaire de Notre-Dame des ardents à Arras* (Arras, 1876)

Chailley, *see* Gautier de Coinci

Chaillou de Pesstain, *see* Gervès du Bus

Le Châtelain de Couci, *Chansons attribuées au Chastelain de Couci*, ed. Alain Lerond (Paris, 1964)

La Chastelaine de Saint Gille, ed. O. Schultz-Gora, *Zwei altfranzösische Dichtungen* (Halle, 1916), 35–69

La Chastelaine de Vergi, ed. F. Whitehead (Manchester, 1944)

La Chastelaine de Vergi, ed. René E.V. Struip (The Hague and Paris, 1970)

Christine de Pisan, *Oeuvres poétiques*, ed. M. Roy, SATF, 3 vols. (Paris, 1886–96)

Complainte d'amors (I), ed. P. Meyer, 'Le Salut d'Amour dans les littératures provençale et française', *BECh*, 28 (1867), 150–54

Complainte d'amors (II), ed. H. Omont, *see* Facsimile editions

La Complainte douteuse, ed. A. Jubinal, *Nouveau recueil de contes, dits, fabliaux et autres pièces inédites des XIIIe, XIVe, et XVe siècles*, 2 vols. (Paris, 1839–42), II, 242–56

Le Comte de Poitiers, ed. B. Malmberg, Etudes romanes de Lund 1 (Lund, 1940)

Li Confrere d'amours: poème avec des refrains, ed. A. Långfors, *Romania*, 36 (1907), 29–35

Correspondance amoureuse (Anglo-Norman), *see* Meyer, Paul

Le Court d'amours (suite anonyme), ed. T. Scully, *Le Court d'Amours de Mahieu le Poirier et la suite anonyme de la 'Court d'Amours'* (Waterloo, Ontario, 1976)

La Court de paradis, ed. Eva Vilamo-Pentti (Helsinki, 1953)

Coussemaker, E. de, *Scriptorum de musica medii aevi*, 4 vols. (Paris, 1864–76)

Dante Alighieri, *Il Convivio*, ed. Maria Simonelli (Bologna, 1966)

Dante's Lyric Poetry, ed. Kenelm Foster and Patrick Boyde, 2 vols. (Oxford, 1967)

Vita nuova, ed. Domenico de Robertis (Milan, 1980)

Le Débat du clerc et de la damoiselle, ed. A. Jeanroy, *Romania*, 43 (1914), 1–17

Deschamps, Eustache, *Oeuvres complètes*, ed. le Marquis de Queux de Saint-Hilaire and G. Raynaud, SATF, 11 vols. (Paris, 1878–1903)

Dinaux, A., *Trouvères, jongleurs et ménéstrels du nord de la France, et du midi de la Belgique*, 4 vols. bound in 3 (Paris, 1837–43; repr. Geneva, 1969)

Douët-d'Arcq, L. C., ed., *Nouveau recueil de comptes de l'argenterie des rois de France* (Paris, 1874)

Eichmann, Raymond and John DuVal, eds. and trans., *The French Fabliau, BN MS 837*, GLML 16–17, 2 vols. (New York and London, 1984–85)

Escanor, *see* Girart d'Amiens

L'Estoire de Joseph, *see* Steuer, Wilhelm

Evrart de Conty, *Le Livre des eschez amoureux moralisés*, ed. F. Guichard-Tesson and B. Roy, Bibliothèque de Moyen Francais 2 (Montréal, 1993)

Faral, Edmond, ed., *Les Arts poétiques du XIIe et du XIIIe siècle* (Paris, 1924; repr. 1982)

La Flour d'amours, ed. J. Morawski, *Romania*, 53 (1927), 187–97

Franco of Cologne, *Franconis de Colonia: Ars cantus mensurabilis*, ed. Gilbert Reaney and André Gilles, CSM 18 (Rome, 1974)

Froissart, *see* Jean Froissart

Galeran de Bretagne, ed. L. Foulet, CFMA 37 (Paris, 1925)

Gautier de Coinci, *Les Miracles de Nostre Dame*, ed. V. F. Koenig, TLF, 4 vols. (Geneva and Paris, 1955–70)

    Les Chansons à la Vierge de Gautier de Coinci (1177/78(-1236), ed. J. Chailley (Paris, 1959)

Gennrich, Friedrich, ed., *Rondeaux, Virelais und Balladen aus dem Ende des XII., dem XIII. und dem ersten Drittel des XIV. Jahrhunderts, mit den überlieferten Melodien*, 3 vols.: vols. I and II, GRL 43 and 47 (Dresden, 1921 and Göttingen, 1927); vol. III, SMMA 10 (Langen bei Frankfurt, 1963)

    Bibliographisches Verzeichnis der französischen Refrains des 12. und 13. Jahrhunderts, SMMA 14, facs. reprint, with added material, of *Rondeaux, Virelais und Balladen*, vol. II (Langen bei Frankfurt, 1964)

    Altfranzösische Lieder, 2 vols. (Tübingen, 1955–56)

Gérard de Liège, *Quinque incitamenta ad deum amandum ardenter*, ed. A. Wilmart, *Analecta reginensia: extraits des manuscrits latins de la reine de Christine conservés au Vatican*, Studi e Testi 59 (Vatican City, 1933), 205–47

Gerard de Nevers: Prose Version of the Roman de la Violette, ed. Lawrence F. H. Lowe, Elliott Monographs 22 (Princeton and Paris, 1928)

Gerbert de Montreuil, *Le Roman de la violette ou de Gerart de Nevers*, ed. D. L. Buffum, SATF (Paris, 1928)

Gervès du Bus and Chaillou de Pesstain, [original *roman*] ed. A. Långfors, SATF (Paris, 1914–19)

    [lyric interpolations (texts)] ed. Emilie Dahnk, *L'Hérésie de Fauvel* (Leipzig, 1935)

    [polyphonic music] ed. Leo Schrade, PMFC 1 (Monaco, 1956)

    [monophonic pieces only, excluding chant] *The Monophonic Songs in the Roman de Fauvel*, ed. Samuel N. Rosenberg and Hans Tischler (Lincoln, Nebraska, and London, 1991)

Girart d'Amiens, *Escanor, Roman arthurien en vers de la fin du XIIIe siècle*, ed. Richard Trachsler, TLF 449 (Geneva, 1994)

    Meliacin ou le conte du Cheval de Fust, songs ed. E. Stengel, ZRP, 10 (1886), 460–76

    Meliacin ou Le Cheval de Fust, ed. A. Saly (Aix-en-Provence, 1990)

Grocheio, *see* Johannes de Grocheio

Guido of Arezzo, *see* Babb, W. and C. Palisca; and Smits van Waesberghe, J.

Guillaume de Dole, *see* Jean Renart

Guillaume de Lorris and Jean de Meun, *Le Roman de la rose*, ed. F. Lecoy, CFMA 92, 95, 98, 3 vols. (Paris, 1965–70)

    ed. E. Langlois, SATF, 5 vols. (Paris, 1914–24)

Guillaume de Machaut, *Le Voir Dit*, ed. Paulin Paris (Paris, 1875; repr. Geneva, 1969)

    Guillaume de Machaut: oeuvres, ed. E. Hoepffner, SATF, 3 vols. (Paris, 1908, 1911, 1921)

    Poésies lyriques, ed. V. Chichmaref, 2 vols. (Paris, 1909)

Musikalische Werke, ed. F. Ludwig, 4 vols.: I–III (Leipzig, 1926; repr. 1954), IV with
 H. Besseler (Leipzig, 1954)
La Louange des dames by Guillaume de Machaut, ed. Nigel Wilkins (Edinburgh, 1972)
Oeuvres complètes, ed. Leo Schrade, PMFC 2–3, repr. in 5 vols. (Monaco, 1977)
Guillaume de Machaut: Le Jugement dou Roy de Behaigne and Remede de Fortune, ed.
 James I. Wimsatt and William W. Kibler, The Chaucer Library (Athens, Georgia,
 and London, 1988)
La Fontaine amoureuse, ed. and trans. Jacqueline Cerquiglini-Toulet (Paris, 1993)
Le Livre dou Voir Dit/ The Book of the True Poem), ed. D. Leech-Wilkinson, trans.
 R. Barton Palmer, GLML 106A (New York and London, 1998)
Le Livre du voir dit: le dit véridique, ed. and trans. P. Imbs; revised J. Cerquiglini-
 Toulet (Paris, 1999)
Guiron le Courtois, unpublished. Consulted in London, BL Additional MS 36673 and
 Paris, BN fr. 350
Hassell, James Woodrow, Jr., *Middle French Proverbs, Sentences, and Proverbial Phrases*
 (Leiden, 1982)
Henri d'Andeli, *Le Lai d'Aristote*, ed. Maurice Delbouille, Bibliothèque de la Faculté
 de Philosophie et Lettres de l'Université de Liège 123 (Paris, 1951)
Hoppin, R. H., ed., *Anthology of Medieval Music* (New York, 1978)
Jacquemart Giélée, *Renart le Nouvel*, ed. H. Roussel, SATF (Paris, 1961)
Jacques Bretel, *Le Tournoi de Chauvency*, ed. M. Delbouille, Bibliothèque de la Faculté
 de Philosophie et Lettres de l'Université de Liège 49 (Paris, 1932)
Jakemés, *Le Roman du castelain de Couci*, ed. M. Delbouille, SATF (Paris, 1936)
Jean de Condé, *Lays dou blanc Chevalier, la messe des oiseaux et le dit des Jacobins et des
 Fremeneurs*, ed. J. Ribard, TLF (Geneva, 1970)
Jean le Court, dite Brisebarre, *Le Restor du Paon*, ed. R. J. Carey, TLF (Geneva,
 1966)
Le Restor du Paon, ed. Enid Donkin, MHRA 15 (London, 1980)
Jean Froissart, *Méliador*, ed. A. Longnon, SATF, 3 vols. (Paris, 1895–99)
La Prison amoureuse, ed. Anthime Fourrier (Paris, 1974)
Jean Renart, *Le Roman de la rose ou de Guillaume de Dole*, ed. G. Servois, SATF (Paris,
 1893)
Le Roman de la rose ou de Guillaume de Dole, ed. R. Lejeune-Dehousse (Paris, 1936)
Le Roman de la rose ou de Guillaume de Dole, ed. F. Lecoy, CFMA 91 (Paris, 1962;
 repr. 1979)
*Jean Renart: The Romance of the Rose or of Guillaume de Dole (Roman de la Rose ou
 de Guillaume de Dole*, ed. and trans. Regina Psaki (New York and London, 1995)
Jeanroy, Alfred, 'Trois dits d'amour du XIIIe siècle', *Romania*, 22 (1893), 45–70
Jeanroy, Alfred, and Henri Guy, eds., *Chansons et dits artésiens du XIIIe siècle* (Bordeaux,
 1898)
Jeanroy, Alfred, L. Brandin and P. Aubry, eds., *Lais et descorts français du XIIIe siècle:
 texte et musique* (Paris, 1901; repr. New York, 1969)
Jehan Acart de Hesdin, *La Prise amoureuse: allegorische Dichtung aus dem XIV. Jahrhun-
 dert*, ed. E. Hoepffner, GRL 22 (Dresden, 1910)

Jehan de la Mote, *Li Regret Guillaume comte de Hainault*, ed. A. Scheler (Louvain, 1882)
    Le Parfait du Paon, ed. R. J. Carey (Chapel Hill, NC, 1972)
Jehannot de Lescurel, *Chansons, ballades et rondeaux de Jehannot de l'Escurel*, ed. Anatole
    de Montaiglon (Paris, 1855)
    Balades, rondeaux et diz entés sus refroiz de rondeaux, ed. F. Gennrich SMMA 13
    (Langen bei Frankfurt, 1964)
    The Works of Jehan de Lescurel, ed. Nigel Wilkins, CMM 30 (Rome, 1966)
Jehan le Teinturier d'Arras, *Le Mariage des sept arts suivie d'une version anonyme*, ed.
    A. Långfors, *Poèmes français du XIIIe siècle*, CFMA 31 (Paris, 1923), 11–26
Johannes de Grocheio, *Der Musiktraktat des Johannes de Grocheo nach den Quellen neu
    herausgegeben mit Übersetzung ins Deutsche und Revisionsbericht*, ed. Ernst Rohloff,
    Media latinitas musica 2 (Leipzig, 1943)
    *Die Quellenhandschriften zum Musiktraktat des Johannes de Grocheio im Faksimile
    herausgegeben nebst Übertragung des Textes und Übersetzung ins Deutsche, dazu
    Bericht, Literaturschau, Tabellen und Indices*, ed. Ernst Rohloff (Leipzig, 1972)
    Concerning Music, trans. A. Seay (Colorado Springs, 1967)
Johannes de Grocheio, *see* Page, Christopher
Le Ju de le capete Martinet, ed. G. Raynaud, *Romania*, 10 (1881), 519–32
Jubinal, A., ed., *Nouveau recueil de contes, dits, fabliaux et autres pièces inédites des XIIIe,
    XIVe, et XVe siècles*, 2 vols. (Paris, 1839–42)
Le Lai d'Aristote, see Henri d'Andeli
Långfors, A., A. Jeanroy and L. Brandin, eds., *Recueil général des jeux-partis français*
    (Paris, 1926)
Langlois, E., ed., *Recueil d'arts de seconde rhétorique* (Paris, 1903)
Legge, M. D., ed., *Anglo-Norman Letters and Petitions from All Souls MS 182*, Anglo-
    Norman Texts 3 (Oxford, 1941)
Lerond, *see Le Châtelain de Couci*
Le Livre du chevalier de la Tour-Landry, ed. A. de Montaiglon (Paris, 1854)
Maillard, J., *Roi-trouvère du XIIIe siècle: Charles d'Anjou*, Musicological Studies and
    Documents 18 (American Institute of Musicology, 1967)
Meliacin, see Girart d'Amiens
Meun, Jean de, *see* Guillaume de Lorris
Meyer, Paul, ed., 'Le Salut d'amour dans les littératures provençale et française', *BECh*,
    28 (1867), 124–70
    'Mélanges anglo-normands: 1. correspondance amoureuse 2. chanson d'amour',
    Romania, 38 (1909), 434–41
Meyer, R., ed., *see* Baude de la Quarière
Monfrin, M. J., 'Piecès courtoises du XIIIe siècle', *Revue de linguistique romane*, 34
    (1970), 133–48
Morawski, J., ed., *Proverbes français antérieurs au XVe siècle*, CFMA 47 (Paris, 1925)
    'Fragments de poèmes et refrains inédits', *Romania*, 56 (1930), 253–63
Nevelon d'Amiot, *Dit d'amour*, ed. A. Jeanroy, 'Trois dits d'amour du XIIIe siècle',
    Romania, 22 (1893), 45–70
Newcombe, Terence, ed., *Les Poésies de Thibaut de Blaison* (Geneva, 1978)

Nicole de Margival, *Le Dit de la panthère d'amours*, ed. H. Todd, SATF (Paris, 1883)

O'Gorman, Richard, 'The *Salut d'Amour* from the La Clayette Manuscript attributed to Simon', *Romance Philology*, 20 (1966), 39–44

Opie, Iona and Peter, *The Singing Game* (Oxford, 1985)

Page, Christopher, 'Johannes de Grocheio on Secular Music: a Corrected Text and a New Translation', *PMM*, 2 (1993), 17–41

Paris, Gaston, ed., 'Le Conte de la rose dans le roman de *Perceforest*', *Romania*, 23 (1894), 78–140

Potvin, Charles, 'La Charte de la Cour d'Amour de l'année 1401', *Bulletins de l'Académie Royale des Sciences, des Lettres et des Beaux-Arts de Belgique*, third series, 12 (1886), 191–220

Psaki, *see* Jean Renart

Raynaud, G., ed., *Recueil de motets français des XIIe et XIIIe siècles*, 2 vols. (Paris, 1881–83)

The Razos de Trobar of Raimon Vidal and Associated Texts, ed. J. H. Marshall (London, 1972)

Reichl, Karl, ed., *Religiöse Dichtung im englischen Hochmittelalter*, Texte und Untersuchungen zur Englischen Philologie, Band 1 (Munich, 1973)

Riley, H. T., ed., 'Regulations of the Feste de Pui', *Munimenta gildhallae Londoniensis*, Rolls Series, 3 vols. (London, 1859–62), II: i, *Liber customarum*, pp. 216–28

Rivière, J.-C., ed., *Pastourelles: Introduction à l'étude formelle des pastourelles anonymes françaises des XIIe et XIIIe siècles*, TLF 213, 220, 232, 3 vols. (Geneva, 1974–76)

Robert de Blois, *Le Chastoiement des dames*, ed. J. H. Fox, *Robert de Blois, son oeuvre didactique et narrative* (Paris, 1950)

Roesner *et al.*, eds., *Le Roman de Fauvel*, *see* Gervès du Bus, Facsimile Editions

Rokseth, Y., ed., *Polyphonies du XIIIe siècle*, 4 vols. (Paris, 1935–39)

Le Roman de Cassidorus, ed. Joseph Palermo, SATF, 2 vols. (Paris, 1963–64)

Le Roman du castelain de Couci, *see* Jakemés

Le Romans de la dame a la lycorne et du biau chevalier au lyon, ed. F. Gennrich, GRL 18 (Dresden, 1908)

Le Roman de Fauvel, *see* Gervès du Bus

Le Roman de Laurin, fils de Marques le Seneschal, ed. Lewis Thorpe (Cambridge, 1960)

Le Roman de Perceforest, Première partie, ed. Jane H. M. Taylor, TLF 279 (Geneva, 1979); *IIIe partie*, 3 vols., ed. Gilles Roussineau, TLF 365, 409, 434 (Geneva, 1988); *IVe partie*, 2 vols., ed. Gilles Roussineau, TLF 343 (Geneva, 1987)

    Les pièces lyriques du roman de Perceforest, ed. J. Lods, Société de publications romanes et françaises 36 (Geneva and Lille, 1953)

Le Roman de la poire, *see* Tibaut

Le Roman de Tristan en prose, ed. R. L. Curtis, 3 vols. (Munich, 1963; Leyden, 1976; Cambridge, 1985)

Le Roman de Tristan en prose, gen. ed. Philippe Ménard, vols. 1–8 (out of 9), TLF 353, 387, 398, 408, 416, 437, 450, 462 (Geneva, 1987–95)

Le Roman de Tristan en prose, Version du manuscrit fr. 757 de la Bibliothèque nationale de Paris, 3 vols., 1. ed. J. Blanchard and M. Quéreuil; 2. ed. N. Laborderie and T. Delcourt; 3. ed. J-P. Ponceau, CFMA 123, 133, 135 (Paris, 1997–2000)

Les Lais du roman de Tristan en prose d'après le manuscrit de Vienne 2542, ed. T. Fotitch and R. Steiner (Munich, 1974)

Le Roman de la violette, see Gerbert de Montreuil

Le Roman de la violette [prose version], see *Gerard de Nevers*

The Romance of Alexander, see Facsimile editions

The Romance of Flamenca, ed. Marion E. Porter, trans. M. J. Hubert (Princeton, 1962)

Rosenberg, Samuel N. and Hans Tischler eds., *Chanter m'estuet: Songs of the Trouvères* (London, 1981), rev. edn with Marie-Geneviève Grossel, *Chansons des trouvères: Chanter m'estuet* (Paris, 1995)

Roy, B., ed., see *Traduction*

Ruggieri, J., 'Deux lettres d'amour', *Archivum romanicum*, 24 (1940), 92–94

Salut d'amours (I), *see* Meyer, P., ed., 'Le Salut d'Amour', 154–62

Salut d'amours (Ia), *see* Meyer, P., ed., 'Le Salut d'Amour', 145–47

Salut d'amours (II), ed. A. Jubinal, *Nouveau recueil de contes, dits, fabliaux et autres pièces inédites des XIIIe, XIVe, et XVe siècles*, 2 vols. (Paris, 1839–42), II, 235–41

Salut d'amours (III), ed. O. Schultz-Gora, *ZRP*, 24 (1900), 358–69

Smits van Waesberghe, J., ed., *Guido of Arezzo: Micrologus*, CSM 4 (Rome, 1955)

Sone de Nansai, ed. M. Goldschmidt (Tübingen, 1899)

Spanke, H., ed., *Eine altfranzösische Liedersammlung; der anonyme Teil der Liederhandschriften KNPX* (Halle, 1925)

Steffens, G., ed., 'Die altfranzösische Liederhandschrift der Bodleiana in Oxford, Douce 308', *Archiv für das Studium der neueren Sprachen und Literaturen*, 97 (1896), 283–308; 98 (1897), 59–80, 343–82; 99 (1897), 77–100, 339–88; 104 (1900), 331–54

Stengel, E., 'Die altfranzösischen Liedercitate aus Girardin's d'Amiens *Conte du cheval de fust*', *ZRP*, 10 (1886), 460–76

Steuer, Wilhelm, 'Die altfranzösische *Histoire de Joseph*', *Romanische Forschungen*, 14 (1903), 227–410

Stimming, A., ed., *Die altfranzösischen Motette der Bamberger Handschrift nebst einem Anhang, enthaltend altfranzösische Motette aus anderen deutschen Handschriften*, GRL 13 (Dresden, 1906)

Thibaut de Champagne, ed. A. Wallensköld, *Les Chansons de Thibaut de Champagne, Roi de Navarre*, SATF (Paris, 1925)

Tibaut, *Le roman de la poire par Tibaut*, ed. Christiane Marchello-Nizia, SATF (Paris, 1984)

Tischler, Hans, ed., *The Earliest Motets (to circa 1270): A Complete Comparative Edition*, 3 vols. (New Haven and London, 1982)

Trouvère Lyrics with Melodies: Complete and Comparative Edition, 3 vols. (to date), CMM 107 (American Institute of Musicology, 1997)

Tischler, Hans, ed., Susan Stakel and Joel C. Relihan, trans., *The Montpellier Codex*, Recent Researches in the Music of the Middle Ages and Early Renaissance 2–7, 4 vols. (Madison, Wisc., 1978–85)

Le Tournoi de Chauvency, see Jacques Bretel

Traduction et commentaire de l'Ars amatoria d'Ovide, ed. B. Roy, *L'Art d'Amours* (Leyden, 1974)

Bibliography

Watriquet de Couvin, *Dits de Watriquet de Couvin*, ed. A. Scheler (Brussels, 1868)

Werf, H. van der, ed., *Trouvères-Melodien, I and II*, MMMA 10–11 (London, 1977 and 1979)

Werf, H. van der, and G. A. Bond, eds., *The Extant Troubadour Melodies: Transcriptions and Essays for Performers and Scholars* (Rochester, NY, 1984)

Wilkins, Nigel, ed., *One Hundred Ballades, Rondeaux and Virelais from the Late Middle Ages* (Cambridge, 1969)

Zink, Michel, ed., *Belle: Essai sur les chansons de toile* (Paris, 1978)

Secondary

Apel, Willi, 'Rondeaux, Virelais, and Ballades in French 13th-Century Song', *JAMS*, 7 (1954), 121–30

Arlt, Wulf, 'Aspekte der Chronologie und des Stilwandels im französischen Lied des 14. Jahrhunderts', *Aktuelle Fragen der musikbezogenen Mittelalterforschung: Texte zu einem Basler Kolloquium des Jahres 1975 = Forum musicologicum*, 3 (1982), 193–280

'Jehannot de Lescurel and the Function of Musical Language in the *Roman de Fauvel* as Presented in BN fr. 146', in Bent and Wathey, eds., *Fauvel Studies* (Oxford, 1998), 25–34

Aubrey, Elizabeth, *The Music of the Troubadours* (Bloomington, 1966)

Aubrey, Elizabeth, 'The Dialectic between Occitania and France in the Thirteenth Century', *EMH*, 16 (1997), 1–53

Avril, François, *Manuscript Painting at the Court of France: The Fourteenth Century (1310–1380)* (London, 1978)

Badel, P.-Y., *Le Roman de la Rose au XIVe siècle*, Publications romanes et françaises 153 (Geneva, 1980)

Bakhtin, M. M., *The Dialogic Imagination*, ed. and trans. Michael Holquist and Caryl Emerson (Austin, Texas, 1981)

Speech Genres and Other Late Essays, trans. Vern W. McGee, ed. Caryl Emerson and Michael Holquist (Austin, Texas, 1986)

Baltzer, Rebecca A., Thomas Cable and James I. Wimsatt, eds., *The Union of Words and Music in Medieval Poetry* (Austin, Texas, 1991)

Barber, Richard, *The Knight and Chivalry* (New York, 1970)

Barker, Juliet R. V., *The Tournament in England 1100–1400* (Woodbridge, 1986)

Baumgartner, E., 'Remarques sur les pièces lyriques du Tristan en prose', *Etudes de langue et de littérature du moyen âge offerts à Felix Lecoy* (Paris, 1973), 19–25

Le 'Tristan en Prose', Essai d'interprétation d'un roman médiéval (Geneva, 1975)

'Les citations lyriques dans le Roman de la Rose de Jean Renart', *Romance Philology*, 35 (1981–82), 260–66

Bec, Pierre, 'Pour un essai de définition du salut d'amour', *Estudis Romànics*, 9 (1966), 191–201

'L'Aube française "Gaite de la Tor": pièce de ballet ou poème lyrique?' *CCM*, 16 (1973), 17–33

La Lyrique française au Moyen Age (XIIe–XIIIe siècles: contribution à une typologie des poétiques médiévaux), 2 vols. Publications du Centre d'Etudes Supérieures de Civilisation Médiévale de l'Université de Poitiers 6–7 (Paris, 1977)

Bibliography

Bédier, Joseph, 'Les Fêtes de mai et les commencements de la poésie lyrique au Moyen Age', *Revue des deux mondes*, 135 (1896), 146–72
'Les plus anciennes danses françaises', *Revue des deux mondes*, 31 (1906), I, 398–424
Bent, Margaret, 'Deception, Exegesis and Sounding Number in Machaut's Motet 15', *EMH*, 10 (1991), 15–27
'Reflections of Christopher Page's *Reflections*', *Early Music*, 21 (1993), 625–33
'Editing Early Music: the Dilemma of Translation', *Early Music*, 22 (1994), 373–94
'Polyphony of Texts and Music in the Fourteenth-Century Motet: *Tribum que non abhorruit / Quoniam secta latronum / Merito hec patimur* and Its "Quotations"', in Pesce, ed., *Hearing the Motet* (Oxford, 1997), 82–103
'The Grammar of Early Music: Preconditions for Analysis', *Tonal Structures in Early Music*, ed. Cristle Collins Judd (New York, 1998), 15–59
Bent Margaret, and Andrew Wathey, eds., *Fauvel Studies: Allegory, Chronicle, Music and Image in Paris, Bibliothèque Nationale MS français 146* (Oxford, 1998)
Boogaard, N. H. J. van den, 'L'Art d'aimer en prose', *Etudes de civilisation médiévale, IXe – XIIe siècles: mélanges offerts à E. R. Labande* (Poitiers, 1974), 687–98
'Les Insertions en français dans un traité de Gérard de Liège', Marche Romane, *Mélanges de philologie et de littérature romanes offerts à Jeanne Wathelet-Willem* (Liège, 1978), 679–97
'Jacquemart Giélée et la lyrique de son temps', *Alain de Lille, Gautier de Châtillon, Jakemart Giélée et leur temps*, ed. H. Roussel and F. Suard (Lille, 1980), 333–53
Nico H.J. Boogaard autour du XIIIe siècle – études de philologie et de littérature médiévale, ed. Sorin Alexandrescu, Fernand Drijkoningen and Willem Noomen (Amsterdam, 1985)
Boogaart, Jacques, 'Love's Unstable Balance', *Musiek und Wetenschap*, 3 (1993), 1–33
Bossuat, R., 'Une prétendue traduction de l'Anticlaudianus d'Alain de Lille', *Mélanges offerts à Alfred Jeanroy* (Paris, 1928), 265–77
'Un débat d'amour dans le roman de Cassidorus', *Etudes romanes dédiées à Mario Roques* (Paris, 1946), 63–75
Boulton, M. B. M., *The Song in the Story: Lyric Insertions in French Narrative Fiction, 1200–1400* (Philadelphia, 1993)
Brownlee, Kevin Seth, *Poetic Identity in Guillaume de Machaut* (Madison, Wisc., 1984)
'Discourse as *Prouesces* in *Aucassin et Nicolette*', *Yale French Studies, Images of Power: Medieval History/ Discourse/ Literature*, 70 (1986), 167–82
'Transformations of the Couple: Genre and Language in the *Jeu de Robin et Marion*', *French Forum*, 14 (1989), 419–33.
'Machaut's Motet 15 and the *Roman de la Rose*: the Literary Context of *Amours qui a le pouoir/ Faus Semblant m'a deceü/ Vidi Dominum*, *EMH*, 10 (1991), 1–14
Brownlee, Kevin Seth, and Sylvia Huot, eds., *Rethinking the Romance of the Rose: Text, Image, Reception* (Philadelphia, 1992)
Brownrigg, Linda L., ed., *Making the Medieval Book: Techniques of Production* (Los Altos Hills, CA, 1995)
Brusegan, Rosanna, 'Le *Jeu de Robin et Marion* et l'ambiguïté du symbolisme

champêtre', *The Theatre in the Middle Ages*, ed. Herman Braet, Johan Nowé and Gilbert Tournoy (Leuven, 1985), 119–29

Busby, Keith, 'Rubrics and the Reception of Romance', *French Studies*, 53 (1999), 129–41

Butterfield, Ardis, 'Interpolated Lyric in Medieval Narrative Poetry', Ph.D diss. (University of Cambridge, 1988)

'Medieval Genres and Modern Genre-Theory', *Paragraph*, 13 (1990), 184–201

'Froissart, Machaut, Chaucer and the Genres of Imagination', *L'Imagination médiévale: Chaucer et ses contemporains: Actes du Colloque en Sorbonne*, ed. André Crépin, Publications de l'Association des Médiévistes Anglicistes de l'Enseignement Supérieur 16 (Paris, 1991), 53–69

'Repetition and Variation in the Thirteenth-Century Refrain', *JRMA*, 116 (1991), 1–23

'The Language of Medieval Music: Two Thirteenth-Century Motets', *PMM*, 2 (1993), 1–16

'*Mise en page* in the *Troilus* Manuscripts: Chaucer and French Manuscript Culture', *Reading from the Margins: Textual Studies, Chaucer, and Medieval Literature*, ed. Seth Lerer (Huntington, 1996), 49–80 = *Huntington Library Quarterly*, 58 (1995), 49–80

'French Culture and the Ricardian Court', *Essays on Ricardian Literature in Honour of J. A. Burrow*, ed. Alistair Minnis, Charlotte C. Morse and Thorlac Turville-Petre (Oxford, 1997), 82–121

'*Aucassin et Nicolette* and Mixed Forms in Medieval French', *Prosimetrum: Crosscultural Perspectives on Narrative in Prose and Verse*, ed. Joseph Harris and Karl Reichl (Cambridge, 1997), 67–98

'The Refrain and the Transformation of Genre in *Le Roman de Fauvel*' and 'Appendix: Catalogue of Refrains in *Le Roman de Fauvel*, BN fr. 146', see Bent and Wathey, eds., *Fauvel Studies*, 105–59

Calin, William, *A Poet at the Fountain: Essays on the Narrative Verse of Guillaume de Machaut* (Lexington, 1974)

Camargo, Martin, 'The Verse Love Epistle: an Unrecognized Genre', *Genre*, 13 (1980), 397–405

Camera, M., 'Bibliografia della biblioteca privata del re Roberto', *Annali delle due Sicilie*, 2 vols. (Naples, 1841–60), II, 402–06

Camille, Michael, *Image on the Edge: The Margins of Medieval Art* (London, 1992)

Cartier, N. R., 'La Mort d'Adam le Bossu', *Romania*, 89 (1968), 116–24

Cerquiglini, Jacqueline, 'Pour une typologie de l'insertion', *Perspectives médiévales*, 3 (1977), 9–14

'Le lyrisme en mouvement', *Perspectives médiévales*, 6 (1980), 75–86

'Le Clerc et l'écriture: le *voir dit* de Guillaume de Machaut et la définition du *dit*', *Literatur in der Gesellschaft des Spätmittelalters*, ed. Hans Ulrich Gumbrecht with Ursula Link-Heer and Peter M. Spangenberg, Grundriss der romanischen Literatur des Mittelalters, Begleitreihe 1 (Heidelberg, 1980), 151–68

'*Un Engin si Soutil': Guillaume de Machaut et l'écriture au XIVe siècle* (Geneva and Paris, 1985)

La Couleur de la mélancolie: La fréquentation des livres au XIVe siècle 1300–1415 (Paris, 1993)

Cerquiglini, Jacqueline, and B. Cerquiglini, 'L'Ecriture proverbiale', *Rhétorique du proverbe*: Special Issue, *Revue des sciences humaines*, 163 (1976), 359–75

Chailley, J., 'La nature musicale du Jeu de Robin et de Marion', *Mélanges offerts à Gustave Cohen* (Paris, 1950), 111–17

Chailley, J., Paul Imbs and Daniel Poirion, eds., *Guillaume de Machaut: poète et compositeur*, Actes et colloques 23, L'Université de Reims (Paris, 1982)

Clanchy, M. T., *From Memory to Written Record: England 1066–1307* (London, 1979)

Clark, Suzannah, 'Refrain', see *New Grove*

Coldwell, Maria Vedder, *see* Fowler

Coleman, Joyce, *Public Reading and the Reading Public in Late Medieval England and France* (Cambridge, 1996)

Cooper, Helen, *Pastoral: Mediaeval into Renaissance* (Ipswich, 1977)

Cosman, M. P. and Bruce Chandler eds., *Machaut's World: Science and Art in the Fourteenth Century*, Annals of the New York Academy of Sciences 314 (New York, 1978)

Crane, Susan, 'The Writing Lesson of 1381', *Chaucer's England: Literature in Historical Context*, ed. Barbara Hanawalt (Minneapolis, 1992), 201–21

Davis, Natalie Zemon, *Society and Culture in Early Modern France* (Stanford, 1975)

Delbouille, Maurice, 'Sur les traces de "Bele Aëlis"', *Mélanges de philologie romane dédiés à la mémoire de Jean Boutière*, ed. Irénée Cluzel and Françoise Pirot, 2 vols. (Liège, 1971), I, 199–218

Derrida, Jacques, 'Living On: Borderlines', Harold Bloom *et al.*, *Deconstruction and Criticism* (New York, 1979), 75–176

Doss-Quinby, E., *Les Refrains chez les trouvères du XIIe siècle au début du XIVe* (New York, 1984)

The Lyrics of the Trouvères: A Research Guide (1970–90) (New York, 1994)

Dragonetti, Roger, *La Technique poétique des trouvères dans la chanson courtoise: contribution à l'étude de la rhétorique médiévale* (Bruges, 1960)

'"La Poésie...ceste musique naturelle", Essai d'exégèse d'un passage de l'Art de Dictier d'Eustache Deschamps', *Fin du Moyen Age et Renaissance: Mélanges offerts à Robert Guiette* (Antwerp, 1961), 49–64

Dronke, Peter, *The Medieval Lyric*, 2nd edn (London, 1978)

Dronke, Peter, *Verse with Prose from Petronius to Dante: the art and scope of the mixed form* (Cambridge, Mass., 1994)

Drzewicka, Anna, 'La Fonction des emprunts à la poésie profane dans les chansons mariales de Gautier de Coinci', *Le Moyen Age*, 91 (1985), 33–51 and 179–200

Dunbabin, Jean, *Charles I of Anjou: Power, Kingship and State-Making in Thirteenth-Century Europe* (London, 1998)

Dufournet, Jean, *Adam de la Halle à la recherche de lui-même* (Paris, 1974)

Sur le Jeu de la Feuillée: études complémentaires (Paris, 1977)

Bibliography

'Complexité et ambiguïté du *Jeu de Robin et Marion*: L'ouverture de la pièce et le portrait des paysans', *Etudes de Philologie Romane et d'Histoire Littéraire offertes à Jules Horrent*, ed. Jean Marie d'Heur et Nicoletta Cherubini (Liège, 1980), 141–59

Durling, N. V., ed., *Jean Renart and the Art of Romance: Essays on Guillaume de Dole* (Gainesville, Florida, 1997)

Dwyer, R. A., *Boethian Fictions: Narratives in the Medieval French Versions of the Consolatio Philosophiae* (Cambridge, Mass., 1976)

Earp, Lawrence, 'Scribal Practice, Manuscript Production and the Transmission of Music in Late Medieval France: The Manuscripts of Guillaume de Machaut' (Ph.D diss., Princeton University, 1983)

  'Lyrics for Reading and Lyrics for Singing in Late Medieval France: the Development of the Dance Lyric from Adam de la Halle to Guillaume de Machaut', in Baltzer, Cable and Wimsatt, eds., *The Union of Words and Music*, 101–31

  'Genre in the Fourteenth-Century French Chanson: the Virelai and the Dance Song', *MD*, 45 (1991), 123–41

  Guillaume de Machaut: A Guide to Research (New York and London, 1995)

Eloranta, M., 'Couplets d'une romance d'Audefroi le Bastard incorporés dans un salut d'amour du XIIIe siècle', *NM*, 43 (1942), 1–6

Empson, William, *Some Versions of Pastoral* (London, 1935)

Enders, Jody, 'Music, Delivery and the Rhetoric of Memory in Guillaume de Machaut's *Remede de Fortune*', *PMLA*, 107 (1992), 450–64

Everist, Mark, 'The Rondeau Motet: Paris and Artois in the Thirteenth Century', *Music and Letters*, 69 (1988), 1–22

  'The Refrain Cento: Myth or Motet?' *JRMA*, 114 (1989), 164–88

  French Motets in the Thirteenth Century: Music, Poetry and Genre (Cambridge, 1994)

  'The Polyphonic Rondeau c.1300: Repertory and Context', *EMH*, 15 (1996), 59–96

Everist, Mark, ed., *Models of Musical Analysis before 1600* (Oxford, 1992)

Falck, Robert, 'Parody and Contrafactum: a Terminological Clarification', *MQ*, 65 (1979), 1–21

Faral, Edmond, *Les Jongleurs en France au Moyen Age* (Paris, 1910)

  'Les Chansons de toile ou chansons d'histoire', *Romania*, 69 (1946–47), 433–65

Ferrante, J. M., 'The Conflict of Lyric Conventions and Romance Form', *In Pursuit of Perfection: Courtly Love in Medieval Literature*, ed. J. M. Ferrante and G. D. Economou (New York and London, 1975), 135–77

Finnegan, Ruth, *Oral Poetry* (Cambridge, 1977)

Fleischman, Suzanne, 'Evaluation in Narrative: the Present Tense in Medieval "Performed Stories"', *Yale French Studies*, 70, *Images of Power: Medieval History/Discourse/Literature*, ed. Kevin Brownlee and Stephen G. Nichols (New Haven, Conn., 1986), 199–251

Fowler, Alastair, *Kinds of Literature: An Introduction to the Theory of Genres and Modes* (Oxford, 1982)

Fowler, Maria Vedder, 'Musical Interpolations in Thirteenth- and Fourteenth-Century French Narratives', 2 vols. (Ph.D diss., Yale University, 1979)

351

Bibliography

Françon, M., 'Rondeaux Tercets', *Speculum*, 24 (1949), 88–92
  'On the Nature of the Virelai', *Symposium*, 9 (1955), 348–52
  'Sur la Structure du Rondeau', *Romance Notes*, 10 (1968), 147–49
  'La Structure du Rondeau', *Medium Aevum*, 44 (1975), 54–59
Frank, Grace, 'The Cues in *Aucassin et Nicolette*', *Modern Language Notes*, 47 (1932), 14–16
Frank, I., 'Mélanges: "Tuit cil qui sunt enamourat", Notes de philologie pour l'étude des origines lyriques, II', *Romania*, 75 (1954), 98–108
Fuller, Sarah, 'A Phantom Treatise of the Fourteenth Century? The *Ars Nova*', *The Journal of Musicology*, 4 (1985), 23–50
  'Tendencies and Resolutions: the Directed Progression in *Ars Nova* Music', *Journal of Music Theory*, 36 (1992), 229–58
  'Guillaume de Machaut: *De toute flours*', in Everist, ed., *Models*
Gégou, F., 'Adam le Bossu était-il mort en 1288?', *Romania*, 86 (1966), 111–17
Gennrich, Friedrich, *Grundriß einer Formenlehre des mittelalterlichen Liedes als Grundlage einer musikalischen Formenlehre des Liedes* (Halle, 1932)
  Bibliographie der ältesten französischen und lateinischen Motetten, SMMA 2 (Darmstadt, 1957)
Gravdal, Kathryn, 'Camouflaging Rape: the Rhetoric of Sexual Violence in the Medieval Pastourelle', *Romanic Review*, 76 (1985), 361–73
  Ravishing Maidens: Writing Rape in Medieval French Literature and Law (Philadelphia, 1991)
Green, D. H., 'Orality and Reading: the State of Research in Medieval Studies', *Speculum*, 65 (1990), 267–80
Greimas, A. J., 'Idiotismes, Proverbes, Dictons', *Cahiers de Lexicologie*, 2 (1960), 41–61
Guesnon, A., 'La Satire à Arras au XIIIe siècle', *Le Moyen Age*, 12 (1899), 156–58, 248–68; 13 (1900), 1–34, 117–68; 15 (1902), 137–73; 22 (1909), 65–93
Guiette, Robert, *D'une poésie formelle en France au moyen âge* (Paris, 1972)
Günther, U., 'Chronologie und Stil der Kompositionen Guillaume de Machauts', *Acta Musicologica*, 35 (1963), 96–114
  'Zitate in französischen Liedsätzen der Ars Nova und Ars Subtilior', *MD*, 26 (1972), 53–68
Gurevich, Aron, *Medieval Popular Culture: Problems of Belief and Perception*, trans. Jànos M. Bak and Paul A. Hollingsworth, Cambridge Studies in Oral and Literate Culture 14 (Cambridge, 1988)
Guy, Henri, *Essai sur la vie et les oeuvres littéraires du trouvère Adam de le Hale* (Paris, 1898)
Hoepffner, E., 'Les Poésies lyriques du Dit de la Panthère de Nicole de Margival', *Romania*, 46 (1920), 204–30
  'Virelais et ballades dans le Chansonnier d'Oxford (Douce 308)', *Archivum romanicum*, 4 (1920), 20–40
Hoppin, R. H., *Medieval Music* (New York, 1978)
Hughes, Andrew, 'The *Ludus super Anticlaudianum* of Adam de la Bassée', *JAMS*, 23 (1970), 1–25

Bibliography

Hult, David F., *Self-Fulfilling Prophecies: Readership and Authority in the First Roman de la Rose* (Cambridge, 1986)
    'Closed Quotations: the Speaking Voice in the Roman de la Rose', *Concepts of Closure, Yale French Studies*, 67 (1984), 248–69
Huot, Sylvia, *From Song to Book: The Poetics of Writing in Old French Lyric and Lyrical Narrative Poetry* (Ithaca and London, 1987)
    The Romance of the Rose and its Medieval Readers: Interpretation, Reception, Manuscript Transmission (Cambridge, 1993)
    Allegorical Play in the Old French Motet: The Sacred and Profane in Thirteenth-century Polyphony (Stanford, 1997)
Hunt, Tony, 'The Rhetorical Background to the Arthurian Prologue', *FMLS*, 6 (1970), 1–23
    'The Prologue to Chretien's *Li Contes del Graal*', *Romania*, 92 (1971), 359–79
    'Precursors and Progenitors of *Aucassin et Nicolette*', *SP*, 74 (1977), 1–19
    'De la chanson au sermon: Bele Aalis et Sur la rive de la mer', *Romania*, 104 (1983), 433–56
Jameson, Fredric, 'Magical Narratives: Romance as Genre', *New Literary History*, 7 (1975), 135–63
    The Political Unconscious: Narrative as a Socially Symbolic Act (London, 1981)
Jauss, H. R., 'Entstehung und Strukturwandel der allegorischen Dichtung', *La Littérature didactique, allégorique et satirique, Grundriss der romanischen Litteraturen des Mittelalters* VI i (Heidelberg, 1968)
    Toward an Aesthetic of Reception, trans. Timothy Bahti (Brighton, 1982)
Jeanroy, Alfred, *Les Origines de la poésie lyrique en France au Moyen Age*, 3rd edn (Paris, 1925)
Jung, Marc-René, 'L'Empereur Conrad chanteur de poésie lyrique: fiction et vérité dans le *Roman de la Rose* de Jean Renart', *Romania*, 101 (1980), 35–50
Karp, Theodore, 'Borrowed Material in Trouvère Music', *Acta Musicologica*, 34 (1962), 87–101
Kay, Sarah, *Subjectivity in Troubadour Poetry* (Cambridge, 1990)
Kelly, Douglas, *Medieval Imagination: Rhetoric and the Poetry of Courtly Love* (Madison, Wisc., 1978)
Kennedy, Elspeth, 'The Scribe as Editor', *Mélanges de langue et de littérature du Moyen Age et de la Renaissance offerts à Jean Frappier*, 2 vols. (Geneva, 1970), I, 523–31
Koenig, V. F., 'Sur une prétendue reverdie de Gautier de Coinci', *Romania*, 99 (1978), 255–63
Kristeva, Julia, 'Word, Dialogue and Novel', *Desire in Language: A Semiotic Approach to Literature and Art* (Oxford, 1981 (first Eng. publn))
    Le Texte du roman (The Hague, 1970)
Kügle, K., *The Manuscript Ivrea, Biblioteca Capitolare 115: Studies in the Transmission and Composition of Ars Nova Polyphony*, Musicological Studies 69 (Ottawa, 1997)
Långfors, A., 'Mélanges de poésie lyrique française, IV, Grans chans du manuscrit d'Oxford', *Romania*, 57 (1931), 312–94

'Les Refrains dans le poème intitulé "D'Amors et de Jalousie", *Romania*, 60 (1934), 204–17

Langlois, Charles-Victor, *La Vie en France au Moyen Age de la fin du XIIe au milieu du XIIIe siècle*, 2 vols. (Paris, 1926; repr., 1981–84)

Langlois, E., 'Le Jeu du Roi qui ne ment et le jeu du Roi et de la Reine', *Mélanges offerts à Camille Chabaneau, Romanische Forschungen*, 23 (1907), 163–73

Lathuillère, R., *Guiron le Courtois: Etude de la tradition manuscrite et analyse critique*, Publications romanes et françaises 86 (Geneva, 1966)

Laurie, I. S., 'Deschamps and the Lyric as Natural Music', *MLR*, 59 (1964), 561–70

Le Gentil, P., 'La Strophe zadjalesque, les khardjas et le problème des origines du lyrisme roman', *Romania*, 84 (1963), 1–27, 209–50, 409–11

Leach, Elizabeth Eva, 'Fortune's Demesne: the Interrelation of Text and Music in Machaut's *Il Mest Avis* (B22), *De Fortune* (B23) and Two Related Anonymous Balades', *EMH*, 19 (2000), 47–79

Leech-Wilkinson, D., 'Machaut's "Rose, Lis" and the Problems of Early Music Analysis', *Music Analysis*, 3 (1984), 9–28

'*Le Voir Dit* and *La Messe de Nostre Dame*: Aspects of Genre and Style in the Late Works of Machaut', *PMM*, 2 (1993), 43–73

'*Le Voir Dit*: a Reconstruction and Guide for Musicians', *PMM*, 2 (1993), 103–40

'The Emergence of *Ars Nova*', *Journal of Musicology*, 13 (1995), 285–317

Legge, M. D., *Anglo-Norman Literature and its Background* (Oxford, 1963)

Lejeune-Dehousse, R., ed., *L'Oeuvre de Jean Renart* (Paris, 1935)

Léonard, E. G., *Les Angevins de Naples* (Paris, 1954)

Linker, R. W., *A Bibliography of Old French Lyrics* (University, Miss., 1979)

Little, Patrick, 'Three Ballades in Machaut's *Livre du Voir-Dit*', *Studies in Music*, 14 (1980), 45–60

Lods, Jeanne, 'Les parties lyriques du *Tristan en prose*', *BBSIA*, 7 (1955), 73–78

Lote, G., *Histoire du vers français: I. Le moyen âge*, 3 vols. (Paris, 1949, 1951, 1955)

Lowe, L. F. H., *Gerard de Nevers: A Study of the Prose Version of the Roman de la Violette* (Princeton, 1923)

Lubienski-Bodenham, H., 'The Origins of the Fifteenth-Century View of Poetry as "Seconde Rhetorique"', *MLR*, 74 (1979), 26–38

Ludwig, Friedrich, ed., *Repertorium organorum recentioris et motetorum vetustissimi stili, Wissenschaftlicher Abhandlung*, 7 (Halle, 1910; repr. New York, 1964)

'Die Quellen der Motetten "ältesten Stils"', *Archiv für Musikwissenschaft*, 5 (1923), 185–222, 273–315

Lukitsch, Shirley, 'The Poetics of the Prologue: Machaut's Conception of the Purpose of his Art', *Medium Aevum*, 52 (1983), 258–71

Machabey, Armand, *Guillaume de Machaut: La vie et l'oeuvre musical*, 2 vols. (Paris, 1955)

Maillard, J., *Evolution et esthétique du lai lyrique des origines à la fin du XIVe siècle* (Paris, 1963)

'Lais avec notation dans le Tristan en prose', *Mélanges offerts à Rita Lejeune*, 2 vols. (Gembloux, 1969), II, 1347–64

Bibliography

'Les Refrains de caroles dans Renart le Nouvel', *Alain de Lille, Gautier de Châtillon, Jakemart Giélée et leur temps*, ed. H. Roussel and F. Suard (Lille, 1980), 277–93

Adam de la Halle: Perspective musicale (Paris, 1982)

Marix, Jeanne, *Histoire de la musique et des musiciens de la cour de Bourgogne sous le règne de Philippe le Bon (1420–67)*, Sammlung musikwissenschaftlicher Abhandlungen 28 (Strasbourg, 1939)

Marshall, John H., 'Textual Transmission and Complex Musico-metrical Form in the Old French Lyric', *Medieval French Textual Studies in Memory of T. B. W. Reid*, ed. Ian Short (London, 1984), 119–48

'Une versification lyrique popularisante en ancien provençal', *Actes du premier congrès international de l'association internationale d'études occitanes*, ed. Peter T. Ricketts (London, 1987), 35–66

McKinnon, James, ed., *Antiquity and the Middle Ages from Ancient Greece to the 15th Century* (London, 1990)

Melli, E., 'I "salut" e l'epistolografia medievale', *Convivium*, s.n.4 (1962), 385–98

Meyer, Paul, 'Le Salut d'Amour dans les littératures provençale et française', mémoire suivi de huit saluts inédits, *BECh*, 28 (1867), 124–70

'Troisième rapport sur une mission littéraire en Angleterre et en Ecosse: D. Douce 308', *Archives des missions scientifiques et littéraires*, second series 5 (1868), 154–62 and 213–44

'Etudes sur les manuscrits du Roman d'Alexandre: P. Oxford, Bodlienne, Bodley 264', *Romania*, 11 (1882), 290–301

Minnis, A. J., *Medieval Theory of Authorship* (London, 1984)

Mölk, U. and F. Wolfzettel, *Répertoire métrique de la poésie lyrique française des origines à 1350* (Munich, 1972)

Montrose, Louis, '"Eliza, Queene of Shepheardes", and the Pastoral of Power', *English Literary Renaissance*, 10 (1980), 153–82

Morawski, J., 'Les Recueils d'anciens proverbes français analysés et classés', *Romania*, 48 (1922), 481–558

Morin, Joseph C., 'The Genesis of Manuscript Paris, Bibliothèque Nationale, Fonds Français 146, with Particular Emphasis on the *Roman de Fauvel*' (Ph.D diss., New York University, 1992)

'Jehannot de Lescurel's Chansons, Geffroy de Paris's Dits, and the "Process of Design" in BN fr. 146', see Bent and Wathey, eds., *Fauvel Studies*, 321–36

Nagler, Michael, 'Towards a Generative View of the Oral Formula', *Transactions and Proceedings of the American Philological Association*, 98 (1967), 269–311

Nathan, H., 'The Function of the Text in French 13th-century Motets', *MQ*, 28 (1942), 445–62

Neilson, W. A., *The Origins and Sources of 'The Court of Love'*, Harvard Studies and Notes in Philology and Literature 6 (Boston, 1899)

The New Grove Dictionary of Music and Musicians, gen. ed. Stanley Sadie, 29 vols. 2nd edn (London, 2001)

New Literary History, 3rd quarterly issue (1977)

Bibliography

Newcombe, Terence, 'The Refrain in Troubadour Lyric Poetry', *Nottingham Medieval Studies*, 19 (1975), 3–15

Noack, F., *Der Strophenausgang in seinem Verhältnis zum Refrain und Strophengrundstock in der Refrainhaltigen altfranzösischen Lyrik, nebst 66 unveröffentlich afr. Refrainliedern aus Pariser HSS.* herausgegeben von E. Stengel, Ausgaben und Abhandlungen aus dem Gebiete der romanischen Philologie veröffentlicht von E. Stengel 98 (Marburg, 1899)

Noomen, W., 'Passages narratifs dans les drames médiévaux français: essai d'interprétation', *Revue Belge de philologie et d'histoire*, 36/ii (1958), 761–85

Nykrog, Per, *Les Fabliaux: étude d'histoire littéraire et de stylistique médiévale* (Copenhagen, 1957; repr. Geneva, 1973)

Olson, Glending, 'Deschamps' *Art de Dictier* and Chaucer's Literary Environment', *Speculum*, 48 (1973), 714–23

'Making and Poetry in the Age of Chaucer', *Comparative Literature*, 31 (1979), 272–90

Orenstein, Herta, *Die Refrainformen in Chansonnier de l'Arsenal (Paris, Bibliothèque de l'Arsenal 5198): Ein Beitrag zur Formenlehre der Troubadour – und Trouvère – Melodien* (New York, 1970)

Pächt, O., and J. J. G. Alexander, *Illuminated Manuscripts in the Bodleian Library, Oxford*, 3 vols. (Oxford, 1966–73)

Paden, William D., 'Rape in the Pastourelle', *Romanic Review*, 80 (1989), 331–49

'Old Occitan as a Lyric Language: the Insertions from Occitan in Three Thirteenth-Century French Romances', *Speculum*, 68 (1993), 36–53

Page, Christopher, 'Machaut's "Pupil" Deschamps on the Performance of Music', *Early Music*, 5 (1977), 484–91

Voices and Instruments of the Middle Ages (London, 1987)

The Owl and the Nightingale: Musical Life and Ideas in France 1100–1300 (London, 1989)

Discarding Images: Reflections on Music and Culture in Medieval France (Oxford, 1993)

'A Reply to Margaret Bent', *Early Music*, 22 (1994), 127–32

'Tradition and Innovation in BN fr. 146: the Background to the Ballades', see Bent and Wathey, eds., *Fauvel Studies*, 353–94

Parkes, M. B., 'The Influence of the Concepts of *Ordinatio* and *Compilatio* on the Development of the Book', *Medieval Learning and Literature: Essays Presented to Richard William Hunt*, ed. J. J. G. Alexander and M. T. Gibson (Oxford, 1976), 115–41

Pause and Effect: An Introduction to the History of Punctuation in the West (Aldershot, 1992)

Peraino, Judith, '*Et pui conmencha a canter*: Refrains, Motets and Melody in the Thirteenth-Century Narrative *Renart le Nouvel*', *PMM*, 6 (1997), 1–16

Pesce, Dolores, 'Beyond Glossing: the Old Made New in *Mout me fu grief / Robin m'aime / Portare*', see Pesce, ed., *Hearing the Motet*, 28–51

Pesce, Dolores, ed., *Hearing the Motet: Essays on the Motet of the Middle Ages and Renaissance* (Oxford, 1997)

Bibliography

Pirro, André, *La Musique sous le règne de Charles VI (1380–1422)*, Sammlung musikwissenschaftlicher Abhandlungen I (Strasbourg, 1930)

Plumley, Yolanda, 'Citation and Allusion in the late *Ars nova*: the Case of *Esperance* and the *En attendant* Songs', *EMH*, 18 (1999), 287–363

Poirion, Daniel, *Le Poète et le Prince* (Paris, 1965)

Räkel, Hans-Herbert S., *Die musikalische Erscheinungsform der Trouvèrepoesie* (Berne, 1977)

Rankin, Susan, 'The Divine Truth of Scripture: Chant in the *Roman de Fauvel*', *JAMS*, 47 (1994), 203–43

Raynaud, G., *Bibliographie des chansonniers français des XIIIe et XIVe siècles*, 2 vols. (Paris, 1884) (*see also* Spanke)

Rea, J. A., 'The Form of Aucassin et Nicolette', *Romance Notes*, 15 (1974), 504–08

Reaney, Gilbert, 'Concerning the Origins of the Rondeau, Virelai and Ballade Forms', *MD*, 6 (1952), 155–66

'The Development of the Rondeau, Virelai, and Ballade Forms from Adam de la Hale to Guillaume de Machaut', *Festschrift Karl Gustav Fellerer zum sechzigsten Geburtstag am 7. Juli 1962*, ed. Heinrich Hüschen (Regensburg, 1962), 421–27

Manuscripts of Polyphonic Music 11th–early 14th century, RISM, Vol.B IV¹ (Munich, 1966)

'Towards a Chronology of Machaut's Musical Works', *MD*, 21 (1967), 87–96

Manuscripts of Polyphonic Music (c.1320–1400), RISM, B IV² (Munich, 1969)

Guillaume de Machaut, Oxford Studies of Composers 9 (London, 1971)

Regalado, Nancy Freeman, 'Gathering the Works: the "Oeuvres de Villon" and the Intergeneric Passage of the Medieval French Lyric into Single-Author Collections', *L'Esprit Créateur*, 33 (1993), 87–100

Reinhard, J. R., 'The Literary Background of the Chante Fable', *Speculum*, 1 (1926), 157–69

Ribard, Jacques, *Un Ménestrel du XIVe siècle: Jean de Condé* (Geneva, 1969)

Richardson, L., 'The Confrérie des Jongleurs et des Bourgeois and the Puy d'Arras in Twelfth- and Thirteenth-Century Literature', *Studies in Honour of Mario Pei*, ed. J. Fisher (Chapel Hill, 1972), 161–71

Roesner, Edward H., *et al.*, 'Introduction', *Le Roman de Fauvel*, see Gervès du Bus (Facsimile editions)

Rouse, Mary A. and Richard H., *Manuscripts and their Makers: Commercial Book Producers in Medieval Paris, 1200–1500* (Turnhout, 2000)

Roussel, H., and F. Suard eds., *Alain de Lille, Gautier de Châtillon, Jakemart Giélée et leur temps* (Lille, 1980)

Ruhe, Ernstpeter, 'A Johenne, ma dame et m'amie', *Romance Philology*, 24 (1970), 259–72

Runciman, Steven, *The Sicilian Vespers* (Harmondsworth, 1960; 1st pub. Cambridge, 1958)

Sabatini, Francesco, *Napoli angioina: cultura e società* (Naples, 1975)

Sahlin, Margit, *Etude sur la carole médiévale: L'origine du mot et ses rapports avec l'Eglise* (Uppsala, 1940)

Bibliography

Salter, Elizabeth, 'The Annunciation to the Shepherds in Later Medieval Art and Drama', *English and International: Studies in the Literature, Art and Patronage of Medieval England*, ed. Derek Pearsall and Nicolette Zeeman (Cambridge, 1988), 272–92

Saly, Antoinette, 'La Chanson dans le *Meliacin*', *Travaux de linguistiques et de littérature*, 23 (1985), 7–23

Schutz, A. H., 'Were the Vidas and Razos Recited?' *SP*, 36 (1939), 565–70

Schwan, E., *Die altfranzösischen Liederhandschriften, ihr Verhältniss, ihre Entstehung und ihre Bestimmung: eine literarhistorische Untersuchung* (Berlin, 1886)

Slocum, Kay Brainerd, 'Confrérie, Bruderschaft and Guild: the Formation of Musicians' Fraternal Organisations in Thirteenth-Century and Fourteenth-Century Europe', *EMH*, 14 (1995), 257–74

Solterer, Helen, *The Master and Minerva: Disputing Women in French Medieval Culture* (Berkeley and Los Angeles, 1995)

Spanke, Hans, 'Das Corpus der ältesten französischen Tanzlyrik', *ZRP*, 49 (1929), 287–309

'Tanzmusik in der Kirche des Mittelalters', *NM*, 31 (1930), 143–70

'Das lateinische Rondeau', *ZFSL*, 53 (1930), 113–48

Spanke, Hans, ed., *G. Raynauds Bibliographie des altfranzösischen Liedes, neu bearbeitet und ergänzt von Hans Spanke*, I (Leiden, 1955; repr. with index, 1980)

Stevens, John, '"La grande chanson courtoise": the Songs of Adam de la Halle', *PRMA*, 101 (1974–75), 11–30

'The Manuscript Presentation and Notation of Adam de la Halle's Courtly Chansons', *Source Materials and the Interpretation of Music: A Memorial Volume to Thurston Dart*, ed. I. Bent (London, 1981), 29–64

Words and Music in the Middle Ages: Song, Narrative, Dance and Drama, 1050–1350 (Cambridge, 1986)

Stevens, John, /Ardis Butterfield, 'Troubadours, Trouvères', see *New Grove*

Strohm, Reinhard, 'How to Make Medieval Music Our Own: a Response to Christopher Page and Margaret Bent', *Early Music*, 22 (1994), 715–19

Sutton, Anne F., 'Merchants, Music and Social Harmony: the London Puy and its French and London Contexts, circa 1300', *The London Journal*, 17 (1992), 1–17

'The *Tumbling Bear* and Its Patrons: a Venue for the London Puy and Mercery', *London and Europe in the Later Middle Ages*, ed. Julia Boffey and Pamela King (London, 1995), 85–110

Switten, Margaret, L., *Music and Poetry in the Middle Ages: A Guide to Research on French and Occitan Song, 1100–1400*, Garland Medieval Bibliographies 19 (New York and London, 1995)

Szkilnik, Michèle, 'Ecrire en vers, écrire en prose: Le choix de Wauchier de Denain', *Romania*, 107 (1986), 208–30

Taylor, Jane H. M., 'The Lyric Insertion: Towards a Functional Model', *Courtly Literature: Culture and Context*, ed. Keith Busby and Eric Kooper (Amsterdam and Philadelphia, 1990), 539–48

'*Le Roman de la Dame a la Lycorne et du Biau Chevalier au Lion*', French Studies, 51 (1997), 1–18

Thomas, Antoine, 'Refrains français de la fin du XIIIe siècle', *Mélanges offerts à Alfred Jeanroy* (Paris, 1928), 497–508

Tischler, Hans, *The Style and Evolution of the Earliest Motets (to circa 1270)*, Musicological Studies 40, 4 vols. (Henryville, Ottawa and Binningen, 1985)

Todorov, Tzvetan, *Les Genres du discours* (Paris: Seuil, 1978)

   Mikhail Bakhtin, The Dialogical Principle, trans. Wlad Godzich, Theory and History of Literature 13 (Manchester, 1984)

Treitler, Leo, 'Homer and Gregory: the Transmission of Epic Poetry and Plainchant', *MQ*, 60 (1974), 333–72

   'Oral, Written, and Literate Process in the Transmission of Medieval Music', *Speculum*, 56 (1981), 471–91

   'Centonate Chant: *Ubles Flickwerk* or *E pluribus unus?*' *JAMS*, 28 (1975), 1–23

Treitler, Leo, *et al.*, eds., *Transmission and Form in Oral Traditions, in International Musicological Society: Report of the Thirteenth-Century Congress* (Berkeley, 1977) (Kassel, 1981)

Trotin, Jean, 'Vers et Prose dans *Aucassin et Nicolette*', Romania, 97 (1976), 481–508

Uhl, Patrice, 'Les "Sotes Chançons" du *roman de Fauvel* (MS *E*): La symptomatique indécision du rubricateur', French Studies, 45 (1991), 385–402

Uitti, Karl D., 'From Clerc to Poète: the Relevance of the *Romance of the Rose* to Machaut's World', see Cosman and Chandler, eds., *Machaut's World*, 209–16

Ungureanu, M., *La Bourgeoisie naissante: société et littérature bourgeoises d'Arras aux XIIe et XIIIe siècles*, Mémoires de la Commission des Monuments Historiques du Pas-de-Calais 8/i (Arras, 1955)

Verrier, P., *Le Vers français*, 3 vols. (Paris, 1931–32)

   'La plus Vieille Chanson de carole', Romania, 58 (1932), 380–421; 61 (1935), 95–97; 63 (1937), 354–76

   'Le Rondeau et formes analogues', *NM*, 34 (1933), 102–25

Wathey, Andrew, 'The Motets of Philippe de Vitry and the Fourteenth-Century Renaissance', *EMH*, 12 (1993), 119–50

   'Myth and Mythography in the Motets of Philippe de Vitry', *Musica e Storia*, 6 (1998), 81–106

Werf, H. van der, *The Chansons of the Troubadours and Trouvères: A Study of the Melodies and their Relation to the Poems* (Utrecht, 1972)

Whiting, B. J., 'The Nature of the Proverb', *Harvard Studies and Notes in Philology and Literature*, 14 (1932), 273–307

   'Proverbial Material in the Poems of Baudouin and Jean de Condé', *Romanic Review*, 27 (1936), 204–33

Wilkins, Nigel, 'The Post-Machaut Generation of Poet-Musicians', *Nottingham Medieval Studies*, 12 (1968), 40–84

   'A Pattern of Patronage: Machaut, Froissart and the Houses of Luxembourg and Bohemia in the Fourteenth Century', French Studies, 37 (1983), 257–84

Bibliography

'Music and Poetry at Court: England and France in the Late Middle Ages', *English Court Culture in the later Middle Ages*, ed. V. J. Scattergood and J. W. Sherborne (London, 1983), 183–204

'The Late Medieval French Lyric: with Music and Without', *Musik und Text in der Mehrstimmigkeit der 14. und 15. Jahrhunderts*, ed. Ursula Günther and Ludwig Finscher (Basel and London, 1984), 155–74

'"En Regardant Vers Le Païs de France": the Ballade and the Rondeau, a Cross-Channel History', *England in the Fourteenth Century: Proceedings of the 1985 Harlaxton Symposium*, ed. W. M. Omrod (Woodbridge, 1986)

The Lyric Art of Medieval France (Cambridge, 1988)

Williams, Raymond, *Culture* (Glasgow, 1981)

The Politics of Modernism, ed. and intro. Tony Pinkney (London and New York, 1989)

Williams, Sarah Jane Manley, 'An Author's Role in Fourteenth Century Book Production: Guillaume de Machaut's "livre ou je met toutes mes choses"', *Romania*, 90 (1969), 433–54

'The Lady, the Lyrics and the Letters', *Early Music*, 5 (1977), 462–68

'Machaut's Self-Awareness as Author and Producer', see Cosman and Chandler, eds., *Machaut's World*

Wimsatt, James I., *Chaucer and the French Love Poets* (Chapel Hill, 1968)

Chaucer and the Poems of 'Ch', Chaucer Studies 9 (Cambridge, 1982)

Chaucer and His French Contemporaries: Natural Music in the Fourteenth Century (Toronto, 1991)

Wright, Craig, *Music at the Court of Burgundy 1364–1419: A Documentary History*, Musicological Studies 28 (Henryville, 1979)

Zink, Michel, *La Pastourelle; poésie et folklore au Moyen Age* (Paris, 1972)

Roman rose et rose rouge: Le Roman de la Rose ou de Guillaume de Dole de Jean Renart (Paris, 1979)

La subjectivité littéraire autour du siècle de saint Louis (Paris, 1985)

'Suspension and Fall: the Fragmentation and Linkage of Lyric Insertions in *Le roman de la rose (Guillaume de Dole)* and *Le roman de la violette*', in Durling, ed., *Jean Renart*, 105–21

Zumthor, Paul, 'De la chanson au récit: La Chastelaine de Vergi', *Vox Romanica*, 27 (1968), 77–95

'De la circularité du chant', *Poétique*, 2 (1970), 129–40

Essai de poétique médiévale (Paris, 1972)

Parler du moyen âge (Paris, 1980)

La Poésie et la Voix dans la civilisation médiévale (Paris, 1984)

'The Impossible Closure of the Oral Text', *Concepts of Closure, Yale French Studies*, 67 (1984), 25–42

Index of Manuscripts

Chansonniers are listed with their standard troubadour or trouvère sigla.

Aberystwyth, National Library of Wales, 5010 C (frag.) (Machaut) 308
Aix-en-Provence, Bibl. Méjanes 572 (*Robin et Marion*) 184, 304
Angers, Bibliothèque Municipale 403 (*Abeïe*) 304
Arras, Bibliothèque Municipale 897 (*La Prise amoureuse*) 310

Bamberg, Staatsbibliothek, Li.115 (olim Ed.IV.6) (*motets*) 228–30, Ex. 12 (230)
Berlin, Staatsbibliothek, Hamilton 25 (*Vergi*) 305
Berne, Burgerbibliothek 218 (Machaut) 308
Berne, Stadt- und Universitätsbibliothek 238 (*Cleomadés*) 304
Berne, Stadt- und Universitätsbibliothek 389 (Trouvère MS *C*) 88, 94–96
Berne, Stadt- und Universitätsbibliothek A.95.I (*La Prise amoureuse*) 310
Besançon, Bibliothèque Municipale 551 (*Miracles*) 185, 186, 306
Blois, Bibliothèque Municipale 34 (*Miracles*) 307
Brussels, Bibliothèque Royale 2475–81 (*Quinque*) 307
Brussels, Bibliothèque Royale 9245 (*Cassidorus*) 312
Brussels, Bibliothèque Royale 9401 (*Cassidorus*) 312
Brussels, Bibliothèque Royale 9411–9426 (Baudouin de Condé) 305
Brussels, Bibliothèque Royale 9574–75 (*Vergi*) 305
Brussels, Bibliothèque Royale 9631 (prose *Violette*) 307

Brussels, Bibliothèque Royale 10747 (*Miracles*) 183, 189, 306
Brussels, Bibliothèque Royale 10988 (Ovid, *Ars amatoria*) 313
Brussels, Bibliothèque Royale II 7444 (*Cleomadés*) 187, 304
Brussels, Bibliothèque Royale IV 319 (*Meliacin*) 307
Burgos, Monasterio de Las Huelgas 326 n.4

Cambrai, Bibliothèque Municipale 1328 (Adam de la Halle) 283
Cambridge, Gonville and Caius College MS 136/76 (sermons) 313
Cambridge, Gonville and Caius College MS 54/31 (flyleaf) (*Correspondance*) 306
Cambridge, Magdalene College, Pepysian Library, 1594 (Machaut) 308
Cambridge, Trinity College B.14.39 (sermons) 313
Copenhagen, Bibliothèque Royale Thott 414 (*Restor du paon*) 309

Dijon, Bibliothèque Municipale 526 (Baudouin de Condé, *Prison d'amours, Rose*) 180, 305
Dijon, Bibliothèque Municipale 526 (*Commens d'amours*) 311, 327 n.34 (*Citations latiries*) 305
Donaueschingen, Fürstlich Füstenbergerische Bibliothek 168

Florence, Biblioteca Medicea Laurenziana, 45, Ashburnham 53 (*Miracles*) 307

Florence, Biblioteca Medicea Laurenziana, Palatinus C.XVII (*Tournoi de Chauvency*) 309
Florence, Biblioteca Riccardiana 2757 (*Meliacin*) 308

Hereford, Cathedral Library P.3.3. (Proverbs) 311

Ivrea, Biblioteca Capitolare 115 (chansonnier) 284

Leningrad, Bibl. Publ. Fr.F. v. XIV 9 (*Miracles*) 80, 306, 320 n.15
Lille, Bibliothèque Municipale 316 (olim 397) (Adam de la Bassée) 120, 177, 304
London, British Library, Additional 16888 (*Restor du paon*) 309
London, British Library, Additional 36673 (*Guiron*) 309
London, British Library, Arundel 292 (*sermons*) 313
London, British Library, Egerton 274 (*Miracles*) 306
London, British Library, Harley 4401 (*Miracles*) 306
London, British Library, Harley 4903 (*Cassidorus*) 312 (*Kanor*) 312 (*Peliarmenus*) 312
London, British Library, Royal 15 E V, Royal 19 E III- 19 E II (*Perceforest*) 311
London, British Library, Royal 20.A.XVII (*Roman de la Rose*) 265

Modena, Biblioteca Estense R 4.4
Modena, Biblioteca Estense g.G.3.20 (= Campori 42) (Ovid, *Ars amatoria*) 313
Mons, Bibliothèque Municipale 330–215 fols. 82–105 v (*Tournoi de Chauvency*) 88, 309
Montpellier, Bibliothèque de l'école de Médicine, H196 (*motets*) 80, 284, 320 n.15
Munich, Bayerische Staatsbibliothek, clm 4660 (*chansons latines*) 187, 305
Munich, Bayerische Staatsbibliothek, Frag. mus. 4775 (chansonnier) 80, 320 n.15

Neuchatel, Bibliothèque Municipale 4816 (B.P. 4816) (*Miracles*) 307

New York, Pierpoint Morgan Library 36 (*Roman de la violette*) 307
New York, Pierpoint Morgan Library, William D. Glazer Coll. G.24 = Donaueschingen, Fürstlich Füstenbergerische Bibliothek 168 (*Restor du paon*) 309
New York, Pierpont Morgan Library, M.396 (Machaut) 293, 308
New York, Wildenstein Collection, MS without shelfmark (Machaut) 308

Oxford, Bodleian Library, Bodley 264 (*Restor du paon*) 173, 309
Oxford, Bodleian Library, Douce 165 (*Restor du paon*) 309 (*Parfait du paon*) 310
Oxford, Bodleian Library, Douce 308 (Trouvère MS *I*) 4, 138, 139, 144, 172, 276, 284, 326 n.5 (*Tournoi de Chauvency*) 44, 59, *60*, 88, 309 (*Bestiaire*) 311

Paris, Bibliothèque de l'Arsenal 2741 (Ovid, *Ars amatoria*) *185*, 313, 328 n.45
Paris, Bibliothèque de l'Arsenal 2776 (*Restor du paon*) 309 (*Manuscrit*) 311
Paris, Bibliothèque de l'Arsenal 3142 (sermon) 184, 186, 313, 327 n.26 (*Cleomadés*) 304 (Baudouin de Condé) 305
Paris, Bibliothèque de l'Arsenal 3483–3494 (*Perceforest*) 311
Paris, Bibliothèque de l'Arsenal 3516 (*Lai d'Aristote*), 309 (*Chastoiement*) 312
Paris, Bibliothèque de l'Arsenal 3517–3518 (*Miracles*) 306
Paris, Bibliothèque de l'Arsenal 3524 (Baudouin de Condé) 305
Paris, Bibliothèque de l'Arsenal 3525 (*Watriquet de Couvin*) 313
Paris, Bibliothèque de l'Arsenal 3527 (*Miracles*) 306
Paris, Bibliothèque de l'Arsenal 5198
Paris, Bibliothèque de l'Arsenal 5201 (*Chastoiement*) 312
Paris, Bibliothèque de l'Arsenal 5203 (Machaut) 308
Paris, Bibliothèque Nationale fr. 93 (*Cassidorus*) 312
Paris, Bibliothèque Nationale fr. 106–109 (*Perceforest*) 311

Paris, Bibliothèque Nationale fr. 146 (*Roman de Fauvel*) 29, 149, 172, 174, 177, 200–14, *210*, *211*, 221, 247, 293, 307, 326 n.17 (chant in) (Lescurel) 310

Paris, Bibliothèque Nationale fr. 338

Paris, Bibliothèque Nationale fr. 345–348 (*Perceforest*) 311

Paris, Bibliothèque Nationale fr. 350 (*Guiron*) 309

Paris, Bibliothèque Nationale fr. 372 (*Renart le Nouvel*) 83, *84*, 138, 176, 187, 309

Paris, Bibliothèque Nationale fr. 375 (*Vergi*) 305

Paris, Bibliothèque Nationale fr. 412

Paris, Bibliothèque Nationale fr. 776 (prose *Tristan*) 184, 312

Paris, Bibliothèque Nationale fr. 790 (*Restor du paon*) 310

Paris, Bibliothèque Nationale fr. 817 (*Miracles*) 307, 327 n.38

Paris, Bibliothèque Nationale fr. 837 (*Court de Paradis*) 88, 237, 306

Paris, Bibliothèque Nationale fr. 837 (*Saluts*) 174, 184, 312, 313 (*Resverie*) 311

Paris, Bibliothèque Nationale fr. 837 (*Chastelaine de St Gille*) 184 (*Chastoiement*) 312

Paris, Bibliothèque Nationale fr. 837 (*Confrere d'amours*) 184, 305

Paris, Bibliothèque Nationale fr. 837 (*Lai d'Aristote*) 184, 237, 309

Paris, Bibliothèque Nationale fr. 837 (*Complaintes*) 231, 305

Paris, Bibliothèque Nationale fr. 837 (*Chastelaine de Vergi*) 237, 305

Paris, Bibliothèque Nationale fr. 843 (Machaut) 308

Paris, Bibliothèque Nationale fr. 844 ('Manuscrit du Roi', Trouvère MS *M*), 31, 39, 81–82, 88, 164, 320 n.15

Paris, Bibliothèque Nationale fr. 845 (Trouvère MS *N*) 326 n.4, 331 n.24

Paris, Bibliothèque Nationale fr. 846 ('Chansonnier Cangé', Trouvère MS *O*) 38

Paris, Bibliothèque Nationale fr. 847

Paris, Bibliothèque Nationale fr. 881 (Machaut) 189, 293 (Ovid, *Ars amatoria*) 313

Paris, Bibliothèque Nationale fr. 986 (*Miracles*) 306

Paris, Bibliothèque Nationale fr. 1149 (Tr. Lud.) 304

Paris, Bibliothèque Nationale fr. 1374 (*Roman de la violette*) 26, 30–31, *32*, 34, 184, 307

Paris, Bibliothèque Nationale fr. 1375 (*Restor du paon*) 310

Paris, Bibliothèque Nationale fr. 1446 (*Kanor*) 184, 312 (Baudouin de Condé) 305

Paris, Bibliothèque Nationale fr. 1455 (*Meliacin*) 180, 184, 308, 327 n.32

Paris, Bibliothèque Nationale fr. 1456 (*Cleomadés*) 180, 304

Paris, Bibliothèque Nationale fr. 1530 (*Miracles*) 34, 306

Paris, Bibliothèque Nationale fr. 1533 (*Miracles*) 327 n.38, 306

Paris, Bibliothèque Nationale fr. 1536 (*Miracles*) 34, 306

Paris, Bibliothèque Nationale fr. 1553 (*Roman de la violette*) 30, 187, 307

Paris, Bibliothèque Nationale fr. 1554 (*Restor du paon*) 173, 184, 310

Paris, Bibliothèque Nationale fr. 1555 (*Vergi*) 305

Paris, Bibliothèque Nationale fr. 1569 (*Robin et Marion*) 176, 304

Paris, Bibliothèque Nationale fr. 1581 (*Renart le Nouvel*) 83, *84*, 138, 176, 309, 327 n.27

Paris, Bibliothèque Nationale fr. 1584 (Machaut) 183, 292, 293, 308

Paris, Bibliothèque Nationale fr. 1585 (Machaut) 308

Paris, Bibliothèque Nationale fr. 1586 (Machaut) 181, 183, *218*, *264*, 308

Paris, Bibliothèque Nationale fr. 1588 (Philippe de Rémi) 311

Paris, Bibliothèque Nationale fr. 1589 (*Meliacin*) 307

Paris, Bibliothèque Nationale fr. 1591 (Trouvère MS *R*) 327 n.39

Paris, Bibliothèque Nationale fr. 1593 (*Renart le Nouvel*) 83, *84*, 138, 176–77, 187, 309 (*Lai d'Aristote*) 309

Paris, Bibliothèque Nationale fr. 1613 (*Miracles*) 307

Paris, Bibliothèque Nationale fr. 1633 (*Meliacin*) 308

Paris, Bibliothèque Nationale fr. 1634 (Tr. Lud.) 304

Paris, Bibliothèque Nationale fr. 1802 (*Court de Paradis*) 88, 187, 328 n.41, 306

Paris, Bibliothèque Nationale fr. 2136 (*Vergi*) 305

Paris, Bibliothèque Nationale fr. 2163 (*Miracles*) 306

Paris, Bibliothèque Nationale fr. 2166 (*Restor du paon*) 310

Paris, Bibliothèque Nationale fr. 2168 (*Aucassin et Nicolette*) 191, *194*, 304

Paris, Bibliothèque Nationale fr. 2186 (*Roman de la poire*) 178, 181–82, *182*, 183–34, 247, 248, 266, 313, 327 n.34

Paris, Bibliothèque Nationale fr. 2193 (*Miracles*) 34, 306

Paris, Bibliothèque Nationale fr. 8541 (Arras, confrérie; *Nécrologe*) 136

Paris, Bibliothèque Nationale fr. 9221 (Machaut) 183, 293, 308, 309

Paris, Bibliothèque Nationale fr. 12467 (sermons) 313

Paris, Bibliothèque Nationale fr. 12483 (Trouvère MS *i*) 81–82

Paris, Bibliothèque Nationale fr. 12562 (*Licorne*) 312

Paris, Bibliothèque Nationale fr. 12565 (*Restor du paon*) 173, 310 (*Parfait du paon*) 310

Paris, Bibliothèque Nationale fr. 12567 (*Restor du paon*) 310

Paris, Bibliothèque Nationale fr. 12599 (prose *Tristan*) 312

Paris, Bibliothèque Nationale fr. 12615 ('Chansonnier de Noailles', Trouvère MS *T*) 80–81, 88, *98*, 233, *234*, 320 n.15

Paris, Bibliothèque Nationale fr. 12786 (rondeaux) 87, 88, 92 (*Roman de la poire*) 178, 247, 248, 313, 327 n.34, 335 n.2

Paris, Bibliothèque Nationale fr. 14968 (Watriquet de Couvin) 184, 313 (*Manuscrit*) 311

Paris, Bibliothèque Nationale fr. 15098 (*Roman du castelain de Couci*) 184, 187, 189, 309

Paris, Bibliothèque Nationale fr. 17000 (*Cassidorus*) 312 (*Laurin*) 312

Paris, Bibliothèque Nationale fr. 19152 (*Lai d'Aristote*) 309 (*Jal.*) 304

Paris, Bibliothèque Nationale fr. 19165 (*Cleomadés*) 180, 304

Paris, Bibliothèque Nationale fr. 20045 (*Restor du paon*) 310

Paris, Bibliothèque Nationale fr. 20050 ('Chansonnier St Germain', Trouvère MS *U*) 30–31, 38, 88, 94–96

Paris, Bibliothèque Nationale fr. 22543 (Troubadour MS *R*) 88, 95

Paris, Bibliothèque Nationale fr. 22545 (Machaut) 293, 308, 309

Paris, Bibliothèque Nationale fr. 22548 (*Laurin*) 312 (*Cassidorus*) 312

Paris, Bibliothèque Nationale fr. 22549 (*Cassidorus*) 312

Paris, Bibliothèque Nationale fr. 22550 (*Kanor*) 312 (*Peliarmenus*) 312

Paris, Bibliothèque Nationale fr. 22928 (*Miracles*) 34, 306

Paris, Bibliothèque Nationale fr. 23111 (*Miracles*) 307

Paris, Bibliothèque Nationale fr. 24042 (*Galeran de Bretagne*) 306

Paris, Bibliothèque Nationale fr. 24300 (*Miracles*) 307

Paris, Bibliothèque Nationale fr. 24301 (*Chastoiement*) 312

Paris, Bibliothèque Nationale fr. 24374 (*Escanor*) 187, *188*, 307, 327 n.34

Paris, Bibliothèque Nationale fr. 24378 (*Roman de la violette*, prose) 327 n.40, 307

Paris, Bibliothèque Nationale fr. 24386 (*Restor du paon*) 310

Paris, Bibliothèque Nationale fr. 24391 (*La Prise amoureuse*) 180, *183*, 184, 189, 310, 327 n.34

Paris, Bibliothèque Nationale fr. 24404 (*Cleomadés*) 304

Paris, Bibliothèque Nationale fr. 24405 (*Cleomadés*) 304

Paris, Bibliothèque Nationale fr. 24406 (Trouvère MS *V*) 30–31

Paris, Bibliothèque Nationale fr. 24429 (*L'Estoire de Joseph*) 326 n.6, 306

Paris, Bibliothèque Nationale fr. 24430 (*Cleomadés*) 304

Paris, Bibliothèque Nationale fr. 24431 (*Roman de la poire*) 178, 187, 313

Paris, Bibliothèque Nationale fr. 24432 (*La Prise amoureuse*) 187, 310

Paris, Bibliothèque Nationale fr. 24432 (*Panthère*) 311

Index of Manuscripts

Paris, Bibliothèque Nationale fr. 25521
  (*Restor du paon*) 310
Paris, Bibliothèque Nationale fr. 25532
  (*Miracles*) 80, 178, 320 n.15, 306
Paris, Bibliothèque Nationale fr. 25532 (*Court
  de paradis*) 81, 88, *99*, 100, 115, 178, 320
  n.15, 327 n.36, 306
Paris, Bibliothèque Nationale fr. 25545
  (*Vergi*) 305
Paris, Bibliothèque Nationale fr. 25566
  (Adam de la Halle, Trouvère MS *W*)
  138, 139, 163, 172, 174–76, 177, 184, *274*,
  283, 293, 294, 304 (Nevelon) 311
Paris, Bibliothèque Nationale fr. 25566
  (*Renart le Nouvel*) 83, *84*, 138, 176, 309
Paris, Bibliothèque Nationale lat. 11331
  (*chansons latines*) 187, 305
Paris, Bibliothèque Nationale lat. 15131
  (*chansons latines*) 305
Paris, Bibliothèque Nationale lat. 16497
  (sermons) 313
Paris, Bibliothèque Nationale lat. 16663 288
Paris, Bibliothèque Nationale n.a.fr. 1050
  ('Chansonnier Clairambault', Trouvère
  MS *X*) 30–31, *33*, 326 n.4
Paris, Bibliothèque Nationale n.a.fr. 1104
  (*Lai d'Aristote*) 309
Paris, Bibliothèque Nationale n.a.fr. 1731
  (*Court d'amours*) 146, 179, 306 (*Ju de le
  capete*) 310
Paris, Bibliothèque Nationale n.a.fr. 4531
  (*Vergi*) 305
Paris, Bibliothèque Nationale n.a.fr. 6295
  (*Miracles*) 307
Paris, Bibliothèque Nationale n.a.fr. 7514
  (*Roman du castelain de Couci*) 309, 328
  n.50 (*Regret Guillaume*) 310
Paris, Bibliothèque Nationale n.a.fr. 10036
  (*L'Estoire de Joseph*) 118, 174, 306
Paris, Bibliothèque Nationale n.a.fr. 10047
  (Tr. Lud.) 304
Paris, Bibliothèque Nationale n.a.fr. 13521
  ('Chansonnier La Clayette') 232
Paris, Bibliothèque Nationale n.a.fr. 24541
  (*Miracles*, 'Soissons') 34, 80, 107, 178,
  320 n.15, 306
Paris, Institut de France 636 (*Cleomadés*) 304
Pennsylvania, French 15 (chansonnier) 334
  n.36
Poitiers, Bibliothèque Municipale 97
  (sermons) 313

Reims, Bibliothèque Municipale 1275
  (*Mariage*) 311
Rome, Biblioteca Apostolica Vaticana Pal.
  Lat.1969 (*Miracles*) 307
Rome, Biblioteca Apostolica Vaticana Reg.
  Lat.1490 (Trouvère MS *a*) 88, 326 n.4,
  327 n.37 (Nevelon) 311
Rome, Biblioteca Apostolica Vaticana Reg.
  Lat.1682 (*L'Estoire de Joseph*) 306
Rome, Biblioteca Apostolica Vaticana Reg. 71
  (*Quinque*) 307
Rome, Biblioteca Apostolica Vaticana Reg.
  1725 (Renart's *Rose*) 19–20, 52, 186, 310,
  328 n.40
Rome, Biblioteca Apostolica Vaticana Lat.
  5232 (Troubadour MS *A*) 31, 34, 41
Rome, Vaticana Borghese 200 (sermon) 186,
  313
Rouen, Bibliothèque Municipale 1057 (O.8)
  (*Restor du paon*) 310

Tours, Bibliothèque Municipale 136
  (*Manuscrit*) 311
Tours, Bibliothèque Municipale 468
  (Proverbs) 311
Tours, Bibliothèque Municipale 948
  (*Miracles*) 307
Troyes, Bibliothèque Municipale 1890
  (*Quinque*) 307
Turin, Biblioteca Nazionale Universitaria
  1626 (*Sone de Nansay*) 313
Turin, Biblioteca Nazionale Universitaria
  1626 L.I.13 (Jean de Condé) 309
Turin, Biblioteca Nazionale Universitaria
  L.V.32 (Baudouin de Condé) 305
Turin, Biblioteca Nazionale Universitaria 1650
  (*Cassidorus*) 312

Verzuolo, Bibl. C. Perrin (*Mémoires*) 311
Vienna, Österreiches Nationalbibliothek
  2542 (prose *Tristan*) 312
Vienna, Österreiches Nationalbibliothek
  2621 (Baudouin de Condé, *Prison
  d'amours*) 180, 253, 327 n.27
Vienna, Österreiches Nationalbibliothek
  2621 (sermon) 184

Wolfenbüttel, Herzog August Bibliothek 677
  (motets, W1) Ex. 7 (110)
Wolfenbüttel, Herzog August Bibliothek
  1099 (motets, W2) Ex. 7 (110)

General index

'*A dieu conmant je mes amors*' 159
'*A l'entrant de mai*' 152
'*A ma dame servir*' 140
'*A mon voloir ont choisi mi eill*' 248
'*A vos, amant, plus k'a nule autre gent*'
    35–36, 39
'*A vous, douce debonnaire*' Ex. 18 (285)
'*Aaliz main se leva*' 45
acrostic 246–47
Adam de la Bassée, *Ludus super*
    Anticlaudianum 29, 119, 174, 177,
    178
Adam de la Halle
    and *Aucassin et Nicolette* 196–97
    as author-figure 259, 260–63, 283–84
    citation in 278–80, 281–82, Exx. 15 (281)
        and 16 (282), 286
    citations of 260–63, 283–84
    grafting processes in 278–81
    Jeu de la feuillée 135, 139, 140 (refrain
        links with *Le Tournoi de Chauvency*),
        148–50, Ex. 9 (148), 151, 163, 280
    Li Jus de pelerin 139, 149, 163
    manuscripts of 138, 179, 184, 293
    motets 279–80, 281–83, Exx. 15–17
        (281–82)
    MS fr. 25566 see manuscripts, Index of
    other works by 164, 279, 281
    polyphonic rondeaux 140 (refrains shared
        by *Renart le Nouvel*), 221, 273–76,
        274, 277, 281–83, Exx. 14 (275), 15
        (281) and 16 (282)
    Robin et Marion 2, 3, 118, 139, 147,
        151–68, Table 9.1 (154–55), Ex. 10
        (157), 163 (and *Le Tournoi de*
        Chauvency), 166–67 (and pastoral),
        280
additamenta 46, 48

Adenet le Roi, *Cleomadés* 179, 180, 187, 189
'*Ai[e] se siet en haute tour*' 148
'*Ainsi va qui amors*' 92
'*Ainssi doit on aler / a son ami*' 87–102, Ex. 5
    (90), 92 (as rondeau), 98, 99, 127
Alain de Lille 119
'*Alés bielement que d'amer me duel*' 54
'*Alés cointement et seri*' 58
'*Amés! Pour avoir goie*' 236
'*Améz moi, blondete, améz*' 62
'*Amis dous / li malz que j'ai me vient de vos*' 115
'*Amour dont tele est la puissance*' 206–07,
    210
'*Amourousement mi tient li maus que j'ai / Hé*
    amours, mourrai je / Omnes' Ex. 12
    (230)
'*An, Diex! Li maus d'amer m'ocit*' 248–49
'*Ancor un chaipelet ai*' 145
Angevin court 163
'*Aprendés a valoir maris*' 54
aristocratic (society) 6
'aristocratisant' 17, 126, 141
Arras
    as cultural centre 7, 125, 133, 151
    Carité des ardents, regulations (see Arras,
        confrérie)
    Cité and Ville 133–34
    confrérie 7, 134, 136–37 (regulations),
        136–37 (founding legend)
    group of works connected with 28, 174
        (in manuscripts)
    patterns of manuscript production in
        174–77, 190
    poetic references to 137, 149
    puy 7, 134, 137
ars antiqua 202, 213
ars nova 202, 213, 218, 276, 277 (ballade),
    289

Arthurian *lai* 27, 29
Arthurian prose romances 26–27
'Au nouviel tans que mais et violette' 36
'Au tens nouvel' 152–53
Aucassin et Nicolette 2, 3, 23, 191–99, *194*
    alternating verse and prose in 192,
      195–96
    and *pastourelle* 196–98
    and *Renart le Nouvel* 195
    and *Robin et Marion* 196–97
    laisses in 191–92
    music in 23, 192, Ex. 11 (193), *194*
    performance of 193
    rubrics of 192, 193–95, *194*
auctor 186 (*auctores*), 262
auctoritas 8, 256
Audefroi le Bâtard 231
Audigier, chanson de geste 149
authorship 7, 41 (among trouvères), 217,
    220 (in *Le Roman de Fauvel* and *Le
    Roman de la Rose*), 245 (and
    language), 263, 267 (*Voir Dit*)
    and anonymity 7, 232, 244–45, 251, 262
    and authority 255–56, 258, 262–63
    and citation 130–2, 220
    represented in manuscripts 31, 34,
      204–05, 293–94
'Aveuc tele compaignie' 155

Bakhtin, Mikhail, on dialogic discourse
    129–31, 145–46, 243
    on speech genres 16, 131–32
ballade 202, 206, 240, 268, 278 (as elegy),
    284 (exchanges of)
    anomalous examples 208, 283
    as *forme fixe* 3, *183*, 202, 209
    in Machaut's Prologue 292
    polyphonic 3
ballettes 284
Baltzer, Rebecca 173
Barthes, Roland 245
Baude de la Quarière (Kakerie), 'Bele Aelis'
    82, 208, 233–35, *234*
Baudouin de Condé, *Li Contes de la rose* 28
    Li Prison d'amours 28, 206, 236, 252–56,
    258, 261
Baumgartner, Emmanuèle 64
Bec, Pierre 17, 44, 104, 126, 127, 128, 129
Bédier, Joseph 42, 44, 47, 48
'Bele Aeliz' topos 47, 107, 113, 145, 184, 186,
    233, *234*, 318 n.55

'Bele Ydoine' 231
'Bele, de fin cuer amée, merci' 255
'Belle Aalis mainz s'en leva' 145
Bent, Margaret 315 n.2
Berger, R. 7, 133, 134
bergerie 118, 143, 152, 159, 167
'Bergeronnete, douche baisselete' 154–55
'Bergeronnete, fetes vostre ami de moi' 153
Bhabha, Homi 7
'Biautez, bontez, douce chiere' 284
'Bien croi que de duel mourrai' 286
Blondel de Nesle 107, 109, Ex. 8 (111)
Boethius 328 nn.1, 2
'Bon jor ait qui mon cuer a!' 82–83, Ex. 3 (83)
'Bone amourete me tient gai' 283
boundary
    between genres or registers 131, 199, 213,
      225, 295
    between kinds of utterance 250, 263
    between lyric and narrative 219, 226, 235,
      236
    between oral and literate 17
    between song and speech 212
    ideas of 7
    in *Le Roman de Fauvel* 201, 213
bourgeois, and clerical writing 134–35, 151
    influence on *confrérie* 137
Brusegan, Rosanna 160

Camille, Michael 203
canso, see troubadour songs
cantefable (as term) see also *Aucassin et
    Nicolette* 191, 227
Carité des ardents see Arras
carole 45, 51, 54, 57, 258 (in Ovid), 263,
    264, 265
'Celui de qui je me fi' / 'La bele estoile de
    mer' / 'La bele en cui je me fi' /
    Johanne' 231
cento, see motet
Cerquiglini, Jacqueline 219, 266, 268
'C'est la gieus, en mi les prez' 69, 144
'C'est la jus' topos 114, 144
'C'est la jus, desoz l'olive' 46
chace 284
Chailley, Jacques 106, 113
Chaillou de Pestain 28, 200, 202, 204, 213,
    220
    identity of 200
    method of revision in *Le Roman de Fauvel*
      201

chanson à refrains 77, 233
chanson avec des refrains 77, 88, 93–96, 228, 233, *234*, 237 (and *saluts d'amour*)
chanson balladée 202
chanson couronnée 137–38
chanson de geste 149, 192
chanson de mal mariée 94, 100 (sacred parody of)
chanson de toile 26, 148, 231
chanson d'éloge 26
chanson d'histoire 68
chanson pieuse 104
chanson, see *grant chant courtois*
chansonniers see manuscripts, Index of
  as *puy* repertories 138–39
  compared with romance 27–42
  first compiled 25
  grouped by author 38, 172
  grouped by genre 172
  layout 182
  survival of music in 29, 30–31
  troubadour 31, 34
  trouvère 30–31, 38
chant royal 137, 221
Charles, Roi de Sicile 163–64
Chastelaine de St Gille, La 89, 184, 333 n.50
Chastelaine de Vergi, La 36, 38–40, 130, 236
Châtelain de Couci (Gui de Couci) 35–36, 83
  songs quoted in romans 35–36, 40
Chrétien de Troyes 19
Christine de Pisan 39
citation 7, 129–30
  and authorship 222, 249–51 (*Roman de la Poire*)
  as self-citation 156, 278–80 (Adam de la Halle), 285–86 (Jehannot de Lescurel)
  practice of 131, 152–56 (in *Robin et Marion*), 222, 267–70 (in *Voir Dit*), 289
Clanchy, M. T. 15
Clark, Suzannah 321 n.11
clausula 109, Ex. 7 (110)
'*Clere blondete sui, a mi*' 62
coeur mangé, legend of the 41, 240
color 288–89
complainte 174, 181, 206, 231 (grafting in), 239, 266
Complainte douteuse, La 238
Complainte I 231, 238

conductus 282
Confrere d'amours, Li 184
confrérie, see Arras
congé 133, 148
contrafacta 29, 78, 84, 103 (definition of)
Court d'amours, Le, anonymous continuation of (Suite) 89, 139, 141 (and *Renart le Nouvel*), 146–47, 165–66, 179 (manuscript of), 236 (rhyme), 250
Court de Paradis, La 50, 81, 88, *99*, 99–101, 115–18, 115 (music in), 139, 187 (initials in)
  and Gautier de Coinci, *Les Miracles* 116–18, 141, 178–79
courtly 6, 17, 105–06 (values), 126 (register), 133–35 (and clerical)
  and popular 7, 142, 143, 151
'Cuers qui par amours n'aime' 253
'*Cui donrrai ge mes amours*' 112, Ex. 1 (80)
'*Cui lairai ge*' 78, 79–80, Ex. 1 (80)
culture
  competing layers 127, 131, 135, 141, 143, 145–46, 151, 163, 167–68
  'internal acculturation' 126, 127, 132, 133, 145
  official 127, 129, 143
  popular 42, 141, 142

dance, as text 45
dance-song 6, *44*, 45, 59 (performance of), *60*, *61*, 65, *264*, *265*, 280 (and rhythm)
  as evidenced by refrains and rondets 45–48, 265–66
  see also carole
  transmission of 6, 50–56
danse robardoise, la (the game of the stolen kiss) 59, *60*, 142–43
Dante, *Vita Nuova* 260
'De ma dame vient' 279
'De ma dame vient / *Diex, comment porroie* / *Omnes*' 279
débat amoureux 238
déjà dit 245, 251, 262
Derrida, Jacques 329 n.1
Deschamps, Eustache 39, 291–92 (on Machaut)
  L'Art de Dictier 292
'*Dex trop demeure; quant vendra?*' 158–59
'*Dieus d'amours, vivrai je longuement enssi?*' 229
'Dieus soit en cheste maison' 283

'*Dieus, quant venra li temps et l'eure*' 265
'*Diex comment porroie*' 273, *274*, Ex. 14
    (275), 279–80, 283
dit 181, 206, 280
dit à refrains 206, 261
dits moraux 133
'Dix et sept, cinq, trese, quatorse et quinse'
    287–88
'*Dont n'ai jou droit que m'envoise*' 58
Doss-Quinby, Eglal 43
'*Douce dame, granz merci!*' 254
Duc de Brabant 120, 136
'D'une amour quoie et serie' Ex. 6 (107),
    107–08
Durling, Nancy 22

'*E non Deu sire se nelai*' 51, *52*
Earp, Lawrence 221, 277–78, 280
Echecs amoureux, Les, Evrart de Conty
    (commentator) 239, 333 n.51
'*Einsi doit aler qui bele amie a*' 91
'*Einsi doit dame aler*' 116
Empson, William 161, 165, 167
'En chantant me veul complaindre' 208
enté 77, 228 (in motets), 231 (saluts), 233,
    249–51 (*Roman de la Poire*), Ex. 13
    (251), 250–51, 269, 286
    definition of 207, 208, 227
Escanor 187, *188*
Estoire de Joseph, L' 2, 118, 172, 174
Everist, Mark 319 n.5, 332 n.31

fabliau 133
fatras, fatrasies 133, 184, 203, 204
fayseur 291, 336 n.3
fête champêtre 50
'Fines amouretes ai, Dieus, si ne sai quant les
    verrai' 283
'Folz est qui trop en son cuidier se fie' 261
form 225 (stability), 236, 289–90
    flexibility 235, 287–88
    irregularity 233, 238
formes fixes 3, 29, 202, 203, 205, 206, 209,
    214, 221, 222 (and first-person *dit*),
    240–42 (in narrative), 262, 270, 277
    (notion of fixity), 287 (relation
    between refrain and strophe)
    earliest examples of 221, 276–77
Froissart, Jean 38–39 (*La Prison Amoureuse*),
    189, 293
'Fui toi, gaite, fai moi voie' 279

Gace Brulé 29, *32*, *33*, 37, 65, 66
Galeran de Bretagne 28, 69
Gautier de Coinci, *Les Miracles de Nostre
    Dame* 1, 8, 28, 104–05 (and secular
    song), 106 (composition of songs),
    106–07 (as compilation), 115–18 (and
    La Court de Paradis), 293–94 (and
    authorship)
    and Renart's *Rose* 23, 105–06, 107,
        112
    contrafacta in 29, 78, 104–15
    manuscripts of 34, 106, 173, 177–79,
        183, 186, 189
    music in 23, 28, 34, Ex. 6 (107), Ex. 7
        (110), Ex. 8 (111), 115, 178
    Prologues 23, 104–05, 106, 227
    versified sermons in 106–07, 112–15
genre 79, 105, 132, 152–56, 161, 167, 213,
    227, 277–78 (and rhythm)
    and performance 15–16, 70–71
    and social meaning 68, 125–32
    as expressed in manuscripts 171, 175,
        187–88
    as forms of utterance 132, 258, 287
    creation of new genres 21, 75, 202, 225,
        276, 284
    generic change 202, 203, 213, 221,
        241–42, 277–78
    medieval terms 172, 187–88, 226–27
    mixing of 18, 75, 167, 199, 207, 213, 222,
        225, 227, 284–85
    questioning of categories of 212, 225, 233,
        242, 269–70
    theory of 15–17, 71
Gerbert de Montreuil, *Le Roman de la violette*
    26, 27 (types of songs in), 29–30, *32*,
    35–38, 54–55 (dancing scenes in), 89,
    130
    Prologue 22, 227
    refrains in 54–55, 57–59, 61, 140, 142,
        207, 286
Gervès du Bus 200, 204
Gillebert de Berneville 136
Gilles de [Viès] Maisons 108, Ex. 6 (107)
'Gracieus temps est, quant rosier' 207,
    208
'Gracïeuse, faitisse et sage' 207, 285–86
grant chant courtois 6, 107, 148, 203, 225,
    256 (in *Ars amatoria*), 270 (and *formes
    fixes*)
    and *chanson avec des refrains* 107–09

grant chant courtois (*Contd.*)
  and music 34–35, Ex. 6 (107), 107–08,
    177–78
  in romance 28, 29–30
Gravdal, Kathryn 160
Greimas, A. J. 243–44
guilds 134
Guilhem de Cabestanh 41
Guillaume d'Amiens, rondeaux of 48
Guillaume de Dole, see Jean Renart, *Rose*
Guillaume de Lorris and Jean de Meun,
    Roman de la Rose, and lyric 221, 224
  carole in *265*, 265–66
Guillaume de Lorris, *Le Roman de la rose* 4,
    59, 221 (glossing of), 239 (discursive
    power of)
  and Renart's *Rose* 4, 105, 220
Guillaume de Machaut 7, 219 (allegory in),
    222–23 (citation in)
  and *Roman de la rose* 219, 265–66
  and Baudouin de Condé 266, 268–69
  and Renart's *Rose* 219, 266
  and self-citation 223, 268–70
  and the *formes fixes* 270, 287–88
  ballades 284, 287
  La Fonteinne amoureuse 266
  La Louange des dames 268, 284, 335 n.57
  Lai de Plour 266
  Le Voir Dit 266–70, 268–70 (refrains in),
    270 (authorship in), 292
    truth and fiction in 267, 268, 335 n.54
  manuscripts of 172, 181, 183, 189, *218*, *264*
  motet 266
  Prologue to collected works 292–93
  Remede de Fortune 2, 217 (as anthology),
    218, 220, 239, 263–66, *264*
    refrain in 263, 265–66
    rondeaux 273–76, Ex. 14 (275), 287
Gurevich, Aron 126, 141, 143, 167

Hainault 146, 278
'Han Diex ou pourrai je trouver' 207–08,
  209, *211*
'Hareu li maus d'amer m'ochist' 85, 320 n.21
'Haro! haro! je la voi la' 229
'Hé Dieus, quant verrai / cele que j'aim?' 280
'Hé! resveille toi, Robin!' Table 9.1 (155), 158,
  159
'Hé! Robin, se tu m'aimes' Table 9.1 (154),
  156
'Hé, amours! mourrai je sans avoir merci?'
  228

'Hé, Dieus que ferai?' 78
'Hier main quant je chevauchoie' 158
Hoepffner, Ernest 212, 217
hoquet 109, Ex. 7 (110)
'Hui matin a l'ajournee' 109, Ex. 7 (110)
Huitace de Fontaine 158
Huot, Sylvia 220

intertextuality 244–45
Ivrea codex 284

'Ja pour hiver, pour noif ne pour gelée' 108,
  109, 112, Ex. 8 (111)
Jacquemart Giélée 121, 139
  Renart le Nouvel 28, 50, 140–41, 152, 206
    (and *Le Roman de Fauvel*)
    and *Le Tournoi de Chauvency* 138, 139
    as playbook 176
    in Adam's complete works MS 174–76
    manuscripts of *84*, 138, 149, 174–77,
      184, 187
    music in 83–84, *84*, Ex. 4 (85), 253
    performances of 138–39 (and *puy*), 177
Jacques Bretel 139, 144
  Le Tournoi de Chauvency 2, 43, *44*, 50,
    59–62, *60*, 65, 90–91, 100, 138, 140,
    142–46, 152, 163, 286
    see also *Jeu du chapelet, danse robardoise*
'J'ai amors a ma volenté' 69, 70, 144
'J'ai amours fait a mon gré' 57
'J'ai, j'ai amoretes au cuer' 254
Jakemés, *Roman du castelain de Couci* 35–36,
  38–39, 41, 130, 143 (rondeau in), 184
  (manuscripts of), 187, 189, 236, 240,
  241
'Jamais amours n'oublierai' 253
Jameson, Frederic 15–17
Jaufre Rudel 26
'Je l'amerai mon vivant' 286
'Je me repairoie du tournoiement' Ex. 10
  (157)
'Je muir, je muir d'amourete' 283, 284
Jean de Meun see Guillaume de Lorris
Jean Renart, 1, 4, 27, 38, 222 (as author)
  Le Roman de la rose 2, 5, 18, 19–20 (music
    for songs), 26 (unique song genres
    in), 27 (as anthology), 50–53 (dancing
    scenes), 66 (irony in), 64–71
    (performance), 314–15 n.8 (date)
    as source for popular song 42, *52*
    grands chants in 35–38, 64–67, 130, 226

influence of 28, 220
manuscript of 19–20, *52*, 173, 186
novelty of 1, 22, 28, 199
Prologue 18–22, 199, 227
relation to Machaut 219, 266
rondets and refrains in 45–53, *52*, 77,
78, 81, 82, 89, 91, 92, 108, 144, 221,
233
Jeanroy, Alfred 42, 44, 45, 47, 129
Jehan Acart de Hesdin, *La Prise amoureuse*
239–41, 252, 276
allegory in 240–41
ballades and rondeaux in 222, 240–41
manuscript of 179, *183*, 184, 187, 189
Jehan Bretel 137, 139
Jehan de la Mote, *Regret Guillaume* 276,
278, 284
Jehannot de Lescurel 146, 284 (lyrics of),
285–87, Ex. 18 (285) (and
polyphony), 285 (and Adam de la
Halle, 285–86 (and self-citation), 289
(and Nicole de Margival)
dits entés 207, 208, 227, 231, 284
Jerome of Moravia 288–89
jeu de mystère, jeux see play
Jeu du chapelet, Le (the game of the circlet of
flowers) 43, *44*, 142–46
jeu-parti 40, 133, 135–36, 139, 172
Johannes de Garlandia, *De mensurabili musica*
288
Johannes de Grocheio 46, 277, 318 n.60,
331 n.24
Johannes de Muris 276
jongleurs 134, 136, 137
Ju de la capete Martinet 146

Kristeva, Julia 333 n.5
Kurzmotetten 97, 98, *98*, 232

'La fontenele i sort clere' 112, 113–14
'La jus, desoz la raime' 92
'*La la voi venir, m'amie*' 46
Lai d'Aristote 89, 91–92, 184
Lai des Amants 193
'*Lai/ La merci Deu, j'ai ataint*' 144
lai, fourteenth-century 181, 203
laisse 191, 192 (in *Aucassin et Nicolette*)
Lambert Ferri d'Arras 120
'L'amours dont sui espris' 107
Langton, Stephen 105, 145
'Lanquan li jorn son lonc en may' 26

Latin and vernacular 84, 121, 130, 178, 203,
208
Le Goff, Jacques 126
'Le pensers trop mi guerroie' 152
'Le plus grant bien qui me viengne d'amer'
268
Leech-Wilkinson, Daniel 287–88, 335 n.54
lemmata 186
letters 26, 175, 181, 238 (*saluts*), 267 (in *Voir
Dit*), 332 n.48
Li Jus du Pelerin, see Adam de la Halle
'Li noviaus tens et mais et violete' 36, 83
'Li plus se plaint d'Amours mès je n'os dire'
109 (melody)
Lille 139
literacy, see orality
litterae notabiliores 186
Livre du Chevalier de La Tour-Landry 39
Lorraine 139
lyric, definition of 213, 217, 217–18 (new
status of), 220, 222, 224 (modern
formulations of)
relation to narrative 220, 224–25, 268,
287

'Ma douce amie, salut, s'il vous agrée' 238
Mahieu le Poirier, *Le Court d'amours*, see
Court d'amours
'Main se leva bele aeliz' 53
'*Mais lasse! [Diex] comment porroie*' 279
'Mal ait cil qui me maria!' 113
mal mariée 113, 247
manuscript layout
illuminations 149, 181, 209, 247
indices in 172
initials in 30, 176, 181–84, *182*, 184, 187,
188, 209, *210*, *234*
paraphs *183*, 184
positurae or 'end-of-section' marks 187,
188, 328 n.48
punctus elevatus 184
sizes and colours of script in 30, 34, 173,
184–85, *185*, 186
speaker markings 118, 175–76, 177
manuscript presentation of songs 7, 14,
19–20, 30–34, *32*, *33*, 46–48
blank staves in 84, 173, 178, 179–80,
181–82, *182*, 247, 253
rubrics and headings 120–21, 173, 177,
181, *183*, *185*, 187–89, *194*, 218
spaces for staves 173, 178, 179, *183*, *188*

manuscripts, and genre 26, 171, 212–13
  and puys 138, 195, 212
  music in 19–20, 83–85, 103, 118, 173–79,
    181, 221, 252, 253
Martin Béquin de Cambrai 120
Meliacin 28, 179, 180, 184, 189
melisma 221, 273
monophony 29, 172, 179, 203
motet 2, 3, Ex. 5 (90), *98*, 130, 173 (layout
    in manuscript), 207, Ex. 12 (230),
    266, 281–83, Exx. 15–17 (281–82),
    284
motet enté, see *enté*
motet, and refrains 77, 82–83, Ex. 3 (83),
    Table 5.1 (88), 96–98, *98*, 232
  centons 77, 228, 232
  definition of 77
  grafting in 228–31, Ex. 12 (230), 278–81
    (Adam de la Halle)
  Latin 109, 208, 231
  music 3, 25, 119–20 (and Boethius), 151
    (register), Ex. 10 (157) (parody), 292
    (*artificiele* and *naturele*)
  and literacy 25, 35
  copying 20, 31, 35, 173 (and genre),
    234
  for songs in romance 19–20, 29, *32*,
    34–35, 177–78, 181, 252, 253
  see also manuscripts, motet, notation,
    refrain, rhythm, song

Naples 152, 163–66 (Angevin court at)
narrative 3 (use of first-person), 196
    (melody)
  as context for song 4, 43–45, 294–95
  in relation to lyric 213, 217
'Ne sont pas achoison de chanter' 29, *32, 33*
'*Ne vos repentez mie*' 49, Ex. 2 (81), 114, 116,
    234
Nevelon Amion, *Dit d'amour* 208
Nicole de Margival, *Dit de la panthere
    d'amours* 28, 221, 259–63, 276, 284,
    286–87 (and Jehannot de Lescurel)
  and Adam de la Halle 259, 260–63, 284
  and poetic authority 260, 262–63
  cites his own songs 259–60
notation, musical, changes in 202, 221
  'noter', meaning of 19–21, 315 n.15
  relation to sound 14, 181
'*Nus n'a joie s'il n'aime par Amours*' 83, Ex. 4
    (85)

'O flour des flours de toute melodie' 291
'On ne porroit penser ne souhaidier' 284
'*Onques n'amai tant comme je fu amée*', see
    also '*Unques*' 250, Ex. 13 (251)
'Or sai ge bien qu'est maus d'amours'
    249
'Or vienent Pasques les beles en avril' 68
orality 16 (genre), 53 (oral performance)
  and literacy 1, 9, 15–17, 55–56
  and music 9, 14, 34–35
organum 109
Ovid, *Ars amatoria*, French translation of
    78, *185*, 186, 189, 256, 258

Page, Christopher 277, 278
'*Par chi va la mignotise*' Ex. 9 (148),
    279–80
'Par Dieu, Amors, fort m'est a consirrer' 40
'Par rire et par biaus dis oÿr' 261
Parfait du paon, Jehan de la Mote 189
Paris 151, 277
Parkes, M. B. *185*, 187
pastoral 132, 142, 146, 160–62, 199 (as
    model of displacement)
pastourelle 78, 109 (as *contrafactum*), 118
    (and *Bergerie*), 120, 131, 142–43, 144,
    147, 148, 151, 161–63, 165, 196–98
    (and *Aucassin et Nicolette*)
pastourelle avec des refrains 233
pastourelle, and *bergerie*
    in *Le Jeu du Robin et Marion* 152–56,
    158–60, 166–68
Perceforest 238
performance 13 (as public event), 15–17
    (genre), 64–71 (and social meaning),
    64 (private and public), 146
    (conditions of)
  as represented in writing 8, 9, 13, 17,
    47–48, 53, 55–56, 59–63, 70–71, 141,
    149, 176–77, 184, 192–96, Ex. 11
    (193), *194*, 201, 207, 212
Perrin d'Agincourt 152, 163
Philippe de Remi, *Salut à refrains* 252
Philippe de Vitry 217, 276, 330 n.1
Pierre d'Alençon 164
play (drama *jeu*) 133, 137–38, 175–76
plica 82
poète 291
polyphony, before ars nova manuscripts of the
    1360s and 1370s 179, 202, 221
  earliest stages of 3, 29, 172–73, 276–78

popular, see also courtly
  meanings of 6, 17, 42, 126, 141–43,
    244–45 (and anonymous writing),
    262
  song 18, 42–63, 142–46 (aristocratic
    appropriation of)
'popularisant' 17, 126, 141
'Pour ce que tous mes chans'
'Pour Dieu, ne vos repentez mie' 113
'Pour ennui ne por contraire' 287
'Pour verdure' 83
propositio 186
prose and verse 267–68 (*Le Voir Dit*)
prose *Tristan* 26, 69, 177, 184, 232, 332 n.48
proses (in *Le Roman de Fauvel*) 203
proverbs, see refrain
  collections of 256
'Providence la senee' 208
Psaki, Regina 20
Pushkin, *Evgenij Onegin* 129
puy, see also manuscripts
  crowning of songs in 137–38
  culture 137–40, 150, 174, 195, 221 (and
    chant royal)
  of Amiens 137
  of Lille 136, 138
  of London 137
  see Arras, *puy*
puys, other towns 136, 137–38

'Quand je ne voy' 273–76, Ex. 14 (275)
'Quant de la foelle espoisse li vergier' 66
'Quant flors et glais et verdure s'esloigne' 37
'Quant li estés et la douce saisons' 237
*Qu'assez reuve/Que qui se complaint assez
  rueve'* 268–69
'Que demandez vos' 67
'Qui a droit veut Amors servir' 260
'Qui bien aim(m)e a tart oblie' 248, 266, 335
  nn.49 and 50

Raoul de Houdenc 20
Raoul de Soissons 120, 163–64
rape 155–56, 158–59, 160
razos 41, 268
refrain, and citation 7, 78, 87–102, 131,
  243–70, 278–90
  and compositional practices 86, 95–99,
    101–02, 228, 255, 279
  and dance-song 43–49 (as fixed element
    in), 280–81

and genre 6, 57, 75–76, 86, 87, 101–02,
  226, 280–81
and proverbs 243–45
and repetition 45–49, 55, 77, 78, 85–86,
  93, 159, 258, 268, 273, 283, 288–89
and the motet 4, 77, 228–31
and transition 63, 167–68, 213, 235, 280,
  294–95
as generating element 49, 57, 62, 99, 159,
  246, 257, 258, 283
definition of 5, 76–77, 85–86, 128
  ('refrain exogène / récurrent')
fragmentary nature of 43, 50, 57, 62, 75,
  128, 213, 228, 322 n.8
in *formes fixes* 273–78, 280–81, 289
in romans 26 (first recorded in), 57–63,
  77–78
issues of identification 49–50, 62, 79–86,
  89, 101, 131, 141–42, 226, 244–45,
  247, 250, 251, 252–53, 277
links between refrains 96–102, 139–40,
  141–42, 147, 152, 279, 284
medieval terms for 108, 172, 187, 226,
  255, 266
music of 5, 29, 35, 48–49, 79–86, 83–85
  (multiple melodies), 107–08, 112,
  157, 206, Ex. 13 (251), 285–86,
  325 n.8
newly composed 108, 142, 144, 206,
  249–52, 256, 268
patterns of metre and rhyme in setting into
  narrative 51, 55, 75, 111, 127–29,
  207, 236–38
performance of 48–49, 51, 61–62, 141,
  252, 280
relation between text and melody 79,
  82–86, 87–88, 95–96, 157, 231, 245,
  252, 253
relation to *rondets de carole* / rondeaux
  43–45, 48–49, 77, 92–93, 128–29
textual character 85, 88–89, 97, 244–45,
  279, 295
Regalado, Nancy 205, 329 n.16
register, changes in 221
  contrasts of 140–47, 160, 161, 232
  definitions of 126, 150 (and social
    meaning), 151 (in music)
Renart le Nouvel, see Jacquemart Giélée
Renart, see Jean Renart
Renaut de Sabloeil 66
'Renvoisiement i voit a mon ami' 97, *98*, *99*

Restor de paon 89, 173, 179, 184
reverdie, reverdie pieuse 113, 148
rhythm 3, 14 (and notation), 202, 203, 273, 283
Richard de Fournival 239, 249–51, Ex. 13 (251)
Robert de Blois, *Chastoiement des Dames* 334 n.32
Robert II, Count of Artois 163, 164
Robert Soumillon 137
'Robins m'aime, Robins m'a' 152, 153, 154 (Table 9.1), 155, 156
Roman de Cassidorus, Le 238, 332 n.49
Roman de Fauvel, Le 3, 4, 29 (polyphony in), 121, 196, 200–14, 204 (author rubric), 220 (and the two *Roses*)
  hybrid character of 202, 209, 269–70
  illuminations in 203, 209, *210*, *211*
  mid-point of 204–05, 329 n.14
  new genres in 201–02 (and generic change), 203
  refrains in 140, 206–09, 212
  'semi-lyric' pieces in 202, 204, 205, 206–09, *210*, *211*
Roman de la poire, see Tibaut
Roman du castelain de Couci, Le, see Jakemés
romans à chansons, compared with chansonniers 27–42
Romans de la dame a la lycorne, Le 28
rondeau 77, 221 (earliest melismatic), 262 (as authored form)
rondeau, as *forme fixe* 3, 202, 206, 221, 240
  polyphonic 3, 221, *274*, Exx. 14 (275), 15 (281), 16 (282) and 17 (282), 277
  see also dance-song, refrain, *rondet de carole*
rondet de carole 26, 43–49, *46–48* (transcription of), 92, 131, 144–45, 258 (principle of alternation in)
  as presented in manuscript 180, 186
  cited in sermons 113, 186
  definition of 45, 317 n.50
  typology, see also 'Bele Aelis' and 'C'est la gieus' 46, 48, 49, 114, 144
  variable form of 46–47, 92–93, 283
Rutebeuf 163

'Sa biele boucete, par un très douc ris' 255
'Sa boucete vermillete m'a mis en prizon' 256
sacred, and secular 100, 103, 104, 112
  see also *contrafacta*

Salter, Elizabeth 119
salut d'amour 131, 140, 146, 152, 174, 206, 207, 237–39, 254–55, 259, 332 n.41
  Salut I 184, 237, 250, 254
  Salut Ia 238
  Salut II 237, 250, 254
  Salut III 237, 238
'Se j'ai amé folement' 100
'Se j'onques a mon vivant' 205
sententia (sentence) 186, 261, 328 n.47
sermons 113, 117–18, 145, 184, 186
'Seulete vois a mon ami' 54
Sicilian Vespers 163, 164
signature 205, 213
Sone de Nansai 69
song, see also music, performance
  and commentary or gloss 34, 186, 187, 258–60
  and memory 69, 96
  and narrative 1, 2–3, 7, 22, 42, 105, 130, 220, 241–42, 294–95
  changes in form 3, 7, 201–02, 213–14, 219, 221–22, 225, 241–42, 262, 276–77
  written character of 1–2, 8–9, 14, 19, 25, 26, 30–35, *32*, 41, 44, 47–48, 51–53, 54–56, 173–90, 214
songs, as authoritative, see also authorship 186–87, 190, 262–63
  musical transmission of 29
sotte chanson 148, 203, 204, 206, 208, 214
'Soutenez moi, li max d'amors m'ocit' 246, 249
'Soyez liez et menez joie' 284
staves, see manuscripts
Stevens, John 6–7, 151, 277
Switten, Margaret 173

Te Deum laudamus 67
'Tendez tuit vos mains a la flor d'esté' 67
Thibaut de Champagne, King of Navarre 34, 134, 136, 293
Tibaut, *Roman de la Poire* 89, 140, 142, 181–83, *182*, 206, 220, 246–52
  acrostic in 246–47
  and Guillaume's *Rose* 246, 251
  music in 178–79
Tischler, Hans 89
Todorov, Tzvetan 132
tornoi de dames 26
Tournoi de Chauvency, Le, see Jacques Bretel

'*Toute vostre gent*' 143
transmission 22, 56, 70–71
treske 147
'*Triquedondele*' 147

'*Unques n'amai tant com ge fui amee*' 248, 250

van den Boogaard, Nico 43, 89, 138, 253, 265
'*Ve qui gregi deficiunt*' / *Trahunt in precipicia* / *Quasi non ministerium* / *Displicebat ei* ' 208
vers de transition 236
verse and prose 30–31, 175, 191–92, 267
verse, lineation of 30–31
vidas 31, 41, 268

'*Vilainnes genz, vous ne les sentez mie*' Ex. 6 (107), 108
virelai 202, 206, 208, *264*
Virgil 232
'*Vos avrois la seignorie*' 247
'*Vos ne vendrez mie*' 46–47
'*Vous ne lairés, le baler, le jouer*' 257
'*Vous ne sentez mie*' 111, 112
'*Vous perdés vo paine, sire Aubert*' Ex. 10 (157)

Watriquet de Couvin 184
words, in relation to music 15, 31, 103, 121, 202

Zink, Michel 4, 19–21
Zumthor, Paul 15–16, 21, 47, 126, 127, 129, 133, 147, 224

CAMBRIDGE STUDIES IN MEDIEVAL LITERATURE

1 Robin Kirkpatrick *Dante's Inferno: Difficulty and Dead Poetry* 0 521 30757 0
2 Jeremy Tambling *Dante and Difference: Writing in the "Commedia"* 0 521 34242 0
3 Simon Gaunt *Troubadours and Irony* 0 521 35439 0
4 Wendy Scase *"Piers Plowman" and the New Anticlericalism* 0 521 36017 x
5 Joseph Duggan *The "Cantar De Mio Cid": Poetic Creation in its Economic and Social Contexts* 0 521 36194 x
6 Roderick Beaton *The Medieval Greek Romance* 0 521 33335 0
7 Kathryn Kerby-Fulton *Reformist Apocalypticism and "Piers Plowman"* 0 521 34298 8
8 Alison Morgan *Dante & the Medieval Other World* 0 521 36069 2
9 Eckehard Simon (ed.) *The Theatre of Medieval Europe: New Research in Early Drama* 0 521 38514 8
10 Mary Carruthers *The Book of Memory: a Study of Memory in Medieval Culture* 0 521 38282 3 (HB) 0 521 42930 (PB)
11 Rita Copeland *Rhetoric, Hermeneutics and Translation in the Middle Ages: Academic Traditions and Vernacular Texts* 0 521 38517 2 (HB) 0 521 48365 4 (PB)
12 Donald Maddox *The Arthurian Romances of Chrétien de Troyes: Once and Future Fictions* 0 521 39450 3
13 Nicholas Watson *Richard Rolle and the Invention of Authority* 0 521 39017 6
14 Steven F. Kruger *Dreaming in the Middle Ages* 0 521 41069 x
15 Barbara Nolan *Chaucer and the Tradition of the "Roman Antique"* 0 521 39169 5
16 Sylvia Huot *The "Romance of the Rose" and its Medieval Readers: Interpretations, Reception, Manuscript Transmission* 0 521 41713 9
17 Carol M. Meale (ed.) *Women and Literature in Britain, 1150–1500* 0 521 40018 x
18 Henry Ansgar Kelly *Ideas and Forms of Tragedy from Aristotle to the Middle Ages* 0 521 43184 0
19 Martin Irvine *The Making of Textual Culture: Grammatica and Literary Theory, 350–1100* 0 521 41447 4
20 Larry Scanlon *Narrative, Authority and Power: the Medieval Exemplum and the Chaucerian Tradition* 0 521 43210 3
21 Erik Kooper *Medieval Dutch Literature in its European Context* 0 521 40222 0
22 Steven Botterill *Dante and the Mystical Tradition: Bernard of Clairvaux in the "Commedia"* 0 521 43454 8
23 Peter Biller and Anne Hudson (eds.) *Heresy and Literacy, 1000–1530* 0 521 41979 4 (HB) 0 521 57576 1 (PB)
24 Christopher Baswell *Virgil in Medieval England: Figuring the "Aeneid" from the Twelfth Century to Chaucer* 0 521 46294 0

25 James Simpson *Sciences and Self in Medieval Poetry: Alan of Lille's "Anticlaudianus" and John Gower's "Confessio Amantis"* 0 521 47181 8

26 Joyce Coleman *Public Reading and the Reading Public in Late Medieval England and France* 0 521 55391 1

27 Suzanne Reynolds *Medieval Reading: Grammar, Rhetoric and the Classical Text* 0 521 47257 1

28 Charlotte Brewer *Editing "Piers Plowman": the Evolution of the Text* 0 521 34250 3

29 Walter Haug *Vernacular Literary Theory in the Middle Ages: the German Tradition in its European Context* 0 521 34197 3

30 Sarah Spence *Texts and the Self in the Twelfth Century* 0 521 57279 7

31 Edwin Craun *Lies, Slander and Obscenity in Medieval English Literature: Pastoral Rhetoric and the Deviant Speaker* 0 521 49690 x

32 Patricia E. Grieve *"Floire and Blancheflor" and the European Romance* 0 521 43162 x

33 Huw Pryce (ed.) *Literacy in Medieval Celtic Societies* 0 521 57039 5

34 Mary Carruthers *The Craft of Thought: Meditation, Rhetoric, and the Making of Images, 400–1200* 0 521 58232 6

35 Beate Schmolke-Hasselman *The Evolution of Arthurian Romance: the Verse Tradition from Chrétien to Froissart* 0 521 41153 x

36 Siân Echard *Arthurian Narrative in the Latin Tradition* 0 521 62126 7

37 Fiona Somerset *Clerical Discourse and Lay Audience in Late Medieval England* 0 521 62154 2

38 Florence Percival *Chaucer's Legendary Good Women* 0 521 41655 8

39 Christopher Cannon *The Making of Chaucer's English: a Study of Words* 0 521 59274 7

40 Rosalind Brown-Grant *Christine de Pizan and the Moral Defence of Women: Reading Beyond Gender* 0 521 64194 2

41 Richard Newhauser *The Early History of Greed: the Sin of Avarice in Early Medieval Thought and Literature* 0 521 38522 9

42 Margaret Clunies Ross *Old Icelandic Literature and Society* 0 521 63112 2

43 Donald Maddox *Fictions of Identity in Medieval France* 0 521 78105 1

44 Rita Copeland *Pedagogy, Intellectuals, and Dissent in the Later Middle Ages: Lollardy and Ideas of Learning* 0 521 65238 3

45 Kantik Ghosh *The Wycliffite Heresy: Authority and the Interpretation of Texts* 0 521 81221 6

46 Mary C. Erler *Women, Reading, and Piety in Late Medieval England* 0 521 80720 4

47 D. H. Green *The Beginnings of Medieval Romance: Fact and Fiction 1150–1220*

48 J. A. Burrow *Gestures and Looks in Medieval Narrative*

49 Ardis Butterfield *Poetry and Music in Medieval France: From Jean Renart to Guillaume de Machaut*

Made in the USA
Lexington, KY
28 February 2013